THE LIMITS TO POWER

SOVIET POLICY IN THE MIDDLE EAST

Edited by YAACOV RO'I

ST. MARTIN'S PRESS   NEW YORK

Copyright © 1979 Yaacov Ro'i, Galia Golan, Amnon Sella, Gur Ofer, Dina R. Spechler, Martin C. Spechler, Oded Eran, Theodore H. Friedgut, Baruch Gurevitz, Itamar Rabinovich and Robert O. Freedman

All rights reserved. For information write:
St. Martin's Press Inc., 175 Fifth Avenue, New York, N.Y. 10010
Printed in Great Britain
ISBN 0-312-48695-2
First published in the United States of America in 1979

Library of Congress Cataloging in Publication Data

Main entry under title:

The Limits to power.

    Includes index.
    1. Near East — Foreign relations — Russia — Addresses, essays, lectures.   2. Russia — Foreign relations — Near East — Addresses, essays, lectures.   I. Ro'i, Yaacov.
DS63.2.R9L55   1979   327.47'056   78-10555
ISBN 0-312-48695-2

CONTENTS

Contents

ACKNOWLEDGEMENTS

This book is the result of a research project carried out by a group of researchers with the help of a grant from the Ford Foundation, and the editor and the other authors are deeply grateful to the Ford Foundation for its support. In addition, we would like to thank Professor Arnold Horelick of the Rand Corporation and Mr David Morison of the Central Asian Research Centre for the time they devoted to reading the draft manuscript and participating in a symposium held to discuss it, and for their enlightening and thought-provoking comments which helped us all to formulate our views more precisely.

We also wish to thank the Russian and East European Research Center of Tel Aviv University and the Soviet and East European Research Centre of the Hebrew University of Jerusalem for providing most of the source material on which our research was based and for their generous secretarial and administrative assistance.

Finally, we are all indebted to Ms. Philippa Lewis for her valuable editorial assistance and advice.

LIST OF ABBREVIATIONS

CPSU — Communist Party of the Soviet Union

FBIS III, V — Foreign Broadcast Information Service, *Daily Report*. Vol. III Soviet Union, Vol. V The Middle East and North Africa

GA OR — United Nations General Assembly, *Official Records*

MFR — Mutual Force Reduction

MENA — Middle East News Agency

N M — Nautical Miles

NYT — *New York Times*

R. — Radio

RPP — Radio Peace and Progress (Moscow)

SWB I, IV — BBC Monitoring Service, *Summary of World Broadcasts*, Part I The USSR, Part IV The Middle East and Africa

TASS — *Telegrafnoe agentsvo Sovetskogo soiuza* (Telegraphic Agency of the Soviet Union)

UNDOF — United Nations Disengagement Observation Force

FOREWORD

Describing and interpreting Soviet policy in the Middle East has its
devotees in many countries, notably and predictably the Soviet Union
itself and the United States, but nowhere is this vocation practised with
such solid research and impressive results as in Israel. It is therefore a
pleasure and a satisfaction for me to write a few words introducing this
volume of Israeli scholarship. The names of many of its authors are
already widely known for past work in the field — Yaacov Ro'i, Galia
Golan, Oded Eran, Theodore Friedgut, to name but a few. All of them
are thoroughly at home in both Russian and Middle East material.
Taken together, their contributions cover the spectrum of Soviet interests and policies since the war of October 1973: how the Soviets have
handled the oil question, military and economic aid, policy toward
Egypt, Syria, Iraq, the Palestinian organisations — and toward Israel.

The chronicle, chapter by chapter, is one of extraordinary lack of
success for the Soviet Union. Measuring success or lack of it, of course,
depends on what Soviet aims were in the first place, and only the
Soviet leaders themselves are authorities on that point. But it is evident
enough that they have been discomfited and humiliated by the turn of
events since 1973, or perhaps we should say since 1972, for it was the
loss of position and of face in Egypt that began, and has continued to
mark, the decline of Soviet influence generally. Moscow might seek
substitutes for the Egyptian connection in Syria, in North Africa or in
the region of the Persian Gulf, but it is not so easy. The Soviets came
into the Middle East in the 1950s through Egypt and by exploiting the
Arab—Israeli conflict; now they can not escape the consequences of the
way in which that conflict has changed, and they obviously have been
unable to control events when their government had no relations with
one party to the conflict and only the most tenuous with the main
party on the Arab side.

The ebb-and-flow of Soviet diplomacy, as it emerges from the wealth
of official statements and press material, is admirably chronicled in
this volume. The policy behind the diplomacy is more difficult to divine.
Internal Soviet discussions and debates on what to do in the Middle
East — unlike what happens in the United States or another democratic
country — are not exposed to public view, and the arcane practices of
Sovietology, by the very qualities of imaginative research which make

them frequently illuminating, can also carry the investigator rather far from the realm of verifiable fact. It is a virtue of this book that its authors have been assiduous in their search for data and restrained in their interpretation of it.

The hostility of the Soviet Union to Israel, in the service of a policy aimed at exploiting opportunities in the Arab world, needs no massive research effort to be demonstrated. These authors — all but one of them citizens of Israel — have certainly documented it, but without exaggeration. There is, one may assume, an Israeli interest in having the world believe the worst about Soviet intentions toward Israel and the magnitude of the Soviet threat to dominate the Middle East. This book does not lend itself to such a political purpose. It is a thorough exposition of evidence and sober interpretation of what it means. Each author, moreover, sticks to his or her own subject and reaches independent conclusions.

The record of Soviet policy in the Middle East since the October war, as I have mentioned, is hardly a brilliant one. It could even be called, with some justice, a near-disaster. Egypt was the fulcrum of Soviet policy, and Egypt under Anwar al-Sadat seems totally to have abandoned the Soviet connection in favour of one with America, which he says holds 99 per cent of the cards for an acceptable settlement of the Arab—Israeli conflict. Syria has not proved a reliable Soviet ally. The Lebanese civil war, which saw Moscow's Syrian and Palestinian 'friends' fighting each other with Soviet weapons, proved a frustration and a failure. Even the Iraqi regime has moved away from exclusive ties, especially since it succeeded in crushing the Kurdish nationalists and in patching up its quarrels with Iran in 1975. The 'rejectionist' forces in the Arab world may win Moscow's ideological favour and accept its arms, but they accept neither Soviet control nor Soviet views on the Arab—Israeli conflict. The Kremlin calls the parties to Geneva, but no Geneva conference takes place. The initiative — such as it is — rests with President Sadat, with Israel, and with the United States.

The Kremlin, however, may have to do no more than wait for events to generate a more favourable situation. There is no inevitability of success for the effort of Sadat to reach a settlement with Israel; indeed the chances seem less than even, given the gap between Israel's position and that of Egypt, to say nothing of those of other Arab confrontation states and the Arab Palestinians, whom Sadat cannot ignore. And the proposition that the Americans hold 99 per cent of the cards remains to be proven.

Soviet interests in the region, regardless of great leaps forward or serious setbacks which put their stamp on any given period, remain a permanent feature of the international scene. They are determined by geography, by ideology, by the arrival of the Soviet Union to the status of a global superpower, by the US—USSR balance, by the inevitable competition for position and influence in the Third World, and perhaps, in time, by a Soviet need for Middle East oil. Shifting Soviet policies toward Israel, toward Egypt, or any other regional state should be interpreted against that background of continuing Soviet interest. Whether the ultimate aim is taken to be a drive for control or domination — a good subject for academic debate — is beside the point, for others, both local states and outside powers, must take account of that 'worst case' possibility in their dealings with the Soviet government, even as they try to influence it in the direction of respect for their independence and legitimate interests. The real problems have to do not with ultimate aims or day-to-day tactics, but with permanent interests and medium-range strategy.

The agreement made by the United States with the Soviet Union on the principles and procedure of an Arab—Israeli settlement, embodied in the joint statement of 1 October 1977, represented neither a denial of the above propositions nor a naive acceptance of Soviet policy as constructive or benevolent in regard to a settlement and the rights and interests of the parties, including Israel. It was a recognition by the United States that it was desirable to associate the Soviets as far as possible with its own efforts (deemed constructive more or less by definition) toward a settlement, and to minimise their power to sabotage and disrupt. The joint statement may have been ill timed and clumsily handled, but in essence it was a recognition of fundamentals and a means of promoting over the long run both the prospects of Arab—Israeli settlement and the chances of controlling great-power competition without danger to the independence of local nations or the security of the West.

It is inevitable that between America and the various states and nations of the Middle East, including Israel, there will be differences of view, of policy, and of interest. That the global interests of a superpower do not coincide with the national interests of a regional state is obvious in the case of the Soviet Union and is true as well for the United States. The result is a complex situation in which the United States, for instance, has continually to seek the balance between competition and co-operation with the USSR, in a region such as the Middle East, that will best serve its interests; and it must seek at the same time to establish and maintain relationships with local states that take due account of their interests.

Thus there is no automatic factor – the persistence of cold war or the hope of détente, ideological difference or ideological solidarity, UN resolutions or traditions of friendship – to predetermine the policy decisions of any of the nations involved, great or small. This is surely one of the lessons of the developments of the past decade.

Such considerations need not cast doubt on the close ties between America and Israel or the many common interests of those two countries. They should, on the contrary, reinforce those ties by a clearer understanding of the interests at stake on both sides. Admittedly, in the tumult and the shouting that accompanies the workings of the democratic process in both countries it is not so easy to achieve understanding or to bring it to bear on foreign policy, but this is a necessary complication that we cannot and should not avoid.

Knowledge of the Soviet Union and of the reasons behind its conduct in the Middle East is important to Israel, to other Middle East countries, and to the United States and its Western allies. Scholarly inquiry which widens and deepens that knowledge should therefore engage the attention of all concerned. Where the results of such research are in the public domain, they can be of use and benefit far beyond the frontiers of the country in which they have been written and published. Accordingly, this product of Israeli scholarship, the most thorough work on the subject yet published anywhere, deserves a thoughtful reading in many countries.

John C. Campbell

INTRODUCTION

The Soviet position in the Middle East in the mid-1970s has declined sharply since the spring and summer of 1970. At the turn of the decade the USSR seemed to be the dominant foreign power in the region. It had a considerable military presence in a number of Arab countries, including air bases and naval facilities and Soviet pilots were flying operational missions in Egypt's War of Attrition against Israel. It was broadening and deepening its political influence in Egypt, Syria, Algeria, Iraq, South Yemen and the Sudan, all of whose leaderships had close working relationships with Moscow. Finally, it had impressive economic investments in most of the major spheres of the economic life of the Arab countries, as well as a significant economic role in Turkey and Iran.

A number of setbacks soon appeared. In September 1970 (Black September) when the situation in Jordan deteriorated, including a shamefaced invasion of that country to help the Palestinians by Syria, one of the USSR's main protégés in the area, it was the USA and not the Soviet Union that had the power to influence events. The same month also saw the death of the USSR's long-time ally, Jamal Abd al-Nasir. Within less than a year the other members of the Egyptian leadership with whom Moscow had had contacts had been ousted, the Kremlin was being pressed by President Sadat for offensive weaponry it had no intention of giving the Arabs, and the short-lived Communist coup in the Sudan had both revealed Soviet and East European political interference in the domestic affairs of an Arab country and brought Moscow into confrontation with a number of Arab leaders. The situation in Egypt underwent a further crisis with the ending of the Soviet military mission in that country in 1972, and although the USSR seemed somewhat to have improved its position by mid-1973, there were clearly major problems in the Soviet–Arab relationship.

Following the October War, the USSR's position suffered new setbacks and an even greater decline. A superpower with vast resources and enormous arsenal at its disposal, it could not translate its power into political influence or diplomatic achievements. The purpose of this book is to depict the USSR's dilemmas in the region and its struggle to halt and reverse the decline in its power. In so doing it not only seeks to describe the options which the Soviet Union has had, the goals it has set

1

itself and the constraints under which it has operated, but also to answer a number of major questions connected with Soviet Middle Eastern policy.

In the first place, this book analyses the reasons for the continued Soviet decline, in particular endeavouring to show how far it was an outcome of the 1973 War, and how far a continuation of developments that had begun earlier and were perhaps simply precipitated by the War.

Another central question which the book seeks to answer is why the Soviet Union continues to devote so much attention to the Middle East. Although there have been important Soviet successes in a variety of other areas (south-east Asia, Angola), and although the military threat to the USSR has been transferred further afield, from the Middle East to the Indian Ocean, the former area still attracts strong Soviet interest. True, this interest has moved from the traditional centres of Soviet activity — Egypt and Syria, both 'confrontation states' — to the periphery of the region (Libya, the Horn of Africa and the Persian Gulf); yet the Soviet Union has continued to lay emphasis on the Arab-Israeli conflict and its settlement. Is it, then, the existence of a major conflict that attracts Moscow to the area, or the inability to concede any region in the inter-bloc competition? Are there permanent Soviet interests in the Middle East and corresponding policy constants, or is Soviet activity a derivative of *ad hoc* decisions relating to changing circumstances in the regional arena?

In discussing these two main issues, the book also seeks to throw light on the two postulates which have guided the USA in its relationship with the USSR regarding the Middle East: on the one hand, that the USSR has the responsibility, as a great power, to co-operate in settling the Arab-Israeli conflict, and, on the other, that it has the ability to undermine any settlement to which it is not a party.

The first section of the book discusses the place of the Middle East in the Soviet–US relationship. It examines global political and military considerations that guide Soviet policy makers in the area and puts the Middle East in the broadest context of superpower politics — whether these be détente or cold war — and of global strategies. It shows, too, how the Soviet Union used or sought to use military supplies to ensure its continued influence in a changing and often unstable environment.

The second part is concerned with the economic factors. This comprises the general topic of Soviet economic aid and investments in the Middle East as well as the more specific one of the Soviet attitude to the various aspects of oil politics. The questions this section deals with are: What are the intentions of Soviet economic aid policies and how successful have they been? What has been the economic price the USSR has had to pay for its influence in the region? How has it fared as a result of the West's energy crisis? Did the oil embargo of late 1973 to early 1974 and the continued threat of future oil embargoes bring it the benefits, direct and indirect, it had long been expecting?

The third part of the book considers a very different set of problems: What has been the Soviet Union's reaction in the realm of theoretical writing to the chain of developments that has|undermined its position in the region? How does it conceptualise the changes that have taken place and explain the reversals? Does it contemplate using the same methods to recover earlier, advantageous positions as it did to build them up originally, or has it re-evaluated its tactics? How does Moscow present its Middle Eastern policies to the Soviet public? Can the reader of the Soviet press discern the Kremlin's anxiety for the future in view of present trends in the Middle East, or guess at the Soviet loss of prestige and influence in the Arab world?

The fourth section deals with the Soviet Union's relations with the main confrontation states and its attitude to the major aspects of the Arab—Israeli conflict. It seeks to trace and analyse the Soviet—Egyptian rift from the end of the October War to Sadat's unilateral abrogation of the Treaty of Friendship and Co-operation in March 1976; was the rift the result of a single factor or moment, such as Sadat's belief after the war that the USA alone could help Egypt in particular and the Arabs in general recover the lands lost in 1967 or was it caused by his domestic policies? Or maybe it was the outcome of a complex interaction between the two states that included political, military, economic and perhaps even psychological elements? This section also intends to clarify what were the differences and similarities between Soviet-Egyptian and Soviet-Syrian relations. Did the Syrians seek to apply the Egyptian model of a rapprochement with the USA to themselves, and if so why did they behave somewhat differently? Was the USSR's reaction to Syrian flirtations with Washington more moderate simply because its options were more limited when this second Arab 'progressive' state threatened to leave the Soviet fold?

As for the Soviet attitude to Israel, was it consistent? Did it have an inner logic of its own and, if so, what was this logic? How did the Soviet Union's declared recognition of Israel's existence accord with its unwillingness to renew diplomatic relations and its calls for the establishment of a Palestinian state? And what did the USSR expect from such a state? Was it fashioning its relationship with the various

Palestinian organisations in such a way as to ensure that when a Palestinian state came into existence, it would be dependent on the USSR and provide a new Soviet military and political base? Or did its relations with these organisations have only short-term goals: for example to strengthen the 'rejection front' and to ensure Palestinian participation in the Geneva Conference?

The final and perhaps most crucial and topical issue (at least at the time of writing – late-1977) deals with the Soviet conception of an Arab–Israeli peace settlement. Did Moscow expect a settlement to be achieved or was talk of a settlement simply intended to set into motion the Geneva Conference of which the USSR was co-sponsor together with the USA? Did it want a settlement and if so, what kind of a settlement? Was a settlement supposed to legitimise the Soviet Union's presence in the region as one of the two superpowers that would be its guarantors? Or did the Kremlin hope that its allies would gain from the settlement and appreciate these gains as the fruit of their relationship with the Soviet Union?

The last section of the book sums up the trends and tendencies that have affected Soviet goals, interests and policies in the Middle East since the October War. It puts into perspective the various individual aspects dealt with in previous chapters and assesses the different constraints put on the USSR in the area. Finally, it seeks to look at the Soviet Union's prospects in the Middle East as they appear at the time of writing in the light of the developments of the preceding four years.

These, then, are some of the problems this book sets out to solve. It does not claim to deal with all the issues in Soviet–Middle Eastern relations. For example, it does not consider the relations between the USSR and the peripheral states, either the non-Arab ones (Turkey, Iran, Somalia) or the Arab ones (Libya, Sudan, the People's Democratic Republic of Yemen, Saudi Arabia, Iraq) – not because these are not interesting or important, but because the book is concerned with what has happened to the USSR's positions, policies and interests in the area in the wake of the October 1973 war. Although the Soviet attitude to Saudi Arabia in particular is of major significance, given the enhanced Saudi status in inter-Arab relations – and indeed it indirectly crops up in connection with the other issues discussed – the crux of the problem is the USSR's relationship with the major states and groupings with which it has traditionally been associated and which are immediately involved in the Arab–Israeli conflict. The Soviet Union and the Middle East's periphery is a legitimate and central problem – for another book.

PART 1   THE GLOBAL CONTEXT

1 THE ARAB–ISRAELI CONFLICT IN SOVIET–US RELATIONS

Galia Golan

Soviet interests and policy in the Middle East have, traditionally, been based on a mixture of regional and global considerations, the two often interacting and occasionally becoming indistinguishable, if not inseparable. Since the early 1960s, with the advent of the American Polaris submarines in the area, together with the accelerated development of the Soviet fleet, the overriding Soviet interest in the Middle East has been a strategic one linked to global considerations of the Soviet–American balance of forces.[1] As the Soviet Union sought bases and support facilities for its new Mediterranean squadron and aircraft deployed in the region, its moves to gain political and economic influence within the region became a subsidiary objective designed mainly to obtain and secure these strategic interests. For these purposes the Arab–Israeli conflict was a convenient and, for some time, helpful vehicle in the pursuit of these ultimately globally-oriented Soviet objectives.

Yet it was just the global aspect of these objectives and moves, specifically the fear of confrontation with the United States, which placed the greatest constraints on Soviet policy in the region and towards the Arab–Israeli conflict. The conflict proved itself increasingly volatile in the 1960s and 1970s, while the Soviet Union had declining control or even influence over its Arab clients in the area. Moreover, the growing American commitment to and involvement in the area — which in itself contributed to (but did not originate) the decline in Soviet influence — rendered the risk of superpower confrontation still greater. At the same time the USSR's primary interests suffered a setback as the actual strategic benefits or return for the Soviet effort in the region declined, with such things as the loss of air and later naval facilities in Egypt, for example. Thus, the Arab–Israeli conflict began to prove disfunctional or, at the least, less worthwhile, considering the growing risks from the Soviet point of view. Moreover, concomitant with the growing constraints and problems, a gradual shift was occurring in Soviet strategic interests. With the development of the US Poseidon and, more important, the Trident missiles, Soviet industrial centres could now be targeted from still greater distances at sea, moving the

7

point of Soviet–American strategic rivalry deep into the Indian Ocean.[2] With this development, as well as growing Soviet capability to service and support its Mediterranean squadron from points farther from Soviet borders, the immediate area of the Arab-Israeli conflict began to assume somewhat less importance in Soviet strategic thinking. This development would explain, at least in part, Soviet unwillingness to pay the price demanded by the Arabs, especially the Egyptians, but also to some degree even the Syrians as well as the Jordanians, in order to improve Moscow's position in the area.[3]

This new situation, which has emerged in recent years, would appear to have altered the more accepted picture of superpower rivalry in the area of the confrontation states in the Arab–Israeli conflict to one in which the Soviet Union has become genuinely interested in and willing to co-operate in a settlement of this conflict. Indeed, events of the post-October 1973 War period, as described in subsequent chapters of this book, may even have rendered co-operation with the United States to this end the only positive option open to the Soviets – if, indeed, the Americans would agree to this – in order to ensure a stable Soviet presence in the region.[4]

The emergence of this option as the optimal if not the only one did not mean that the USSR was to abandon all competition with the United States in order to achieve such co-operation. Indeed, to play a role in the negotiating process Moscow not only had to prove its usefulness to the parties involved, but, presumably, it also had to take certain steps to ensure itself some benefits from the final product. For this purpose, the USSR allied itself with the more radical demands and groupings of the Arab world, not only to discredit American efforts in the area (and bring pressure on those, such as the Egyptians, who showed signs of moving towards Washington), but also for tactical purposes – so as to appear indispensable to the achievement of a settlement, that is, indispensable to the Arabs as the only superpower pressing for *all* the Arab demands, indispensable to the United States as that factor which controlled the war option. At the same time, occasional declarations for the benefit of Israel were even employed to present the Soviets as an acceptable partner for what was steadily emerging as an exclusively American bargaining process. Similarly, the Soviet Union was increasingly to invoke détente in connection with settling the Arab–Israeli conflict and the need to apply détente to this region.

Such a linkage of détente, i.e. the superpower relationship, with the Arab–Israeli conflict was understandable in terms of the underlying

concern lest the conflict draw the superpowers into direct
confrontation. Beyond this, however, the degree and manner in
which this basic superpower relationship could affect or be affected by
the conflict was open to conjecture. Past Soviet manipulation of the
Arab–Israeli conflict in the 1950s and 1960s and the apparent
competition between the superpowers in the area might lead to the
conclusion that détente did not or would not apply to the Middle East
and, indeed, might even be negatively affected by the superpowers'
policies in the area. At best it could be said that the crisis-control
element of détente was applicable to the Middle East but not the
aspects of détente concerned with a non-crisis situation, co-operation
and reduction of tension. Before attempting to determine the validity
of these impressions one must examine the Soviet definition of détente,
for this definition was rather more flexible and broad (regarding what is
included or excluded) than often perceived in the West.

Primarily in justification of Soviet behaviour in Angola and American
accusations of Soviet violations of détente, but also in response to
criticism from the Third World, China, and, possibly, domestic
opponents to détente, the USSR exerted some effort, particularly in
1975–6 to define the limitations of détente as it saw it.[5] And this
definition most certainly did *not* rule out ideological-political
competition, or for that matter the USSR's attempts to improve its
economic and even military positions. Rather, it perceived détente as
the securing of an atmosphere which would reduce the possibility that
such competition would reach a crisis point of the type to create
superpower tensions. One Soviet definition even went so far as to say
that détente meant nothing beyond the idea that the 'inevitable
struggle' between the two social systems would be placed in a
non-military framework.[6] It was also seen as the securing of certain
world conditions which would permit economic co-operation of the
type needed by the Soviet Union, arms limitations also needed by the
Soviet economy, and the possibility of co-operation for crisis control,
without abandoning or even subordinating Soviet strategic interests.
Indeed, Soviet strategic interests in some areas such as Western Europe
might conceivably even be better served by the pursuit of détente. The
greatest difference between this concept of détente and the former
Soviet policy of peaceful co-existence – which also sought a reduction
of world tensions in order to render competition less dangerous – was
the new element of co-operation, primarily in the economic but also in
other spheres such as arms limitations. Thus, Moscow's usual
calculation as to the possible American response to this or that action (be it

in Angola or the Middle East) was to be guided not only by the none the less primary consideration — the probability of American intervention — but now also by the possibility of irreparably damaging chances for co-operation. The brief experience of détente so far would indicate that here, too, the Soviets saw détente as a very flexible concept, certainly a hardy one, to which the USA was sufficiently dedicated (at least under President Nixon and even Ford) as to tolerate a good deal of stretching. Thus, when the Soviets spoke of applying détente to the Middle East (in the context of the Arab—Israeli conflict), the concept need not be as restraining an element on Soviet behaviour as it sounded. Indeed, in the post-October War context it may even be seen as intended, rather, to restrain the United States. If, in the prewar period and even later, the Soviet Union argued defensively that détente was not a restraining factor upon its efforts on behalf of the Arabs, after the war, when Moscow found itself something of an underdog, virtually excluded from the major activities concerning the Middle East, it insisted, as it were, that détente be applied to the area so as to create and justify a Soviet role there.

The USSR has sufficiently discussed its view of the relationship between détente and the Arab—Israeli crisis to provide a relatively good idea of the degree to which it does indeed mean superpower co-operation. It has insisted that peace is indivisible and, therefore, by implication, détente in all its aspects must apply to the Middle East as well. This was expressed on a theoretical level in an article in *Mezhdunarodnaia zhizn'* entitled 'Détente and International Crises.'[7] The Middle East conflict, along with Vietnam, was categorised as a 'protracted crisis' which, like all crises today, was particularly dangerous to world peace and security because of the following: (1) the existence of nuclear weapons; (2) the universal nature of crises, which rapidly, almost instantaneously, involve directly or indirectly the major powers of the world and the military coalitions, and because of the 'global system of communication, mass media and military and technical means that make it possible to concentrate forces in the crisis area in unprecedented short times'; (3) 'substantial danger is presented by the "uncontrolled element" within international crises, that is, a package of factors which allow various local aggressive forces to create situations sharpening the conflict and pushing the major imperialist powers to more vigorous action than they had been prepared to engage in. Israel's numerous aggressive acts offer striking examples of such actions'; (4) crises 'lead to explosions of international tensions, a revival of the cold war and can slow down the process of détente and

sharpen relations between the great powers'; (5) 'they [crises] whip up
the arms race, involving not only conventional weapons which are used
in local armed conflicts, but also strategic weapons'; (6) crises 'can
seriously undermine international economic relations'. The article
concluded that for all the diversity of the above, the threat of war
generated by crises remained the main danger, citing again the Middle
East as an example of the need for the application of détente to crises.
Without entering into such detail, the general idea of the inclusion of
the Middle East in the framework of détente was reiterated in
innumerable articles, commentaries and also speeches by Soviet leaders,
usually from the point of view that this was a dangerous 'hotspot'
which threatened world peace. Often the idea of the 'indivisibility of
peace' was introduced to make the same point.

Détente in the Middle East was not only advocated because of the
risks involved in the continued crisis, but also cited as that factor which
could benefit all concerned. This took the form of the argument that
the atmosphere of détente – the progress already made elsewhere in the
relaxation of tensions and the co-operation of the superpowers in the
Middle East, as well – provided more favourable conditions for
achieving a settlement. There was an element of defensiveness in this
particular claim, for the Soviet Union was sensitive to Third World
criticism (encouraged by the Chinese) that détente would render
Moscow less willing to support its clients, constituting in this sense a
policy of capitulation or 'collusion' which froze the status quo so as to
permit the Soviet Union to pursue its own interest in improved
relations with the United States. Egyptian President Sadat, for one,
believed not only that the USSR was serious in its declarations of the
necessity of détente for the Middle East, but that this meant a virtual
'freezing' of the Middle East status quo (in favour of Israel). This had
been Sadat's interpretation of the 1972 US–Soviet summit declaration
regarding a relaxation of tensions in the Middle East and he cited this
as part of Moscow's opposition to what was called a 'military
solution' (as distinct from a political one), as one of the reasons for his
expulsion of the Soviet advisers in July 1972.[8] Even after the October
War, the Soviets remained somewhat defensive on this point, for in
addition to their criticism of American initiatives in the area and
warnings to the Arabs not to be taken in by the Americans, they found
it necessary to accompany Soviet–US summit meetings and the like
with assurances that the Soviet Union had remained (despite and in the
course of these meetings) a firm supporter of the Arabs' demands. Party
Secretary-General Brezhnev, for example, apparently found it necessary

to reassure the Syrians on this point in his speech honouring Syrian President Asad in April 1974; subsequent references to détente in Soviet–Syrian statements suggested that this remained a touchy point.[9]

This defensiveness, however, may have been directed at another source of attack, an internal one. Immediately following the October War there appeared to be two camps in Soviet explanations of the relationship of the war to détente. The view was expressed then that the war had proved the aggressive nature of imperialism and just how far the world was from peace and security.[10] Presumably what was behind these interpretations was not, specifically, opposition to the application of détente to the Middle East crisis but, rather, more general opposition to détente itself (although during the war there were some signs of discontent within certain circles over Moscow's restraint in helping the Arabs[11]). In counter-distinction to this attitude, Brezhnev and most of the Soviet leadership and press stressed the positive role détente had played in the war, specifically crediting the atmosphere created by détente and the Soviet–American co-operation thereby facilitated with having prevented a disaster. For example, Brezhnev told the Indian parliament:

> . . . matters would look quite different were it not for this factor of détente in the world, which emerged in the last two or three years. If the current conflict had flared up in a situation of universal, international tension and aggravation of relations, say, between the United States and the Soviet Union, the clash in the Middle East might have become more dangerous, it might have assumed a scope endangering world peace.[12]

This line was the predominant one and was to become, in time, the only official one on this subject. Thus, it was repeated in long articles in *S.Sh.A.* and *Mezhdunarodnaia zhizn'* as part of a long list of examples of Soviet–US co-operation in the quest for a solution to the Middle East crisis and in subsequent articles which appeared even after the USSR had little to present as signs of such co-operation.[13] In time such references to the value of détente and Soviet–American co-operation, sprinkled upon occasion with quotes of American admissions that the USSR was playing an essential part, were probably designed to lay claim to a Soviet role which did not entirely exist. Nonetheless, the fact that Moscow chose this line of persuasion (with its potentially negative ramifications amongst the more radical Arabs and others) itself indicated the Soviet interest in applying détente in the Middle East.

There was one further element of détente, that of 'military détente', which the Soviet Union was increasingly to emphasise. Eventually this, too, was applied to the Middle East, most officially when Brezhnev, at the Twenty-Fifth CPSU Congress in February 1976, called for a limitation on the arms race in the Middle East. Although the Soviet leaders, including Brezhnev himself,[14] had raised this issue before, the 1976 mention was hailed as a new Soviet initiative, to be repeated relatively frequently thereafter. Given the reported profitability of Soviet arms sales to the Middle East (i.e. hard currency payments) — and the generally believed, though by now disproved, conception that Soviet arms supplies created Soviet control — such a proposal was surprising. This even fuller application of détente to the area probably reflected Soviet concern over the introduction of nuclear weapons into the area, as well as the realisation that America was becoming increasingly important in the realm of arms supplies.

These Soviet declarations about the applicability and desirability of détente with regard to the Arab—Israeli conflict coincided with an apparent Soviet preference for co-operation rather than mutually exclusive superpower competition in the area. Yet, as we have pointed out, even co-operation — or détente in the Soviet interpretation — need not rule out competition of *all* types. Moreover, Soviet declarations are meant to serve many purposes (including tactical ones), not all of which are necessarily reflected by actual Soviet behaviour. Thus, to answer the question to what degree détente as such has influenced actual Soviet policy towards the Arab—Israeli conflict or, conversely, to what degree the Arab—Israeli conflict has affected détente or the basic superpower relationship, the following case studies may be enlightening.

1. The October War and Immediate Aftermath

During the October War itself the general view of Soviet aid to the Arabs created the impression that détente had become totally inactive, at least as a restraining measure. Yet the Soviet Union not only sought to preserve and protect its relationship with the United States, it actually risked its future relationship with the Arabs by its efforts to obtain a ceasefire and its willingness throughout most of the war to co-operate with similar US efforts.[15] This behaviour may well have been dictated more by the overriding consideration of avoiding a military confrontation with the United States than by détente (and in this respect was similar to Soviet behaviour during the 1967 conflict), but Soviet hesitation throughout much of the war to identify the United States as the major villain in the conflict suggested Soviet concern for détente as well. The major risk to détente came with the

Soviet ultimatum to the US on 24 October 1973 to send a peacekeeping force (although there is some question whether the Soviets thought they were risking more than this, i.e. that their move would elicit the American reaction it did). At this point the USSR was very much on the defensive with the Arabs, having engineered a ceasefire against the will of Syria and Iraq, which was based on Resolution 242 and contained the idea of negotiations (both of which were unacceptable to the radical Arab groupings), and which was not holding on the one front where it was most needed: the Egyptian front. It would appear that Moscow made a calculation at the time as to its future position with the Arabs versus the limitations imposed by détente, arriving at the conclusion that the former demanded some Soviet action and that the latter would most likely survive. At any rate, considerations of détente certainly did not prevent the Soviet Union from issuing its ultimatum even if they did, perhaps, cause the USSR to couch this ultimatum in somewhat restrained terms. This was not, however, necessarily a question of priorities, in which the Middle East took precedence over the Soviet–American relationship, but rather a calculated risk of an *ad hoc* nature – similar to other Soviet moves on specific problems (such as Angola) – from which Moscow assumed it could emerge victorious at relatively little cost.

Whatever Soviet reasoning, Soviet behaviour during the war, specifically the crisis of 24–25 October, did hurt détente. Opponents to the policy in both the Soviet Union and the United States were now strengthened, and both governments were hard put to justify continued (or past) pursuit of détente. It was, therefore, immediately after the war that the Soviet Union returned to the priority of détente, almost entirely avoiding mention of the American alert or even the American role in the Israeli war effort, emphasising, rather, Soviet–American co-operation and the contribution of détente in bringing the war – and crisis – to a close. As pointed out earlier, this was not the line of all Soviet officials, suggesting that there were those who hoped to use the Arab–Israeli conflict to dampen the Soviet–American relationship.

The official line generally linked détente favourably with Soviet behaviour in the Middle East, criticism of the United States being relatively limited, employed for tactical purposes upon occasion but even then relatively mildly. Whether this was the result of the priority of the pursuit of détente, or merely the function of the Soviet preference for superpower co-operation, rather than all-out competition, is a moot point. That Soviet regional objectives were linked with global considerations at this point was evidenced not only by this effort at co-operation but also by the nearly opposite propaganda line pursued with regard to the area south and south-east of the Arab–Israeli conflict. For here Soviet strategic interests took precedence and competition with the United States was still the watchword, as the USSR sought to prevent both the abandonment of the oil boycott against the United States and American military entrenchment in the Indian Ocean. Nor was it unwilling, both in its propaganda and, apparently, in its dealings with the various Arab states, to refrain from linking these American interests with the Arab–Israeli conflict by claims that the efforts of the United States in the latter arena were motivated only by its ambitions *vis-à-vis* the Persian Gulf and Indian Ocean. This type of juggling of Soviet policy and tactical lines was not unusual; the important point was that in late 1973 and early 1974, the USSR did not permit this to overshadow its main line, and practical policy, of détente – co-operation with the United States – with regard to the Arab–Israeli conflict. While it might be argued that it indeed had no other option, inasmuch as the United States had the upper hand at the moment, the fact that the Soviet Union did not adopt an obstructionist posture or even seek to wrest the initiative from the United States (by offering its own alternatives) may have reflected certain Soviet priorities whereby settlement of the potentially dangerous conflict took precedence over the less pressing issue of Soviet–American confrontation south-eastwards. Indeed, in terms of eventually facing the latter contingency, regulation of the Soviet–American relationship over the more immediate (both in time and space) Arab–Israeli issue would be higher on the agenda.

2. Israeli–Syrian Disengagement

A certain risk to the Soviet–American relationship as a result of Soviet policy towards the conflict may have arisen in the spring of 1974, during the negotiations for a Syrian–Israeli disengagement. The Soviet Union, fearful that these negotiations would take the same American-dominated road as the Egyptian–Israeli disengagement, significantly augmented its criticism of the Americans' efforts. While some of this was directed against the Egyptians, with whom Soviet relations were reaching a new low, the direct criticism of Secretary of State Kissinger, even to the point of calling his efforts 'a mountain that produced a mouse', was of broader intent.[16] While this did not find an echo in the more general Soviet foreign pronouncements at the time, or even those pronouncements dedicated to US–Soviet relations as such, it was of sufficiently serious proportions to cast a shadow over Kissinger's

Moscow talks in March 1974 (according to the Americans, at least, but denied by the Soviets).[17] Nonetheless, the major topic of these talks — and the major problem in Soviet–US relations at the time — reportedly was the stalemate reached in the SALT talks, together, possibly, with the US–Soviet Trade Agreement.[18] Regarding the Middle East, the two sides were apparently satisfied with a new declaration of co-operation, probably the result of American assurances that Moscow would not be totally excluded from negotiations, in exchange for Soviet assurances that it would not try to obstruct them.[19] It is, of course, possible that the two were simply unable to reach any greater accord (the Geneva Conference was mentioned, for example, without any reference to its reopening) and that this disagreement did in fact affect other issues between them. Yet the reference to co-operation, and the effort in Soviet propaganda to emphasise the success of détente (an effort which however, necessitated explanations to the Third World that Moscow was not colluding with the US to the disadvantage of the Arabs, for example[20]), indicated that the Middle East was not to blame for whatever the continued difficulties were with regard to such issues as SALT or the trade bill.

This was in fact the picture throughout the Syrian–Israeli disengagement talks: Kissinger and Soviet Foreign Minister Gromyko met several times, ostensibly on the disengagement issue, in order to satisfy Moscow's demand for 'participation', but the major issue of some of these talks may well have been the détente-related subjects of Nixon's forthcoming visit. Similarly, Soviet criticism of Kissinger's efforts continued, but the official and unofficial conclusion of both the Kissinger–Gromyko meetings as well as the Soviet response to the disengagement itself emphasised the superpowers' co-operation and the beneficial effect of détente on the situation in the Middle East, specifically progress towards a settlement. The overall impression was that, whatever ups and downs détente was suffering on strictly bilateral Soviet–American issues, it was still operative (or to be presented as operative) on the level of the Arab–Israeli conflict, allowing room as always for a certain amount of competition of a more tactical nature (i.e. the anti-American propaganda aimed particularly at the Egyptians). This conclusion would appear to have been confirmed by Brezhnev in his 14 June 1974 speech just as Nixon was visiting the Middle East. While this speech admitted to problems with détente, the Middle East was in fact cited in connection with the *positive* results achieved by détente, while problems in Soviet–American relations were explained only in strictly bilateral terms, i.e. economic problems and, particularly, the issue of SALT (which Brezhnev analysed in relative detail).[21] Brezhnev was to repeat just this formulation, including the crediting of détente for the progress made towards an Arab–Israeli settlement, in his speech honouring Nixon two weeks later.[22] Thus the net result was that the Arab–Israeli conflict was not to be permitted to influence negatively the pursuit of détente but rather the idea of détente was to be used to further Soviet interests in this region, i.e. some role in the American-dominated search for a settlement.

3. The Vladivostok Summit

A third case of possible interaction between détente and the Arab–Israeli conflict might have been the Vladivostok summit in autumn 1974 in which the Soviets most likely sought, above all, reassurances that Ford would maintain Nixon's détente policy.[23] The summit itself took place in an atmosphere of severe Middle East tensions due primarily to the Syrian refusal to reveal its intentions regarding renewal of the UNDOF mandate at the end of November 1974. These tensions were aggravated by the successful Arab–Soviet campaign on behalf of the PLO which included the Rabat Conference's recognition of the PLO as the sole legitimate representative of the Palestinian people, the pro-Palestinian resolutions and appearance of Arafat at the UN, Moscow's own upgrading of the PLO by agreeing to open an office in Moscow and raising the demand for a Palestinian state. None of these last measures need have directly affected Soviet–US relations in the Middle East, except that they were seen to a large degree as a means of blocking Kissinger's latest initiatives to negotiate a Jordanian–Israeli agreement and/or a second Egyptian–Israeli agreement, without reconvening the Geneva Conference. And it was the desire for a reconvening of Geneva which dominated Soviet policy towards the Arab–Israeli conflict at this time. Soviet exaggeration of the tension in the area – even to the point of accusing Israel of planning to launch an all-out attack – could be seen as part of this blocking tactic, as well as the creation of an atmosphere more favourable to the USSR's demand regarding Geneva.

In this atmosphere one could hardly continue to speak of the progress made in the area due to détente, as had been appropriate following the Syrian disengagement. The line therefore shifted to a more standard reference to the Middle East as one of the remaining 'hotspots', along with Vietnam and Cyprus, which were yet to be quietened, although *Izvestiia* of 22 November 1974, for example, argued that even these hotbeds would be worse if not for détente. Upon occasion the 'remaining hotspots' idea was linked with the call for the extension of détente to all areas. For example, Politburo member A. P. Kirilenko reiterated the earlier crisis theory when he said that stable peace in the world was impossible if such hotbeds as Vietnam, the Middle East and Cyprus remained, as did an *Izvestiia* commentator in a *New Times* article entitled 'Détente and Conflicts'. Indeed, the latter clarified the shift in emphasis by explaining that détente had not been developed enough to prevent the conflict of October 1973, but had made possible Soviet–US co-operation during the conflict and now created favourable conditions for the elimination of this remaining, together with Vietnam, 'hotbed'.[24] Some went further by claiming that the fact that such obstacles as the lack of a settlement in the Middle East remained was due to the work of opponents to détente in the West.[25] At the same time, apparently in the interests of safeguarding (or defending) détente, Soviet domestic media were much more reticent than Soviet broadcasts to the Third World about identifying the United States as the factor behind Israel's obstinacy regarding a settlement.[26] The fact that the above comments, as well as the Soviet exaggeration of the tensions in the Middle East, came at the time of Kissinger's October preparatory visit to Moscow and just prior to the Vladivostok meeting itself, suggested that in addition to its blocking tactics *vis-à-vis* the United States and the creation of a general atmosphere favourable to its demand for the reconvening of Geneva, Moscow sought in particular to set the stage for Vladivostok.[27] Yet the Middle East was by no means the main topic scheduled for or in fact discussed at the summit; the pre-Vladivostok Soviet propaganda emphasised SALT and Soviet–US trade without mentioning the Middle East as a scheduled topic at all, or mentioning it only after much (positive) attention to SALT.[28]

Although the USSR vastly exaggerated the tensions in the Middle East, its optimistic emphasis upon SALT prior to and during the summit made|it difficult to believe that the Middle East problem in fact negatively affected these talks. The only genuinely disturbing issue was probably the Soviet–US trade bill, but even this matter was minimised by the Soviet Union in its attempt to present the summit in the most glowing terms – as proof that détente was still viable and worthwhile. Much of this optimism was probably intended as justification of Brezhnev's policy, but at the same time there were indications that Moscow did not intend to permit Soviet–American difficulties in areas such as the Middle East to impede its progress. Thus Brezhnev did not mention the Middle East, specifically, in his public speech at Vladivostok (he spoke only of SALT and related issues), urging only

more generally that Soviet–US co-operation be applied to the solution
of remaining hotbeds of tension.[29] Similarly, the final communiqué of
the talks placed the Middle East next to last (the last place was held by
the even thornier issue of US–Soviet trade and technical-economic
co-operation[30]), after not only SALT, disarmament, limits on nuclear
tests, etc., but also European security, MFR and Cyprus.[31]

While the poor situation in the Middle East would not appear to
have affected détente at this stage (as expected by the Soviet Union,
significant SALT agreements were reached), it is more difficult to
determine to what degree, if any, Soviet interest in détente affected the
discussions on the Arab–Israeli conflict. Did the success in the area of
SALT affect the statement or agreements reached on the Arab–Israeli
issue? Did the bargaining over SALT involve Soviet concessions
regarding the Middle East? Commentary on the Vladivostok talks did
mention that the two sides had agreed that their co-operation should be
extended to this topic as well, and, as in the past, Soviet propaganda to
the Third World considered it necessary to deny that such co-operation
meant 'collusion' at the expense of Soviet support for the Arabs.[32] One
commentary even claimed that 'the Soviet stance has greatly influenced
the attitude of the United States leadership' which 'shows that
improvement of Soviet–US relations is based on principles and is not at
the expense of other peoples'.[33] Indeed, Brezhnev's speech
immediately following the summit – and at a time when PLO leader
Yasir Arafat was visiting Moscow – dwelt at some length on the Arab,
particularly Palestinian, demands in what may have been compensation
for the *lack* of any genuine Soviet effort on their behalf at the
summit.[34] The summit communiqué added nothing to previous joint
Soviet–US declarations on the Middle East, including no more specific
call for the reconvening of Geneva than the general 'as soon as possible'
heard before. The only concession the Soviet Union may have gained
from the US regarding the Middle East formula concerned Palestinian
participation in Geneva. For the communiqué omitted the phrase used
in the July 1974 summit, that additional participants (read, the
Palestinians) would be discussed at the conference itself – suggesting, at
the least, that the Soviet Union was no longer willing to agree that
Palestinian participation be postponed. Whether this was in fact a
concession wrested from the United States or not, Moscow was
nonetheless to claim that the summit had proved a victory for the
positive effect of détente on such crises as the Middle East, creating
favourable conditions for a solution.[35] One commentary explained that
'some' saw the Middle East as a 'testing ground' for détente, but, the

commentary continued, the Vladivostok statement on a Middle East settlement disproved such pessimism.[36] In a somewhat more indirect way the Soviet Union could benefit from the impression of a successful link between détente and the Middle East conflict when, just two days after the summit, Syria announced its willingness to renew UNDOF for a further six months, thereby greatly reducing tensions in the area. This action was not determined by Moscow; indeed, it may not even have been co-ordinated with it, but the announcement, following one just two weeks earlier of a forthcoming Brezhnev trip to Syria, might have created a positive impression of the Soviet Union's role because of – or in spite of – détente. This was indeed the conclusion drawn by some Western observers, yet the overall picture tended more to the conclusion that while the tense situation in the region was not allowed to harm the détente relationship, success in the latter had little effect on regional matters, little having been achieved or perhaps even attempted on that score at Vladivostok, with Moscow merely hoping for a positive spillover, to its advantage.

The positive linkage of détente with the Middle East via the argument that it had created favourable conditions for a settlement continued somewhat, even after the Soviet cancellation of the trade agreement with the US, at which time détente itself appeared badly shaken.[37] More common, however, was the line that hotspots such as the Middle East endangered world peace (*Krasnaia zvezda*, 3 January 1975, repeated the theory linking local and global conflicts) and had to be settled in order to deepen détente.[38] Moreover, the deterioration in Soviet–US (and Soviet–Egyptian) relations at this time could be felt in the intensified Soviet accusations against the Americans regarding such matters as a partial settlement, the arming of Israel, and plans to invade the oil-producing countries.[39] Yet, just as most commentaries and speeches were positive, even optimistic, on the continuation of détente (using the argument (1) that Ford and Kissinger were still interested; and (2) that all would simply have to try harder now) so, too, with regard to the Arab–Israel conflict the overall line did not change, and the Vladivostok–Geneva Conference idea of superpower co-operation was maintained.[40] The Soviet Union chose this path (over that of obstructionist competition) to regain a foothold.

4. European Security Conference

In the summer and early autumn of 1975, Soviet foreign policy appeared to concentrate first on the long-sought European Security Conference (CSCE) and then on the issue of disarmament (and the stalemate in SALT). While this by no means led to a suspension of Soviet concern for activities in the Middle East, it did lead to speculation that Moscow wanted temporarily to freeze this thorny issue lest it interfere with the progress of the above détente-related moves. Moscow's sudden hesitation on reconvening the Geneva Conference, once Kissinger's spring efforts for a second Egyptian–Israeli agreement failed, seemed to confirm (if not create) this impression.[41] This appraisal of Moscow's priorities was probably accurate; the Soviet Union had been striving for a European Conference for over ten years, seeing it primarily as a means of securing official recognition of the results of World War Two, i.e. of the territorial-political changes in Eastern Europe. Yet, while the Soviet Union may not have wished to jeopardise (by a clash at a Geneva Middle East Conference) the American goodwill necessary for convening the CSCE finally, in the summer of 1975, the major reason for Moscow's hesitation may well have been somewhat less complicated. The difficulties of Soviet–Egyptian relations, the differences between the Soviets and the other Arab groupings over the settlement, as well as the disagreement among the Arabs themselves in the spring of 1975, were such that the USSR appears to have concluded that it could not forge a line sufficiently consistent with its own to risk the reconvening of Geneva. Moreover, the whole issue of Palestinian participation was far from settled, even amongst the Palestinians themselves or between the Palestinians and the USSR. Moscow most likely wished to enter such a conclave with at least as much leverage as the Americans, while nonetheless determined to have some sort of progress made there so as to justify the use of this forum. Thus, even before Moscow consulted with the Arabs in April and May 1975 it issued its cautionary formula on the need for 'preparations', and following these consultations spoke of different attitudes towards the conference and a settlement amongst the Arabs themselves.[42] This caveat continued well after the successful conclusion of the CSCE; for example, Gromyko's major foreign policy article in *Kommunist*, September 1975 (reprinted in *International Affairs*, December 1975) called for 'thoroughgoing and serious preparations', suggesting that Moscow still felt unsure of its position with the Arabs.[43]

At the same time, Soviet concern for the success of the CSCE may have influenced what was an albeit slight reduction in criticism of US policy in the Middle East, particularly around the time of Gromyko's meetings with Kissinger in May and July, in Vienna and Geneva respectively, primarily apparently for talks concerning SALT and the

CSCE. By and large favourable articles appeared on Soviet–American co-operation – one in *Mezhdunarodnaia zhizn'*, June 1975, even positing the favourable attitude of the two superpowers as the basis for progress in almost all areas, 'be it a political settlement in the Near East, European security and co-operation, the reduction of armed forces and armaments in Central Europe, the prevention of the spread of nuclear arms over the planet, or strategic arms limitation'. A *Pravda* article of 17 June 1975 used the line that although the Middle East was a serious hotspot, the atmosphere of détente was making it harder for anti-détentists to work. Similarly, some papers were careful to shift the brunt of their criticism regarding the Middle East to Israel, referring only to 'Israel's patrons' rather than the United States directly.[44] Most of the numerous speeches by the Soviet leaders in June 1975 did not even mention the Middle East, while the few that did made no comments critical of partial solutions or anything connected with US efforts in the area. Kirilenko even claimed that détente was creating the 'necessary prerequisites' for a political settlement.[45] Nonetheless, direct criticism of the United States, only slightly moderated, did continue to appear.[46] Moreover, it was also difficult to determine if this relative moderation was caused by détente (CSCE) considerations or merely a general (though by no means total) slackening of Soviet interest in the Arab–Israeli conflict following the failure of its consultations with the Arabs and during Washington's reassessment of its own policy.

5. The Israel–Egyptian Interim Agreement

The Israeli–Egyptian Interim Agreement concluded at the close of August 1975, with its clause for the stationing of American technicians in Sinai, offered another possible point of conflict between Soviet pursuit of détente and its policy towards the Arab–Israeli conflict. The Soviet Union opposed this agreement – the most striking expression of this opposition being the refusal even to appear to be participating, by boycotting the signing ceremony in Geneva – yet Moscow's opposition did not take the form of strong attacks on the United States of the type apparent prior to the Syrian disengagement, for example. Rather, the Soviet attacks were against the agreement itself, i.e. partial settlements that left basic questions unresolved, and, as could be expected, against the use of American technicians (and, later, against American promises to Israel, specifically in the area of arms). For all this, however, there were no leadership speeches accusing Kissinger or the Americans of 'ersatz plans' or of producing 'mice' from 'mountains'. Indeed, for all the propaganda directed against the move, a number of

official Soviet statements (speeches and communiqués) at the time of
and for over a month following the agreement, even failed to mention
the Middle East, while most of those that did, made no reference to
partial settlements.[47]

Rather, Soviet official utterances at this time devoted much
attention to the issue of détente as a whole, the question of general
disarmament and related topics, pursuant to proposals put to the UN
General Assembly by Moscow in September and probably also
connected with the bogged-down SALT talks. Even speeches by
Gromyko and Podgornyi which did criticise partial settlements placed
this in the context of the danger that the ongoing Middle East conflict
constituted for world peace. Gromyko told the UN General Assembly,

> There is no need to tell you how great the danger is when a
> particular hotbed flares up and develops into a crisis. The world has
> repeatedly encountered such a turn of events and is well aware what
> trouble it takes to extingush the flames of war.[48]

Podgornyi, in his speech honouring visiting Portuguese President
Gomes, said that the 'interests of world peace' required a settlement
and that a settlement 'would no doubt have the most favourable effect
on normalising the situation in the entire basin of the Mediterranean
Sea'.[49] This was, of course, a far cry from the earlier linkage of the
direct positive effects détente had already had on the Middle East
situation itself, but the relative moderation regarding the United States,
at the Soviet leadership level, was nonetheless notable.[50]

The more regionally dictated responses of the Soviet Union to the
interim agreement are discussed in several chapters below. Of interest
here is the possible link between this relatively mild response to an issue
well laden with potential Soviet–American discord, and Soviet–US
détente, but this link is impossible to prove. That the differences over
the agreement did *not* affect either Soviet utterances on or interest in
détente was quite obvious; Soviet comments favouring détente,
disarmament, Soviet–US co-operation and the like remained a very
bulky component of the Soviet line. That it was the interest in détente,
the desire to produce a positive atmosphere for Soviet disarmament
proposals to the UN and, more important, for the SALT talks
conducted in part by Gromyko during his September trip to the United
States and more thoroughly in the Soviet–US meetings held in the
following months, remains only a hypothesis. Kissinger claimed to have
received a mild reaction from Gromyko to the interim agreement

during their September talks, with both sides claiming (and emitting) a generally congenial atmosphere.[51] Moreover, Soviet propaganda preparation for the UN General Assembly session at the close of September rarely elaborated on the Middle East issue but concentrated, like the speeches and communiqués cited above, on détente, disarmament and the like. The Soviet Union strove to present a positive picture of continued and generally successful efforts in all matters concerning détente,[52] and, from this point of view, may simply not have wished to draw too much attention to an area where Soviet fortunes were declining.

It was only after this, with Soviet concern lest the Syrians conduct a similar agreement with the Americans and the launching of the Syrian initiative at the UN on behalf of the Palestinians, that Soviet behaviour became somewhat obstructionist in the context of the Arab–Israeli conflict. Yet, even with the USSR's pressures to prevent a Syrian move towards the United States and its renewed emphasis on the Palestinians (first to please the Syrians and later, during the Lebanese War, to pressure them and the United States), Moscow countered this with ostensibly moderate statements regarding Israel (for example, Brezhnev's speech to the February 1976 CPSU Congress) and renewed proposals for reconvening Geneva. Moreover, the Soviet Union continued to evoke détente, even in its criticism of the United States, claiming that the Americans were flagging in the application of détente to the Arab–Israel crisis – i.e. failing to agree to Soviet participation in the quest for a settlement.[53] Conversely, the overall line on détente remained unchanged, even to the point of excluding any mention whatsoever of the Middle East when trying to make the point of how successfully détente was progressing.[54] Indeed, even in the spring of 1976, when numerous articles on détente appeared in the Soviet media in response to growing criticism of US policy,[55] the Soviets refrained from mentioning the Middle East, concentrating on positive developments or using other examples of potential obstacles.

A renewed optimism regarding Soviet–US relations appeared to prevail in Moscow in the first year or so of the Carter administration, despite the early temporary deterioration in Soviet–American relations. The deterioration, which was primarily felt in the area of SALT, and precipitated by President Carter's 'Human Rights' demands, did not generate a harder Soviet line on a settlement of the Arab–Israeli conflict. Although American moves on a Middle East settlement occasioned Soviet concern over the diminishing possibility of Soviet–American co-operation (and, therefore, Soviet inclusion) in the Middle

East peace efforts, Moscow welcomed the American abandonment of the step-by-step method in favour of a comprehensive solution and the Administration's commitment to a reconvening of the Geneva Peace Conference. Soviet criticism of American Middle East policy – and a somewhat more radical Soviet line at least with regard to the Palestinians – did emerge when the Americans appeared to be reaching a compromise position with the PLO. Nonetheless, the May 1977 Soviet–US talks, which marked the beginning of an improvement in overall Soviet–American relations, reportedly also occasioned a more co-operative Soviet attitude regarding the Middle East in general, and the Palestinian question in particular.[56]

While it is difficult to prove any direct connection with the gradual amelioration of Soviet–US relations, especially in the area of SALT, over the summer and early autumn of 1977, the joint Soviet–US statement on the Middle East on 1 October sparked much speculation in the West that Soviet concessions on SALT had been made in exchange for the inclusion of Moscow once again in the Middle East peace process. American willingness to bring the Soviets back into the Middle East picture may indeed have been encouraged by the general improvement in Soviet–US relations at that time, but the actual decision was probably prompted by specific American tactical considerations, *vis-à-vis* Israel, on the one hand, and Syria and the PLO on the other.

On a more general level, the move was at least consistent with National Security Adviser Zbigniew Brzezinski's conviction that the Soviet Union would have to have an active role in a Middle East settlement eventually.[57] Moreover, the idea of trade-offs on such important issues as SALT did not appear to be part of either Soviet or American policy strategies. In any case, Sadat's visit to Jerusalem in November 1977 and the new peace-making momentum it initiated made the joint Soviet–US statement irrelevant. As long as the USSR remained opposed to Sadat's moves and supported Syria and the rejection front, while the USA remained committed to the Egyptian–Israeli negotiations, Soviet–US co-operation on the Middle East was obviously ruled out.

The foregoing would suggest that while the Soviet Union sought to use the policy of détente as a justification for and means of obtaining a role in the Middle East, it was careful not to permit either negative spill-overs from one to the other or the possibility of trade-offs between them. This was particularly the case with regard to preventing Soviet–American discord in the Arab–Israeli context from affecting the overall Soviet–American détente relationship. The opposite was also generally – but not always – the case. Similarly, whatever the ups and downs in one policy sphere, there was no basic change in the second. Thus, it would seem that on the whole the Soviets strove, whenever possible, to maintain a certain compartmentalisation (the October War itself having been a case when this was *not* possible). Yet, the two areas – détente and Middle East policy – were not always or totally unrelated with regard to very short-term tactical-propaganda manoeuvres; nor were they segregated when some benefit could be produced (or claimed) by linking them. On the whole, however, it is most difficult to prove such linkage or even interaction; it is much easier to investigate Soviet policy in each sphere according to the parameters of that sphere. The priority of the détente policy, with its global implications and importance, would appear obvious, just as Soviet–American co-operation in the regional conflict has emerged as Moscow's preferred option. One cannot say definitely that the last was the result of the moderating effects of détente or merely the lack of alternative options. The very paucity of options acceptable to the Soviet Union derives from several concomitant circumstances: the increased risk (including risk to détente) of the Arab–Israeli conflict, with the increased involvement of the United States, *together* with Moscow's declining interest in and benefits from the conflict. Yet the Soviet Union is not the sole actor in either sphere, thus necessitating, upon occasion, competitive moves which are apparently – or even in reality – potentially detrimental to superpower co-operation and even détente. Moreover, Soviet policy, both in the sphere of détente and even in the sphere of the Arab–Israeli conflict, is linked to other, sometimes conflicting, interests in still other spheres, the most important and obvious being Soviet strategic interests, e.g. in the Indian Ocean. This, too, can and has produced what would appear to be the opposite of a policy of co-operation or détente. Yet, even in recent years after the Yom Kippur War, when Soviet influence and possibly interest in the area of the Arab–Israeli conflict has been on the wane, the Soviet Union's pronouncements and actual policy initiatives have tended on the whole to give priority to a positive Soviet–American relationship as a means of achieving Soviet objectives.

Notes

1. For a discussion of Soviet interests in the area see Galia Golan, *Yom Kippur and After: The Soviet Union and the Middle East Crisis* (London:

Cambridge University Press, 1977), chap. 1. The forward deployment of the Soviet navy dates back to the 1960s, traceable, possibly, to the Soviet failure in the Cuban missile crisis, but, more specifically, to the deployment of American nuclear submarines. See Michael McCguire (ed.), *Soviet Naval Developments: Context and Capability* (New York: Praeger, 1975).

2. Ibid., and Geoffrey Jukes, 'The Indian Ocean in Soviet Naval Policy', *Adelphi Papers* (London), 87 (1972).

3. For example, the Soviet refusal to agree to a moratorium on Egypt's military debt; Soviet willingness to criticise and employ a degree of arms blackmail against Syria during the Lebanese civil war; Soviet demands for cash payments and the stationing of certain personnel in Jordan in exchange for a Soviet air-defence system.

4. A settlement, to which the Soviets were a party and co-guarantor, might put a halt to Moscow's declining role in the area; it could provide formal international recognition of their interests there as well as a continued presence – even military – as co-guarantor, without necessarily eliminating the possibility of political competition with the US in the area, in a much less volatile atmosphere.

5. See, for example, the entire issue of *Mezhdunarodnaia zhizn'*, 11 (1975) in preparation for the 25th CPSU Congress.

6. V. E. Chiskin, 'A Symposium on International Relations: Politics and the Individual', *Voprosy filosofii*, 2 (1975), pp.141–9.

7. V. Zhurkin, 'Détente and International Crisis', *Mezhdunarodnaia zhizn'*, 6 (1974), pp.95–104 (quotes from English version: *International Affairs*, 7 (1974), pp.89–97).

8. See Sadat speeches, *R. Cairo*, 23 July 1973/*SWB IV*, 25 July 1973; *R. Cairo*, 3 April 1974/*SWB IV*, 5 April 1974 and interviews, *al-Hawadith*, 6 October 1972/*SWB IV*, 11 October 1972; *TANYUG*, 26 May 1973/*SWB IV*, 30 May 1973.

9. Sadat pointed out the contradictory nature of the USSR's pursuit of détente with the US while opposing any similar policy on the part of the Arabs – *R. Cairo*, 1 May 1974/*SWB IV*, 3 May 1974.

10. Speeches of Suslov, *R. Vilnius*, 28 November 1973/*FBIS III*, 29 November 1973; Grechko, *Krasnaia zvezda*, 12 October 1973; General Petrov, *R. Khabarovsk*, 7 November 1973/*FBIS III*, 8 November 1973; Admiral Smirnov, *R. Vladivostok*, 7 November 1973/*FBIS III*, 8 November 1973; Col.-Gen. Salmanov, *R. Kiev*, 7 November 1973/*FBIS III*, 8 November 1973.

11. Shelepin's speech to WFTU, *Trud*, 18 October 1973; Grechko's speech in Warsaw, *Krasnaia zvezda*, 18 October 1973; *Krasnaia zvezda*, 13 and 20 October 1973. See also Dina Spechler, 'Internal Influences on Soviet Foreign Policy: Elite Opinion and the Middle East', The Soviet and East European Research Centre, Hebrew University of Jerusalem, Jerusalem, 1977.

12. *Izvestiia*, 1 December 1973. See also Kosygin, *Sovetskaia Belorossiia*, 15 November 1973, or *Pravda* commentary, 16 November 1973 or Soviet message to Algiers Conference of Arab heads of state, *R. Moscow* in Arabic, 26 November 1973/*FBIS III*, 27 November 1973.

13. A. Kislov, 'Soviet–American Relations in the Middle East', *SShA* 9(57) (1974), pp.63–8; V. Alexandrov, 'Middle East: A New Step Towards Peace', *International Affairs*, 8 (1974), pp.86–8. See also Viktor Matveyev, 'Détente and Conflicts', *New Times*, 46 (1974), pp.4–5; *R. Moscow*, 23 February 1975/*FBIS III*, 24 February 1975; M. V. Valerianov, 'The USSR–USA: Results, Difficulties and Prospects', *SShA*, 1 (1976), pp.3–10.

14. *Pravda*, 15 February 1975.

15. For Soviet behaviour during the war, including the issue of détente, see Golan, *Yom Kippur and After*, chap. 2.

16. *Pravda*, 17 March 1974.

17. *New York Times,* 22 March 1974; *Izvestiia, R. Moscow* and TASS, 29 March 1974/*FBIS III,* 1 April 1974; *Pravda,* 3 April 1974 (the last did add, however, that differences existed between the two countries because of opponents to détente).

18. See *Le Monde,* 29 March 1974.

19. TASS, 28 March 1974/*FBIS III,* 28 March 1974 (joint communiqué). They agreed to meet again in Geneva in April and it may even have been decided to meet regularly during the disengagement negotiations and, possibly, to have the signing of the agreement in Geneva, so as to provide for at least the appearance of Soviet participation. (*New York Times,* 30 March 1974, carried the State Department announcement of the April meeting to be held prior to Kissinger's departure for the Middle East; *New York Times,* 29 March 1974, quoted a US official on Kissinger's agreement to consult with the Russians.)

20. E.g. *R. Moscow* in English to Africa, 29 March 1974/*FBIS III,* 1 April 1974; *R. Moscow* in Arabic and *R. Peace and Progress* in Arabic, 29 March 1974/*FBIS III,* 1 April 1974; *R. Moscow* in Arabic, 30 March 1974/*FBIS III,* 1 April 1974.

21. *Pravda,* 15 June 1974 (Brezhnev speech); *R. Minsk,* 10 June 1974/*FBIS III,* 11 June 1974 (Gromyko speech).

22. TASS, 2 July 1974/*FBIS III,* 3 July 1974.

23. During the summer Moscow had tried to link the Cyprus crisis with what it called US–Israeli collusion, and Brezhnev used the opportunity to issue a call on 21 July 1974 for a nuclear-free Mediterranean – *R. Moscow,* 21 July 1974/*FBIS III,* 22 July 1974 (Brezhnev to the Polish Sejm). This linkage of regional and global as well as détente and Arab–Israeli conflict issues was, however, tactical and primarily propagandistic in nature. There were also infrequent Soviet references to the inclusion of the Middle East in the idea of an Asian security pact, e.g. *R. Moscow,* 5 January 1975/*FBIS III,* 6 January 1975 or Kosygin's speech, *Pravda,* 3 November 1974.

24. Matveyev, 'Détente and Conflicts', pp.4–5; *Pravda,* 16 November 1974 (Kirilenko). See also *R. Moscow* in Finnish, 16 October 1974/*FBIS III,* 18 October 1974 (Podgornyi) and *Pravda,* 3 November 1974 (Kosygin), though the long comments by Kosygin on extending détente to all areas, including the Middle East, were in the general context of Asia.

25. See Gromyko, *R. Moscow,* 6 November 1974/*FBIS III,* 7 November 1974; Podgornyi, TASS, 18 October 1974/*FBIS III,* 21 October 1974; *Izvestiia,* 30 November 1974. Ukrainian Communist Party Secretary V. V. Shcherbitskü also linked 'anti-détentists' with such 'reactionaries' as Zionists, Fascists, etc. but this position was somewhat more standard for him – *Pravda Ukrainy,* 19 October 1974.

26. See, for example, *Izvestiia,* 2 November 1974, which referred only to Israel's 'NATO patrons' while foreign broadcasts were more direct.

27. Also prior to Vladivostok there were the usual attacks on US oil ambitions (e.g. Lev Tolkunov, 'The Middle East Crisis and the Ways of Solving It', ibid., *Kommunist,* 13 (1974), pp. 97–105, and 'Oil and Politics', 16 (1974), pp.114–24) and something of a campaign, primarily in foreign broadcasts but also in domestic media, regarding American bases and plans in the Indian Ocean (including a reference to the Trident missiles in D. N. Konavalov, 'The Trident Programme', *SShA,* 11 (1974), pp. 66–9). The latter, however, was probably directed towards the visit of Sri Lanka President Bandaranaike to the USSR in mid-November 1974. At any rate, both oil and the Indian Ocean were relatively standard lines in Soviet propaganda to the Third World, directed at Soviet interests beyond the Arab–Israeli conflict, though linked with détente and the Soviet–American relationship.

28. See, for example, *R. Moscow*, 3 and 17 November 1974/*FBIS III*, 4 and 19 November 1974; *R. Moscow*, 12 November 1974/*FBIS III*, 13 November 1974; TASS, 22 November 1974/*FBIS III*, 22 November 1974; *R. Moscow* in Arabic (e.g. 19 November 1974/*FBIS III*, 20 November 1974) did, however, mention this as a topic of the talks.

29. *R. Moscow*, 24 November 1974/*FBIS III*, 25 November 1974.

30. Admitted by *R. Moscow*, 24 November 1974/*FBIS III*, 25 November 1974 as still a difficult problem.

31. Communiqué, TASS, 24 November 1974/*FBIS III*, 25 November 1974.

32. On co-operation, see the communiqué and Brezhnev's speeches as well as commentary, *R. Moscow*, 24 November 1974/*FBIS III*, 25 November 1974; regarding collusion, e.g. *R. Moscow* in Arabic, 25 November 1974/*FBIS III*, 26 November 1974 or *R. Moscow* in English to Africa, 25 November 1974/*FBIS III*, 26 November 1974 which argued that détente and Soviet–US co-operation could solve the remaining hotbeds of tension in the world.

33. *R. Peace and Progress* in Arabic, 28 November 1974/*FBIS III*, gave as an example of the positive influence of détente the inclusion in the communiqué of the phrase on the Palestinians' interests, even though this phrase had been in the communiqué after the 1973 summit and even in the Nixon–Sadat communiqué in June 1974 (and considered unsatisfactory by the Palestinians because of the use of the word 'interests' rather than 'rights').

34. *Pravda*, 27 November 1974.

35. *Pravda*, 9 December 1974; *Izvestiia*, 31 December 1974.

36. *R. Moscow*, 1 December 1974/*FBIS III*, 30 December 1974.

37. V. Larin, 'Middle East: Two Tendencies', *New Times*, 1 (1975), pp.12–13, used the unusual argument that as détente asserted itself more the Israeli military would find it harder to act.

38. E.g. *Krasnaia zvezda*, 5 January 1975; *Pravda*, 15 January 1975 (Kosygin). See also D. Antonov, 'Urgent Task', *New Times*, 7 (1975), p.6: '. . . evolution of the international climate is dependent in a large measure on developments in that region [Middle East].' A settlement would 'understandably give impetus to the development of détente'.

39. *Pravda*, 5 7, 18 January 1975, 2 February 1975; *Izvestiia*, 23 January 1975, 1 February 1975; *Krasnaia zvezda*, 31 December 1974, 12 January 1975; *R. Moscow*, 29 December 1974/*FBIS III*, 30 December 1974, and *R. Moscow*, 5 January 1975/ *FBIS III*, 6 January 1975.

40. See *Pravda* and *Izvestiia*, 18 January 1975; V. Kuznetsov, 'Détente: Deep Roots', *New Times*, 5 (1975), pp.4–5; G. Troin and V. Babak, 'International Review – Current Problems of World Politics, Détente Gains Momentum', *Mirovaia ekonomika i mezhdunarodnye otnosheniia*, 1(1975), pp.91–7; N. D. Turkatenko, 'An Important Stage in the Development of Soviet–American Relations', *SShA*, 1 (61) (1975), pp.8–15; editorial, '1975', *SShA*, 1(61), 1975, pp.3–7; D. Tomashevskii, 'The Scientific and Technological Revolution and American Foreign Policy', *Kommunist*, 2 (1975), pp.117–20.

41. Just a few days after Kissinger's failure, the Soviet media began to speak of the need for 'thorough preparations' before Geneva could be reconvened. *Pravda* and *R. Moscow*, 30 March 1975/*FBIS III*, 1 April 1975; *Izvestiia*, 1 April 1975; *R. Peace and Progress*, 31 March 1975/*FBIS III*, 1 April 1975.

42. For problems with Syria, see Galia Golan and Itamar Rabinovich, 'The Soviet Union and Syria: the Limits of Co-operation', in this volume; for problems in connection with the PLO, see Galia Golan, 'The Soviet Union and the PLO', *Adelphi Papers*, 131 (1977). For Soviet admissions of differences with the Arabs, see Kosygin and Gromyko, *Pravda*, 14 and 15 May 1975 respectively.

43. A. Gromyko, 'Peace Programme in Action', *Kommunist*, 14 (1975),

pp.3–20.

44. For example, *Pravda*, 6 and 17 June 1975.

45. Kosygin on 11 June 1975 only said that the Soviet Union was helping the Arabs in the liquidation of Israeli aggression and pursuit of a just peace, following this with remarks on the need for détente in order to shift from tensions to co-operation between the different social systems in the world. Brezhnev and Kirilenko's speeches (*R. Moscow*, 13 June 1975/*FBIS III*, 16 June 1975 and *R. Leningrad*, 20 June 1975/*FBIS III*, 19 June 1975 respectively) made no mention of the Middle East.

46. Direct criticism appeared, for example, in *Krasnaia zvezda*, 22 June 1975; *Sovetskaia Rossiia*, 6 June 1975; A. Alov, 'The Way to a Middle East Settlement', *New Times*, 28 (1975), pp.18–19; Lev Tolkunov, 'Détente Enters a New Phase', *Kommunist*, 13 (1975), pp.96–104 (otherwise giving a very positive assessment of détente, with no mention of the Middle East). See also, *R. Moscow* in English to North America, 13 June 1975/*FBIS III*, 16 June 1975 against Rabin's talks in the West; and TASS, 11 June 1975/*FBIS III*, 12 June 1975 on US oil interests (at the time of an OPEC meeting).

47. Some statements which did not mention the Middle East: Kosygin, TASS, 2 September 1975/*FBIS III*, 3 September 1975; MTI, 21 October 1975/*FBIS III*, 28 October 1975; Gromyko, communiqué with GDR, *Pravda*, 30 September 1975 and speech in *Rude pravo*, 29 September 1975. Statements which mentioned the Middle East very briefly but made no reference to partial settlements: Soviet–Hungarian communiqué, *Pravda*, 25 October 1975; Soviet–Portuguese communiqué, TASS, 3 October 1975/*FBIS III*, 6 October 1975; Brezhnev, TASS, 17 September 1975/*FBIS III*, 18 September 1975; Podgornyi, TASS, 1 October 1975/*FBIS III*, 2 October 1975.

48. Gromyko to UN, *Pravda*, 24 September 1975; Podgornyi, TASS, 1 October 1975/*FBIS III*, 2 October 1975. A *New Times* editorial at the beginning of October 1975 also said that détente should be continued to include the Middle East (and other issues such as Cyprus), 'Pressing on in the Cause of Peace', *New Times*, 40 (1975), p.1.

49. TASS, 1 October 1975 (Podgornyi)/*FBIS III*, 2 October 1975.

50. Even now, however, Soviet broadcasts to the Arabs were much more critical, especially as American overtures to Syria began and, later, when the Syrian initiative in the UN was underway.

51. *Jerusalem Post*, 21 September 1975.

52. For example, V. V. Kortunov, 'Relaxation of Tensions and the Battle of Ideas in Present Day International Relations', *Voprosy istorii KPSS*, 10 (1975), pp.16–30; Gromyko, 'Peace Programme in Action', or above speeches.

53. See, for example, M. V. Valerianov, 'The USSR–USA: Results, Difficulties, and Prospects', *SShA*, 1 (1976), pp. 3–10; D. Volsky, 'Struggle to Eliminate Hotbeds', *International Affairs*, 12 (1975), pp.39–44; Leonid Medvedko, 'High Time for a Middle East Settlement', *New Times*, 52 (1975), pp.24–5; Kosygin in Turkey, *Pravda*, 30 December 1975; N. Lebedev, 'The USSR's Effort to Reconstruct International Relations', *International Affairs*, 1 (1976), pp.3–13; A. Svetlov, 'The Soviet Union's Struggle for Military Détente', *International Affairs*, 2 (1976), pp.92–101; N. Inozemtsev, 'The Unity of Theory and Practice in the Leninist Peace Policy', *Kommunist*, 18 (1975), pp.43–53; editorial, 'The Communist Party and the Mandate of Peace', *Kommunist*, 17 (1975), pp.3–15; E. D. Dimitryev, 'The Middle East: An Important Factor of Settlement', *Kommunist*, 2 (1976), pp.99–105; I. P. Beliaev, 'The USA and the Middle East Crisis', *SShA*, 3 (1976), pp.16–17; L. Vidyasova, 'Inter-Imperialist Contradictions and Western Foreign Policy', *International Affairs*, 3 (1976), pp.98–108, accused Western political strategists of procrastinating and of maintaining conflict situations, such as the Middle East, so as to claim that the

socialist states and the Soviet Union were obstructing détente (p.107). As in the past, statements by military people ignored the idea of co-operation, pointing to the Middle East as a sign of the imperialists' continued aggressiveness and the need for vigilance (e.g. Col.-Gen. A. V. Gerasimov, *R. Kiev,* 7 November 1975/*FBIS III,* 10 November 1975).

54. K. Chernenko, 'The Leninist Strategy of Peace in Action', *International Affairs,* 5 (1976), pp.4–12 (who even spoke of opponents to détente in Europe, NATO, the USA and China), or *Izvestiia,* 29 April 1976, in a long article entitled 'Rhythm of Détente' or A. Vakhrameyev, 'Socialism and Peace are Indivisible', *International Affairs,* 7 (1976), pp.4–12, (who cited only good examples of détente, ignoring the Middle East on this point).

55. This was the time of Ford's 1 March 1976 declaration that he would no longer use the word 'détente'.

56. In his May talks with Vance, Gromyko was reportedly flexible with regard to the timing of PLO participation in a reconvened Geneva conference; Brezhnev had reportedly conveyed this position to Arafat during the latter's Moscow visit a few weeks earlier. See TASS, 7 April 1977; *Le Monde,* 14 April 1977, and Karen Dawisha, 'The Soviet Union in the Middle East: Setback or Comeback?', *The Middle East,* 33 (July 1977), p.27.

57. See *New York Times,* 14 December 1977; also Zbigniew Brzezinski, François Duchéne and Kiichi Saeki, 'Peace in an International Framework', *Foreign Policy,* 19 (Summer 1975), pp.3–17. In particular this point had been made in the Brookings Institution report on the Middle East in December 1975, in the composition of which Brzezinski had participated.

2 CHANGES IN SOVIET POLITICAL-MILITARY POLICY IN THE MIDDLE EAST AFTER 1973

Amnon Sella

The Middle East forms only part of Soviet global deployment and although not the most important link, it draws heavily on Soviet sources. Ideally the Soviet government would have liked to deploy its strategic forces independent of regional forces, but for historical and practical reasons it cannot do so. The historical reasons are that the Soviet Union managed to obtain a foothold in the Middle East owing to rivalries between Egypt and Iraq and Iraq's alignment with the West, and it consolidated its position by taking the Arab side in the Arab-Israeli conflict. As time went by, the USSR found itself deeply involved in the region's disputes and policies. Encroachment on to what used to be a Western domain turned into various commitments from which it was impossible to disentangle without loss of face, money or both. The practical reasons were that to date the Soviet military has had to work under tight constraints. For instance, lack of aircraft carriers forces the Soviet government to seek good relations with as many Middle Eastern countries as the military deems necessary to provide adequate air cover for a growing navy.

The Soviet military aims in the Middle East on the strategic level are the following:

1. Securing targets deep inside the USSR against the 'second strike capability' of the Sixth Fleet.
2. Securing the southern border of the USSR against any potential hostile coalition.
3. Securing water passages and sea-routes for Soviet merchant and war ships.
4. A Soviet presence along the same to apply pressure on Western traffic when the need arises.
5. Building and expansion of a strategic infrastructure: harbours, airfields, command-and-control networks, all designed to extend the 'defence-perimeter' of the USSR.
6. Forward deployment of sea and air forces that can join the inner line of Soviet defence with the far reaches of its current deployment.
7. Securing the existing Soviet bases on friendly territories like

Yugoslavia, Iraq, Syria, Libya, Yemen and others.

This paper seeks to analyse the intermediate level between the strategic aim and the tactical politicking in the post-October 1973 period. The assumption is that if a distinctive line exists between a 'grand strategy' design and a daily political bargaining, the USSR has failed to toe this line, as indeed the British and the French failed to do in the past. The paper examines changes in the USSR's bargaining strategies in its attempt to maintain a balance between its global need to avoid direct confrontation with the USA and its need to keep and to enhance Soviet influence in the region. The paper also attempts to single out the USSR's weapon supply policy in order to show the implications of this particular phenomenon in a rather complicated political environment.

The Soviet Strategic Plan before 1973

In the period between 1955 and the end of 1973 the Soviet Union invested over three billion dollars in military aid to Egypt.[1] Most of this aid was given as long-term loans at low interest rates or else in exchange for Egyptian cotton. However, the real return reaped by the Soviet Union was its growing presence in Egyptian harbours and airfields and its considerable influence over the configuration of Egypt's armed forces. The latter was achieved by many Soviet advisers and technicians and by the types of weapon systems supplied to Egypt which moulded its military doctrine. While the Soviet government was still deliberating whether to build aircraft carriers on a large scale, a question which also involved the nagging problem of the auxiliary ships that would be needed, the Mediterranean squadron found shelter in Egypt's harbours, and painful decisions could be put off for the time being, although not for long. The lessons of 1967 hastened the building programme of some auxiliary ships and may have modified the design of the Kuril class, the first Soviet aircraft carrier.[2] A large complex of airfields under exclusive Soviet control provided shore-based air cover for the Soviet fleet and a jumping-off board for reconnaissance flights over NATO ships in the Mediterranean.[3] The basis in Egypt once established, it could be combined with the one gradually expanding in Syria to form the infrastructure for a Soviet 'forward deployment' that could outflank NATO in the Eastern Mediterranean and bring pressure to bear against the 'soft under-belly' of Europe. This infrastructure of course helped also to promote Soviet interests in Arab countries.

The USSR had every reason to want to secure this posture for itself. The US Sixth Fleet with its aircraft carriers and Polaris submarines presented an ugly threat to vast urban and industrial areas deep inside Soviet territory.[4] Furthermore, conscious of its growing prestige as a superpower, the Soviet Union could not leave the Americans unchallenged in the Mediterranean. Increased presence in Arab countries *ipso facto* involved an increase in Soviet traffic. Soviet prestige everywhere was nurtured by the impressive presence and friendly visits of large, sleek, modern warships.[5] And last but not least, a well-buttressed presence in the Mediterranean could be utilised in the service of still more ambitious plans. A stable presence in the Indian Ocean can benefit considerably by a safe and strong rear echelon in the Mediterranean and a measure of control over the Suez Canal, and such a presence may prove vital for the USSR when the US 'Trident system' is put to sea.

This formidable strategy, which for a while seemed to be materialising, was jeopardised even before it got off the ground when Egypt expelled the Soviet advisers in July 1972. Since 1973 a great deal of Soviet political, diplomatic and economic effort has been invested in salvaging the foundation of what had promised to be a remarkably advantageous Soviet bastion in the Middle East.

The October 1973 War: Egypt

On 16 October 1973, when Sadat voiced the threat that if Israel attacked Egypt in depth he had the means to retaliate against Tel Aviv, he changed the whole problem of the balance of power in the Middle East.[6] The terms of the balance were altered in more ways than one. He inaugurated a limited version of the 'balance of terror' through conventional arms, but at the same time he indicated *inter alia* the possibility of a nuclear 'balance of terror'. His threat also amounted to a formal pledge that Israel would not be allowed to penetrate deep into Egypt with immunity and that the penalty for trespass might be destruction deep inside Israel.[7] Sadat later elaborated this idea to the effect that an attack on the reconstructed cities of the Canal would also be considered an attack on Egypt proper and would be answered in kind.[8] Thus a whole new edifice arose of ideas of deterrence, with the concept of 'hostage cities' as its cornerstone: if any Egyptian town were attacked, an Israeli town would be attacked in retaliation.

Whether Sadat on 16 October 1973 did or did not have the ground-to-ground missiles needed to back up his threat is a matter of conjecture. What is certain is that the threat had its weight in the deliberations over Soviet readiness to support Egypt, and so contributed to the superpower crisis of 24 October, when the US government decided on a 'nuclear alert'.[9] Some sources have it that the USSR was committed to guaranteeing Egypt against Israeli bombing in depth and that two SCUD missile battalions were actually shipped from a Soviet Black Sea port to Egypt on 12 September 1973.[10] The first inference could be drawn from an interview given by Sadat to an American journalist in April 1973, though he gave no definite date for the installation he hinted at.[11] In the course of the fighting in October, when Egypt's military situation deteriorated sharply and Syria was knocked out of the war, the USSR is alleged to have transferred a further two SCUD battalions in haste, thus bringing the Soviet missile establishment in Egypt up to brigade strength.[12] These last two battalions, which may have been pulled out of the Soviet defence system in Europe and sent sailing off to Egypt, could have been accompanied by full teams to operate them and their nuclear warheads according to the book. This would be no more than organisational routine, even if not exactly prudent from the political point of view. It is a fact that all the rumours pinpoint the dates 16 or 17 October for the passage through the Bosphorus of a mysterious ship emitting radio-active signals.[13] 16 October was a crucial date because it was then that the Israeli forces crossed the Suez Canal, decisively seizing the initiative, and that Sadat made his 'hostage city' speech.

Egypt's desire to have her armed forces furnished with an independent deterrent force presented the Soviet government with a complex problem. This desire not only ran counter to traditional Soviet policy in supplying weapon systems but also increased the risk of another round of hostilities in the Middle East, and one which would be even more liable to get out of hand than the previous ones. It amounted to a ground-to-ground missile force under Egyptian command, which in its turn went several steps towards a possible nuclear posture some time in the future. The Soviet Union has always refused to give or sell weapon systems unless Soviet advisers and technicians go with them to train the recipient army in their use and thereby exert a measure of political influence as well.[14] Moreover, tactical missiles are the most sophisticated ground weapon systems, short of full-scale nuclear capability. Ground-to-ground missiles must be incorporated into a whole system of defensive and offensive weapons, including the air force. The USSR could not agree to any radical change in its arms supply policy before 1973, nor yet for quite a long time afterwards, because as the result of any such change the USSR might find itself with no say at all in Egyptian foreign or even military policy and still be called upon to render assistance in an emergency and shoulder responsibility for failure or for a crisis on a global scale.[15]

Egypt's Postwar Dilemma: Soviet Military Support or American Diplomacy

Thus on 16 October 1973 Sadat explicitly shifted the Middle East arms race into high gear. He could no longer retreat from the advanced posture of deterrence that he had adopted without losing face with the Arab states or credibility with Israel. But to make this deterrent credible he had to find a reliable arms supply source, and one that would give him a free hand in trying to restore his lost territories without having to resort to war again. Moscow insisted on supply of arms as an 'instrument of political leverage'[16] which, broadly interpreted, could also cover the reincorporation of Egypt in a Soviet general strategy for the Middle East. Washington, on the other hand, promised to put pressure on Israel in order to make her give up some or all of the occupied territories.[17] Unfortunately for Egypt, these two lines were hardly compatible with each other. The choice between them was difficult and no immediate resolution of the dilemma was in sight. Sadat therefore decided on a long-range manoeuvre which tried to embrace both alternatives: to maintain low-keyed relations with the USSR, avoiding any deliberate deterioration, while offering a warm welcome to American initiatives without surrendering the option of backing out. At the same time Sadat started on a long-term programme of 'rearmament for the eighties'.[18]

Egypt had been the mainstay of the Soviet Union's Middle Eastern policy since 1955. After the blow dealt by the expulsion of Soviet advisers in July 1972, Soviet policy in Egypt seemed to lose both orientation and momentum. During the year preceding the October War there was a revival born of expediency between the two countries, but this was followed after the war by an almost immediate eclipse.[19] From 24 October a series of events snowballed into a remarkable transformation of the superpower-to-client relationship, which is dealt with in detail elsewhere in this volume. What concerns us here is the impact of this change on Soviet military policy in the area.

The date of 24 October is doubly significant since it is probable that on that date the USSR may have been on the brink of introducing Soviet forces into the area (perhaps armed with nuclear weapons) in order to save the Egyptian Third Army.[20] Readiness or the possibility of readiness to use a nuclear threat in the Middle East was only one of a series of Soviet moves during the war, mainly towards its end. Soviet troop carriers were sighted in the Mediterranean, landing craft were said to have been spotted not far from the Egyptian coast. There were rumours of intense activity at an airfield near Budapest, where elements of Soviet airborne divisions were allegedly located. By 24 October the number of Soviet naval units in the Eastern Mediterranean had reached the staggering figure of eighty-five.[21] Any one of these moves would have created a stir at USA HQ. Put together they were definitely alarming. Despite the 'hot line', despite the fact that Ambassador Dobrynin was in constant touch with the US administration, and despite the exchange of signals between the two superpowers before each escalation, by 24 October no little uncertainty had been generated as to Soviet intentions.[22] The only way to make it clear to the Soviet government that the USA was seriously worried and to let the Soviet leaders off the hook without their losing face was to alert the Strategic Air Command. The nuclear alert did bring tension to a peak but it also allowed the Soviet government to demonstrate that they were 'sane', 'peace-loving' people and put the onus for the scare on the US 'warmongers'. In the light of this extraordinary crisis — only a degree less acute than the Cuban missile crisis — the twists and turns of Soviet-Egyptian 'friendship' since 1973 appear all the more surprising.

Faced with its declining position in Egypt, the Soviet government was well aware that it would be impossible to carry on as though nothing had happened. While trying to maintain a low profile in Egypt, the USSR groped vainly for a new initiative in its Middle Eastern policy. From the shambles of the old policy Brezhnev tried to salvage some vestige of a 'common political front' with Egypt. He also tried to bring pressure to bear on Sadat by using Syria, Libya and later even the PLO.[23] The Soviet government in its exasperation tried to trade its former monopoly in weapon systems for something less than that, like control over the supply of spare parts for the main weapon systems, but found out that it was being asked to take its place as an ordinary customer seeking favour in the eyes of a country that can afford to choose. At the same time there was less and less political consultation with the USSR, while US diplomacy was scoring many successes. Sadat wanted to prevent a new outbreak of war after October 1973 by keeping up the pace of the American 'momentum' but without relaxing his military vigilance in case his political manoeuvres did not succeed.[24] The Americans were happy to help. They had nothing to gain from a new round of fighting and they were therefore willing to bring about a disengagement of forces. Once the Egyptian and Israeli armies were no longer confronting each other, there would be a breathing space for further negotiations. Since the Egyptians could not lose by the

disengagement of forces that was taking shape in Secretary of State
Kissinger's mind and since the Americans could only gain by it, there
was common ground for American–Egyptian agreement.

With the end of the war and the subsiding of tension between the
superpowers[25] the Soviet government found that it had no way of
making any constructive contribution. It could not serve as a mediator
between Israel and Egypt for the simple reasons that it had no relations
with Israel and the job of mediator was firmly in Kissinger's hands. All
the advice the Soviet government could give was negative, warning
Egypt not to trust the USA and vaguely propounding a general
settlement for the Arab–Israeli conflict.[26] In actual terms this policy
meant doing nothing for the time being except to apply more pressure
on Israel to make it give way. Egypt had no objection to certain points:
Sadat was perfectly ready to replenish his arsenals and have the Soviet
Union make up for his war losses, provided he was given a free hand to
go along with the Americans.[27] Understandably, the USSR did not like
the dichotomy between a military option based on a steady flow of
Soviet-made equipment to Egypt and a political option based on better
understanding between Sadat and Kissinger.

By April 1974, Sadat had succeeded in mobilising a great deal of
international goodwill for Egypt. The West was interested in good
relations with the country that had challenged Israel on the field of
battle and not been defeated. It was interested in oil, in order, in some
sort of peace. It was eager to invest in reconstruction and if possible
also in military aid.[28] The West European countries, having castigated
the USA for maintaining the balance of power in the Middle East in
defiance of the Arab oil embargo, were prepared to profit from the
results of the American power game. With every Western initiative, the
Soviet monopoly position in Egypt was shaken more and more. For
some time Sadat investigated Western sources to find out whether he
could obtain any weapon systems in the West.[29] With his
announcement in April 1974 that after almost two decades of complete
reliance on the USSR he had decided to diversify his armament
sources,[30] Sadat struck a blow at the very foundation of Soviet-
Egyptian friendship, unstable as it had become. Despite all the USSR's
political exertions, military aid had been its main contribution to Egypt
and the other Middle Eastern countries.[31] The Soviet reaction was
immediate: resumption of arms supplies to Egypt, as reported by many
sources during the last week of May.[32] The event was even played up a
bit as 'coinciding' with the 'arrival' of the new Soviet Ambassador –
whose nomination had been announced in Cairo a month earlier.

Replacing Vinogradov, who had left early in November 1973, V. P. Poliakov was said to have brought a very friendly message from Brezhnev. This may have been the first feeler put out regarding a possible state visit by Brezhnev to Cairo.

The Syrian Equation

Many of the Soviet Union's activities in Egypt in this period, although apparently of a purely military and economic nature, were directed towards its main political goal: the reconvening of the kind of Geneva Conference which would be of benefit to the Soviet Union. For this it needed at least the consent of Egypt and Syria.

Early in 1974 the Soviet Union was reported to be putting pressure on Syria to agree to attend a renewed Geneva Conference by threatening to stop arms supplies.[33] However, Syria did not waver in its declared policy of not negotiating with Israel and maintained a belligerent posture. No sooner had Sadat returned from his tour of Arab capitals and Fahmi from his visit to Moscow than the Syrians began warming up their border with Israel with skirmishes and artillery duels.[34] In the south tension was gradually easing: Israeli forces were withdrawing from the west bank of the Canal, and the siege of the town of Suez itself was lifted by the end of January 1974. Israel had started on the biggest gamble in its history — giving back territory by agreement; Sadat was implementing his long-range policy of a lower profile for Soviet-Egyptian relations and more room for American initiative. Thus in the south the danger of renewed warfare was receding perceptibly, while it flared up in the north. On both the southern and the northern fronts there had been sporadic outbursts of firing, artillery duels, commando raids and exchanges of small-arms fire that on occasion threatened the fragile truce, but by the end of January 1974 the Egyptian front was finally calm. The Syrians, moreover, had a trump card: the Israeli prisoners-of-war. They had little to lose from a controlled war of attrition. If the Kremlin was reluctant to be involved in another round of full-scale hostilities, it made no display of this fact, and duly replenished Syria's depleted stocks of tanks and aeroplanes.[35] President Asad was free to agree to American mediation any time he chose to do so and in the meantime he could step up clashes along the border with Israel. Syria's Foreign Minister Khaddam declared that Syria was waging a war of attrition in order to keep Israeli reserves mobilised and paralyse Israel's economy.[36]

The Syrians felt they had good reason to take a tough line. War damage to the country's economic infrastructure was estimated

officially at about 1·8 billion dollars.[37] In addition, Asad was in
the grip of a host of constraints. He could not afford to achieve
less than his Egyptian ally as a result of the war. He was proud that
Syria had been instrumental in conceiving and planning the war and
intended that its result should have the appearance of a victory for
Arab nationalism: only such a victory could put him ahead of Sadat in
their unremitting contest for the championship of the Arab world.
Sadat could play up the Palestinian cause or play it down as he pleased,
but Asad had the Palestinians encamped on the border of his own
country. Last but not least, by the end of 1973 Syria's relations with
the Soviet Union had become not unlike those between Egypt and the
Soviet Union at the height of the 1969–70 war of attrition, involving a
good measure of dependence. The rules of the Soviet–American game in
the Middle East dictated a considerable Soviet presence on Syrian soil,
namely, as far as the USSR was concerned, in Syrian ports and airfields.
Asad complied with this presence as long as he wanted to play up his
belligerent posture against Israel.

Asad knew perfectly well that had it not been for the Soviet airlift
and the Soviet presence during the October War, his position might
have been far worse.[38] He also knew that in order to restrict the Israeli
Air Force in case of war, he needed Soviet anti-aircraft (AA) weapons
and crews.[39] He wanted the Soviet Union to reconstruct his wrecked
oil installations, his bombed harbours and his badly mauled armoured
forces. His air force wanted more and better aircraft and these could
only come from the USSR, where a number of his pilots were being
trained on the most modern MiG-23s.[40] By its own account, the Syrian
Air Force had performed better in the war than the Egyptian, and Asad
was particularly sensitive to his pilots' demands.[41] Nor could he forgo
the gound-to-ground missile option: he needed the military leverage
provided by the SCUD missiles, and what was more – Sadat already
had them. Yet while all this pointed to a continued pro-Soviet
orientation, Sadat was proving that the way to bring pressure to bear on
Israel was through Washington.

The Kremlin was beginning to lose its grip on the Middle East early
in 1974, in spite of the fact that the October War had produced better
results for the Arab cause than all previous clashes. Despite the Soviet
contribution to these achievements,[42] Moscow's allies in the region,
Egypt and Syria, preferred to deal with the USA. Sadat was brazenly
opting for a political solution, namely the American one, while Asad
was doing much the same in his own style. The Kremlin could not
advise Asad to 'hang tough', for he was already doing so, nor could it

advise him to negotiate, as he was doing that too. It could not refuse him new supplies of weapon systems either, for military equipment was the only commodity with which the USSR could hope to maintain its influence in Syria. Besides, as the Soviet dispute with Egypt became more unpleasant day by day, it was only prudent to make sure of the naval and air bases in Syria. The Soviet Navy could provide the huge reinforcements it did in October only because shore-based aeroplanes were able to give its vessels at least the appearance of air-cover to countermand to a modest extent the prodigious might of the US Sixth Fleet. Thus the USSR had to give its backing to Syrian-style negotiations, although it had little if any influence over their course.[43] The Soviet government had no way of keeping Kissinger from coming to Damascus where he arrived for the first time on 15 December 1973, the first American Secretary of State to do so since the visit of Dulles in 1953. If Egypt was not willing to resume the war, Syria could not hope to go to war alone, and the Soviet Union was certainly not prepared to commit its own forces side by side with those of Syria. But it could not suggest any other, better, way of recovering the lost territories.

The alternatives before Syria were now clear enough. By tough negotiations with Israel it must produce a 'victory' of some kind as impressive as the Egyptian one, while still upholding the Palestinian cause. If war were to ensue as a result of this tough bargaining, Egypt might find itself in an impossible position and be obliged to join in the fighting, and the USSR for its part would find it difficult to do less than it had done during the October War.[44] The contours of a deal were taking shape amid the welter of efforts to keep up the pressure of the oil embargo, maintain Arab unity and produce an atmosphere of permanent crisis on the Golan Heights, all accompanied by numerous and impossible demands. In the last resort Syria was willing to exchange POWs and sign a strictly military disengagement of forces, in return for Quneitra.[45] The longer Syria could go on fighting after a fashion while Egypt was busy disengaging itself, the better for the Syrian posture as the rising leader of Arab nationalism. The USSR had no alternative but to go along with this policy, pledging itself more and more firmly to the PLO cause under Syrian pressure.[46]

This was especially so since the only substitute for another round of war in the Middle East was at least the expectation of a settlement. Kissinger succeeded in persuading Egypt, Israel and also to some extent Syria that they could not lose anything by trying to achieve a settlement step by step. This was easier for the Arabs because it did not commit them to making peace with Israel, and it was acceptable to

Israel because it prevented war and did not force her to give away very large chunks of territory at one go in return for vague political concessions. The 'step-by-step' policy became anathema to the USSR. Brezhnev wanted a full-blooded Geneva Conference where a Soviet-Arab common front would teach the USA and Israel a lesson, and where the USSR would play a role of no less importance than the USA. Yet on the one hand Syria was unwilling to attend a reconvened Geneva Conference unless certain preliminary conditions were fulfilled, and, on the other, the Egyptian-Syrian alliance was under desperate strain which seriously lessened, under these conditions, the chances for a wide Soviet-Arab common front. The linchpin of such a common front still had to be Egypt.

Problems of Military Aid – The Ceiling of Sophistication

Meanwhile, Moscow spelled out the nature of the new weapon systems being supplied to Egypt and even hinted at the need for reorganisation of the Egyptian armed forces (of course, not without generous Soviet advice) – perhaps a piece of wishful thinking.[47] In the wake of these deliveries, Egypt displayed and probably also deployed some new types of weapon systems that had not been shown before and were said not to have been in the Egyptian arsenal during the October War.[48] Up to the end of 1974, however, the USSR did not supply Egypt with overtly offensive systems; indeed, after the first deliveries Sadat was soon complaining again that he had received nothing since the end of the airlift. Sadat actually introduced another subject for complaint by claiming that the USSR had not fulfilled its obligations under old contracts and that Egypt had not received supplies that were supposed to arrive at the end of 1973.[49]

Soviet military supply policy had indeed undergone many changes over the years. Despite all the ups and downs in Soviet-Egyptian relations, however, the USSR did have a policy regarding supplies, a policy dictated by intentions and capabilities, and which was the outcome of a process of trial and error over two decades and through three major (if limited) local wars, 1967, 1969–70 and 1973. It was based on the following major considerations: availability of the matériel, cost, absorption capacity of the recipient, sophistication, political control and the risk of a global flare-up. The problems of Soviet military aid – and their solutions – depend on the correlation between these variables. For instance, a given recipient's enlarged absorptive capacity increases the demand on availability and raises the 'ceiling of sophistication', but it may decrease political control and increase the risk of a global flare-up. If the cost of the equipment is too high, the competition with other suppliers becomes sharper and this in turn weakens the bargaining posture of the USSR, that is to say the political control. As the absorption capacity of the Arab countries steadily improves, sophistication reaches the ceiling of conventional arms, which in turn raises the cost and reduces political control as the recipient country is less dependent on advisers and on spare parts. It also sharpens the competition still more and increases the risk of global flare-up. With the tremendous technological advances of recent years in, say, AA devices and penetration aids, the cost of wars becomes so high that economic constraints dictate shorter wars, even though political considerations may favour prolonging them.[50]

From 1956 on, the USSR was never willing to agree to a formal system of arms control in the Middle East on a regional basis, even though from time to time vague suggestions were bandied about for de-nuclearisation of the Mediterranean, or in other words, the elimination of the presence of the US Sixth Fleet.[51] Yet, as the USSR became increasingly interested in a dialogue with the West and first and foremost with the USA, the Soviet government did respect a certain tacit arms control, never openly seeking to produce gross imbalances in major offensive systems. After the lessons of the Six Day War, moreover, the USSR had no interest in provoking further full-scale warfare in the area and refused to let any one Arab country become strong enough to challenge Israeli air supremacy on its own.[52]

An illustration of that policy can be found in the supply of aeroplanes. Air supremacy has been deemed essential for strategic offensive. Israel has enjoyed such supremacy for many years. A war may, of course, be won without air supremacy or lost with it, but military prudence will always seek to optimise probable gains by obtaining supremacy in the air. The ratio of Israeli and Egyptian–Syrian air forces, according to available sources, was 1:2·5 at the beginning of the October War. With that ratio Israel kept its air space clear of enemy planes and managed also to inflict heavy punishment on Egyptian and Syrian air forces and installations. Given the quality of Israeli and Egyptian-Syrian machines and the assessed quality of their respective pilots and command-and-control systems, in order to achieve air supremacy the Arab countries will need a ratio of about 1:5. In absolute figures, a ratio of 1:5 calculated according to the number of planes in 1973 means that Egypt and Syria needed 2,480 first-line aeroplanes in order to achieve air supremacy. The USSR found it either difficult or imprudent to supply such numbers, and preferred to strengthen air defence.

The war of attrition after the Six Day War showed, however, that in the eyes of the Kremlin there was also a limit to the damage that Israeli air power could be allowed to inflict. When Egypt failed in its attempt to draw a line beyond which the Israeli air force could not deepen its penetration into Egypt, the USSR thereupon prepared to step in to force and plug the gaps in Egypt's sagging AA defences.[53] The resulting Soviet build-up in Egypt in 1969–70 introduced the missile era into the region. The missiles themselves – and the fact that the USSR had reached the point of supplying such advanced weapons – set new rules for the regional game, and that at a time when détente was becoming common currency in political parlance (though what was involved was still unsure). The creation of the heaviest anti-aircraft missile belt in the world meant a new reality in the Middle East and of course in Soviet-Egyptian relations as well. The missile belt could only be effective if it included all the necessary components: radar systems to cover every possible angle of attack, command and control points, a variety of launchers, missiles in sufficient amounts, an assortment of AA guns and an adequate number of modern aircraft squadrons along with the defence system. At one stroke the sophistication of the necessary systems almost reached the ceiling.

Over the years, the USSR found it increasingly difficult to hold its clients clear of the ceiling of sophistication. From one war to the next, the task became more complicated. The period of time from the design of an advanced weapon system like an aircraft till its delivery is about ten years.[54] In that period of ten years a variety of new designs, advanced models and experimental models reaches operational units: the best types are kept and the rest are shelved. A war is, of course, the best laboratory for testing out new designs. There have been four major wars in the Middle East (apart from endless skirmishes) since the first military agreement between Egypt and the Eastern bloc: the Sinai Campaign of 1956, the Six Day War of 1967, the War of Attrition of 1969–70 and the October War of 1973. The wars increased in scale and in sophistication. If most of the equipment used during the Sinai Campaign was of World War Two vintage, a very large part of the equipment deployed by both sides in the Six Day War was far more advanced. The War of Attrition marked the first step into the missile era, and the October War produced the rudiments of the balance of terror.[55] Consequently, the time elapsing between the procurement of a certain model of aircraft by operational units of the Soviet armed forces and its appearance in the arsenals of one or more of the Arab countries became ever shorter. The same applied to tanks, armoured personnel carriers (APCs), guns, missiles and electronic systems. The superpowers, for all their interest in testing out new ideas in military technology on each other, were nevertheless not happy when their respective clients' demands encroached on their well-guarded secrets. After what Sadat considered his great military victory in October 1973, it became his ambition to close the technological gap between Egypt and Israel.[56] To achieve this he was ready to diversify his sources of supply and to try to incorporate Western systems in his old Soviet-made ones.[57] If at that time he had been able to 'promote' his Soviet-made systems by creating a 'symbiosis' between them and Western-made ones, the Soviet Union would have found itself willy-nilly sharing technological secrets with its sworn adversaries.

The MiG-23 is a case worth studying. This advanced aircraft entered service in units of the Soviet Air Force no earlier than 1971. Since it is estimated that the USSR produces about a thousand first-line machines of all types annually, not many MiG-23s could have been around when the Egyptians first showed interest in purchasing them in 1971.[58] Moscow must have considered it an impertinence on the part of Sadat to demand the MiG-23 at such an early date and it was well-nigh impossible for the USSR to deliver the goods at that time. The MiG-23 was nowhere to be found outside the borders of the USSR and the Soviet government refused the Egyptian request. Brezhnev was busy during 1972 working out his détente policy and the Arab-Israeli conflict was relegated to a very low place on the list of priorities. This fact, together with the configuration of the Egyptian armed forces as they were shaping up in preparation for the October War, did not predicate offensive weapon systems such as the MiG-23.[59] Egyptian requests for ground-to-ground missiles were met only partially. FROGs were supplied in some quantities but SCUDs arrived only in small numbers on the eve of the war. No MiG-23 took part in the October War. In fact, the role assigned to the Egyptian Air Force at the beginning of the war was a limited one.[60] Ground-to-ground missiles (SCUD) under Soviet command did appear on the scene but not as part of an offensive strategy.

During 1974 the situation changed radically. By that time the Soviet Union was in a position to supply the MiG-23 to Egypt, Syria, Iraq and its other allies, and it could also present the USA with some awkward problems, since the F-14 and F-15, the American counters to the MiG-23, were not yet ready for delivery in any significant numbers.[61] Furthermore, even if the Americans had been able to sell the F-15, there remained the additional problem of its missile ordnance. The F-15 can effectively encounter the MiG-23 if it is armed with the advanced air-to-air Phoenix, and this system the Americans were reluctant to sell. However, in 1974 the USSR chose not to enter into an open arms race that would change the balance of power in favour of the Arab countries.

The Soviet government still adhered to a modicum of restraint, which comprised at most three self-imposed restrictions: (a) not to allow any one Arab country to become so strong that it could go to war against Israel alone; (b) not to allow the Arab countries a configuration of their armed forces that might tempt them to go for an all-out offensive war; and (c) to maintain a measure of control over the supply of arms to the Middle East that would allow the USSR at least some leverage in its bargaining with the Arab countries. After the October War, with the Arabs filled with a new sense of pride and power, the Soviet government found it difficult to keep within these limitations, especially since it was now faced with the choice of trading off failing political influence for much-needed hard currency. Thus Algeria was willing to pay dollars for tanks for Egypt, Saudi Arabia contributed 100 million dollars to Egypt for Soviet weaponry, and Libya was also prepared to buy large amounts of Soviet equipment.[62] The commercial nature of some of these latter-day Soviet dealings simplified USSR policy in the Middle East and provided some compensation for wounded pride and loss of influence, but it was also another step forward in the break-up of what used to be the virtual complete Soviet monopoly of arms supplies to several Arab countries.

Soviet Reassessment – In Search of a Middle Eastern Policy

Following Nixon's visit to the Middle East in June 1974, the Soviet government (while carefully preparing a Brezhnev 'counter-visit') engaged in some soul-searching concerning the whole of its Middle Eastern policy. There were at least six major issues demanding assessment and decision: the results of the Nixon visit; possible new American moves after Nixon was replaced by Ford; the wisdom of Brezhnev's 'counter-visit' to the region; the approaching Arab summit meeting at Rabat; the debate that would follow at the UN; and the first fruits of Egypt's decision to diversify its arms supply. The Soviet ambassadors to Egypt, Syria and the Lebanon were therefore called to Moscow for consultations at the beginning of September.[63] While Poliakov, Mukhitdinov and Azimov were conferring in Moscow, a secret visit was made to the Middle East by Vladimir V. Snegirev, head of the African sector in the administration of foreign policy planning in the Soviet Foreign Ministry (*Upravlenie po planirovaniiu vneshne-politicheskikh meropriiatii*). Since he was to be a member of the Soviet UN delegation at the next session of the Assembly, it was important for him to familiarise himself with the problems of the region and get to know Moscow's friends at first hand.[64]

Nixon's visit was still reverberating in Arab diplomatic quarters, signalling the immense popularity still enjoyed by the USA despite its steadfast support for Israel, when he was replaced by Ford. The presidential changeover did not, however, mean any faltering in Kissinger's tireless efforts to reinforce the American victories in the Middle East and add new ones to the list. So when President Ford and Foreign Minister Gromyko issued a joint communiqué (20 September) emphasising 'the importance of continuing efforts for a lasting and equitable peace in the Middle East', the Soviet government could feel with some relief that it was at least nominally a partner to peace negotiations in the area.

The Palestinians, meanwhile, were being brought increasingly into the picture. The Arab countries made the request on 13 September that the UN Assembly discuss the 'Palestine Question' as a separate item. It is now known that several Arab countries were already absolutely sure what would be the outcome of the Rabat Conference in October. It seems almost certain that it was on the basis of this sure foreknowledge that the Soviet special envoy to the Middle East, Vladimir Snegirev, talked with Arafat at length about developments in the Middle East and the problem of Palestine. Israel had long before made it clear that it would not negotiate with the PLO, and the PLO was certainly not going to recognise the State of Israel.[65] The USSR had given a growing measure of backing to the PLO since the 1973 war.[66] When in due course the Rabat Conference decided (28 October) that the PLO was the 'sole legitimate representative of the Palestinian people on any liberated Palestinian territory',[67] the Soviet government had thus already laid the groundwork for a better understanding with this organisation.

The real troublemakers, from the Soviet point of view, still remained the Egyptians. Well before the end of August, when France officially terminated its 1967 embargo on arms supply to countries in active confrontation in the region, Sadat had announced that he had taken measures towards 'diversification of arms sources'. He showed interest in certain advanced weapon systems that could make a considerable change in the configuration of the Egyptian armed forces: aircraft for attack on ground targets, heavy-load bombers, air-to-ground missiles, anti-tank helicopters and a variety of other sophisticated items.[68]

Since even if all this equipment were bought by the end of 1974, it could not be delivered in operational quantities before 1977, it was obvious that Egypt was making its interest in these items public for political reasons. Indeed, Sadat told *an-Nahar* at the beginning of September: 'The USSR has now begun to respond to our demands again.'[69] Sadat's ploy succeeded and the USSR was responding at least partially and temporarily. A week later *Akhbar al-Yawm* reported that agreement had been reached with the USSR to 'turn over a new leaf' in Soviet-Egyptian relations. Following Egyptian Foreign Minister Fahmi's October visit to Moscow,[70] reportedly to discuss political, economic and military affairs,[71] the USSR was prepared to deliver some spare parts and the first batch of MiG-23s. Fahmi was saying that it was in Egypt's interest that the USSR should play a bigger role in peacemaking efforts — and also declared that the Soviet Union was Egypt's 'principal arms supplier'.[72] Amid rumours that Egypt had already received several MiG-23s[73] the NATO Military Council reported a considerable increase in Soviet arms shipments to Egypt.[74]

With the postponement of the Brezhnev visit at the very end of December 1974 and Sadat's embitterment as he came to appreciate early in the new year that the postponement was tantamount to cancellation, it was clear that no new leaf had been turned. The change in Egyptian policy conceived by Sadat at the end of 1973 was now put into effect at a fast pace. Sadat's reliance on the USA, as virtually the sole mediator between the Arab countries and Israel, became consistent and demonstrative. The USSR also set about implementing decisions taken during its 'reassessment' of September 1974. The new Soviet policy was a good deal less complicated than the Egyptian one, because the USSR was left with practically no alternatives. The USSR became less and less inclined to support Sadat's overt 'Western orientation'. It did not want to yield its bases and influence in Egypt unilaterally but it became ever more persistent in its demand for material or political compensation for its past and present efforts. The closer Sadat drew to the USA, the less helpful the USSR became. Concomitantly, Cairo was left with less leeway to play the two superpowers against each other, while the scope for Soviet political manoeuvre was narrowed.

Open Rift between Moscow and Cairo

Egypt disclosed some details of its dispute with the Soviet Union at the beginning of 1975. Sadat's new policy restricted Egyptian-Soviet relations within narrower confines than at any time since 1955.

According to Sadat, there were two major problems in relations between the two countries: Egypt's debts to the USSR and the problem of arms supply.[75] The problem of arms supply fell under three heads: compensation for loss of equipment during the 1973 war; arms supply and delivery under contracts signed with the USSR before the war and not fulfilled in time; and modernisation of the Egyptian armed forces, meaning more MiG-23s, more T-62s, more advanced electronics and more ground-to-ground missiles. A glance at the figures in table 2.1 shows clearly that at the time Sadat was voicing these complaints, Egypt was better armed than before the October 1973 War. Nonetheless, careful study of Sadat's accusations and the Soviet leaders' retorts reveals that the dispute between them was one not susceptible of simplistic interpretation. Actually, Sadat was not saying that the USSR had not compensated him for the losses suffered during the war, but that the losses had not been fully made up. He was not saying that the USSR had not fulfilled its obligations under contracts signed by the two countries but only that the contracts were not fulfilled on time. Last but not least, it was not that the USSR was refusing to modernise the Egyptian army but that the technological gap between Egypt and Israel was not being narrowed.[76] Moscow still would not allow the Egyptian Army to be turned into a truly modernised machine with far-reaching offensive capabilities. This was the real bone of contention. The Egyptians wanted to be able to decide for themselves whether they would attack Israel in order to destroy it, or just in order to break a political stalemate. Yet the Soviet military had analysed the lessons of the last war and well informed as it was on the capabilities of the Egyptian soldier and the Egyptian command and control system, had come to the conclusion that it was premature to equip the Egyptian armed forces for an all-out offensive. Uncertainty as to whether Israel did or did not have a nuclear capacity made the Soviet military even more reluctant to take responsibility for a war machine that might stumble into a nuclear confrontation with all the global implications involved. In other words, the USSR was refusing to meet the upper limit of Sadat's demands, but was willing to maintain the balance of power in the Middle East. Sadat's aim was to be able to start a war of a different nature from the one he launched in October 1973, if and when he decided to do so, while the Soviet leadership was prepared to allow Egypt to start a war only slightly different from that of 1973. The USSR allowed a considerable improvement in anti-aircraft defence, was willing to supply advanced tanks and MiG-23s and also gave more ground-to-ground missiles, but it still was not ready to bring Egypt to the point at which it would be able to go to war alone and change the face of the Middle East. The USSR was slowly feeling its way towards an overall equality between a combination of Arab countries and Israel and was even prepared to envisage Arab superiority in due course, but the key to the success of the Arab combination was to be given to Syria and Libya.[77] If Egypt were ready to go along with Syria, a country which the USSR had more control over for the time being, then — with the possible addition of Jordan and the arsenals being built up in Libya — all these forces combined could work wonders (from the Soviet point of view). Libya was, of course, an additional bonus for the USSR — it was paying for piles of equipment for which it had no immediate use, and which were being kept there for use either in the Middle East or in

Table 2.1: Egyptian and Syrian Arms

	Egypt — 1976	Prior to October 1973	Syria — 1976
Armoured vehicles	5,000	3,850	3,400
T-55	1,500	1,650	1,000
T-62	1,000	100	1,300
APC	2,500	2,100	1,100
Artillery pieces	1,760	1,400	1,340
Ground-to-ground missiles (launchers)	24 SCUD; 24 FROG F3; 50 F7	ND	30 SCUD; 24 FROG
A.A. missiles (launchers)	30 SA-2; 30 SA-3; 5 SA-6	ND	24 SA-2/SA-3; 14 SA-6
Aeroplanes	640	600	380
MiG-23	48	ND	52
MiG-21	210	ND	200
SU-7	120	ND	60
Other aeroplanes	262	ND	68
Submarines	12	12	2
Missile boats	16 (?)	19	ND
Komar	5	6	3
Osa	38	(?)	3
Destroyers	5	5	ND

ND — No data available

Sources: *New York Times; Financial Times; Time; Aviation Week; Flight International; Air International; Armies and Weapons; IISS; SIPRI; Ha'aretz; Bamahaneh; International Defence Review.*

Africa. Thus, if Sadat wanted to 'play safe', reconstruct his economy in capitalist fashion and rely on Kissinger to get back his lost territories for him, he would have to be satisfied with a military leverage at the October 1973 level or something only a little beyond that. If he were to decide to follow the Soviet lead, that is to agree to convene the Geneva Conference immediately (in March 1975)[78] and set a limit to American influence in Egypt, he could rely on having a better trained army as well as the steady flow of ammunition and spare parts that is the key prerequisite for waging war on a modern scale of manpower casualties and matériel attrition. However, had he decided to follow that course he would have had to put up with at least some of the Soviet demands. When Fahmi said that Egypt would not go to Geneva until it was compensated for all its war losses, he was revealing that a major Soviet political demand was an immediate Geneva Conference orchestrated by the USSR.[79]

Arms Supply Policy towards Syria

Even before the signing of the Syrian–Israeli disengagement of forces agreement the USSR was helping to rebuild the Syrian armed forces and most probably also to reorganise them. It is not unlikely that Saudi Arabia helped the Syrian government to meet part of the Soviet financial demands. The aim of Saudi policy was to regulate Soviet arms supply to the area with a view to moderating the more radical Soviet clients and perhaps extricating them altogether from complete dependence on the Soviet Union. Very soon a new pattern of arms supply was interleaved with the old one. On the one hand, the Syrians claimed that they had paid for the equipment they had received, thus emphasising their independence, and on the other, several hundred Soviet advisers and then some thousands of them were reported to have arrived in Syria, marking the growing Soviet influence in the country. By the end of 1974, the amount of Soviet arms supplied to Syria since the October 1973 war had reached staggering proportions. There were hundreds of tanks, including T-62s, hundreds of armoured personnel carriers, and hundreds of pieces of artillery. The whole anti-aircraft system had been reconstructed, complete with new, improved missiles and radar installations, many of them, especially in the more sensitive areas such as harbours and the environs of Damascus, manned by Soviet personnel. Intensive work was done during 1974 on the airfields, notably in reinforcing aircraft hangars. By the beginning of 1975 Syria's war-depleted arsenals had been 'substantially replenished', to use Secretary of Defence Schlesinger's expression.[80] In fact, not only were losses made good in several key items but old model aircraft were replaced by the new MiG-23, and Syria too received SCUD ground-to-ground missiles. All this was delivered to Syria at a time when the USSR was busy re-equipping its own first-line armoured and mechanised divisions in Europe and in the Soviet Far East with at least partially the same types of equipment.[81] One can only deduce that a great deal of the equipment that was shipped to Syria must have been brand-new and must have come straight off the production line. A number of Syrian pilots were being trained on the MiG-23s, but even so quite a few aeroplanes must have stayed on the ground, since a thorough pilot's course on an advanced aircraft takes at least a year.[82] The question then presents itself as to why the Soviet Union was so prompt in piling up all this equipment in Syria, when there were neither pilots to fly the planes nor enough crews for the tanks and when the Syrian Army was altogether unprepared for war.

The reasoning behind the large-scale Soviet stockpiling in Syria was complex. Soviet interests could be served by a client state's yielding to Soviet influence, either by moving lock, stock and barrel into the Soviet orbit or else by going half-way towards meeting Soviet political or military needs. The Soviet Union has always been in need of dollars, and although at times it was generous, giving arms away or forgoing payment, since 1973 it has no longer been prepared to do this for countries that did not enter the fold. Thus, the Soviet benefits reaped could sometimes be a combination of political returns together with partial payment for the arms supplied under more or less convenient terms, although the USSR would officially deny any such 'mean' interest.[83] A cardinal consideration which cut across many others was, of course, Soviet dependence on the goodwill of a given country, the Soviet need, for instance, for naval facilities or shore-based aeroplanes either for reconnaissance or for air cover for its maritime squadrons.[84] Apart from all this, there were the customer's demands and the Soviet estimate of the customer's capacity to learn to handle modern weapon systems. There was also the overall aspect of the arms race in the Middle East. The USSR had no wish to let Syria become strong enough for it to be tempted to start a war against Israel in the hope of producing a chain effect. If Moscow ever harboured such a wish it had to discard it when Sadat made it clear that he was not going to join Syria in a war precipitated by Asad. Although it could prove well-nigh impossible to discern who started a war and Sadat might find himself fighting a 'Syrian' war, the uncertainty involved did not allow the Kremlin to work out any long-range policies.

The answer to the whole riddle is to be found in the precarious position of the USSR in the Middle East after 1973. As we have seen, Egypt had already gone its own way, and Syria was threatening to do the same. This gave additional force to its demand to be allowed to wage a war of attrition. Yet a war of attrition could very easily turn into a full-scale war. In that event, by piling advanced arms on Syrian soil right away, the USSR could avoid the risks involved in an airlift during the turmoil of fighting or of shipment on unsafe seas. In this way the Soviet Union strengthened the hand of the aspiring champion of Arab nationalism, helping to isolate Egypt while making its own presence more secure in Syria. At the same time, it worked hard at training the new Syrian pilots of the MiG-23s, in the teeth of unpleasant complaints from the Syrians about the cost of maintenance and spare parts of the new machines.[85] The Soviet advisers also had to overcome considerable shortcomings that were revealed in Syrian Army logistics and in command and control. For the time being, then, it was a marriage of convenience. The Soviet Navy found a haven in Latakia and Tartus, as was designedly demonstrated in the form of a friendly but formidable visit in November 1974 by a navy flotilla under the flag of Vice-Admiral Khovrin, Commander of the Black Sea Fleet.[86] With all its Soviet supplies, the Syrian Army was by now almost as fully equipped as the much larger Egyptian one — and in some respects even better so. Last but not least, the presence of Soviet personnel on Syrian soil created the same uncertainties for Israeli decision-makers as had their presence in Egypt during the 1969—70 War of Attrition.

The New Balance of Forces

The year 1975 brought no change in the fortunes of Soviet Middle Eastern policy. The USSR could still offer nothing to outbid Kissinger's step-by-step diplomacy just as long as the parties concerned were ready to follow the American line. The USSR's best policy was to bide time and wait for one or more of the volatile forces in the region to make a blunder. It would, of course, keep its ear close to the ground and not let slip any chance to strengthen the hand of a bellicose Syria or a radical Libya. A huge, combined effort was put into Libya to prepare the infrastructure for Soviet air and naval facilities in that country, which opened new vistas due west in North and even West Africa. One such base, moreover, was no more than twelve miles from the border with Egypt. As an intra-Arab ploy, Soviet aid to Syria and Libya helped to isolate Egypt and make it difficult for Sadat to negotiate a separate settlement with Israel; but it also had another, further-reaching and subtler aim. If the USA were to blunder or if it failed to maintain momentum, thus marring Kissinger's great reputation as 'peace wizard', the USSR could immediately make its appearance with ready-made military leverage. If this were to happen, a whole reaction process could be set in motion. Syria could orchestrate an eastern front relying on Iraq, and probably also on Jordan, and on some forces inside the Lebanon. Egypt would be able to draw supplies from Libya. Meanwhile, however, there were more immediate tasks to hand, and Gromyko was sent to the area at the beginning of February 1975. He visited Syria and then Egypt, forestalling the forthcoming Kissinger visit to the Middle East. The Syrians duly agreed to the Geneva Conference's being convened in March with the Palestinians present.[87] Egypt, however, did not change its policy, though prepared to use this new Soviet effort in order to impress the Americans and probably the Syrians, the Libyans and the PLO as well. Despite the arrival of MiG-23s and the promise of more military aid, Sadat preferred to give Kissinger a chance to obtain by diplomacy what the USSR was implicitly saying would have to be got by threatening the use of force.

It cannot be established from the evidence available whether or not the USSR realised that the rules of the game were different now. Egypt had opted out of a war deliberately begun by the Arabs. 'We [Egypt and Syria] will never start a war unless Israel attacks us first', *Europe Radio One* quoted Sadat as saying.[88] Egypt was ready to prepare for a war in the 1980s, while for the time being maintaining capability for another round of limited war, perhaps an improvement on the Ramadan (1973) performance. As long as Sadat was not going to be involved in a war in the near future, let alone initiate one, as long as he could tell his military that the armed forces would get all the equipment they needed, as long as he could assure the Arab world that he was not going to sign a separate peace agreement with Israel, and as long as he could persuade the West that he was 'moderate', he could take a tough line with the Soviet Union.[89] Indeed, at the beginning of 1975, the USSR could no longer think in terms of augmenting its influence in Egypt: it was rather a matter of how to cut its losses, hold on to existing assets, and avail itself of opportunities.

The difficulties in the way of reconvening the Geneva Conference were mounting higher day by day, and in attempting to overcome them the USSR devised a somewhat ambiguous policy. On the declamatory level, it promoted the idea relentlessly, but in practice it was interested in having a conference only if staged and conducted by the USSR. An opportunity to achieve precisely such a conference presented itself when Kissinger failed to secure another Israeli-Egyptian partial agreement. Kissinger announced on 22 March 1975 that he was suspending his efforts, and he called for a 'period of reassessment'. Two days later the Soviet media started to work up the theme of the Geneva Conference. Moscow tried to depict the conference as the only way to a settlement in the Middle East and to emphasise the need for urgency. The formula that emerged at the end of March 1975 was that the conference should be convened immediately, with representatives of the PLO taking part. The technique was the familiar one: ample quotations from 'progressive' and 'responsible' circles, from newspapers and declarations in the West and in the 'Third World', all indicating the urgent need for a conference to be held post-haste.[90] There was also the usual sprinkle — sometimes swelling to a flood — of denunciations of the 'unrealistic attitude' of Israel, which could not grasp the true situation.[91] Israel was seemingly not alone in its 'unrealistic' view. Sadat, too, was unobtrusively putting a spoke in the wheels. Even at the peak of supposedly restored cordiality during Fahmi's April visit to Moscow, Gromyko had to accept a crucial reservation on the part of the Egyptians: a Geneva Conference indeed, and with the PLO, but carefully prepared in order to guarantee its success. Thus the joint statement was like the double-headed snake of Osiris, looking both left and right: an immediate conference — but only after serious and detailed preparation.[92] The statement showed what the Egyptian mood was. The Egyptians had been taken aback by the Israeli refusal to accept their conditions for an interim agreement; it was not in line with either the Americans' interpretation or theirs of the Israeli attitude nearly two years after the war. However, the prize was still there to be had — the oil of Abu Rodeis and the Mitle and Gidi Passes — if only the right formula could be found.

What the Soviet Union was saying meant starting all over again without the benefits of Kissinger diplomacy. The Egyptians knew that even if the conference proposed by the USSR were ever convened, its result could well be stronger Soviet influence in the area and the possibility of military tensions, all this entailing the risk that Egypt would lose its foothold on the eastern side of the Canal, that the Canal would be closed again and that the psychological effect of the 'Ramadan victory' would vanish into thin air. Despite the resumed arms supply, Sadat was well aware that during the October War he had won first and foremost a political and not a military victory. Therefore he was determined to go along with the American initiative even after the Israeli refusal in March. By the end of April, the Soviet initiative to reconvene the Geneva Conference had petered out. Moscow retreated, though still brandishing the conference as a propaganda ploy. In fact, Brezhnev had had to give in to Sadat. By May, the Moscow line was identical with the Egyptian: there would have to be very careful preparation before a Geneva Conference could convene.

Even before Kissinger's next visit to the Middle East, the Soviet Union suffered another setback in Egypt. Sadat put curbs on the Soviet Union's access to naval facilities in Egypt that it had enjoyed for years. By July, the USSR could use only the port of Alexandria and even that only with permission.[93] Even though still in October 1975 Sadat pointed out that it was not true that the USSR and the USA had equal rights in Egyptian ports and instanced naval facilities given to Soviet ships only, Soviet–Egyptian relations had apparently taken a sharp about-turn and were now very strained. They reached their lowest ebb in March 1976 when Sadat abrogated the 1971 'Treaty of Friendship and Co-operation', leaving the USSR with no political or military privileges in Egypt.

Conclusion – the Soviet Military Posture in the Middle East – 1977

During the October 1973 crisis, the Soviet Navy had shown considerable operative capability; it had transferred reinforcements rapidly and efficiently and given the US Sixth Fleet several uneasy days. It was clear that in any future crisis in the Mediterranean no force would be able to ignore the Soviet Mediterranean squadron. All the same, the very large establishment it assembled at the height of the crisis showed how vulnerable the squadron would be if a global war should break out, or even if a naval skirmish were to occur while it was being deployed. Once out of the Bosphorus and away from home ports, it was dependent on shore-based air-cover. The loss of the bases in Egypt did not greatly hamper the effectiveness of the navy on the high seas, but it did raise the cost of supporting it there, apart from depriving naval personnel of shore leave. As far as the Eastern Mediterranean was concerned, the squadron remained well within the range of shore-based MiG-23s (MiG-23B with three external tanks – range perhaps 2,200 n.m.)[94] or even MiG-21s. Its main problem was the possible danger of having its retreat cut off by a blockade of the Dardanelles, and the lack of air-cover if it sailed further west. By the end of 1975, the Soviet squadron in the Mediterranean was a formidable force, but it still lacked organic air-cover. At any point in the Mediterranean it was closer to home ports than the Sixth Fleet, but it still had to rely on volatile and unpredictable Arab regimes in Syria or

Libya for port facilities and air-cover. Thus, while the Mediterranean squadron served as a 'forward deployment' of the Black Sea Fleet and could reinforce itself at will without any apparent diplomatic friction, if war were to break out it would be out on a limb. It might indeed be intended for exactly this task in an extreme situation, namely to kill enemy aircraft carriers and cause as much damage as possible, even if the squadron were to be wiped out in the process.

The navy also does its share of intelligence work, using its special ships both for passive collating and for the active jamming or confusing of signals. In addition, the impressive development of Soviet electronics allows the Soviet military to enjoy a steady flow of information of a strategic nature; much of this information can be gathered by satellites and a great deal more by the MiG-25s. This information is not a substitute for the minute detail necessary for understanding the opponents' process of decision-making, but between 16 and 19 October 1973 it was sufficient to give Soviet intelligence a better picture of the Israeli crossing of the Suez Canal than that available to the Egyptian intelligence services on the ground.

Soviet logistics capability, too, has improved to such an extent recently that the USSR should not find it difficult to supply an ally involved in a local war. By tacit mutual agreement, airlifts and the shipment of military equipment do not imply direct involvement of the superpowers in a local war. Airlift and shipment have, of course, a regulatory effect, but by and large they prolong the fighting and intensify the losses in men and|matériel,|and this under circumstances not conducive to crisis management or political controls. In a situation like this, military daring may carry the day against the better judgement of the policy-makers.

From a political point of view, the October War brought a considerable increment to the credit of American diplomatic initiative. The Soviet position in Egypt, a key country in the Arab-Israeli conflict, has been weakened. Deprived of access to Egyptian ports, the Soviet Navy can only maintain its former posture in the eastern Mediterranean at a higher premium. Given this choice between maintaining its previous posture in the region at a higher political and economic cost or else making concessions of a political and strategic nature, the Soviet Navy opted for the second alternative: the USSR has been investing greater efforts in its newly-acquired base in Libya, which represents a shift of weight, and negotiating the treacherous shoals in Syria. No very striking changes in Soviet naval deployment in the Mediterranean have as yet given even a clue to future Soviet policy: the clues to be watched for would be a sudden rise in the number of auxiliary ships, the stationing of the aircraft carrier *Kiev* in the Mediterranean for long periods or an increase in the number of nuclear submarines there, all of which may increase Soviet strength and bring it closer to parity with the Sixth Fleet.

Put together, all this means that for the time being the USSR is not prepared to pay as high a price for its positions in the Middle East as it did in the past for four complementary reasons: (a) owing to the anticipated appearance of the Trident submarines with their longer-range missiles the Soviet Navy must also move further afield to the periphery of the Middle East, namely the western Mediterranean, North Africa and the Indian Ocean; (b) the October 1973 nuclear crisis was another signal that a regional war fought among client states may turn into a global confrontation, especially where oil and prestige are involved; (c) the Arab countries proved unreliable from the Soviet point of view. USSR foreign policy failed to translate economic, military and political aid into permanent Arab support for Soviet interests in the Middle East; (d) the USSR has not been compensated economically for its prodigious investment in the Arab countries.

The Soviet strategic aim is apparently to keep pushing the 'defence perimeter' as far away from the Soviet frontiers as possible, at the same time attempting to maintain a continuous line of fighting units and logistic operations from the Black Sea round and down to western Africa. The Soviet Navy cannot yet defend each and every square mile of this huge stretch of water, but it is striving towards that end, contenting itself meanwhile with subtle pressures on the Adriatic Sea[95] and less subtle ones on North and West Africa. The Soviet Navy in a time of crisis will rely on differences of opinion in the NATO camp to restrict the freedom of manoeuvre of the American Navy and Air Force, and it is confident of its ability to reinforce itself in the Mediterranean quickly and efficiently from one or other of the North, Baltic or Black Sea Fleets.[96] Tactical capability in the Mediterranean may prove to be a problem of control of sea passageways: the Dardanelles, the Straits of Gibraltar, the waters between Sicily and Libya, and the Red Sea.

Thus, since October 1973 the USSR has a changed military posture in the region, with its multi-purpose squadrons in the Mediterranean and the growing flotilla in the Indian Ocean. Even though new aircraft carriers have yet to put in an appearance, the navy's radius of activity increases with its better, longer-range aircraft; the 'Backfire' strategic bomber is still rare and precious, but it has recently appeared with navy insignia. Reorganisation of airborne divisions, coupled with a considerable improvement in airlift capacity, allows the cautious Soviet policy-makers to take bigger risks.[97] In other words, many of the political constraints that used to dictate military restraint may no longer be available to the policy-makers to justify their urging caution in their deliberations with the military because now they are present in the area with a great force. Given the present Soviet military and naval capability in the Middle East, all that the Soviet military needs in order to change the rules of the game as fixed during the October War is just one successful intervention in the region which does not provoke American fury.

Notes

1. Roger F. Pajak, 'Soviet Arms and Egypt', *Survival*, July/August 1975, p.165, covers only part of the sum total.

2. Since the Soviet Navy was somewhat straitened regarding surface warship construction, as shown by Michael MccGwire (ed.), *Soviet Naval Developments* (New York: Praeger, 1973), p.194, it could delay preparations for a proper 'forward deployment' squadron in the Mediterranean until such time as a few aircraft carriers with their escorts and auxiliary ships were ready to put to sea. For decisions taken in the USSR in 1968–71, see Michael MccGwire, Ken Booth, John McDonnell (eds.), *Soviet Naval Policy* (New York: Praeger, 1975), pp.521–2.

3. John Erickson, 'Soviet Military Power', p.58, in *Strategic Review* (United States Strategic Institute, Spring 1973).

4. American fighter-bombers on board the aircraft carriers in the Mediterranean plus the Polaris submarines can between them cover the whole of southern Russia.

5. MccGwire *et al.*, *Soviet Naval Policy*, chap.21.

6. Until the October War no ground-to-ground missiles were used in the Middle East. Up to 16 October 1973 there were no open threats to use missiles strategically and no veiled threats of unspecified weapons implying the use of nuclear warheads. See Sadat's speech of 16 October 1973 in *al-Ahram*, 17 February 1973: '. . . but we understand the grave consequences of the use of certain types of weapons and we refrain from using them. They are bound to remember what I have said once and am still saying today: eye for eye, tooth for tooth and depth for depth.'

7. In his speech Sadat said: 'Our missiles . . . which are capable of overflying Sinai . . . are right now on their launching-pads ready to fire, when the signal is given, into the depth of Israel.'

8. *Ma'ariv*, 26 August 1974, p.1; also Sadat to American television, 6 April 1975; Ali Amin, *al-Ahram*, 16 April 1974; *New York Times*, 17 April 1974, p.11; *New York Times*, 18 April 1974.

9. Marvin Kalb and Bernard Kalb, *Kissinger* (New York; Dell, 1975), p.555.

10. Lawrence L. Whetten, *The Canal War* (Cambridge: The MIT Press, 1974), pp.234, 276–7; see also *Aviation Week*, 22 October 1973, p.14, 5 November 1973, p.12, and 3 December 1973, p.17.

11. An exclusive interview granted by Sadat to *Newsweek* senior editor Arnaud de Borchgrave, *Newsweek*, 9 April 1973, p.11.

12. Whetten, *The Canal War*, p.277. Whetten, however, does not reveal his sources; also Chaim Herzog, *The Atonement War* (Jerusalem: Edanim, 1975) (in Hebrew), p.34, says that the SCUD missiles arrived in Egypt in March 1973 and helped Sadat to arrive at his decision, taken in April, to start the October War; Zeev Schiff, *Earthquake in October* (in Hebrew, Tel Aviv: Zmora, Bitan, Modan, 1974), p.236, also does not specify the date.

13. Schiff, *Earthquake in October*, p.236.

14. The October War may have meant a change in this policy. Under the double pressure of Western competition and loss of influence, the USSR may face the choice of giving up political influence altogether or else trading it off for hard currency. If it chooses the latter course its arms supply will become a matter of purely commercial transactions like those of so many other countries for years past.

15. Note Soviet insistence on payment for arms deliveries to Egypt, Syria, Libya. Cf. Yaacov Ro'i, 'The Soviet Union and Egypt: the Constraints of a Power-Client Relationship', in this volume.

16. *New York Times*, 19 April 1974, p.1.

17. Officially, Washington has never endorsed the Israeli line on the territories occupied during the Six Day War, but there have been fluctuations in the American pressure put on Israel to make her withdraw from all or most of the territories. One such case was the Rogers Plan. Kissinger's diplomacy as it was shaped during the October War envisaged a complete or almost a complete Israeli withdrawal from Arab lands in return for peace, or even less than peace. See, for instance, Kalb and Kalb, *Kissinger*, pp.592–3.

18. The reference is to the types of weapon systems Sadat was interested in, like the F1, for instance, their approximate dates of delivery and the likelihood of training the troops to use them in a given period of time.

19. As early as November 1973 the USSR was excluded from any substantial role in Israeli-Egyptian negotiations.

20. See Schiff, *Earthquake in October*, p.236; also Herzog, *The Atonement War*, p.223; also Insight Team, *The Yom Kippur War* (London: Deutsch, 1975), pp.409–12.

21. The exact number of Soviet ships in the eastern Mediterranean at the height of the crisis is a subject of controversy; see, for instance, interview with Admiral Worth H. Bagley, *US News and World Report*, 24 December 1973, p.28. The figure quoted is nearly 100 ships. *Ma'ariv*, 11 November 1973, quoting Vice-Admiral D. Murphy, gives the figure of 90 ships. *Ha'aretz*, 1 November 1973, puts the number at 95. The latest account is given by Admiral Zumwalt in his book, *On Guard*, several chapters of which were published in *Ma'ariv*. See *Ma'ariv*, 3 June 1976, p.32. He claims that on 24 October the Soviet squadron in the Mediterranean numbered 80 ships and on 31 October the number was 96.

22. I deliberately do not discuss the often heard speculation that the real reason for the American alert was Nixon's Watergate predicament and his wish to divert public opinion from internal to external policies. The idea cannot be easily dismissed but we must deal with decision-makers as they are and not as they could have been if it were not for the constraints within which they must operate. Uncertainty is still the reason most often quoted for the American nuclear alert. See, for instance, Insight Team, *Yom Kippur War*, pp.408–12; also Kalb and Kalb, *Kissinger*, p.555. I have not been able to find any hard evidence to substantiate the rumours that the USSR actually brought nuclear heads to Egypt.

23. The USSR embarked on a course of developing intensive relations with Libya when Egypt made known its new policy of 'diversification of weapon

sources'. See, for instance, *Economist*, 18 June 1975; see also *Financial Times*, 29 April 1974, p.5; also *New York Times*, 5 May 1974, p.3. I have dealt with the use made by the USSR of its rapprochement with Libya to bring pressure to bear on Egypt.

24. Note the endless stream of Egyptian threats, boasts and declarations regarding Egypt's military prowess.

25. The USA ended its nuclear alert on 16 November 1973.

26. *Pravda*, 25 March 1974.

27. The Soviet-Egyptian joint statement of 25 January 1974 on the conclusion of Fahmi's visit (see below) is a striking example of this policy of Sadat's.

28. *Flight International*, 19 September 1974, p.341; *Yediot Aharonot*, 10 September 1974, p.1; *New York Times*, 30 January 1975, p.3; *Flight International*, 6 February 1975, p.162; *Aviation Week*, 3 March 1975, p.17; for economic aid see, for instance, *Middle East Economic Digest*, 19 November 1973.

29. *SIPRI*, 1975, pp.222–3. In late 1973 Egypt bought several Mirages (probably III and not F1) through Kuwait. Six Westland Sea-Kings were bought by Saudi Arabia and delivered directly to Egypt.

30. *New York Times*, 19 April 1974, p.1. See Ro'i, 'The Soviet Union and Egypt', pp.186–7.

31. *Communist States and Developing Countries: Aid and Trade in 1974* (Bureau of Intelligence and Research, Report No. 298, 27 January 1976), p.20, Tables 2, 8. If one subtracts the aid for south-east Asia the picture becomes even clearer.

32. *Financial Times*, 24 May 1974, p.8; *New York Times*, 25 May 1974, p.1; *Pravda*, 27 May 1974, p.6.

33. *New York Times*, 2 February 1974, p.1, and 4 February 1974, p.5, for reported Soviet pressure on Syria to pay cash for arms; *Financial Times*, 7 March 1974, p.7. The Syrians are paying cash for arms supplies.

34. See, for instance, *Pravda*, 28 January 1974, p.3.

35. *New York Times*, 12 January 1974, p.3; *Ma'ariv*, 5 March 1974, p.2; *Financial Times*, 8 March 1974, p.7; joint statement issued at the close of Gromyko's visit to Damascus; *Times*, 28 March 1974, p.9.

36. Interview with Saudi paper *al-Riyadh*, 2 February 1974.

37. Statement by the Syrian Minister of Economy, Muhammad al Imadi, on 4 December 1973. *The Middle East Economic Digest* reported on 15 March 1974 that the USSR was prepared to pay for all the damage inflicted on Syria during the October War, damage estimated at one billion dollars, see *Mezhdunarodnaia zhizn'*, 3 (1976).

38. There was Soviet personnel in Syria in command and control posts during the October War. The ominous presence of the Soviets in Syria must have been taken into consideration by the IDF during the war.

39. The visit of Marshal A. I. Pokryshkin to Syria in the middle of February 1974 could be precisely an indication of what was happening; see *Krasnaia zvezda*, 16 February 1976, p.1. Perhaps this is what Brezhnev had in mind when he made his speech during Asad's visit to Moscow in April; see *Pravda*, 12 April 1974, pp.1, 2.

40. *New York Times*, 2 April 1974, p.3, and 17 April 1974, p.13.

41. Asad himself used to be in the air force.

42. The Soviet Union was not slow to emphasise the role of Soviet military and political aid in these achievements – *Pravda*, 8 December 1973 and 30 January 1974.

43. See *Pravda*, 2, 4 and 12 February 1974; see also *New York Times*, 4 March 1974, p.4, and 17 April 1974, p.13; also London *Times*, 8 March 1974, p.9.

44. I.e. once a threatening posture has been assumed by a superpower it is difficult not to assume the same posture under similar circumstances.

45. According to the *Washington Post*, 21 February 1974, quoting the Beirut daily *al-Bayraq*, Syria was prepared to return Israel's POWs if Israel allowed 17,000 people to return to Quneitra.

46. *New York Times*: 22 March 1974, p.11, rumours about a possible Arafat visit in Moscow, 22 May 1974, p.11, Soviet–Libyan pledge at the end of Jallud's visit to Moscow; 28 May 1974, p.6, and 30 July 1974, p.5, first official invitation by Brezhnev to Arafat.

47. *Pravda*, 27 May 1974, p.6.

48. *Flight International*, 18 July 1974, p.50 and 25 July 1974, p.83. The Long Track radar of the SA-4 may not have been in Egypt's arsenal during the October War; see also *Aviation Week*, 26 August 1974, pp.14–19.

49. *Times*, 29 August 1974, p.7.

50. For a detailed discussion of local wars, see General of the Army I. Shavrov, 'Local Wars and Their Place in Imperialism's Global Strategy' *Voenno-istoricheskii zhurnal*, 3, 4 (1975). For the problem of the duration of wars, see ibid., 4, p.96.

51. Donald W. Mitchell, *A History of Russian and Soviet Sea Power* (New York: Macmillan, 1974), pp.544–5.

52. Nadav Safran, *From War to War* (New York: Pegasus, 1969), pp.217–28; for the balance of forces between Egypt and Israel during the War of Attrition, see Whetten, *The Canal War*, pp.95–110; also Zeev Schiff and Eitan Haber (eds.), *Israel, Army and Defence* (Hebrew) (Tel Aviv: Zmora, Bitan, Modan, 1976), pp.175–6, 182–5. The closest the USSR military ever came to the idea of a balance of forces in the air was when it committed its own forces to the defence of Egypt; for the balance of forces in the air prior to the October War, see *Strategic Survey 1973*, IISS, p.26. These figures are not entirely accurate but the ratio of forces illustrates the point.

53. Whetten, *The Canal War*, pp.95–110; Schiff and Haber, *Israel, Army and Defence*, pp.175–6, 182–5; also Heikal, Road to Ramadan, pp.86–90.

54. MccGwire, *Soviet Naval Developments*, p.180; for the interrelations between budget, education, R & D and new military technologies, see *Impact of New Technologies on the Arms Race* (Proceedings of the 10th Pugwash Symposium held at Wingspread, Racine, Wisconsin, 26–29 June 1970), in particular F. A. Long, 'Growth Characteristics of Military Research and Development', pp.272–302. For some of the political reasons behind military development, see Kenneth Galbraith, *The New Industrial State* (Penguin Books, 2nd edn, 1972), chap.29.

55. Galbraith, *New Industrial State*, Chap.29, nn. 6 and 7.

56. *Al-Anwar*, 8 January 1975, interview with Sadat.

57. *Aviation Week*, 9 June 1975, p.9, 4 August 1975, p.11, 18 August 1975, p.11; *Flight International*, 13 November 1975, pp.710, 717; *Aviation Week*, 1 December 1975, p.16, and 26 January 1976, p.13.

58. *Jane's All the World's Aircraft*, 1972–1973, p.465.

59. Whetten, *The Canal War*, pp.234, 246–9, 254–8; also Edward Luttwak and Dan Horowitz, *The Israeli Army* (London: Penguin Books, 1975), pp.347–8.

60. Ibid. For Syrian views on the war in the air, see *Military Review*, 2 (1976); for Egyptian Air Force performance, see *National Defence*, May–June 1975.

61. *Flight International*, 17 October 1974, p.494. The first F-15s were due to be delivered to the USAF on 15 November 1974; *Flight International*, 21 November 1974, p.710. In November 1974 the first twenty F-15s reached USAF operational units, while the USSR had already delivered two or three squadrons

of MiG-23s to the Middle East before that date.

62. *Ha'aretz*, 14 April 1974, p.2; *al-Anwar*, 8 January 1975, interview with Sadat; *New York Times*, 19 April 1974, p.1; *Economist*, 18 June 1975, p.7; *Pravda*, 15 and 21 May 1974.

63. *An-Nahar*, 8 September 1974, pp.1, 14.

64. *MENA*, 7 September 1974.

65. The Soviet position in 1974 was and has remained to date a recognition of Israel's right of existence, to which the PLO could not agree. See, for instance, *New York Times*, 7 March 1974, p.4; also *Daily Star* (Beirut), 4, May 1975.

66. This was on the whole true, but there still remained several differences between the USSR and Syria; see, for instance, *The New York Times*, 17 April 1974, p.13.

67. *New York Times*, 29 October 1974, p.1.

68. For diversification of arms sources see *as-Sayyad* (Lebanon), 29 August 1974; *Ha'aretz*, 19 August 1974; *Flight International*, 19 September 1974, p.341; *New York Times*, 30 January 1975, p.3. It should be taken into consideration that there is a period of time between negotiations, placing of orders and delivery of weapon systems, and further that many items never become a matter of public knowledge.

69. *New York Times*, 8 September 1974, p.11.

70. For Fahmi's visit see Ro'i, 'The Soviet Union and Egypt', pp. 189—90.

71. *FBIS V*, 4 October 1974, p.D4. The Soviet side in these discussions was represented by Gromyko, First Deputy Foreign Minister V. V. Kuznetsov, M. D. Sytenko, V. P. Poliakov and First Deputy Chief of Staff M. M. Kozlov — *Krasnaia zvezda*, 15 October 1974; *New York Times*, 16 October 1974, p.3; *Financial Times*, 19 October 1974.

72. Ibid., 10 December 1974, p.1.

73. *Air International*, November 1974, p.216; *Financial Times*, 12 September 1974, p.8.

74. *New York Times*, 10 December 1974, p.13.

75. *Al-Anwar*, 8 January 1975. For the question of Egypt's debts, see Yaacov Ro'i, 'The Soviet Union and Egypt, the Constraints of a Power-Client Relationship', in this volume, pp. 181—212.

76. These points came out in a series of articles appearing on the pages of *al-Ahram*, 11 June, and 16 July 1975. Prior to this, the same points were revealed by Sadat in an interview he gave to *al-Anwar*, 8 January 1975.

77. The USSR was building up a huge arsenal in Libya apparently because it was absolutely sure that that country could not go to war with Israel. Syria was also given equipment, because the Kremlin could rest assured that Asad would not go to war alone. On the other hand, the equipment and spare parts poured into these countries could sustain the momentum of a war started by a coalition of Arab countries. See note 63 above.

78. *Pravda*, 24 and 27 March 1975.

79. *New York Times*, 20 February 1975, p.3.

80. Ibid., 27 June 1975, p.3.

81. J. Erickson, 'Soviet Arms: The Grim Truth', *Sunday Times*, 8 February 1976.

82. According to *R. Monte Carlo* in Arabic, 10 October 1974, the first MiG-23s were seen flying in Syria at the end of a pilots' course in Aleppo.

83. *Izvestiia*, 25 January 1974.

84. This Soviet dependence is diminishing with the advance of aircraft carriers and auxiliary ships and with better capability at sea.

85. *Aviation Week*, 7 April 1975, p.9. A most biting complaint in the light of the Indian Air Force complaint about the same aircraft. See *Flight International*,

6 February 1975, p.164.

86. *Times*, 18 November 1974; *New York Times*, 19 November 1974, pp.5, 42. The flotilla arrived on 20 November for a five-day visit.

87. See Soviet-Syrian joint communiqué, *Pravda*, 4 February 1975.

88. *New York Times*, 30 January 1975.

89. See, for instance, an interview with Jamasi on *Radio Cairo*, 6 October 1975/*FBIS V*, 7 October 1975; Sadat in an interview to a Saudi newspaper, as quoted by the Middle East News Agency, 20 February 1976.

90. *Pravda*, 24, 25, 26 March and 16 April 1975; *Izvestiia*, 16 April 1975.

91. *Pravda*, 27 March 1975.

92. Ibid., 20, 23 and 27 April 1975.

93. *New York Times*, 29 July 1975. According to Brian Crozier, the Soviet Navy was denied access to Marsa Matruh as early as the beginning of 1975, but that would seem to be too early a date: 'The Soviet Presence in Somalia', *Conflict Studies*, 54 (February 1975), p.9.

94. *Flight International*, 15 May 1976, p.1311.

95. *See Yediot Aharonot*, 28 April 1975.

96. See, for instance, *Rapport Annuel sur le mouvement des navires à travers les Detroits Turcs* (Ankara), January 1975.

97. *Aviation Week*, 24 January 1977, pp.43–4.

PART 2   ECONOMIC DIMENSIONS

3 ECONOMIC ASPECTS OF SOVIET INVOLVEMENT IN THE MIDDLE EAST*

Gur Ofer

In a recent article on the Soviet programme of military aid to the Middle East, it was suggested by this author that the larger flow of military supplies to the region in the last years may reflect the development of a new Soviet economic interest rather than an intensifying of the existing strategic or political ones.[1] Since this increased stream represents a lighter economic burden on the Soviet Union than the military aid used to impose, it can at least point to a decline in the importance of the strategic goals. The strategic and political goals themselves, which are by no means assumed gone, seem to have shifted from the centre of the region – the Near East and the eastern Mediterranean to the periphery – to the central and western Mediterranean, to the Indian Ocean, to the Persian Gulf and the so-called Northern Tier: the countries on the southern flank of the Soviet Union.

These propositions were based on an analysis of the economic and political changes that took place in the region during the early 1970s, the shifts in the strategic deployment of the great powers, and the development of the economic situation of the Soviet Union. The propositions were substantiated by evidence on shifts in the geographical distribution of Soviet military supplies – from the centre to the periphery and towards rich oil countries – and on changes in the terms demanded from recipients of Soviet military supplies – more cash-hard currency deals and heavier pressure to observe repayment schedules on arms deals or loans. Since this paper is mainly concerned with providing more evidence in support of the above proposition, we restate here in short the main arguments linking changes in the region with the observed shifts in the structure of Soviet interests.

1. During the 1960s the Soviet Union faced a strategic threat from the American nuclear forces in the Mediterranean, a threat to which it lacked a suitable answer. The Soviet Union badly needed naval bases to compensate for the deep inferiority of its naval capabilities. Since then the main strategic nuclear competition has shifted towards the larger seas, the Mediterranean threat has declined as Soviet counter-measures were developed, and the position of the Soviet fleet has been

*There is a postscript to this article on p.368.

strengthened. The Mediterranean, while still an important arena for big-power confrontation, no longer represents an acute nuclear threat to the Soviet Union. According to this argument, therefore, the Soviet Union should no longer be obliged, nor should it be willing, to pay a very high economic (and political) price in order to acquire a foothold along the Mediterranean. It thus may redirect some of its aid efforts to regions of increasing importance.

2. The political and economic leverage of the Soviet Union, by which it successfully expanded its role and influence in the region, has declined in recent years for three main reasons: first and foremost the energy crisis, by greatly increasing the wealth of the region, has also enhanced its political independence and created an alternative source of economic (and indirectly also military) support for the poorer countries, some of which were the Soviet Union's best friends. Secondly, the turn of the Israeli—Arab conflict towards negotiations, at least for the time being, has drastically reduced the potential Soviet contribution to the Arab cause, while enlarging that of the United States; and thirdly, the energy crisis has raised Western and especially American interests in the region. The Western powers are thus ready to compete more fiercely against any Soviet effort to penetrate the area, by offering to the countries in the region a wealth of political, military and economic aid. The intensified Western interest has thus raised the unit price the Soviet Union has to pay for any asset it is interested in keeping or acquiring in the region. With its interests shifting elsewhere in any event, why should the Soviet Union pay a higher price?

3. Finally, the ever-growing need of the Soviet Union for hard currency meets in the Middle East a rare, or rather unique, situation where countries which are economically underdeveloped possess an almost unlimited supply of hard currency. At least for the time being, this situation presents the Soviet Union with an opportunity to try to earn hard currency by selling industrial — military and civilian — products. Less developed countries may find that Soviet equipment (especially of the military and heavy industries) is in some respects more attractive than comparable Western products and in other respects not as inferior as developed countries may consider it to be.

It may well turn out that whereas in the past the main question regarding the economic aspect of Soviet involvement in the Middle East concerned the size of the economic sacrifice the Soviet Union was willing to make in order to advance its other interests, we are now observing a turning point. It may be that the Soviet Union is now trying not only to cut these economic costs — and thus to adapt them to its more modest list of goals in the area and its reduced chances of success – but also to reverse the previous situation and attempt to win economic gains at the expense of strategic and political interests.

The main purpose of this paper is to examine to what extent the changes in the amounts, structure, terms and geographical distribution of the various aspects of the economic relations between the Soviet Union and the Middle East correspond to the changes in the Soviet military aid (MA) programme and to our proposed outline of Soviet interests and goals. A summary of Soviet MA to the region is also included.

In the next section we review various trends in the Soviet Union's economic relations with the Middle East. In the last section these trends are analysed with respect to the initial hypothesis, and the prospects of success are evaluated for what is believed to be the new pattern of Soviet economic interests in the region.

A Review of Soviet Economic Relations with the Middle East

Table 3.1 presents a summary of Soviet economic relations with a widely-defined Middle Eastern region[2] in the context of Soviet economic relations with all the less-developed, non-Communist countries of the Third World over the period 1954(5)–1975. Tables 3.2–3.5 elaborate on the various aspects of these relations, with special emphasis being placed on the changes in the structure of aid and trade within the region and over a period of time.

The aspects covered by the tables are: the actual amount of military and economic aid delivered; economic aid extensions or agreements, and the volume of trade. Table 3.1 also contains data on economic aid agreements and the amount of aid granted by the East European countries. Each of the aspects listed above represents different measures of the economic burden and political commitment accepted by the Soviet Union in order to achieve its purposes; each aspect also reflects, therefore, Soviet expectations for rewards. When extended as aid, military assistance seems to be the most burdensome on the Soviet Union from both the economic and political points of view. Less burdensome in that order are deliveries of economic aid, aid agreements (which are generally only partly consummated), and finally trade relations, which are in general beneficial to both sides and may constitute, from the Soviet point of view, the fruits of its previous aid efforts. It should be emphasised, however, that the military aid series also contains the sale of armaments, and that the proportion of arms sales in total military aid has increased lately. This fact changes the

Table 3.1: Soviet (and East European) Aid to and Trade with LDCs and with the Middle East[a] (Billions of current rubles and per cent)[b,c]

	Period				
	1954/5/-75	1954/5/-66	1967-70	1971-73	1974-75
a. *Less developed countries*					
1 (2 + 3) Total aid delivered	14·1	3·9	3·4	4·1	2·7
2 Military aid delivered	9·5	2·4	2·2	3·0	1·9
3 Economic aid delivered	4·6	1·5	1·2	1·1	0·8
4 (2 ÷ 1 x 100) Per cent military aid	67	61	64	74	71
5 6 + 7 Trade volume	45·7	13·0	9·5	11·1	12·1
6 'Civilian trade'	35·7	11·1	7·4	8·0	9·2
7 'Export residual'	10·0	1·9	2·1	3·1	2·9
8 Economic aid extensions	7·9	3·3	1·2	2·1	1·3
9 East European economic aid extensions	5.8	2·0	0·9	1·8	1·1
10 East European economic aid delivered	1·7	0·6	0·5	0·4	0·3
b. *The Middle East region*					
1 (2 + 3) Total aid delivered	9·9	1·8	2·4	3·3	(2·4)
2 Military aid delivered	7·2	1·3	1·7	2·5	1·8
3 Economic aid delivered	2·7	0·5	0·8	0·8	0·6
4 (2 ÷ 1 x 100) Per cent military aid	72	71	69	76	74
5 (6 + 7) Trade volume	25·5	5·1	5·6	7·3	7·5
6 'Civilian Trade'	17·7	4·1	4·0	4·7	4·9
7 'Export residual'	(7·8)	(1·1)	(1·6)	(2·6)	(2·6)
8 Economic aid extensions	4·0	1·5	0·8	1·1	0·6
9 East European economic aid extensions	3·3	0·9	0·7	1·2	0·5
c. *(b ÷ a x 100) Share of ME Region*					
1 Total aid delivered	71	48	71	81	(86)
2 Military aid delivered	76	55	76	84	(90)
3 Economic aid delivered	59	36	62	75	76
4 Trade volume	56	39	59	65	63
5 'Civilian trade'	50	37	55	58	54
6 'Export residual'	(76)	(55)	(76)	(84)	(90)
7 Economic aid extensions	49	45	63	52	45
8 East European economic aid extensions	57	44	81	69	43

burden-benefit calculation of military aid as is shown below.

The tables cover the period since 1954, when the first Soviet—Egyptian economic agreement was signed, or 1955 — the year of the first arms deal between Egypt and Czechoslovakia (in lieu of the Soviet Union). The internal periodisation of the tables follows more or less the military history of the region or rather of the Arab—Israeli conflict. This periodisation, while closely connected with the shipment of arms supplies and military aid, is also very significant in mapping the main stages in the development of overall Soviet involvement in the area. It must be added, however, that other events, such as changes in regimes in the area, changes in the Soviet leadership, developments in world power relations and the arms race, the energy crisis, etc., all affected Soviet—Middle East relations, and such events can serve as a basis for alternative or supplementary periodisation. Whenever such an event is believed to be especially significant the tables are supplemented in this respect. Since the paper concentrates mainly on recent years, we present data for the entire 1954(5)—66 period and then divide the second decade into 1967—70 (from the 1967 war to the end of the War of Attrition and the death of Nasir in 1970) and then 1971—3 and 1974—5 with the 1973 war serving as the dividing line.

In addition to data for individual countries the tables also present figures for groups of countries within the region, the groups being formed on the basis of geographical, national (Arab) and economic (oil) criteria. A fourth criterion — the ideological one — is more difficult to apply consistently over the entire period (as countries changed their ideological colour or the Soviet Union altered its definition of what

Notes:
a. The Middle East 'Region' is defined to include: all countries in North Africa, the Arabian Peninsula, the countries along the coast of the Red Sea and Somalia, Iran, Turkey, and countries of the Middle East proper.
b. Except in lines 9 and 10 where billion current US dollars are used. Dollar figures are converted to rubles at the official exchange rates for the relevant period. See Table 3.6.
c. Figures in parentheses are rough estimates. Apparent inaccuracies in totals and percentages reflect rounding.
Sources: Lines 2 and 7: part (a), see Table 3.6. Part b, based on the share of the region in military aid extended as in Table 2 and on rough estimates of the above shares in 1975. Lines 3, see Table 3.3. Lines 6, see Table 3.5. Lines 8, see Table 3.4. Lines 9 and 10, based on US Central Intelligence Agency, *Communist Aid to Less Developed Countries of the Free World, 1975* (Washington, DC, 1976), pp.5—9 and Table 7, pp.32—3, and on earlier issues of the same title issued annually by the Bureau of Intelligence and Research of the Department of State.

makes a country 'progressive'); the ideological motive will, however, be discussed in the text. This grouping of countries is designed to help identify Soviet motives or interests in establishing relations in the region. Since the groups of countries are not mutually exclusive and there is a problem in identifying precisely the Soviet interest in giving aid to a country belonging to more than one group, it is hoped that the discussion will clarify this question.

The figures in Table 3.1 are all expressed in current rubles. The figures on economic aid (line 2) and on trade are either given in rubles directly or the source and the other series are converted from current dollars into rubles at the official exchange rate for the relevant period. Although the ruble figures contain a small element of inflation, they are closer to constant prices than are current dollar figures. Because we were unable to find a good price index by which to deflate the series, and since we are mostly interested in the *relative* distribution of aid and trade, we have used the current ruble figures.

Over the period 1954—75 the Soviet Union has delivered to LDCs some 14 billion rubles worth of military and economic aid (Table 3.1). Together with aid supplied by the Communist countries of Eastern Europe, the figure tops 15 billion rubles or roughly more than 20 billion dollars. The annual flow of total aid rose significantly from an average of about 350 million rubles during the first decade to some 1·5 billion rubles during the first half of the 1970s; only a relatively small part of the increase reflects the rise in prices. Over the entire period military aid constituted some two-thirds of the total aid extended; its share rose from some 60 per cent of the total in the first decade to almost three quarters in recent years. Thus military supplies constituted the major share of the increase in the annual aid provided by the Soviet Union. Total Soviet trade with LDCs expanded even more rapidly, rising from some 1 billion rubles during the first decade to some 6 billion rubles for 1974—5; the rise reflects both the development of Soviet relations with LDCs and the general Soviet policy of expanding trade relations especially with the non-Communist world. All the above-mentioned developments are characterised by rates of growth that are significantly higher than the growth rates for internal Soviet economic and military magnitudes; thus both aid to and trade with LDCs have become somewhat more important elements in the Soviet economy and planning.

Over the entire period the Middle East region as defined here received over 70 per cent of total Soviet aid and accounted for more than half of Soviet trade with LDCs. The region's share in Soviet military aid is even higher – more than 75 per cent of the total. Moreover, the region's share of all Soviet aid and trade has increased in course of time. The share of total aid delivered rose from less than half during 1955–66 to about 85 per cent during 1974–5, that of military supplies from 55 per cent during the first decade to nearly 90 per cent lately; economic aid to the region climbed from 59 to 76 per cent; and the proportion of trade has risen from 56 to 65 per cent during 1971–3 and to 63 per cent during 1974–5.

Such close aid and trade relations maintained and intensified over the past two decades certainly reflect on the one hand the desires and preferences of the partners to these relationships in the region; but there can hardly be any doubt that they also represent Soviet priorities revealing as they do a persistent general trend of ever-increasing interest in the region.

But while the general trend is most certainly there, the aggregate data presented so far may hide many changes in the nature and structure of those interests and in the goals of the recipient countries. Such changes may be indicated by intra-regional shifts in aid and trade relations, in changes in the relative role of the various kinds of aid and trade with respect to individual countries, and in the conditions, economic and other, under which aid and trade relations are carried out. Tables 3.2–3.5 explore the extent of such developments.

1. Military Aid

Estimates on the amount of military supplies delivered by the Soviet Union to LDCs come from two sources (not necessarily independent of each other), one Soviet and one American. The estimate based directly on the Soviet source is made up of the export residual (ER) to developing countries, that is the difference between total exports to these countries and the sum of the exports reportedly sold to these countries and the sum of the exports reportedly sold to the individual countries. As claimed by Kostinsky, the bulk of this residual constitutes arms supplies.[3] The American estimate[4] lists both 'agreements' and actual 'deliveries' of arms supplied by the Soviet Union both on credit terms and for cash, as I assume is also the case with respect to ER. The inclusion of cash sales of arms under the name 'aid' may be justified on the grounds that at least in principle there is no free market for the more sophisticated armament systems, so that even an agreement to sell them constitutes a concession on the donor's part.

The difference, however, between the extension of MA in the form of grant (*ex post* if not *ex ante*) or on favourable credit terms to be paid back in 'soft goods' and the outright sale of arms in return for hard currency or 'hard goods' is extremely significant. Offering grants or loans on easy terms imposes an economic (and possibly political) burden on the Soviet Union and most likely places some strategic and political obligations on the recipient. Selling arms for hard currency, however, is the best kind of economic bargain the Soviet Union can hope for; while there may also be some political exchange, clearly the recipient's non-economic obligations cannot be very large. We shall thus have to follow changes in the terms of the Soviet MA programme alongside the shifts in its volume and distribution.

When the American estimates are converted into rubles at the exchange rates prevailing in the relevant periods, the two series prove to be reasonably similar, as such estimates go. The results are shown in lines 2 and 7 of Table 3.1, and in Appendix Table 1. The ER series gives an overall figure only 500 million rubles larger than the American one, a difference that is made up of a lower Soviet figure of about 500 million rubles during 1955–66 and a higher Soviet figure for 1974–5 of about 1,000 million rubles. Of the two this difference for the last two years for which there are data is the more conspicuous. It might reflect arms supplied to such countries as Libya, Egypt or Somalia, or else supplies beyond what the CIA knows about or cares to report on at this point. These two discrepancies are the only significant deviations between the two series since 1965.

For the distribution of Soviet MA by country a third series must be used. For arms delivered a series estimated by the US Arms Control and Disarmament Agency (ACDA) is available which is similar though not identical with that of the CIA presented in Table 3.1. Another CIA series is also used, based on MA 'extensions' that apparently do not include cash sales.[5] In Table 3.2 we present the ACDA and CIA series (both up to 1974) and discuss the differences between these series and the CIA 'deliveries' and the Soviet ER series presented in Table 3.1.

The increase in the relative share of the region as a whole in total Soviet MA has already been noted. The main recipients of MA within the region – Egypt, Syria and Iraq – raised their combined shares over the period from about half of the total during 1955–66 to about two thirds during the early 1970s. Both the level of the shares and their upward trend represent in the first place the Soviet exploitation of the Arab–Israeli conflict in order to build up and maintain its hold in the region, especially in the east Mediterranean. The setback to Soviet–Egyptian relations is reflected in the shift of the centre of gravity of Soviet aid from Egypt to Syria and Iraq. This shift is much more

marked following the 1973 war, when supplies to Egypt plummeted.[6]
By 1975 the supplies to both Syria and Iraq had also dropped off.[7]

Although the increase in Iraq's share of Soviet MA is at least
somewhat connected with the Arab—Israeli conflict, it can also be seen
as part of two other trends unrelated to that conflict. First there is a
marked increase in the MA shares of two groups of countries to which
Iraq belongs: the share of the oil countries grew from 23 to 33 per cent
according to the CIA series and from 18 to 28 per cent according to
ACDA, and a similar increase occurred with respect to the Persian Gulf
countries. Both trends seem to indicate quite significant shifts in Soviet
economic and strategic interests. The geographical shift towards the
Persian Gulf group includes, in addition to Iraq and Iran and some more
recent military supply deals with Kuwait,[8] the southern tip of the Red
Sea — North and South Yemen, Somalia, Ethiopia and the Sudan. It is
true that the share of MA going to the 'Red Sea' group dipped during
the last years shown, but this decline reflects mainly the sharp drop in
supplies to the Sudan. The proportion of MA received by South Yemen
and Somalia has increased. Supplies to Somalia have risen even more, it
would seem, since 1975; one also has to add to these figures the costs
of the Soviet military presence there. Most recently there has also been
a resumption of cordial relations between a new 'Marxist' government
in Ethiopia and the Soviet Union. In December 1976 they signed a
100—200 million dollar MA agreement and later in 1977 an economic
aid agreement of unspecified amount.[9]

A second aspect of what may constitute a geographical shift of the
Soviet Union's MA programme is apparent in its attempt to send
supplies to Iran. In addition to being an oil country, Iran is also part of
the so-called 'Northern Tier' of countries bordering the Soviet Union.
The increase in supplies to Iran during 1971—4 has been reinforced by a
new programme of MA for Afghanistan begun in 1975.[10]

The third geographical shift of the MA programme is only marginally
apparent in the tables, but in reality it is shaping up strongly and
quickly: this is the move to Libya and westwards along the
Mediterranean coast. Although the CIA figures do not as yet show any
such supplies and the ACDA series contains only about 170 million
dollars' worth of supplies to Libya for 1971—4, the latest CIA report
on Soviet aid to LDCs amends the 'extensions' figures given in previous
reports to include cash sales, thus adding 1,210 million dollars for 1974
as well as 725 million dollars in extensions and 1,275 million dollars in
deliveries during 1975 — much of it directed to Libya. As mentioned
above, the Soviet export residual figure is still much higher (by about 1

Table 3.2: Military Aid Delivered to LDCs and the Middle East 1954–1975: Groups of Countries, and Countries

(Per cent)

Country, group of countries[a]	CIA (SD) estimates[c]				ACDA estimates[d]		
	1955-74	1955-66	1967-70	1971-74	1961-66	1967-70	1971-74
Total (million US$)[b]	12,010	4,505	2,300	5,205	2,875	2,318	5,191
Annual average (million US$)	601	375	575	1,301	479	580	1,298
Per cent	100·0	100·0	100·0	100·0	100·0[e]	100·0[e]	100·0[e]
Region	73·0	55·4	75·9	86·8	48·3	77·0	81·2
Main 3	59·6	50·7	56·2	68·7	37·1	64·6	63·9
Egypt	28·7	32·3	43·9	18·9	22·6	44·0	23·9
Syria	17·5	8·3	4·7	31·0	3·4	8·2	26·6
Iraq	13·3	10·0	7·6	18·7	11·1	12·4	13·3
North Africa[f]	3·3	3·4	6·7	1·7	6·8	3·4	5·4
Red Sea countries	2·8	1·1	5·3	3·3	3·8	3·8	2·9
Iran	7·1	–	7·2	13·2	–	5·2	9·0
Arab countries	65·7	55·2	68·2	73·7	47·7	71·7	72·2
Persian Gulf	23·2	11·1	20·1	35·2	14·9	21·4	25·2
Oil countries	23·3	13·1	21·5	33·0	17·6	21·0	27·7
Afghanistan Central Asia	16·6	19·2	23·2	11·4	21·9	23·0	12·8
Others[g]	10·4	25·3	0·8	1·8	29·7	–[e]	0·6[e]

Notes and Sources:

a. The 'Region' is a widely defined Middle East ranging from Turkey and Iran in the north and north-east, to Somalia in the south and Morocco in the west. The Main 3 are Egypt, Syria and Iraq; North African countries include Morocco, Algeria, Tunisia and Libya; Red Sea countries include South and North Yemen, Ethiopia, Sudan and Somalia; oil countries are Iran, Iraq, Libya and Algeria; the 'Persian Gulf' includes Iran, Iraq and the Red Sea countries; Arab countries are all the regional countries with the exception of Iran (Turkey) and Ethiopia; finally, Central Asia includes Afghanistan and the countries in the Indian subcontinent.

b. The percentage distribution is based on the dollar figures. Since the ruble/dollar exchange rates changed over the period (and also within sub-periods), the distribution based on ruble figures could, in principle, be different. In fact, however, the differences are very small and seldom larger than one percentage point.

c. Based on US Department of State, *Communist States and Developing Countries Aid and Trade in 1974*, Bureau of Intelligence and Research Report No 298 (Washington DC, January 1976) (henceforth SD 1976), Table 7; and on earlier annual issues of the same publications (henceforth CIA estimates). This source does not provide a full breakdown of MA received by each country for each year, instead each year's report contains new cumulative figures for aid extended to each country covering one additional year. However, each new annual report contains, in addition to data for one more year, also corrections, based on new information, for previous years (SD 1976, p.iii). Therefore, presenting yearly figures for each country involves making adjustments based on other sources on arms deals and also some heroic assumptions. For this reason the figures should be looked upon with caution. Grouping of yearly figures into four-year periods (since 1967) reduces significantly the potential mistakes.

d. Based on US Arms Control and Disarmament Agency (ACDA), *World Military Expenditures and Arms Transfer 1965–1974* (Washington DC, 1976), Tables IV and V; and *The International Transfer of Conventional Arms* (1973) and *World Military Expenditures of Arms Trade* (1963–1973, 1974) issued by the same agency. The underlying figures for the distribution, as well as the totals for the LDCs for individual years and sub-periods, were estimated from information on (a) total MA received by each country from *all* suppliers every year over 1961–4, and (b) the total MA extended to each recipient country over the entire 1961–71, 1964–73 and 1965–7 periods. The 'missing' link was filled by outside information on arms-supply agreements and by a 'proportionality principle', that is dividing Soviet MA over the years in accordance with the proportion constituted by Soviet MA in the total MA received by the given country during the relevant period.

e. Totals do not include aid to a few countries included under 'Other' which amount to 1–3 per cent of the total.

f. SD figures do not include cash deliveries of arms to Libya. According to ACDA they amounted to $125 million during 1971–3, about 2·4 per cent of total Soviet MA during 1971–4.

g. 'Other' includes south-east Asia, Sub-Saharan Africa, with the exception of Somalia and Latin America.

billion rubles), so that even under the most conservative assumption
Libya acquired during 1974–5 at least an additional 1–1·5 billion
dollars worth of arms. This addition raises the share of North Africa in
Soviet MA from 20 to 25 per cent of the total;[11] the real figure could
be even higher, and it certainly increased even more during 1976.

If the Libyan deal is also included in the MA received by the oil
countries, their share would exceed 40 per cent of total Soviet arms
supplies for 1971–4 or 1971–5; for the last two years the share would
be even higher.

The increased emphasis on military assistance to the oil countries,
the rising proportion of arms sales instead of their supply on credit (a
shift that applies to non-oil countries, such as Syria, Egypt, and perhaps
others, as well as to the oil producers), and the increased Soviet
pressure on the recipient countries to pay for previous deals (see below)
all represent efforts to economise on MA and turn arms supplies into a
money-making endeavour. Indeed, it is more than plausible that most
of the Soviet military aid during 1974–5 represented profitable
commercial deals.

2. Economic Aid

The data available on Soviet economic aid (EA) include, first of all,
information on agreements between the Soviet Union and the recipient
countries. The sums mentioned reflect the intention of the two sides to
use Soviet aid for various development plans. The actual execution of
these plans, the delivery of equipment, materials and technical services,
is reported as a special category in the official Soviet foreign trade
statistics. As is not the case with military aid, there are substantial
lapses of time as well as monetary differences between the economic
aid as agreed upon and what is actually executed. Thus, whereas the
total sum of EA agreements signed up to the end of 1973 amounted to
about 6·6 billion rubles, the total amount of aid actually delivered by
the end of 1975 stood at only 4·6 billion rubles.[12] Although this
lead-time has many built-in and objective explanations, the gaps of time
and money between extension agreements and execution may also
indicate any changes in the relations between the parties in the period
following the signing of the agreement. In addition, since agreements
precede execution they can serve as early signs of any changes in Soviet
priorities. The nature of the extension agreements, however – a
one-time signature on long-term plans – makes the breakdown of the
data series into short periods much less meaningful.

Table 3.3 presents data on the distribution of Soviet EA deliveries, while Table 3.4 gives the breakdown of EA extension agreements.

The share of the region in actual EA deliveries has risen over the period covered from just about one third of the total during 1955—66 to three quarters of all deliveries during 1971—5. The extension share, however, shows a different trend — rising moderately at first but then declining back to its earlier level of just under half of total extensions. The difference between the two trends partly reflects the lead-time

Table 3.3: Economic Aid Delivered to LDCs and the Middle East, 1955—75: Countries and Groups of Countries

						(Per cent)
Countries and Groups of Countries[a]	1955— 75	1955— 66	1967— 70	1971— 75	1971— 73	1974— 75
Total (million rubles)[b]	*4,566·3*	*1,488·9*	*1,213·9*	*1,863·5*	*1,067·8*	*795·7*
Annual average	(217)	(124)	(303)	(372)	(356)	(398)
Per cent	*100·0*	*100·0*	*100·0*	*100·0*	*100·0*	*100·0*
Region	59·0	36·1	62·0	75·4	74·9	76·0
Main 3	30·7	31·6	28·3	31·7	30·7	32·9
Egypt	19·8	23·6	20·9	16·0	16·5	15·3
Syria	5·1	1·7	6·2	7·0	7·0	6·9
Iraq	5·9	6·3	1·1	8·7	7·2	10·7
North Africa	4·4	1·0	5·3	6·6	5·8	7·7
Algeria	3·7	0·6	4·4	5·8	4·4	7·5
Red Sea countries	2·0	2·8	1·6	1·5	1·1	2·1
Northern Tier	23·9	0·7	26·7	35·6	37·3	33·3
Iran	15·0	0·3	21·9	22·2	16·8	29·4
Turkey	6·9	0·4	4·8	13·4	20·5	3·9
Arab countries	36·8	34·7	34·8	39·7	37·5	42·6
Persian Gulf	22·9	9·4	24·6	32·4	25·1	42·2
Oil countries	24·6	7·2	27·2	36·6	28·5	47·6
Afghanistan	7·8	12·8	6·1	4·9	6·1	3·3
Central Asia	35·5	55·3	36·4	19·0	16·9	21·7
Sub-Saharan Africa	4·1	4·3	1·6	5·7	8·2	2·2
South-east Asia	1·4	4·3	—	—	—	—
Latin America	—	—	—	—	—	—

Notes

a. Official Soviet figures. For explanation, see text.

b. For the definition of groups of countries, see note a to Table 3.2. The Northern Tier includes Iran, Turkey and Cyprus.

Sources: USSR Ministry of Foreign Trade, *Vneshniaia torgovlia SSSR* (The Foreign Trade of the USSR) (Moscow: annual issue).

factor mentioned above, but it may also signify some problems in signing new agreements or a trend towards expanding the scope of Soviet EA to other regions. If, however, Afghanistan is brought into the region, even the extension share is on the rise.

Over the entire period the region's share of actual deliveries (59 per cent) was higher than its proportion of extended aid (48·6 per cent). These figures may be the reflection of a more efficient execution of EA agreements, but they might also be the result of the region's smaller share in recent agreements as mentioned above. EA deliveries have grown at a faster rate than have the region's MA shares, perhaps indicating also a trend to 'economise' the Soviet aid relations with the region. It should be noted, however, that in the absence of any new agreements this trend may halt in the future.

The main three recipients of MA are also major EA recipients, but their shares of EA are uniformly smaller than that of MA. Moreover, unlike the MA share, the combined EA share of Egypt, Syria and Iraq has been fairly constant over the period at roughly 30 per cent, even though their share in economic aid agreements declined from about a quarter of the total during 1955—66 to about 15 per cent during the second decade. The group's constant share of EA deliveries masks the sharp decline in the share going to Egypt and a build-up first in that of Syria and more lately in that of Iraq. The decline in the group's extensions share applies entirely to Egypt, with only small changes taking place in the shares of Syria and Iraq. It should be emphasised, however, that even for Egypt the decline is only in the *share* of EA, not in its absolute level. Since the annual flow of EA in both series has risen markedly, the absolute level of EA to Egypt more than doubled between 1955—66 and 1971—5 or even 1974—5.

In contrast to the decline in the Egyptian share of EA, that of all the other sub-regions of the Middle East has tended to increase; Soviet involvement has spread outwards from the centre — very similar to the geographical changes observed in the direction of MA. Thus the increase in Iraq's share is definitely part of the redirection of the Soviet efforts towards the Persian Gulf. This group of countries, which received no more than 9·4 per cent of total aid deliveries during 1954—66, increased its share to about one quarter during 1967—70 and to a third during 1971—5. During 1974—5 the countries included in this group received fully 48 per cent of all Soviet EA deliveries. This rising stream of EA deliveries is based mostly on agreements reached during 1967—70. Yet since then the share of the group in new agreements has declined considerably.[13] It should also be mentioned that the shares of the Red Sea countries, which are also part of the Gulf group, have remained fairly constant over the period with some internal shifts occurring from Ethiopia to the countries lying on the shore of the Indian Ocean.

Table 3.4: Economic Aid Extensions to LDCs and the Middle East, 1954—75: Countries and Groups of Countries

Country and Group of Countries[a]	1954— 75	1954— 66	1967 70	1971— 75	1971 73	(Per cent) 1974— 75
Total (million US$)[b]	10,859	5,398	1,335	4,098	2,259	1,839
Annual average	494	415	338	820	753	920
Per cent	*100·0*	*100·0*	*100·0*	*100·0*	*100·0*	*100·0*
Region	48·6	45·1	63·0	48·4	51·6	44·5
Main 3	20·9	26·3	10·7	17·2	26·8	5·4
Egypt	12·0	18·5	—	7·3	13·2	—
Syria	3·8	4·3	—	4·5	3·7	5·4
Iraq	5·1	3·4	10·7	5·4	9·8	—
North Africa	5·1	5·8	3·3	4·6	8·4	—
Algeria	3·9	4·4	—	4·6	8·4	—
Red Sea countries	4·0	5·2	4·2	2·3	1·2	3·8
Northern Tier	18·6	7·8	44·8	24·3	15·3	35·3
Iran	6·9	6·1	17·4	4·6	8·3	—
Turkey	10·9	0·1	27·4	19·7	7·0	35·3
Arab countries	29·0	35·4	18·2	24·1	36·2	9·2
Persian Gulf	16·0	14·7	32·3	12·3	19·3	—
Oil countries	15·9	13·9	28·1	14·6	26·5	—
Afghanistan	11·6	10·5	10·1	13·7	5·6	23·8
Central Asia	39·3	43·4	18·0	40·9	39·6	42·6
Sub-Saharan Africa	5·1	7·3	8·9	1·0	0·6	1·4
South-east Asia	1·4	2·8	0·1	—	—	—
Latin America	5·5	1·4	10·0	9·6	8·2	11·4

Notes
a. For the definition of groups of countries, see note a to Table 3.2.
b. The sub-period totals do not exactly add to the overall total due to difficulties in reallocating the changes in sums extended to individual countries that appear in more recent issues of the sources. So while the figures given for total extensions are the most recent, those for sub-periods have not been fully adjusted. The percentage distribution should be only marginally affected by the differences.
Sources: US Central Intelligence Agency, *Communist Aid to Less Developed Countries of the Free World,* 1975 (Washington DC, 1976), pp.5—9 and Table 7, pp.32—3; and earlier issues of the same title issued annually by the Bureau of Intelligence and Research of the Department of State.

Iran, which drew most of the additional aid to the Gulf countries, is also a member of the Northern Tier sub-region which also benefited from significantly greater Soviet aid. In addition to Iran, Turkey also received substantially more in Soviet EA, with this aid reaching a peak during 1971–3. Iran and Turkey constituted together the group with the fastest growing share of all the sub-regions in the area. As late as 1974–5 these two countries alone received fully one third of all Soviet EA. With the signing of new large-scale agreements with Turkey and Afghanistan during 1975, this trend is certain to continue at least for the rest of the 1970s.[14]

Another sub-region which sharply increased its share in Soviet EA is North Africa. It received a mere 1 per cent of the total during 1955–66 as compared to almost 8 per cent in recent years. While the main Soviet target for MA in this region is Libya, the main recipient of EA is Algeria (a large-scale agreement was signed in 1972).

Cutting across the geographical redistribution of EA, there is a definite trend towards increasing the share of Soviet EA awarded to the oil (and gas) producing countries. These countries, which from 1955 to 1966 received only 7 per cent of the total Soviet EA, accounted for almost half of all deliveries during 1974–5 (with Afghanistan included in this group the figures are 20 per cent and 51 per cent respectively). Here again, however, the peak in reaching aid agreements with countries in this group occurred during 1967–73, and no new agreements (except the one with Afghanistan) were signed during 1974–5, that is following the increase in the price of oil. It remains to be seen whether the absence of new agreements indicates a deliberate change in Soviet aid policy.

We see, therefore, that although in some cases MA and EA are granted to the same countries (Egypt, Syria, Iraq, Iran, Afghanistan, etc.) whereas in other cases only one or the other form of aid is awarded (Libya, Turkey), the general trend is evident: more aid is being granted to North Africa, the Persian Gulf–Indian Ocean and Northern Tier countries, while the share of aid to Egypt is declining and that to the countries involved in direct conflict with Israel is kept relatively constant. In addition there is a clear movement of aid towards countries rich in oil and gas.

Given the increasing tendency of Soviet aid agencies to fund projects that pay back the aid with part of their own production, the shift to the oil countries provides not only better assurance that the aid will be repaid in time, but also guarantees that at least part of the goods with which payments are to be made will be hard goods, especially oil (from

Iraq) and gas (from Iran and Afghanistan). The shift may also represent an interest in promoting additional trade on top of and in conjunction with aid agreements. If the absence of any new agreements in the region is intentional, it may reflect difficulties in adapting the agreements to the higher prices now commanded by oil and gas. Alternatively, it may indicate the reluctance of the now richer aid recipients to sign new agreements with the Soviet Union.

3. Trade

The expansion of Soviet trade with LDCs shows trends similar to those observed in Table 3.5. Table 3.5 is based on data concerning the total volume of trade of the Soviet Union with various countries as presented in official Soviet sources. The data thus do not include the 'export residual' discussed above which comprises mainly arms exports to LDCs.[15] Soviet trade with LDCs was in line with the two clearest trends in the development of Soviet trade during the past two decades: the rapid increase in the value of trade and a rise in the proportion of trade with non-Communist countries (relative to changes in Soviet GNP). Thus while the share of LDCs in total Soviet trade grew considerably (from 8·4 per cent in 1955—66 to 13·4 per cent during 1974—5), their share in total Soviet trade with non-Communist countries remained fairly constant at 35 per cent over most of the period and then even dropped to 30 per cent following the increase in oil prices and the jump in Soviet trade with the West.[16]

Of the increased trade relations with the LDCs the Middle East region accounted for just over a third during 1954—66, rising to 54—58 per cent during the first half of the 1970s. As with respect to EA this upward trend was interrupted by post-1973 changes.

Most sub-regions in this area benefited during the 1960s from an increasing share of the Soviet Union's trade with the Third World. Trade with the 'main three' — especially Egypt — and with the Red Sea countries experienced the slowest rate of expansion. These are also the same groups and countries whose trade shares declined after the October War. Thus Egypt's share declined from 23·6 per cent during 1967—70 to just 15·7 per cent during 1974—5. For other groups — the Northern Tier countries and North Africa and Syria — the peak levels attained during the late 1960s have been maintained during the 1970s. The only countries that continued to increase their share in Soviet trade throughout the period are the oil countries, mainly Iran and Iraq, which are also the main members of the Persian Gulf sub-region. The share of Soviet trade with oil countries increased from a mere 7·7 per cent

Table 3.5: Soviet Trade Volume with LDCs and the Middle East
1954—75: Countries and Groups of Countries

					(Per cent)
Countries and Groups of Countries[a]	1954—75	1954—66	1967—70	1971—73	1974—75
Percentage trade with LDCs of total trade		9·9	12·3	13·7	13·4
Percentage trade of total non-Communist trade		35·1	36·1	36·5	30·0
Total trade with LDCs (million rubles)[b]	45,697	13,058	9,436	11,125	12,078
Total identified trade with LDCs (million rubles)[b]	35,351	10,945	7,329	7,944	9,133
Annual average of total identified trade with LDCs	1,607	842	1,832	2,648	4,567
Percentage of total identified trade with LDCs	*100·0*	*100·0*	*100·0*	*100·0*	*100·0*
Region	50·1	37·2	55·0	58·6	54·0
Main 3	29·5	24·6	30·1	32·7	30·9
Egypt	20·3	20·1	23·7	21·4	15·8
Syria	3·2	2·1	3·4	3·9	3·7
Iraq	6·0	2·4	2·9	7·4	11·4
North Africa	6·0	2·3	7·5	8·0	7·3
Algeria	3·3	0·7	4·4	4·4	4·6
Red Sea countries	1·9	2·1	2·7	1·8	1·1
Northern Tier	11·5	6·4	12·6	14·6	13·9
Iran	8·1	4·3	8·5	9·4	11·0
Turkey	3·0	1·9	3·6	4·7	2·4
Arab countries	38·3	30·5	42·1	43·7	40·1
Persian Gulf	30·3	8·8	14·2	18·6	23·6
Oil countries	18·3	7·8	17·1	23·1	27·6
Afghanistan	3·8	5·5	3·6	2·7	2·8

Notes
a. For the definition of groups of countries, see note a to Table 3.2.
b. Soviet official statistics present overall figures for trade value with 'developing countries' which are larger than the sum of the volume of trade with all individual developing countries. Total trade with LDCs in the table refers to the former and total identified trade with LDCs, to the latter. As explained in the text most of the differences are in unidentified exports rather than in trade with unidentified countries. (For 1954—75 total unidentified trade is 10,346 million rubles of which 10,013 million rubles is the export residual while only 333 million rubles are unidentified imports.)
Sources: See sources to Table 3.3.

during 1954–66 to 27·5 per cent during 1974–5, including an increase from 4·2 to 11·0 per cent with Iran and from 2·4 to 11·0 per cent with Iran and from 2·4 to 11·4 per cent with Iraq over the same period.

It thus seems that while the relative shift of Soviet trade within the region resembles that of MA and EA, the tendency towards the oil countries is stronger. Since trade contains the smallest aid component as compared to MA and EA, this specific trade shift to the oil countries is another sign of the increased importance and weight of economic considerations in the Soviet Union's relations with the region.

This same tendency is also apparent from the changes in the *balance of trade* of the Soviet Union with the region. In order to understand the significance of changes in this variable let us recapitulate the arithmetic relations between the main aid and trade magnitudes. Soviet official trade statistics with any individual country include on the Soviet export side all the economic aid (but not MA) delivered in the form of goods and apparently connected technical services. Soviet imports from any individual country include all the back payments by the recipient countries – on both interest and principle accounts and for both MA and EA insofar as it is paid in goods. Not included in the trade balance in addition to MA are back payments paid in the form of services supplied or in cash, all trade in services, Soviet cash aid payments and third party transactions. If all the above were negligible, the Soviet trade balance with each country would measure the stream of *net* Soviet economic aid (new aid less back payments). As it stands, even if we assume that all non-goods transacted are relatively small, and that if there are cash back payments they cover MA, the trade balance still includes back payments in goods for MA and in this respect it diverges from a pure measure of net economic aid. However, since MA does not create economic benefits the net trade balance may be considered as a rough measure of the net economic benefits (if positive) or burden (if negative) to the recipient country.

With these assumptions in mind the following points are made: first, the Soviet export surplus to the region as a whole rose from 465·3 million rubles during 1955–66 to 1,011 million rubles during 1967–70, but dropped to 484 million rubles during 1971–3 and turned into an import surplus, of 194 million rubles, during 1974–5.[17] As pointed out by Orah Cooper this change is partly an outcome of the ageing of the Soviet aid programme – more payments for past aid are coming in.[18] It certainly reflects the larger repayments in goods made in return for the increased flow of MA in past years; but the change also demonstrates that the Soviet Union is not keeping up its economic aid

programme even on a constant net-aid level. That this has happened
well before many of the recipients of Soviet aid in the region are ready
to become net exporters may indicate, moreover, that Soviet aid
priorities are undergoing modification and that the Soviet Union is
putting higher pressure on the recipient countries to pay their debts.
The most striking example of the change is, of course, Egypt; the
Egyptian import surplus with the Soviet Union declined from 454
million rubles during 1967—70 to 203 million rubles during 1971—3
(while the trade volume increased) and then turned into an export
surplus of 312 million rubles during 1974—5. Similar trends
characterise trade with Iraq (182 million rubles, 73 and —143,
respectively), Syria (67 million rubles, 56 and —2), Turkey, and to a
lesser extent Iran, where a new relatively small export surplus
developed during 1974—5. The only exceptions to this development are
the Red Sea countries and North Africa. While in the former net aid has
genuinely increased, the larger export surplus to North Africa is, of
course, superfluous as Libya is known to be paying large sums of cash
for Soviet arms, thus turning the North African trade balance into one
with a Soviet import surplus.

That the Soviet Union provides negative net aid to countries with
which it has long-standing relations reveals more than just a Soviet
tendency to economise. In such a situation any existing trade and
aid relations can be interpreted as a Soviet effort to cut losses incurred
from previous investments that went sour at least from the political or
military point of view. It may well be that if no debts were outstanding
the Soviet Union would be willing to cut its economic relations even
further. Egypt is, of course, the most striking example: it lately has a
negative net aid flow from the Soviet Union — on the combined civilian
and military accounts — and the signing of the annual trade agreement
with the Soviet Union is regularly bogged down on the issue of how
much Egypt is going to repay (net) on its outstanding debt.[19] It may
well be, therefore, that the observed shifts in the distribution of Soviet
aid and trade would have been sharper if the Soviet Union did not have
to collect debts on past investments. Even without adding this factor,
however, it is clear that all aspects of Soviet aid and trade relations with
the region demonstrate similar trends: a centrifugal geographical
movement away from the centre to the periphery and an emphasis on
'economisation' as reflected in the shift to the oil-rich countries,
in attempts to increase the proportion of MA sold, and in efforts to
collect old debts at a faster rate.

Discussion and Temporary Conclusions

The presentation of the findings in the previous section implied that they reflect only Soviet priorities. Not only in principle but also in reality this is clearly not the case. Changes in patterns of aid and trade result from a meeting of interests and preferences of both sides. There is no question that many decisions to sever or strengthen economic or MA relations with the Soviet Union over this period were made by countries in the region as well as by the Soviet Union. Thus the failure of the Soviet-supported Communist coup in the Sudan in 1971 led to a decline in the Soviet–Sudanese relations, and the increased influence of Saudi Arabia in North Yemen similarly affected the Soviet position. In both cases, however, the Soviet Union found adequate substitutes in line with its interests in Libya, South Yemen, Somalia, and most recently also Ethiopia.

A much more central issue is the turn of events in Soviet–Egyptian relations, to which we shall soon return, but even here adequate substitutes were found for the time being, first in Syria and then more and more in Libya. Another example where supply factors mattered is the Soviet MA to countries directly engaged in the Arab–Israeli conflict; it may well be that the Soviet Union found itself supplying more arms and aid than it had really intended or was ready to supply. Had the situation developed as the Soviets wished, it is possible that the figures on MA would show both a more moderate uptrend and a more drastic shift towards countries that pay for their arms. Or alternatively, the Soviet Union may have hoped that through the principle of Arab unity, which it worked very hard to support and enhance, the richer Arab countries would pay more than they actually did to finance Soviet military supplies to the confrontation states.

The degree of readiness of some of the oil-rich countries to co-operate with the Soviet Union and sign mutual trade and aid agreements is, of course, another major supply-side issue that will determine the success of what I believe has become an important Soviet regional interest. In the previous paper mentioned above, some of the concerns of the oil countries themselves are discussed.[20] The natural tendency to spend available hard currency earnings on what is considered top-quality Western equipment and arms may be balanced by the attractiveness of the much lower Soviet prices and the sometimes higher adaptability of Soviet equipment to the needs and capabilities of the developing countries in this region. The importance of the lower prices charged by the Soviet Union and its willingness to receive goods that are or may become non-tradeable in the West (it may even happen to oil supplies above a certain limit in the future) has increased lately as even some of the oil countries have begun to feel the financial pinch of their ambitious economic development plans and military build-up.[21]

It is quite clear that at this point the Soviet Union has managed to harness only a small part of the region's wealth to its own economic efforts. The only countries which *buy* most of their arms from the Soviet Union are Libya and Iraq, and with respect to both, especially Iraq, it is becoming clear that the Soviet share will go up. The Soviet Union has only a marginal share of the huge Iranian military acquisition programme and none at all in the no smaller build-up of the countries of the Arabian Peninsula, especially Saudi Arabia. On the economic front, the Soviet Union plays a relatively larger role in Algeria, Iraq, Iran and Afghanistan, but here too most of the orders for new equipment have until now gone to the West.

Although Soviet access to the region's wealth and trade is still relatively limited, the amounts involved are not insignificant in the context of Soviet economic problems. A conservative estimate of the Soviet cash earnings from arms sold in the region must be put at 0·5—2·0 billion rubles during 1973—5; in addition, the Soviet Union exchanged during 1974—5 more than 1 billion rubles of Soviet goods for oil and gas alone for which it probably received — through direct or indirect re-export — some 1·3—1·4 billion dollars.[22] If these estimates are close to the mark then the region helped the Soviet Union to finance about 15 per cent of its hard currency imports during 1974—5 and more than half its hard currency trade deficit over the same period. Other favourable signs from the Soviet point of view are Iran's financing of a paper plant in the Soviet Union and the multilateral enterprise to develop and ship Iranian gas to West Europe via the Soviet Union. But whether these achievements have lived up to Soviet expectations or not — I believe the latter — there is a clear case for a continuing Soviet economic interest in the region.

The redirection of Soviet aid and trade towards the oil countries raises the issue of whether and to what extent there is a Soviet economic interest in the oil as such and not only as a potential source of income. Since this is a topic of a separate paper of this volume,[23] I shall only state my view here: I find it very hard to believe that the Soviet Union will at any point allow itself to become dependent on external sources of such an essential material as oil. In addition, the present high price for oil certainly encourages the Soviets to make even greater efforts to develop their own resources, efforts that are indeed apparent in the new Soviet five-year plans. On the other hand, the Soviet Union is apparently urging the East European members of CMEA to seek larger shares of their oil from the Middle East. For the present, such a move frees more Soviet oil and gas for export to the West in return for hard currency. The shift may also be directed towards the future, however, when the Soviet Union may not be able to meet the increasing East European demand.

The Soviet effort to gain influence over some of the oil-rich countries is of course motivated also by political and strategic considerations. The extreme dependence of the West on oil coming from a region neighbouring the Soviet Union offers the latter a natural opportunity in the Big Power and East–West competition. This is clearly also one of the reasons for the shift in the centre of gravity of its efforts to the oil countries in the area and along the oil transport routes. Here, however, the Soviet Union impinges on a highly sensitive, top-priority, strategic interest of the West, and it should therefore expect to meet very stiff resistance to any step that would endanger the supply of oil.

The intensified Western interests in the region, the turn to negotiations as part of the Arab–Israeli conflict, and the changes (not entirely independent of the above) in the political orientation of Egypt and possibly also of Syria are among the major 'supply' factors that affected the shift in the Soviet deployment in the region, especially its reduced activity in Egypt and later in Syria. It is both natural and obvious that the Soviet Union was not happy to see its status in Egypt decline and that it is still interested in restoring to itself a stronger position there. The real question, however, is not whether a given interest exists, but how much the holder of the interest is willing to pay in order to pursue it.

Irrespective of whether the Soviet exit from Egypt was caused by a push or a pull (most likely it had elements of both), the new situation in which the Soviet Union found itself was that the price it had to pay in order to keep its position in Egypt became too high to be worth the value of the interests it was supposed to secure. The importance and acuteness of those interests had been on the decline, and already on the eve of the 1973 war the Soviet Union was paying more than what it should have considered enough.[24] In the aftermath of the war the minimum price needed to pay to 'stay in the game' increased by a sizable order of magnitude. In addition to the increased cost of the military aid required, it was high time, certainly in the minds of the

Egyptian leaders, to start solving Egypt's pressing economic problems. It was (and is) clear to everyone that such a goal involves sums much greater than those spent on the Aswan Dam, or the Hielwan steel works or the annual stream of economic aid of 50, 60 or even 80 million rubles as in past years. Egypt was in urgent need of many billions of dollars worth of aid of all kinds, amounts that the Soviet Union could not or would not grant.

Aggravating the Soviet problem was the fact that alternative aid was available and coming from the rich oil countries as well as from Western Europe and the United States. These two groups of countries, indeed the United States alone, have been pouring into Egypt during the last few years more economic aid than the Soviet Union gave during the last two decades. In just three or four years this alternative aid has topped the total Soviet assistance to Egypt, both military and civilian, since 1955. Although it is not impossible that the Soviet Union with little but well placed aid will reap the fruits created by aid from other sources, the odds against it happening in the Egypt of today are very high.

It is claimed, therefore, that given the present situation the Soviet Union decided to back away rather than try to outbid its competitors at a very high economic cost. A better strategy under the circumstances was to look for a less expensive substitute that would enable the Soviet Union to secure — even if less effectively — its interests and permit it to wait in the meantime for the failure of Egypt's alternative path. Such a substitute was first found in Syria. Although it had the advantages of being smaller, in a basically better economic situation, and more favourable ideologically to the Soviet Union, Syria was essentially vulnerable to the same forces that helped erode the Soviet position in Egypt.

The Soviet Union found a better substitute in Libya which seems to provide the service required at a price that matches what it is willing to buy in return. Libya needs the Soviet Union in order to protect it against Egypt and is able to buy for hard currency all the armaments it needs and more. In Libya the Soviet Union is getting back its lost Mediterranean bases — actually they are now much better situated — as well as a more suitable base from both the geographical and political points of view from which to advance its new African interests and to keep a watchful eye on southern Europe, all at a very low economic cost, indeed with an added economic gain.

Clearly there is an ideological price being paid, and there is a feeling that this unholy alliance can only be temporary. It seems, however, that by now not only the Soviet Union itself but also the analysts of its actions are accustomed to the use of the ideological issue as just another tool of international relations by the Soviet Union. If it can be used positively, so much the better; if not, the show must go on despite the inconvenience. As to the temporariness of Soviet–Libyan relations, the Soviet Union has certainly learned that planning based on the assumption of permanency at this stage of development of the Middle East is bound to end in frustration. When compared with the interests protected by the Libyan deal, the price charged makes it highly profitable even if for only a few years.

The above discussion makes it appear that even if the Soviets did not pull out of Egypt intentionally and turn to Libya instead, they should have done just that. This may be an exaggeration, Egypt was and is the centre of gravity of the Middle East, and the Soviets definitely regret losing it even for the time being. But given the relative prices, they could hardly afford to stick with Egypt even if it were possible politically. Their present purpose in Egypt seems to be, in addition to collecting Egypt's past debt and waiting for a change, to acquire a stable low-cost, low-returns status until present conditions change, or are changed.

The Egyptian–Libyan switch, unintentional as it may have been, symbolises the change in the Soviet profile in the region: an effort to reduce costs and earn hard currency (both on arms deals and civilian projects – the latter not yet present in Libya) even at the cost of putting aside ideological considerations; but still pursuing important strategic and political interests.

In pursuing these interests the Soviet Union is of course also ready, where necessary, to extend aid even when there is no immediate economic payoff. Such readiness is presented in Soviet economic aid to Turkey[25] and in its military and economic aid efforts in the north-western tip of the Indian Ocean – especially in South Yemen, Somalia and, lately, Ethiopia. In both cases while the aid is significant from the point of view of the recipient countries, it does not impose a significant burden on the Soviet Union. The Soviet Union has not yet given up its efforts to sustain its position in Syria and, with the right conditions, it should be ready to extend more aid there. Other countries with which the Soviet Union seems to have deeper long-standing relations – Algeria, Iraq and Afghanistan – are all resource-rich countries in which the aid burden on the Soviet Union cannot be high; the Soviet Union has already reaped some economic gains from these relationships and there should be more to come.

The present standing of the Soviet Union may be less secure and well-established than might be desired. The Soviets are probably ready to raise their level of commitments if their position can be enhanced. In the near future, however, the economic interest will definitely have a prominent place in any Soviet considerations regarding its policy in the region.

Notes

1 Ofer, 'Soviet Military Aid to the Middle East — An Economic Balance Sheet', in US Congress Joint Economic Committee, *Soviet Economy in a New Perspective* (Washington, DC, 1976), pp.216–39.

2. Including all the countries of North Africa, the countries along the shores of the Red Sea down to Somalia, the countries of the Arab Peninsula, Iran, Turkey and all other countries of the Middle East proper.

3. B. L. Kostinsky, *Description and Analysis of Soviet Foreign Trade Statistics*, US Department of Commerce, Foreign Demographic Analysis Division, Foreign Economic Reports, No. 5 (Washington, DC, 1974), pp.66–9.

4. US Central Intelligence Agency, *Communist Aid to Less Developed Countries of the Free World* (Washington, DC, 1971), p.1.

5. US Arms Control and Disarmament Agency (ACDA), *The International Transfer of Conventional Arms* (Washington, DC, 1973), *World Military Expenditures and Arms Trade 1963–1973* (Washington, DC, 1974); US Department of State, *Communist States and Developing Countries, Aid and Trade in 1974,* Bureau of Intelligence and Research Report No. 298 (Washington, DC, January 1976), Tables 7 and 8.

6. Note that the decline in Egypt's share is less steep according to the ACDA delivery series, for the simple reason that arms continued to be supplied under old agreements.

7. CIA, *Communist Aid,* pp.1–2.

8. *International Herald Tribune,* 30 November 1976.

9. Ibid., 18 April 1977, p.5; 7–8 May 1977, p.1.

10. CIA, *Communist Aid,* p.2.

11. Ofer, 'Soviet Military Aid', p.223,n.14; CIA, *Communist Aid,* pp.2, 12–13.

12. See also James R. Carter, *The Net Cost of Soviet Foreign Aid* (New York: Praeger, 1971), pp.29, 98–9, and Orah Cooper, 'Soviet Economic Aid to the Third World', in US Congress Joint Economic Committee, *Soviet Economy in a New Perspective* (Washington, DC, 1976), pp.190–1.

13. The significance of these two divergent trends is discussed below.

14. In addition to the agreements included in the Tables the Soviet Union signed, early in 1977, a new 1·2 billion ten-year economic aid agreement with Turkey. *International Herald Tribune,* 27 April 1977, p.6.

15. The corresponding 'import residual' is very small and probably made up of trade with countries having a very small volume of trade with the Soviet Union that are not listed. The entire 'import residual' for 1954–75 stands at 333 million rubles or about 0·7 per cent of the total.

16. There is a sharper decline in the share of identified trade due to the increased volume of the arms trade (compare lines 1a and 1b).

17. Author's computations based on official Soviet foreign trade data.

18. Cooper, 'Soviet Economic Aid', p.193.

19. See for example a statement to this effect by Foreign Minister Fahmi of Egypt, as quoted by Yaacov Ro'i, 'The Soviet Union and Egypt: The Constraints of a Power–Client Relationship:, in this volume.

20. Ofer, 'Soviet Military Aid', pp.236–7.

21. A case in point is Iraq, which apparently has finally decided to turn its main demand for arms towards the Soviet Union.

22. Soviet official foreign trade statistics.

23. Dina and Martin Spechler, 'The Soviet Union and the Oil Weapon: Benefits and Dilemmas', in this volume.

24. Ofer, 'Soviet Military Aid', pp.232–6.

25. On the Soviet efforts in Turkey see *International Herald Tribune,* 27 April 1977, p.6.

Appendix Table 1 Soviet Military Aid to LDCs: Different Sources 1955–75

	'Export Residual'[a]		CIA Estimates[c]			ACDA[d]	5 – 2	6 – 2
	Rubles	US $[b]	'Aid'	Aid+Cash US $	'Deliveries'	Deliveries		
	1	2	3	4	5	6	7	8
1955–75	10,006	13,057	–	14,350	12,475	–	–582	8
1955–74	8,640	11,128	12,010	13,625	11,200	–	72	–
1955–66	1,935	2,804	4,505	4,475	3,575	–	771	–
1961–66	1,465	1,628	3,220	(3,200)	(2,601)	2,875	973	1,247
1967–70	2,065	2,295	2,300	2,400	2,450	2,318	155	23
1971–75	6,006	7,958	–	7,475	6,450	–	–1,508	–
1971–74	4,640	6,029	5,205	6,750	5,175	5,191	–854	–838
1971–73	3,107	3,903	3,940	4,275	3,725	3,521	–178	–382
1974	1,533	2,126	1,265	2,475	1,450	1,670	–676	–456
1975	1,366	1,929	–	725	1,275	–	–654	–

Notes

a. The 'export residual' (ER) is the difference between total reported Soviet exports to developing countries and the sum of exports reported for each of these countries separately.

b. Ruble figures in column 1 are converted to current dollar values in column 2 by the official exchange rates prevailing at the respective years in rubles per dollar: 1955–60: 0·4; 1961–71: 0·9; 1972: 0·829; 1973: 0·746; 1974: 0·721; 1975: 0·708. It is *assumed* that this is also the practice used in compiling the two other series.

c. Aid in column 3 includes *extension* of credit for military aid and excludes down payments or cash sales (source SD up to 1976; see below). 'Aid Cash' in column 4 includes all MA *extensions* whether on credit or cash terms as updated to July 1976 (CIA 1976). The differences between the figures in columns 3 and 4 result from both definitional changes *and* updating. Column 5 gives MA as actually delivered.

d. Soviet arms delivered to LDCs as aid or cash sales according to ACDA 1976. The differences from the figures in column 5 result apparently from differences in estimation.

e. The distribution between 1955–60 and 1961–66 is a rough estimation.

Sources

Column (1) USSR Ministry of Foreign Trade: *Vneshniaia torgovlia SSSR* (The Foreign Trade of the USSR) and similar *compendia* for groups of years.

Column (3) US Department of State, Bureau of Intelligence and Research, *Communist States and Developing Countries: Aid and Trade in 1974* (Washington, DC, 1976), Table 7.

Column (4) and (5) US Central Intelligence Agency, *Communist Aid to Less Developed Countries of the Free World, 1975* (Washington DC, 1976), Table 4, p.5

Column (6) Based on US Arms Control and Disarmament Agency, *World Military Expenditures and Arms Transfers, 1965–74* (Washington DC, 1976), Tables III–V; *World Military Expenditures and Arms Trade, 1963–1973* (Washington DC, 1974), Tables III–IV; and *The International Transfer of Conventional Arms* (Washington DC, 1973), Tables I–III.

4 THE SOVIET UNION AND THE OIL WEAPON: BENEFITS AND DILEMMAS

Dina R. Spechler and Martin C. Spechler

When the Arab oil-producing states and their allies in OPEC[1] resolved to wield their 'oil weapon' during the October 1973 War in the Middle East, their would-be Soviet patrons were quick to express their pleasure. The Soviet Union welcomed Iraq's announcements on 7 and 21 October that it was nationalising the shares held by Exxon, Mobil and Shell in the Basrah Petroleum Corporation. The 16 October decision by the six major Persian Gulf producers[2] to increase posted prices by 70 per cent and the declaration on the following day of a 5 per cent monthly cut in oil exports by the OAPEC[3] producers were widely praised in the Soviet press. The total embargo declared by Saudi Arabia on sales to the United States and the Netherlands was likewise hailed as a positive and desirable step. The Soviets and Western observers as well regarded these moves as offering the USSR a major opportunity. To a very considerable extent, however, this opportunity has eluded the Soviet Union politically and diplomatically, and even economically the benefits have been quite limited (well below 1 per cent of national product) for the world's largest producer.

This paper first examines Soviet attitudes and policy towards the threefold use of the 'oil weapon' — the embargo and cutbacks, the nationalisations of assets and facilities, and the doubled and redoubled price increases to world markets. It reviews the expectations entertained by the Soviets and Western observers with regard to the implications of Arab and OPEC oil policy for the USSR. Then it analyses the actual impact of that policy on the Soviet Union and Soviet global interests.

The Soviets have attempted to portray the oil weapon as an extension of the anti-imperialist struggle by more militant but not qualitatively new means. OPEC is never depicted as a cartel or oligopoly which is taking advantage of the low demand-and-supply elasticities for petroleum in the world to extract monopoly profits. On the contrary, OPEC represents in the Soviet view an 'anti-cartel'[4] — the most

*The authors would like to acknowledge the able research assistance of Ida Isaac and Ruth Yanai and the helpful comments of John Hardt, Marshall Goldman, Herbert Sawyer, Arnold Horelick, David Morison, and our fellow contributors. Final responsibility must, of course, rest with us.

successful of the Third World attempts to overthrow and defy the capitalist monopolists (in this case the international oil companies, which have controlled refining, distribution, pricing, and exploration and development of new wells).

Does this Soviet position represent misperception and self-deception, or is it rather all-purpose propaganda designed to impress the Third World have-nots while temporising with the newly-rich Arab producing states? While this question remains open, we suggest that the Soviets have not yet developed a clear stance *vis-à-vis* the rich oil producers in particular, or towards commodity hold-ups in general. This points to a lack of Soviet imagination no less damaging than that in the West towards this phenomenon. Rather, as they have in the past with diamonds, platinum and other commodities, the Soviets are seeking to ride along with the cartel, to turn a quiet profit, and to be ready for opportunities. For the most part, however, Soviet ability to exploit the new oil situation has been limited. Moreover, we argue that the oil weapon may harm the not so innocent Soviet bystander as much as the intended victim. Already Eastern Europe finds it difficult to meet its oil bills, while Soviet friends in the Middle East like Iraq, Syria and Libya eye what their oil revenues will buy in the West in place of what Soviet largesse has provided.

1. Embargo and Cutbacks as a Weapon

The most jolting aspect of the oil weapon, but also the shortest-lived, was the refusal of Arab oil-producing states to maintain previous levels of oil supply to Western Europe and Japan or even to sell oil to the United States and the Netherlands until concessions had been imposed on Israel. This dramatic move delighted the Soviet Union in proportion to the discomfort and division it aroused among the Western allies. The embargo stirred fears that Sixth Fleet oil supplies would be jeopardised. The announced OAPEC export cuts – which by December 1973 amounted to 25 per cent of the September 1973 level – deepened doubts about the military preparedness of Western Europe. Disagreements between the United States and its European allies on Middle Eastern policy were intensified by the OAPEC measures, and the European Economic Community (EEC) was thrown into disarray.[5] Britain and France were anxious to woo the Arabs, the Netherlands unwilling to support such a policy, and the West Germans clearly embarrassed by it.The supply restrictions (together with OPEC price rises) precipitated major diplomatic shifts favourable to the Soviets' allies in the Middle Eastern conflict. On 6 November 1973, the

Council of Ministers of the EEC issued a declaration recognising the 'rights' (not merely the 'aspirations') of the Palestinian people; Japan followed suit on 22 November, when she took a pro-Arab position. Even the United States, previously content with the status quo in the Middle East, now began insisting on Israeli concessions to facilitate a resolution of the conflict.[6] All this put considerable pressure on Israel and gave urgency and persuasiveness to Soviet calls for a settlement which would meet Arab demands. In view of these developments, it is not surprising that the Soviets lauded the embargo and cutbacks. Calling them a fitting 'means of defence against Israeli aggression'[7] on the part of the Arabs, the USSR in Arabic broadcasts[8] urged their continued use until political concessions agreeable to Syria and other Soviet friends were achieved. Brezhnev called on Iraq, the Arab oil producer closest to the Soviet Union, to hold back needed oil.[9] In the same vein the Soviets criticised Libya − unfriendly to the USSR at that point − for breaking ranks.

As an exporter of some 50 million metric tons annually to non-Communist countries (see Table 4.1), the Soviets had more than words to wield. Yet when it came to deeds, they made no effort to reinforce the embargo. Rather, they chose to turn it to their own advantage. Possibly, the Soviets served as intermediary for some of the Middle Eastern oil which flowed into Western Europe during the cutback period, lessening the pressure on the Arabs' customers. Moreover, despite Arab criticism of their behaviour[10] they apparently shipped $40 million worth of oil to the United States − a previously negligible customer − during the embargo and $135.6 million to the Netherlands.[11] The benefits accruing to the USSR from these shipments were small[12] especially when weighed against the political cost of angering the Arabs.[13]

It soon became apparent to everyone that the boycott and export reductions would force the West to seek alternative sources of energy, even at considerable sacrifice. It would have to find ways to counter present and possible future restrictions on the supply of Middle Eastern oil. This would put the Soviet Union, possessor of some 12 per cent of the world's proven petroleum reserves and around one third of the reserves of natural gas, in an enviable bargaining position. The Soviet Union could, many assumed, obtain Western investment, capital and technology against delayed payment in kind. Although Western and Soviet interest in foreign participation in oil and gas development in Siberia dates back years before October 1973, high costs and political implications had restrained enthusiasm on both sides. Since the boycott

Table 4.1: Sources and Uses of Soviet Petroleum[a]

	1960	1965	1970	1971	1972	1973	1974	1975	1976	1980 (planned)[b]
Sources:										
1 Domestic production (million metric T)	147·9	242·9	353·0	377·1	400·4	429	452	491	521	620 to 640
2 Annual growth rate[c]		10%	8%	7%	6%	7%	5%	9%	6%	
3 Of which W. Siberia mmT		17	64		104			148		300 to 310
4 Imports (mmT)		1·9	4·6	6·5	9·1	14·7	5·4	7·6	7·2	
5 TOTAL SOURCES 1 + 4		244·8	357·6	383·6	409·5	443·7	457·4	498·6	528	
Uses:										
6 Consumption		180·4	261·8	278·6	302·5	325·4	341·2	368·3	379·5	
7 Annual growth rate[c]		8%	8%	6%	9%	8%	5%	7%	3%	

	1960	1965	1970	1971	1972	1973	1974	1975	1976
8 Exports (mmT)	33·2	64·4	95·8	105·1	107·0	118·3	116·2	130·3	148·5
9 Annual growth rate[c]		14%	8%	10%	2%	11%	−2%	12%	14%
9a Ruble value (billions)		0·9	1·3	1·6	1·7	2·4	4·4	5·9	7·7
10 Of which: 5 East European countries (mmT)[d]	9·2	20·5	40·2	44·8	48·9	55·3	58·7	63·3	68·4
11 Annual growth rate				11.4%	9.2%	13.1%	6.1%	7.3%	8.1%
12 All socialist countries (mmT)[e]	15·2	26·5	50·4	55·4	60·2	67·6	71·7	77·7	84·0
13 Annual growth rate[c]		12%	14%	10%	9%	12%	6%	8%	8%
14 All non-socialist (mmT)	18·0	37·9	45·3	49·6	46·8	50·5	44·5	52·5	64·5
15 Annual growth rate[c]		16%	4%	9%	−6%	8%	−12%	18%	23%

16 Export to advanced capitalist countries (mmT)	32	42	33	36·13	30·4	39·1	50·2
17 Annual growth rate	—	31·2%	−21·5%	10·3%	−16·5%	25·7%	31·4%
18 TOTAL USES 6 + 8	244·8	357·6	383·6	409·5	443·7	457·4	498·6	528

Notes:

a. Includes gas condensate of 1% to 2% (except for 1976 estimate).
b. 1976—80 plan – final version.
c. Geometric average growth rates for five-year intervals.
d. Bulgaria, Czechoslovakia, German Democratic Republic, Hungary and Poland.
e. CMEA, Yugoslavia, North Korea, North Vietnam and China.

Sources:

Line 1   Joint Economic Committee, *Soviet Economy in a New Perspective*, October 1976, p.462. *Pravda*, 23 January 1977.
Line 4   *Vneshniaia torgovlia*, various issues.
Line 8   *Ekonomicheskaia gazeta* 19 (1976), pp.20—1; *Vneshniaia torgovlia*.
Line 10 *International Oil Developments*.
Line 11 *Radio Liberty Report*, 5 August 1974; *Vneshniaia torgovlia*.
Line 16 *Vneshniaia torgovlia*, annual issues, sum of Austria, Belgium, Britain, Canada, Denmark, France, Germany (Federal Republic including Berlin), Greece, Iceland, Ireland, Italy, Japan, Netherlands, Norway, Portugal, Spain, Sweden, Switzerland, and the United States of America.

and cutbacks, however, numerous articles in Soviet journals have elaborated the high and rising dependence of Western Europe, Japan, and even the United States on Middle East and other overseas sources of oil energy.[14] While the more sophisticated Soviet writers were aware of substitutes for oil, these were not considered immediate relief at then-current price levels.[15] Soviet observers minimised possibilities for fuller exploitation of existing fields and conservation by the United States and others[16] and maintained that the North Sea would provide only a fraction of European needs, at a relatively high cost. It is generally believed by Soviet writers that the ocean floor, while a rich source of energy resources, cannot profitably be exploited in the near future.[17] Clearly the Soviets could expect a substantial windfall in terms of heightened Western interest in the development of Soviet oil resources.

The Soviets' expectations were realised. American and Japanese firms opened discussions on development of Soviet oilfields and pipeline construction. But the USSR was excessively optimistic about the terms on which it could obtain Western capital and technology. This optimism, combined with pressure from domestic groups opposed to capitalist exploitation of Siberian resources,[18] led the Soviet Union to stiffen the conditions on which it was willing to offer its oil. In May 1974 the Western press reported that a Japanese offer of about $2 billion in pipeline investments in exchange for 40 million tons of oil per year was sandbagged.[19] The Soviet negotiators apparently demanded that an additional $3 billion in railway investment fortify the Japanese commitment.[20] In the same month, Oil Minister V. D. Shashin declared that the Soviet Union would no longer be interested in 'big deals' such as had been bruited with major American concerns.[21] In February 1975 negotiations broke down with the USA over large-scale Siberian oil exploration. By the end of 1976, only much smaller deals were still alive. During 1976 the Japanese signed a delayed compensation deal for prospecting the Sakhalin shelf, a difficult enterprise which may require American aid as well.[22] Japan and the Bank of America may lend about $25 million for Yakutsk oil development, but this could hardly suffice for a modest housing project in Siberian conditions.[23]

Large purchases of equipment have been agreed to with a number of Western countries, but credits are a bottleneck because of US Eximbank restrictions and rising indebtedness in Western Europe. On this matter, the Soviets today (mid-1978) seem to be content to wait for the lenders to queue up, arguing that credits are the accepted way of doing business. West European bank credits can plausibly cover their immediate needs.

Thus to date the new situation created by OAPEC's supply restrictions has not actually brought the Soviets much of the Western aid they sought. Possibly the leadership as a whole has had second thoughts on the desirability of such deals. Their behaviour may be interpreted as reflecting a shortage of Soviet oil (as opposed to gas) for future delivery,[24] or as a reluctance to grant long-term ownership commitments at all.[25] Alternatively, they may simply be waiting for the West to see things their way. Time may prove them adept bargainers. Or (as we expect) it may demonstrate that ideologically-encouraged predictions of crisis in the capitalist system were not a useful basis for policy.

2. Nationalisation as a Weapon

Although at the beginning of the 1970s the posted price system of the Western oil companies was revised to increase prices and taxes, the Western companies remained concessionaires. The moves by Libya, Iraq and Algeria to nationalise these concessions before the events of 1973, and Iraq's actions during the war, were viewed by the Soviet Union as important achievements in themselves because nationalisation 'strengthens the state sector' in these transitional societies, asserts social control over national wealth, and ultimately undermines Western political and economic influences.[26] Moreover, if an embargo were to be considered again, national companies would be more likely to deny oil to the West. At the same time, they would make Soviet and East European access to Middle Eastern oil more secure. Nor could it have escaped Soviet understanding that the nationalised oil companies would be open to Soviet offers of technical and marketing assistance and might thus serve as a basis for Soviet political and economic penetration.

Nationalisation would end the system according to which foreign companies paid low prices for crude and reaped monopoly profits largely at the processing stage.[27] Hence a policy of taking over Western concessions could finance development in Soviet style and with Soviet equipment. Several Soviet articles of this period praised their own country's role in restraining the West and facilitating nationalisations.[28] This aid would have a beneficial effect on Soviet—Arab relations, even if European, Japanese and American firms continued to do business with the nationalised operations. Furthermore, an inevitable side-effect of nationalisation, hallowed in Leninist thinking, would be intensified competition of the monopolies for supplies and markets. They would be forced to buy dear and sell cheap, reaping smaller and smaller profits, until they, too, would have to be nationalised.[29] The USSR could only gain, it was assumed, from this new stage in the crisis of capitalism.

3. Price Increases as a Weapon

As a consequence of attaining and defending their monopoly position through unopposed nationalisations and some measure of success in embargo and cutbacks, OPEC naturally wanted to continue the high prices achieved during the embargo period, to the extent that excess supplies would not erode the unity among the members. In the longer view, this would require discipline and even cutbacks from some exporters, not necessarily OPEC members alone, to support the price for this (relatively) homogeneous and footloose commodity. Moreover, it would surely harm the interests of oil importers, including Third World nations.

The Soviet Union, like the oil producers themselves, refuses publicly to acknowledge OPEC responsibility for this situation. The Soviets portray OPEC as an 'anti-imperialist' organisation,[30] which constitutes 'the main strike force of developing countries in their struggle for fair oil prices and a revision of terms of payment with the monopolies'.[31]

According to the Soviet view, the Western monopolies kept prices 'artificially' low on extraction and took profits downstream from distribution operations, which remain in their control. These profits, as well as national taxes, explain high retail prices for petroleum products in the West up to 1973.[32] Soviet articles appearing just before and contemporaneously with the first great price rise show that the Soviets expected only a gradual rise of oil prices during the middle and later 1970s,[33] on the basis of straitened Western supplies. Subsequent to the discontinuous increase which actually occurred, Soviet writers emphasised the *continuity* in OPEC policy and justified it in terms of scarcity, higher costs, oil-company profiteering, and political aspirations.[34] Production cutbacks and higher prices, they added (in 1974–5 when the Arabs and Iranians were saying the same), would conserve oil in the ground instead of exchanging it for depreciating dollars. Moreover, higher oil prices were needed to offset higher machinery prices. On these points, though, they offered no substantiation.

Soviet and Western observers were quick to conclude that the political and economic advantages of vastly multiplied oil bills would not merely accrue to the Arabs alone. There was much to please the

Soviets in the new situation. By late 1974 the payments for oil orders at the new price of over $11 per barrel began to affect the balance of payments of Western nations, especially of the weaker and more dependent of the Western allies, like Italy.[35] In view of the terms of trade effect, real domestic incomes had to fall in the importing countries as a whole. Offsetting loans to *all* of them were impracticable, or seemed so before the conservative oil producers began to invest in the main financial centres. The choice confronting these countries was therefore either recession or aggravated inflation or both – neither discomfiting to the USSR.[36] (The Soviets ignored the possibility that Western purchases of Soviet raw materials would be likely to grow less quickly in an economic downturn.[37]) Some of the initial responses of the Western nations, like discussion of cutting NATO troop levels or raising exports, quickly created dissension and promised to engender exacerbated competition among them. The price rises soon led to major disputes over policy towards the Middle East, energy conservation measures and aid to the less developed countries. In Italy and France the local Communists seemed to be making major gains from their countries' economic plight. Within the Communist bloc, higher world prices for a major Soviet export appeared to strengthen the hand of the USSR in its friendly game with its socialist neighbours, as it had long been agreed in principle that CMEA trading would be cleared at world prices. And, most important from the Soviet point of view, Soviet terms of trade with the West would surely improve with the revised prices in operation.

4. The Benefits from the Oil Weapon: Real and Elusive

The opportunities created by the new situation were, indeed, promising. One needs to ask, however, to what extent has the Soviet Union been able to translate these opportunities into actual benefits, political and economic? With regard to the crisis of capitalism so eagerly heralded in Soviet prognoses, it may, of course, be premature to draw conclusions. However, even Soviet observers have begun to acknowledge an unanticipated resilience in the economies of the West. As they themselves have argued, the recession in the capitalist world was not due solely to OPEC price increases, but to cyclical trends inherent in market economies as well. Key industrial states – West Germany, Japan, the United States and France – appear to have withstood the cycle and begun a process of recovery. The capitalist countries have recognised their own interdependence, and those in an economically stronger position have been forthcoming with aid to the weaker. Petrodollars have not remained in desert coffers but have found their way back to the economies of the West and may, indeed, play a role in their recovery.[38] While there has been no complete meeting of minds on the issues dividing the Western alliance, there has been a greater convergence than seemed possible in the first months after the oil price increases and export reductions were announced.[39] Thus despite ardent efforts begun even before the October War, the Soviet Union has advanced little in its campaign to persuade the USA's friends that their true interests lie in disentangling themselves from an encumbering alliance. If anything, the energy crisis may have generated a stronger sense of the need for co-operation. The social strain the Soviets anticipated has indeed materialised, but the results have not been entirely an unmitigated benefit to the USSR. Economic woes in Britain and West Germany have strengthened the Right, not the Left. The German reaction has jeopardised the fragile structure of détente so carefully constructed by Brandt and Brezhnev. Where the local Communists have gained, they have recognised the need to assert their independence from Moscow, and the prospect of power has made them all the more willing to do so. The impact on Eastern Europe of this new brand of 'Eurocommunism' has been profoundly disturbing to the Soviets, as evidenced by their assiduous efforts to condemn and combat it.

If the use of the oil weapon has not been of much help to the Soviets in their political competition with the West, it did bring them tangible economic benefits in the short run (see Table 4.1, lines 9a, 14). The Soviet deficit in sales to hard-currency areas was nearly cut in half in the first year after the quadrupling of oil prices at the end of 1973.[40] However, it soon became evident that OPEC policy would not solve the Soviets' balance of payments problems.[41] In part this is owing to their growing demand for Western products. But certain constraints on their ability to benefit from the new situation have also been responsible for this.

For the Soviets to benefit directly from higher world prices, they must continue to expand their oil exports to hard-currency areas and produce that oil at incremental costs lower than foreign trade values. This means that production at such costs must be expanded beyond desired levels of domestic consumption plus export to soft-currency and barter buyers.

The benefits accruing to the Soviet Union in 1974–5 from the price increases (on actual export levels to all customers) it obtained over the 1973 average price was 5·3 billion rubles, of which 3·4 billion came from the fact that the price per ton obtained in *hard currency* markets rose from 26 rubles to 60–63 rubles. These benefits are therefore about ¾ per cent of net material product in those years (353 billion rubles in 1974). In 1976 hard currency receipts jumped to a total of 3·5 billion rubles by virtue of a 28 per cent increase in volume and a 10 ruble price increase obtained per ton. The 1977 total was $4.55 billion rubles, but volume figures have been withheld thus far.

The Soviets have been able to produce enough oil for profitable export to hard currency buyers for some time now. However, in the period from the initial large price increase until 1976 they had been unable to increase the rate of oil production growth significantly more than the rates of growth of consumption and sales to non-hard-currency customers. The real question is whether they will be able to continue in the intermediate term and at what price. Production has grown since 1965 at an average of over 7 per cent annually to a 1976 level of 521 million metric tons (see Table 4.1). If the planned level of at least 620 million metric tons were to be achieved by 1980, this would represent somewhat less than 5 per cent yearly growth during the Tenth Five-Year Plan.

The enormous levels achieved already, making the USSR the world's leading producer of petroleum, and the fact that the rate of production growth peaked in 1963, would in themselves suggest that significant acceleration is unlikely.[42] Moreover, Western experts have noted some special factors which will increase the cost of any production growth and probably delay or limit it. During the period of the Tenth Five-Year Plan nearly all the 'new oil' available from expanded production rates and exploitation of new fields will come from the West Siberian region.[43] This continues a strong shift eastwards established since the early 1960s, as a result of gradual depletion of fields in the Caucasus, Urals, Volga, and other regions within the European part of the Soviet Union.[44] Of the 10–11 billion metric tons of proven and prospective reserves within Soviet borders, according to Western calculations, the vast majority is located in eastern, inhospitable areas.[45] To increase the amounts from such places will require expensive pipelines, which will be time-consuming and difficult to construct in northern tundra and taiga. Estimates of the cost of extracting this new oil vary. Robert Ebel of Washington, DC, an oil specialist, believes the costs are about 52 kopeks per barrel, while the Soviet writer Probst said in 1971 that Tiumen oil cost about 59 kopeks per barrel at the well-head, with another 20 per cent in pipeline transportation charges. At the unrealistically overvalued ruble of 1976, these estimates agree with the

Adelman—Bradley figure of roughly $0·80 per barrel.

While these costs might curb the rate of increase of production, they certainly do not in themselves preclude production growth. The profit margin on incremental Soviet oil delivered to ocean ports would still be very substantial to society overall — more than ten times the incremental costs! One should perhaps discount Soviet oil slightly for its high sulphur and high paraffin content and its undesirable specific gravity, but even so the social returns from expanding production in the Soviet Union suggest that this is feasible and desirable.

These calculations do not, however, take into account the question of the availability of new technology and equipment necessary for oil exploration, drilling and transportation in extremely cold and inaccessible regions. American intelligence sources anticipate a 3 to 8 per cent shortfall relative to planned output for 1976—80, as a result of Soviet inability to develop such technology and equipment in the time allotted.[46]

If exploration is inherently uncertain, exploitation of existing wells is less so. Yet here, too, the Soviets face major problems. Labour productivity is, by their own admission, extremely low, owing to high turnover and uncertain supply.[47] Moreover, the Soviets waste a great deal, impeding their efforts to increase production and exports. According to one source 37 percent of all oil and gas is lost at the production stage.[48] By the nature of the process, all oil producers leave as much oil in the ground as they manage to raise. But evidently technological innovations can improve things, thereby prolonging or renewing the use of depleted wells.[49] Recent Soviet articles call for more automated programming, better chemicals, as well as more qualified personnel to solve this problem.[50] Such innovations are not developed or diffused quickly. Moreover, it is essential to give oilfield managers an incentive to adopt them, in order to raise the percentage of their fields which is exploited. As it stands, incentives centre on output with no attention to conservation or fuller (albeit higher cost) exploitation. It is conceivable that the Soviets could do better in this area without resorting to Western-type share-ownership or rental charges, but we do not expect immediate progress here either. Although the urgency of the issue is apparent to the Soviet authorities,[51] workable solutions do not seem to be in the offing at this time.

If the Soviets' ability to benefit from OPEC price policy has been and is likely to be limited by exploration, transportation and exploitation problems, this makes a reduction in consumption all the more imperative if the USSR is to gain more than minimally from the new oil situation. Notwithstanding the natural growth of demand for oil at all prices, which continues, there ought to be a rationing of oil and partial switch to other fuels in certain uses and certain locales, since the value of the Soviet oil, if exported, is now several times higher than previously, while its value in replacing coal or natural gas has presumably changed little.

What has, in fact, happened to domestic Soviet consumption of petroleum? Apparently, consumption has resumed its growth but at lower levels than before, when domestic use doubled within a decade. Although it is impracticable to shift away from using petroleum within a short span of years, what is noteworthy is that little movement is *planned* in this direction. Crude oil and condensate constituted about 42·5 per cent of the fuel used in the Soviet Union in 1975 (as compared with 39·4 per cent in 1970 and only 28·9 per cent in 1960); this is due to increase marginally to 42·7 per cent by 1980. Such a level would still be about three percentage points below the average oil usage in the global fuel balance. While atomic energy is to be pressed, the pace in the much vaster coal industry is evidently not to be accelerated significantly despite previous hopes to cut the use of petroleum for fuel by a sizable amount.[52] Natural gas is planned for further growth of 44 per cent over the 1975 level, only a slight deceleration from the rate achieved in the previous quinquennium.

Rising numbers of cars and trucks on Soviet roads account for the enlarged petroleum demand in significant measure, and planned output of vehicles was actually raised from nil to 17 per cent during the drafting process for the Tenth Five-Year Plan.[53] Having more than doubled car output since 1970, further increases will apparently be minor. The auto revolution is one popular movement which is not to be suppressed. Regular petrol still costs only|$0.38| per gallon to the Soviet public. Apart from this, deficiencies of the success indicators facing the Soviet manager impede any rational and wide-ranging programme to conserve petroleum in favour of coal or natural gas. Constructing plants and buildings with cheaper operating costs does not accrue to the credit of ministries and construction agencies or increase the bonuses of managers contemplating major alterations; therefore, price-induced shifts away from petroleum are not to be expected spontaneously in the Soviet economy. Soviet householders pay a nominal or actually nil charge for extra heat or cooking gas; constantly 'exposed to reports of economic successes in oil and gas production [they] have responded casually to the absence of an energy pinch'.[54] Nonetheless, the restricted consumption rise in 1976 is worth mentioning.

Another factor which has limited Soviet ability to take advantage of OPEC price policy has been the difficulty of diverting exports from Soviet allies and soft currency or barter buyers to hard-currency, capitalist customers. The capitalist countries in 1975 received less Soviet petroleum than in 1971, the peak year, although of course the revenues of about $3·2 billion in 1975 exceed very considerably the revenues from this commodity in the early 1970s. Oil alone now provides 28 per cent of total Soviet export revenues, but the proportion is nearly half of its exports to hard-currency markets. Taken together, all non-socialist countries received 52·5 million metric tons of petroleum from the Soviet Union in 1975. While this is a record amount, which represents an 18 per cent rise from the previous year, it is only 4 per cent above 1973 (the highest year prior to 1975). In 1976, owing to restricted consumption, the non-socialist countries received a record 64·5 mmT of Soviet oil and oil products.

The major room for manoeuvre in an effort to divert exports would be Soviet shipments of petroleum to the East European countries, which, aside from Roumania, have remained almost totally dependent on their Soviet ally for this raw material.[55] However, up to 1976 sales to these 'fraternal' countries have grown even more rapidly than Soviet production, with exports to hard-currency countries advancing modestly and spasmodically by comparison (see Table 4.1). Preliminary reports indicate a greater squeeze on CMEA countries in 1977 to help Soviet hard-currency revenues.

As for the future, some signs point to pressure from the Soviet Union on these allies to conserve and to be satisfied with less Soviet oil in relation to their total needs. Already before 1973 the Soviet Union told Eastern Europe that past rates of increase could not be sustained.[56] Reportedly the Tenth Five-Year Plan calls for petroleum exports to the CMEA of 364 million metric tons during the quinquennium. On the basis of recent trends, Eastern Europe is likely to receive seven-eighths of this total or 318·5 million metric tons. At a yearly rate this is 63·7 million metric tons, which scarcely exceeds the amount it obtained in 1975.[57] Apparently the Soviets are planning to hold exports to this area constant. There has also been pressure from the USSR to employ substitutes for its oil. In an important article S. Pomazonov and A. Iakushin, specialists on the CMEA economies, lectured East Europeans on their extravagant use of (other peoples') energy.[58] Much can be done in Eastern Europe, according to them, to conserve Soviet oil imports. Coal, lignite, shale and tarsands — as well as hydro-electric sites — are underutilised. Power stations achieve only 30 to 35 per cent fuel efficiency. Ferrous metallurgy, aluminium and ethylene industries – all energy-intensive – might be curbed, they imply. High world prices for petroleum would make gasification and hydrogenation of solid fuels worthwhile.

This pressure has produced some response from Eastern Europe. Czechoslovakia, Bulgaria and Poland have been cutting petroleum use by administrative means. Poland and Czechsolovakia reportedly plan to reduce dependence on the USSR, in part by favouring alternative fuels and in part by importing more from the Middle East.[59] There is a limit, however, to how much is likely to be done in this direction, especially in the short run. Administratively generated fuel scarcities carry considerable political risks. Fuel substitution is a costly process, requiring substantial changes in plant and equipment and unusual flexibility on the part of managers and bureaucrats. It is far from clear that the USSR will tolerate high levels of East European dependence on extra-bloc energy sources.[60]

The very increases in oil prices which have made hard-currency oil exports attractive to the USSR make oil imports onerous (and hence politically problematic) to Eastern Europe. Ultimately, imports from the Middle East will be limited by Eastern Europe's ability to export and OPEC's willingness to import from this region. The Middle Eastern oil producers have little incentive to accept East European goods when Western counterparts are available to them, and the USSR's bloc allies cannot simply sell millions of dollars of gold to obtain the imports they need. Nor are large-scale credits likely to be forthcoming to finance such purchases. The countries of Eastern Europe are already suffering severe balance of payments problems. The bloc (excluding the Soviet Union) had a Western debt of $6·6 billion in December 1975, a rise of about $4 billion during that year.[61] Net borrowing during 1976 was running at an annual rate of $10 billion. Owing to the Communists' refusal to supply information on foreign currency and gold supplies, Western banks are beginning to view these sums and especially their growth with concern. And direct Arab credit to the Soviet bloc is still a curiosum.[62]

In the light of these problems, Eastern Europe is likely to continue importing Soviet oil in large amounts. Given the possible domestic political repercussions of fuel shortages, the USSR has little choice but to supply its allies in the style to which they have grown accustomed. The loss of political leverage which would probably accompany reduction of economic dependence gives the USSR additional reason to do this.

Now would it actually make economic sense to do otherwise. A 10 per cent cut in oil made available to Eastern Europe would be worth about $550 million in the free market, gross of the value to the Soviet Union of the counterpart goods obtained from Eastern Europe in exchange for the 6·3 million tons of petroleum. As compared with OPEC exports of more than 1,000 million tons, in 1976 such an amount could not break the cartel,[63] but it might put downward pressure on prices − which would not benefit the USSR. If we therefore put the marginal dollar revenue[64] from a shift of 10 per cent of Soviet exports from CMEA to the West at perhaps $275 million, it is immediately evident that this can hardly offset the added military and political costs of the discontent which such a move would arouse.

If the Soviets cannot appreciably increase their hard-currency sales of oil, might they at least receive better terms of trade with soft-currency customers as a result of OPEC price policy? To some extent this has already occurred. The Soviets have begun to increase the price of their supplies to Eastern Europe in accord with the 'Bucharest principle' that oil should be shipped at the average world price of the past five years, including a transportation adjustment. This formula, assert Soviet writers, is 'free of monopoly effect and day-to-day fluctuation'. (We should remember in this connection that the Soviet Union does not treat OPEC and its price as monopolistic.) The world price allegedly reimburses Soviet outlays and 'encourages stable deliveries'.[65] Pursuant to these formulae, negotiations beginning in 1974 led to a price rise in 1975 to a nominal $7 per barrel, still below the contemporary world price.[66] It is probable that prices paid *to* Eastern Europe for its goods also rose recently, but not as much as oil, which represents such a large share of Soviet exports to these countries.[67] Further price increases were effected in 1976−7, and the average realised price rose from 34 to 37 rubles per ton sent to Eastern Europe, compared with some 69 rubles on every ton sent to hard-currency destinations. Sizable increases are due each year according to the Bucharest formula. Moreover, *above*-plan deliveries are to be priced according to the *current* world price. Thus OPEC measures have strengthened the Soviets' hand in trading with Eastern Europe.

In the negotiations with Eastern Europe, furthermore, the Soviet Union has been insisting on East European investment and labour participation in building up the production and transportation infrastructure for supplying oil.[68] For example Czechoslovakia and East Germany have committed themselves to send machinery for the West Siberian fields; and the Hungarians and Czechs are participating in the

construction of the pipeline linking Soviet fields with the Adriatic. The
Poles have agreed to send their own workers to lay 900 kilometres of
pipeline and build pumping stations. In all, the East European allies are
to put up $6 billion for joint CMEA projects in the period 1976–80.
The Soviets' success in eliciting such co-operation may well be a result
of the improved bargaining position which OPEC price policy has won
for them.

However, as in the case with Soviet attempts to reduce East
European oil imports from the USSR, Soviet gains — actual and
potential — from higher prices and increased investment are limited by
political and economic constraints. The USSR has carefully refrained
from raising the price of the oil it sells to Eastern Europe to the level
of current world prices — even though the world price is the accepted
price for most CMEA trade.[69] Key East European states — Poland,
Czechoslovakia and East Germany — have been experiencing grave
economic difficulties since 1973, including declining rates of growth
and improvement in living standards. It is widely assumed that the
political restiveness in these countries — riots in Poland and anti-regime
protests in East Germany and Czechoslovakia — has been sparked at
least in part by this economic decline. And there is no doubt that the
economic difficulties are largely a result of the increases in petroleum
product prices. Comparing 1976 with 1973 the five dependent CMEA
countries in Eastern Europe spent nearly three times as much for Soviet
oil — 2·54 billion rubles in 1976. In 1977 they spent $3·3 billion. The
Soviets, though, have been and will be wary of pressing Eastern Europe too
hard by raising prices too far too fast. As for the investment commitments,
these are not, apparently, being fulfilled. With their higher fuel bills, the
USSR's CMEA allies lack the resources for projects of this sort. The
capital inflows the Soviets anticipated have largely failed to materialise,
and Socialist Co-operation has not flowered as a consequence of
OPEC policy.[70]

5. Soviet Penetration of the Arab Oil Sector

Insofar as the Soviets have sought to deny Middle Eastern oil to the
West and/or obtain it for themselves, the benefits they have received
from the nationalisations have been disappointingly small. Nor have the
Middle Eastern oil producers, newly rich as a result of oligopolistic
pricing, been willing to spend substantial amounts of hard currency on
Soviet goods. Some Soviet 'penetration' of the oil sector in several Arab
economies has occurred. But the political gains which have accrued to
the USSR from the expansion of state ownership of oil facilities have

been extremely limited.

In the three years since the lifting of the embargo and cancellation of the cutbacks in 1974, sales to the West by the Middle Eastern producers have recovered, their rise having been limited only by the lower demand levels which the price increases and recession generated. There has been no interest on the part of OAPEC members in denying oil to the West on a long-run basis, even though Arab political demands have not been met. (Of course this aspect of the oil weapon may be invoked again in the future.) Thus the Soviets' chief suppliers — Iraq, Algeria and Lybia — no longer particularly need this market and may even regret their long-term arrangements with the USSR.[71]

It is alleged, doubtless on Soviet-supplied information, that OPEC producers once expected to send some 50 to 100 million tons per year to the Soviet bloc, but later it became evident that this was not to be.[72] These deals were almost always on a barter basis; they continue to be attractive only to the extent that Soviet equipment for oil, hydro-electric facilities and general economic development remains attractive in quality and implied price as compared with similar Western products.

The past three years have seen energetic Soviet efforts to push such exports to oil-producing states, with only limited success. Oil and gas exploration and extraction equipment exported to all developing countries amounted to 36·7 million rubles in 1973 and 45·9 million rubles in 1974.[73] Of the major customers, only Syria, Algeria and Iraq could offer the USSR oil (or divert it from the West) in the short term, and only the latter two possessed the substantial hard-currency resources eagerly sought by the USSR.[74]

Soviet—Syrian co-operation dates from at least 1971 in the petroleum area, with a big deal for aid to the power generation, petroleum and petrochemical industries signed in early 1973, in connection with the Euphrates River dam project.[75] The Soviets have encouraged their East European allies similarly to become involved in the development and reconstruction of the Syrian oil sector. After the war, the Czechs agreed to re-equip the destroyed Homs refinery for the sum of 190 million crowns — about $3·2 million — while the Romanians were supposed to rebuild the Banias refinery.[76] The Soviets also have signed several deals with Libya since 1974 for atomic power stations, water desalination and arms, presumably in exchange for oil.

By 1975, though, Soviet attention was centred on Iraq, the largest exporter among the 'progressive' Arab oil producers. Aid was to go for developing the North Rumailia and Nahr-Umr fields and prospecting elsewhere.[77] The Soviets were scheduled to complete a pipeline from Baghdad south to Basra by 1976 and are committed to build an oil depot at Nahr-Umr. Various deals involving power and irrigation equipment and arms have also come about in recent years, and in 1976 a protocol was signed for the exchange of road and construction vehicles, metals and chemicals for Iraqi oil and dates.

All together, the Soviets assert they have assisted in adding to oil output in these countries by 22 million metric tons (commissioned by 1975), while as of 1 January 1975 another 28 million tons of output expansion were stipulated in agreements.[78]

Depending on sources not mentioned by name, the *Economist* of London, which generally takes an anti-Soviet but not markedly anti-Arab stance, has called the Soviet oil exploration record in the Middle East 'not impressive', in comparison with the American companies.[79] The Soviets are known to be slow to devise and execute aid projects, and their technicians, selected on political grounds rather than merit, perform poorly in exploration and refining. (The Soviets themselves are extremely defensive on this issue, insisting that Middle Eastern governments 'have expressed a high opinion of the Soviet oil geologists in their analysis and survey of geological samples and data'.[80] Yet even Soviet sources admit the USSR would do well to reduce lead times on aid deliveries and completions.[81])

The poor performance of Soviet technicians and equipment as compared with Western counterparts is one reason why the Soviets have not made significant political gains as a result of the movement within OPEC to nationalise the oil sector. Iraq had shown a definite preference to diversify its economic contracts and acquire Western goods with its hard currency.[82] Even Syria has been moving in this direction.

If anything, the success of the oil weapon has worked against Soviet political interests and ambitions in the Middle East. The effect of the price increases has been to decrease Soviet leverage (never very great) over clients and potential clients in the region. Oil revenues (Saudi Arabia alone netted $25 billion in 1975) have allowed Egypt, Syria and the Palestinians to enjoy a greater degree of independence *vis-à-vis* the Soviet Union and Soviet policy than would otherwise have been possible. This has been all the more true as France, Britain and the United States, confronted with rising oil bills and trade deficits, have been increasingly willing to sell arms to Israel's opponents.[83] Iraq and Libya, with substantial oil incomes of their own, have been able to maintain more extreme positions than the Soviets in the Arab–Isareli conflict in part because of their new financial strength. The USSR has had to mute its criticism of the two 'radical' states in order to preserve its stake in their oil sector and economy generally. All these regimes have kept the Soviet Union politically at arms' length, carefully limiting the number and type of Soviet advisers and technicians they admit and cultivating good relations with the United States and Western Europe. Thus, OPEC policies have not enabled the USSR to acquire in any of these countries the kind of political influence they enjoyed in Nasir's Egypt and sought elsewhere in the Middle East after 1972.

An even greater setback for Soviet policy has been the marked growth of Saudi influence in the region in the wake of the oil price rises. A conservative, anti-communist alignment has emerged, subsidised by Saudi oil money. Prompted by their wealthy donor in the Arabian Peninsula, Egypt and the Sudan have been taking an increasingly hard line towards the Soviet Union, denouncing it for intervention in their domestic affairs. In Southern Yemen and Jordan the Saudis have made substantial offers of aid, specifically to reduce or prevent a Soviet role as arms supplier.[84] One cannot rule out similar Saudi moves in Syria and even Iraq in the future. If the USSR continues to be unable or unwilling to compete with Saudi offers, it will find itself more and more superfluous to its erstwhile and potential friends in the Arab world. OPEC price policy may not merely fail to serve, but ultimately subvert, Soviet political interests in the Middle East.

Some early growling in the direction of Saudi Arabia and its Gulf allies has recently been reported. When Saudi Arabia failed to support the majority OPEC decision to raise prices, the Soviet press called Saudi readiness to supply an additional 100 mmT a 'threat' to the other members. The same article spoke of 'neo-colonialist' pressure on Saudi Arabia and the United Arab Emirates.[85] The Kuwaiti daily *as-Siyasa* has reported that Soviet agents approached Algeria to set up a rival, 'progressive' petroleum exporters' organisation to act in parallel to OPEC. It is believed that the Soviet Union has been dissatisfied with OPEC and has attacked it as being a US-dominated organisation which is blocking producers' rights to price increases.[86]

6. The Plight of Third-World Consumer Nations

While the Soviet Union has preferred to see OPEC as the leading edge of the Third World group — what OPEC has done, others can and should do[87] — more sober and detailed analyses published in the Soviet press take note that most countries of the underdeveloped world are losers in the oil game.[88] On the whole, Soviet writers still blame the West for the jump in commodity prices in 1974—5 without reference to this as a major cause of the recession at the time. While oil is mentioned as the cause of LDC external debts and declining incomes,[89] the oil companies and not OPEC are held responsible. Only very recently have the Soviets begun to suggest that the oil producers ought to provide economic aid to the less well-endowed representatives of the Third World. Iran and Saudi Arabia have been singled out for mild criticism, and this only in connection with purchases of American arms.[90] In general the Soviets seem embarrassed by and ideologically unequipped to deal with the fact that independent, even socialist and generally pro-Soviet developing countries can be responsible for the economic plight of other developing countries, even in part. This conflict of interest is simply not provided for in the Marxist-Leninist canon.

The policy dilemma which this situation has generated is no less acute than the ideological one. Soviet allies in the Third World who have relied on the USSR for oil are among the countries hardest hit by OPEC policy. India's oil bill, for example, has climbed to over one billion dollars yearly since 1974.[91] This development appears to have presented more problems than opportunities. Soviet oil shipments to their customers Sri Lanka and Cuba, as well as India, are more desperately needed, but they are also more expensive to provide now. The chances for repayment are slimmer than ever, and the Soviet Union has no credible threat against defaults. What is more, Third World oil consumers have been turning to the World Bank, Western private banks and Arab oil magnates for aid and stabilisation of export receipts. Suddenly the ante has been raised in the aid game, and fresh bank rolls have appeared around the table. Obviously Saudi interests in the Middle East are anti-communist, though publicly the Soviets have not quite decided how to counter them.

7. Conclusions

The three-pronged trident of the oil weapon projected from the Persian Gulf northwards and westwards has not served Soviet interests as at first it seemed it would. The embargo and cutbacks did not last long enough and did not seriously affect the United States. On the contrary, oil stringency may have strengthened the position of the American leadership in the Western Alliance, and the high prices of the recent three years may in the more distant future make production cutbacks less effective. This clearly depends on conservation efforts and technological change in the West, as well as new oil discoveries. Partly for political reasons but mainly for economic—technical ones, the Soviet Union was not able or willing to replace OPEC deliveries.

Nationalisation, the second prong, has not led to denial of a Western role in Middle East developments. Paradoxically, nationalisation may serve to stabilise relationships between the countries giving and receiving technical help, because the latter have asserted their self-respect. Nationalisation has fed nationalism and pan-Islamic, as opposed to pro-communist, tendencies as well. Higher oil prices have improved Soviet terms of trade, but withdrawing and diverting precious oil from Eastern Europe and the Third World pauper states has not proved worthwhile or even possible in the short term. At the same time the Soviet Union does not have enough new oil to threaten the OPEC oligopoly's more anti-Soviet members, as long as they are willing to cut their own supplies. Assuredly a number of Western countries have been weakened by the oil price rise, affecting primarily their level of national income but also their defence capacity and political stability. Yet Western and international banks and American leadership have answered Third World calls for finance and assistance not less than the Soviet Union — indeed, we would say, a good deal more. The balance of influence, therefore, has not swung towards Moscow up to now in Western Europe, the Middle East or the Third World as a whole. Whatever the hopes of Third World commodity producers and their Soviet well-wishers, OPEC success shows little tendency to spread to other commodities. A successful strike by the exploited hewers of wood and drawers of water — a commodity which is, alas, still more common than oil — is more unlikely than ever. This is the reality which the Soviet Union has yet to conceptualise and turn to its own use.

Notes

1. Organisation of Petroleum Exporting Countries. Members are Algeria, Ecuador, Gabon, Indonesia, Iran, Iraq, Kuwait, Libya, Nigeria, Qatar, Saudi Arabia, United Arab Emirates and Venezuela.

2. Abu Dhabi, Bahrein, Iran, Kuwait, Qatar and Saudi Arabia. Posted prices were increased from $3·01 to $5·11 a barrel.

3. Organisation of Arab Petroleum Exporting Countries. Members are Algeria, Bahrein, Egypt, Iraq, Kuwait, Libya, Qatar, Saudi Arabia, Syria, and the United Arab Emirates.

4. *Mirovaia ekonomika i mezhdunarodnye otnosheniia*, 7 (1974), p.37.

5. Romano Prodi and Albert Clô, 'Europe', in Raymond Vernon (ed.), *The Oil Crisis* (New York: Norton, 1976), pp.91–112.

6. See the speech by President Nixon at his press conference on 26 October 1973.

7. *SShA*, 7 (1974), pp.9–21.

8. Arthur Jay Klinghoffer, 'The Soviet Union and the Arab Oil Embargo of 1973–74', *International Relations*, V, 3 (May 1976), pp.1011–23. The *New York Times* correspondent C. Sulzberger asserted (edition of 29 December 1973) that the Soviets advocated the embargo. See also 'Soviet Radio Beamed to Arabs Backs Those Favoring Oil Ban', *New York Times*, 13 March 1974, p.24.

9. *Pravda,* 9 November 1973, p.1.

10. *Radio Liberty Research Bulletin,* 3 (1974), p.8.

11. Marshall Goldman, *Détente and Dollars. Doing Business with the Soviets* (New York: Basic Books, 1975), pp.91ff. Some $76 million of oil exports during that year are unaccounted for in the *yearly* breakdown published in *Vneshniaia torgovlia.*

12. Total sales to hard-currency consumers were $1·3 billion in 1973. Goldman, *Détente and Dollars,* p.91.

13. The Soviets appear to have regarded this cost as high. They took great pains to defend themselves to their Arab critics, insisting that 'the Soviet Union is not a competitor of the Arab oil-producing countries but is their partner, because its international prestige and strength lead to the point where new principles of relations will crystallise in the oil market'. (This assertion was made on 30 November 1973.) See *Radio Liberty Research Bulletin* 3 (1974), p.8.

14. E.g. *Mirovaia ekonomika i mezhdunarodnye otnosheniia,* 11 (1973), 3 (1974); *International Affairs,* 10 (1973), pp.75–6; *SShA,* 7 (1974), pp.9–21.

15. Substitution would require serious changes in transport facilities, plant and equipment, and machine-building industries. *Mirovaia ekonomika i mezhdunarodnye otnosheniia,* 3 (1974), p.82, and 2 (1974), p.68.

16. Greater exploitation by the American oil companies of resources in the United States is too costly, even with the increases in the world price of oil. Ibid., 2 (1974), p.67.

17. Ibid., 3 (1974), p.79.

18. There had been a long-standing debate within the Soviet leadership and among concerned citizens how much, if any, of the riches of Siberia should be 'mortgaged' to foreign capitalists. *New York Times,* 28 May 1974.

19. *Le Monde,* 29 May 1974.

20. Joseph A. Yeager and Eleanor Steinberg, *Energy and US Foreign Policy* (Cambridge: Ballinger, 1974), pp.202ff.

21. *Economist,* 1 June 1974, p.91; *New York Times,* 28 May 1974.

22. *International Affairs,* 8 (1975), p.64.

23. Economist Intelligence Unit, *Economic Review* (February 1976).

24. *Petroleum Economist,* 3 (1976).

25. Leslie Dienes, 'Soviet Energy Resources and Prospects', *Current History,* 420 (October 1976), pp.116ff.

26. *Mirovaia ekonomika i mezhdunarodnye otnosheniia,* 11 (1974), p.135; *SShA,* 7 (1974), p.32. Cf. also Oded Eran, 'The Soviet Peception of Influence: The Case of the Middle East', in this volume.

27. *Mirovaia ekonomika i mezhdunarodnye otnosheniia,* 11 (1975), pp.132–3.

28. *International Affairs,* 11 (1973), pp.32ff; *Mirovaia ekonomika i mezhdunarodnye otnosheniia,* 11 (1974), p.132; *SShA,* 7 (1974), p.27.

29. *Mirovaia ekonomika i mezhdunarodnye otnosheniia,* 12 (1974), p.25.

30. *Mirovaia ekonomika i mezhdunarodnye otnosheniia,* 11 (1973), p.44; 7 (1974), p.37.

31. *International Affairs,* 11 (1973), p.58; *Foreign Trade,* 10 (1973), pp.30–9 (Part II).

32. *Mirovaia ekonomika i mezhdunarodnye otnosheniia,* 2 (1974), p.83; 11 (1974), p.132.

33. Y. Yershov in *Foreign Trade,* 10 (1973), pp.33–4.

34. *Mirovaia ekonomika i mezhdunarodnye otnosheniia,* 2 (1974), p.77; *Pravda,* 7 January 1975, p.5; *SShA,* 7 (1974), p.24.

35. The embargo and cutbacks implied a theoretical 12 per cent cut in European energy supplies, about eight times the supply effect possible with respect to the USA. In the event, the cuts were neutralised. Prodi and Clô,

'Europe', p.98. 'Excess' oil costs engendered in 1974 by the 1974 price rises were about $30—36 billion for Western Europe alone; this represented an ominous threat to the international reserves of these countries which in December 1973 stood at $82.2 billion. T. M. Rybczynski and George G. Ray, 'Historical Background of the World Energy Crisis', in T. M. Rybczynski (ed.), *The Economics of the Oil Crisis* (New York: Holmes and Meier, 1976), p.8. By 1976, though, the *financial* drain had been staunched to a great degree, except for the chronic vulnerability of U. K. sterling deposits.

36. The Soviets happily catalogued the likely impact of the energy crisis on the economies and social systems of the West: decline in industrial production, slower growth rates, foreign exchange problems, breakdown of the entire system of economic ties among capitalist countries, rise in unemployment, increased social strain, and sharper class struggle. *Mirovaia ekonomika i mezhdunarodnye otnosheniia,* 3 (1974), p.81.

37. Actually, Soviet exports to advanced capitalist countries grew handsomely, both the 47 per cent represented by oil in 1975 and all other commodities.

38. Cf. *Columbia Journal of World Business* (Fall 1976), esp. pp.28ff.

39. The two countries furthest apart on a range of crucial issues, the United States and France, have moved closer together. Their positions on the Arab—Israeli conflict, arms sales to the Middle East, treatment of the oil-producing states and measures to aid developing countries are much more alike than in 1973.

40. The deficit on hard-currency visible trade was $1·7 billion in 1973, $0·9 billion in 1974. CIA, *Recent Developments in Soviet Hard Currency Trade* (January 1976), p.2.

41. The trade deficit climbed to $6·3 billion in 1975, despite oil revenues of $3·2 billion in that year. Ibid. See also Economist Intelligence Unit, *Quarterly Economic Review,* 3 (1976), p.7. So defined, the 1976 deficit was $5·1 billion though unregistered arms sales and services may reduce this by $2 billion. Thus the accumulated hard-currency debt was still in excess of $7·5 billion registered by the end of 1975, unless gold sales have been seriously underestimated. Ibid., 4 (1976), p.3, and 3 (1977), p.12. Based on returns through June 1977, it is estimated that the trade deficit may run to $4·1 billion owing to curtailed grain purchases.

42. *Pravda,* 23 January 1977.

43. Ibid., 6 January 1975.

44. Yeager and Steinberg, *Energy,* pp.195ff. The 1976—80 plan calls for 300—310 mmT to be extracted in West Siberia, nearly half of the 620—640 mmT aggregate figure. The West Siberian share was a mere 18 per cent as late as 1970. *Ekonomicheskaia gazeta,* 22(1976), p.4.

45. Arthur Meyerhoff, 'Economic Impact and Geopolitical Implications of Giant Petroleum Fields', *The American Scientist,* LXIV (September—October 1976), pp.536—40. It might well be supposed that 'ultimately recoverable' reserves will likewise occur in the relatively less explored areas of the country, including offshore Arctic and Pacific fields.

46. Emily E. Jack, J. Richard Lee, and Harold H. Lent, 'Outlook for Soviet Energy', in *Soviet Economy in a New Perspective* (Washington, DC: Joint Economic Committee, 1976), pp.460—78.

47. *Trud,* 215 (1976), p.2. Too little attention is given to social facilities and basic amenities in bleak, isolated areas.

48. Walter Gumpel, 'The Energy Policy of the Soviet Union', in Curt Gasteyger (ed.), *The Western World and Energy,* (The Atlantic Papers, 1974).

49. *International Herald Tribune,* 27 April 1977. Admiral Stansfield Turner, the director of the US Central Intelligence Agency, has testified that Soviet use of water-flooding technique has cut the ultimate recovery from oil wells. Admiral

Turner provided no source for his statement. Two oil experts have contended that the Soviets now use gas injection (ibid.), though we have seen references to the water-flooding technique being given to the Iraqis. D. Shpilev, 'Soviet Geologists in Other Countries', *Foreign Trade* (1977), p.37. Recent reports indicate pressing interest by Soviet officials in importing appropriate technology to improve secondary recovery rates.

50. *Ekonomicheskaia gazeta,* 22 (1976), p.4.

51. *Pravda,* 6 January 1975.

52. *Izvestiia,* 2 February 1975 (article by L. Grafov, deputy minister of the fuel industry). Lignite produced by Siberian strip mining will generate more electricity. Coal will make a comeback as a basic boiler fuel. *International Herald Tribune,* 27 April 1977, p.2; *Ekonomicheskaia gazeta,* 28 (1976), p.2. Planned coal output for 1980 is put at 790—810 mmT, a 14 per cent gain over five years compared with 701 mmT in 1975. The Ninth Five-Year Plan achieved a 12 per cent growth in coal output.

53. *Petroleum Economist,* 12 (1976), p.453. The final 1980 plan calls for a 10 per cent growth, predominantly in heavier vehicles.

54. Christopher Wren in *International Herald Tribune,* 27 April 1977, p.2.

55. A. I. Zubkov in *Istoriia SSSR,* 1 (January—February 1976), pp.52—70.

56. SIPRI, *Oil and Security* (New York: Humanities Press, 1974), appendix to chap. 2; *Petroleum Economist,* 3 (1974), pp. 99—101.

57. *Ekonomicheskaia gazeta,* 19 (1976), pp.20—1. Other fuels will be increased, however, bringing the total for *all* fuels to 780 mmT of standard fuel, an increase of 50 per cent. M. Loshakov and A. Poliyenko, 'Soviet Trade with the European Socialist Countries: Results and Prospects', *Foreign Trade,* 12 (1976), pp.6ff.

58. *Voprosy ekonomiki,* 6 (1976), pp.70—9. According to these authors, energy consumption by the USSR's partners in the CMEA will rise from 580 million metric tons of standard fuel in 1975 to 780 mmT in 1980 and 1 billion metric tons in 1990. In view of limited internal supplies, half of this will have to come from abroad — as against about 30 per cent at present.

59. *Petroleum Economist,* 12 (1976), pp.453—4; 1 (1974), p. 13. This information has been confirmed by Marshall I. Goldman, in Vernon (ed.), *The Oil Crisis.* Bulgaria and the German Democratic Republic are already purchasing a great deal on the world market. In 1974, Eastern Europe, including Romania and Yugoslavia, imported around 14 mmT of free market oil. George Hoffman, 'Energy Politics in Eastern Europe: Structural Changes in Production and Consumption and Resources Dependence', from *Proceedings:* International Ex-Students' Conference on Energy, Center for Energy Studies, University of Texas at Austin, 26—30 April 1976, p.145.

60. The Soviet Union and Comecon together recorded a surplus of 0·87 million barrels per day in 1975 (approximately 43·5 mmT for the year). This is more than the 0·70 of 1973 though lower than the 0·98 million b/d surplus of 1971. *International Oil Developments* (1976), pp.23—8. (We are indebted to Aaron Lapidoth for the reference.) In the light of this, recent CIA predictions of a net bloc deficit in 1985 of 3·5—4·5 million b/d — resting on unsubstantiated forecasts of a violent fall of Soviet production in the early 1980s — must be viewed with suspicion. *New York Times* 16 April 1977, p.G—11.

61. *International Herald Tribune,* 17 November 1976. By March 1976 the entire bloc apparently had a debt of $18 billion. According to a report from Brussels by Eliahu Salpeter, Western estimates of Communist debts to the West range from $27 billion to as high as 40 billion, a growth of around $9 billion during 1976. Since many loans are indirect 'third-party' ones, these figures are vague estimates. *Ha'aretz,* 27 December 1976, p.9.

62. Kuwait seems to be the only country interested in loans to Eastern

Europe. It has provided Hungary with $40 million and agreed to finance one-third of a Yugoslav–Czechoslovak–Hungarian pipeline. It discussed a $34 million credit with the USSR in early 1976. *Middle East Economic Digest*, 4 July 1975, and 12 March 1976; *Foreign Trade*, 9 (1975).

63. But Saudi Arabia in 1974 threatened to dispose 150mmT in order to restrain a price rise – the Soviet Union has no such thrust potential. While the Soviet Union produced 82 per cent of Europe's *refined* imports of 26·9 mmT in 1976, OPEC-supplied European refineries have ample capacity to replace the Soviet product at present. *Economist*, 2 March 1977, p.76–7.

64. Marginal revenue from the dollar area (current price times the contemplated diversion *minus* the induced cut in price times the *total* Soviet dollar exports of oil) less the 'dollar' value of the East European exports received in return. We assume these two elements offset about one half of the dollar revenue of approximately $12 per barrel.

65. *Voprosy ekonomiki*, 6 (1975), pp.3–13; *Planovoe khoziaistvo*, 6 (1976), pp.47–53. No mention or provision for reconciling these price principles is typically made.

66. *Petroleum Economist*, 4 (1975), p.138. The nominal price for 1975 represents an unexpected doubling by the Soviets within the five-year plan, but our calculations show they collected only half of it. Where trade is bilaterally cleared and where one side typically exports machinery inherently difficult to assign a 'world price', the price for the commodity import – in this case, Soviet oil – is less meaningful than in multilateral trade. Apparently both Soviet imports and Soviet exports have historically been underpriced when taken separately!

67. Economist Intelligence Unit, *Quarterly Economic Review – USSR*, 3 (1976), p.10.

68. Yeager and Steinberg, *Energy*, p.203; *Istoriia SSSR*, (January–February 1976), pp.52–70. Other CMEA countries are said to be contributing $6 billion to projects within the Soviet Union during the current five-year plan.

69. During 1975 the average price for oil supplied to the advanced West was 59 rubles per metric ton as against 31 rubles to Cuba! During 1974 the five East European countries paid only 18 rubles per ton, and in 1973, 16 rubles per ton, on average. Computed from *Vneshniaia torgovlia*, various issues.

70. *New York Times*, 24 February 1977.

71. Imports of crude oil to the Soviet Union in 1975 amounted to only 7·6 million tons, almost all from Algeria and Iraq. The peak occurred in 1973, when the Soviets took 14·7 million tons (re-exports are not known precisely but undoubtedly occurred) as a political gesture to Iraq after it nationalised foreign shares in its Basrah Petroleum Corporation. Iraq and possibly others as well were reluctant to send oil to their usual customers during the period of the embargo and production cutbacks. See Table 4.1 and *New Times*, 48 (1973). The amounts of oil flowing to the Soviet Union from Syria, as well as from Iraq and other countries, might well be understated in the official figures to the extent that they are cleared in special accounts against arms. Gumpel, 'The Energy Policy of the Soviet Union'.

72. *Middle East Economic Digest* (August 1974), pp.902–64; *Petroleum Economist*, 3 (1975).

73. *Foreign Trade* 6 (1975), pp.51–5. In 1976 the Soviets exported only 846 million rubles of all civilian goods to these five countries – Iraq, Iran, Syria, Algeria and Libya. In 1974 the figure was 657 million rubles and in 1973, 430 million.

74. For a £2·4 million deal with Afghanistan for gas field equipment and exploration aid, see *Middle East Economic Digest,* (July 1974), p.819; Ibid., 13 April 1973. For the South Yemen exploration deal, see *The Petroleum Economist,* 7 (1975), p.394. For a recent deal to help Algeria with technology and personnel training, see *International Affairs,* 11 (1973). Morocco similarly agreed to a Soviet offer of oil exploration around July 1974. *Middle East Economic Digest* (July 1974), p.797.

75. Ibid., April 1973. May 1976 saw the signing of a further oil-extraction protocol. *Foreign Trade,* 1 (1977), p.37.

76. *Petroleum Economist,* 10 (1974), p.394. The Czechs agreed to lend $100 million in all for various projects. *Middle East Economic Digest,* August 1974, p.388.

77. *Foreign Trade,* 6 (1976), pp.2–11; and 10 (1975), pp.2–16. In addition, general development projects were in various stages of completion. *Foreign Trade,* 3 (1976), p.14.

78. Ibid., 6 (1975).

79. *Economist,* 1 June 1974, p.91. Reference here was to Egypt in particular.

80. I. Khotsialov, 'Soviet–Iraqi Co-operation: Results and Prospects', Ibid., 10 (1975), pp.8–16.

81. Ibid., 9 (1975).

82. *US News and World Report,* 25 August 1975, p.53.

83. The American arms export drive, for example, was stepped up by Presidents Nixon and Ford as a way of strengthening the American trade balance after the quadrupling of oil prices in 1974. *International Herald Tribune,* 29 March 1977, p.1.

84. *International Herald Tribune,* 18 March 1977, p.1.

85. *Ekonomicheskaia gazeta,* 4 (1977), p.27.

86. *Middle East Economic Development,* 28 January 1977, p.14.

87. *SShA,* 7 (1974), p.32. However, the Soviets recognise the difficulties this presents. They may also wish to avoid the embarrassment which they, as exporters of raw materials, would face should they wish to remain outside future cartels as they have remained outside OPEC. Between 25 and 30 per cent of non-fuel raw materials are found in socialist countries, they point out. Therefore they advocate international commodity agreements as the preferred method of aiding developing countries. *Mirovaia ekonomika i mezhdunarodnye otnosheniia,* 7 (1974), p.38.

88. *Foreign Trade,* 1 (1976), notes that in 1974 the yearly deficit of non-oil LDC's was about $25 billion.

89. *Mirovaia ekonomika i mezhdunarodnye otnosheniia,* 7 (1974), pp.31–2.

90. *Voprosy ekonomiki,* 6 (1976), pp.70–9. Previously the Soviets criticised the oil producers for not using oil revenues to improve the living standard of their own people. *Mirovaia ekonomika i mezhdunarodnye otnosheniia,* 7 (1974), p.35.

91. *Petroleum Economist,* 2 (1974), p.47.

PART 3   DOMESTIC PERSPECTIVES

5 THE SOVIET PERCEPTION OF INFLUENCE: THE CASE OF THE MIDDLE EAST 1973–1976

Oded Eran

Introduction

It is apparent to any observer that since the Yom Kippur War the Soviet Union has suffered a series of severe setbacks in the Arab world. The war may not have triggered the decline of Soviet influence but it certainly accelerated its tempo. Evidently the impact of the American performance during the fighting in October 1973 and the feeling, on the part of several leading Arab states, that only the United States was capable of modifying behaviour patterns in the area, has been destructive to the Soviet regional position.

One would expect that the series of events which led to the deterioration of the Soviet regional position would leave a deep impression on the Kremlin's thinking concerning the premises, objectives and techniques of its policies in the Middle East and elsewhere in the Third World. More specifically, it would appear inevitable that after 1973 the operational conceptions and methods, which traditionally have been used by Moscow to establish, promote and maintain Soviet influence over the countries of the region, would urgently require a thorough reappraisal. Tracing such a Soviet reappraisal is the aim of this paper; it seeks to determine what impact the post-October 1973 developments in the Middle East have had on Soviet thinking concerned with the building and preservation of influence in client states in general and in the Arab countries in particular.

In order to obtain reliable data on Soviet perceptions and political thinking regarding these issues, this study focuses on the 'scientific research' establishments of several institutes of the USSR Academy of Sciences and of several state universities which deal with foreign and international problems. These are: the Institute of Oriental Studies (IVAN), the Africa Institute, the Institute of the USA and Canada, the Institute of World Economics and International Relations (IMEiMO), the Institute of the International Workers' Movement (IMRD) – all of which belong either to the Department of Historical Sciences or the Department of Economic Sciences of the USSR Academy of Sciences.[1] Attention was paid also to the Institute of the Countries of Asia and

Africa of the Moscow State University and the Chair of the Economy of Contemporary Capitalism of the Leningrad State University, both of which conduct research on contemporary problems of the Third World, including the Middle East.

These academic establishments were chosen because of the special role which they play in the forming of Soviet policy and the special services which they perform for the Soviet political elite. They are in charge of feeding the Soviet decision makers with expert opinions in their specific fields of specialisation as well as of providing the official line with 'scientific' endorsement; they also tend to reflect the current Soviet state of mind on the issues they are responsible for.

While these scholarly establishments have always been preoccupied with problems of Soviet policies towards the Third World — the Middle East included — their activities since 1973, in the form of conferences, symposia and discussions of various types, have indicated a major intellectual and practical effort, probably commissioned by the party leadership, to look thoroughly into the questions involved in the policies conducted towards these parts of the world. Most prominent in this apparent and intense effort were the following: a First Conference of Young Scholars held in the Institute of the Countries of Asia and Africa of the Moscow State University on 24–25 December 1973 with the participation of research associates from the IVAN. At least one of the papers presented at that conference dealt specifically with the Arab world.[2] On 22 February 1974 the Scholarly Council of the Africa Institute of the USSR Academy of Sciences, which deals in particular with problems of the North African Arab countries, including Egypt, held a debate on 'revolutionary democratic' parties, and in April 1974 a special session on the subject of 'ideological currents in developing countries'.[3] The same institute sponsored on 23 April 1974 a conference devoted to 'the state sector in the countries of North Africa' which concentrated mainly on current developments in Egypt. The IMRD sponsored on 23–25 April 1974 a scientific conference on the problems of 'class development and class struggle' in the Afro-Asian countries in which research associates from the IVAN, the Africa Institute and the Leningrad State University participated.[4]

The IVAN itself was also active. Several formal and informal discussions were held there in 1974 and eventually led to the convening of an inter-institutional 'scientific theoretical' conference on the 'social and bureaucratic structure of the Eastern countries' sponsored by the Historical Section of the Scholarly Council and the Department for General Problems of Contemporary Development of that Institute.

Among the other institutes which participated in that conference were IMEiMO, IMRD, the Africa Institute and the Institute of the Countries of Asia and Africa of the Moscow State University.[5] In January 1975 the IVAN, jointly with the editorial board of *Rabochii klass i sovremennyi mir* (The Working Class and the Contemporary World), published by IMRD, held another conference in which A. I. Sobolev, editor-in-chief of the journal and head of the Department for the International Communist Movement in the Institute of Marxism-Leninism of the CPSU Central Committee, delivered a central and most significant paper on the relationship between 'revolutionary democratic' regimes and the indigenous Communist parties, covering the Arab countries among others.[6] The scholars operating in these institutes, and appearing on their behalf in the conferences, have extensively published material interpreting the official positions on the issues concerned.[7] Of that material, the most authentic source of information about the evolving Soviet state of mind concerning questions of influence has been the articles and reports included in the theoretical-professional journals. They have been more useful than newspaper articles or even recent books because commentaries in the press tend to represent immediate (and sometimes hasty) responses to events, without much thought given to broader conceptual and operational matters, while books are, as a rule, somewhat too distant from the events simply because of the time necessary for their preparation for press. In contrast, the theoretical journals have provided a more balanced picture of the relationship between 'theory and practice' inside the Soviet elite and they will serve therefore as the primary source of this paper.[8]

The apparent wealth of Soviet material reflecting current thinking in the Kremlin on the issues of our concern posed a methodological problem of identifying the Soviet terminology equivalent to the concept of influence in currency in the West.[9] Though the Soviet sources occasionally employ the concepts of 'influence' and 'authority' (*vliianie* and *avtoritet*), in relation to the Soviet Union or to an individual communist party, what they usually mean is the general importance, impact or prestige of the Soviet state, or of the given communist party, in the context.[10] These concepts are not used in the sense of Soviet ability to modify or change concrete policy decisions, let alone to force Soviet will upon a foreign government.

Naturally, Soviet theoreticians are not likely to employ Western concepts in developing their theory of influence because these would contradict the official Soviet ideology and undermine the

Marxist-Leninist legacy of Soviet foreign policy. In theory the Soviet
Union is pursuing a selfless policy of supporting the national liberation
movements of the post-colonial countries in their struggle against
neo-colonialism and therefore any desire to achieve influence for the
sake of promoting Soviet political or strategic interests is heretical.
Consequently, in order to understand the Soviet theory of influence
one has to look for the Soviet conceptual equivalents, namely the
concepts of 'solidarity' or 'union' (*soiuz*) between the world socialist
system and the developing nations.[11]

In accordance with that terminological guideline, in order to trace
the evolution of the Soviet perception of influence we must analyse
Soviet assessments of those political factors and circumstances which,
in Soviet opinion, strengthen or weaken 'solidarity' and 'union'
between the USSR and the Afro-Asian nations; in our case, the Arab
countries.

The pertinent Soviet material has traditionally presented the
'solidarity' or 'union' between 'World Socialism' and the 'National
Liberation Movement' as a consequence of both domestic and
international circumstances. On the domestic scene of each national
state the crucial factor was the assumption of power by political and
military circles oriented against the West and towards co-operation with
the Soviet bloc, and pursuing a policy, encouraged by the Soviet Union,
of internal economic socialisation, uprooting neo-colonialism and
capitalism. The political participation of the indigenous communist
party has been regarded as an additional guarantee. On the international
scene, the growing might of the Soviet bloc and the change in the
'correlation of forces' between East and West have allegedly presented
the Afro-Asian nations with the genuine option of an independent path
of development towards closer alignment with the socialist bloc. In
accordance with that conceptual framework, the analysis of the state of
'solidarity' and 'union' between the Soviet Union and the Arab states
should be related to Soviet appraisals of the political orientations of the
military and civilian elites which are ruling the radical Arab countries,
and to the Kremlin's thinking on the effectiveness of Soviet economic
and military support provided to client Arab regimes, as well as on the
role of the Arab communist parties in their domestic politics. The
analysis should also be related to problems which affect the
international balance of power and thereby the conduct of the client
regimes, such as regional disputes, the energy crisis and the capability of
American diplomacy.

'Deformatsiia' of a 'Sotsorientatsiia'

The first question which emerges is how great the Soviet sources believe the decline of Soviet influence in the client Arab states to be, particularly in those countries which since October 1973 have been exposed to the American diplomatic offensive. In dealing with Soviet assessments of this kind we must recognise that to admit a major setback, let alone a reversal of a certain historical trend, is very problematic in any apocalyptic ideology. The integrity of such an ideology is threatened by any practical development which appears to contradict the anticipated historical flow of events. Therefore, the Soviet evaluations of the current state of affairs in the Arab world have been understated and somewhat apologetic. On the one hand, references to unidentified setbacks, failures and disappointments have increased significantly in the Soviet material pertaining to the Arab world and the Third World in general. On the other hand, the same reports have aimed at placing everything in the right perspective, i.e. emphasising that setbacks are the exception, that the positive trend continues to prevail and that the historical balance has so far been positive.

More specifically, if before 1973 infrequent references to the likelihood of retreats and fiascos in the Third World could be found in Soviet sources,[12] since 1973 there has been hardly an article on the subject which avoided reference to occasional disappointments. Most of the pertinent statements have taken a general theoretical approach to the subject. As stated in one article: 'retreats, cases of restoration (*restavratsiia*) − in a word − defeat of the National Liberation Revolution are possible.'[13] Another article argues that 'the possibility of a temporary departure of some countries from a socialist orientation should not be ruled out'.[14] Other sources speak of 'historical surprises',[15] of the 'zigzags of History', of the 'deformation of the socialist orientation'[16] and of the fact that 'occasionally the neo-colonialists succeed in guiding the foreign policy of some individual liberated states on to a path desired [by the neo-colonialists]'.[17]

While most of the sources speak of the subject in general terms, some of them do refer to Egypt specifically as the major setback of the era where 'the rightist tendency assumed an almost pro-imperialist character'[18] and where the forces in power think that the process of 'revolutionary-democratic development' can be stopped or reversed.[19]

To be sure, as a rule the specific and nonspecific references to setbacks and failures are immediately qualified. Retreats and departures from the socialist path are always temporary, accidental, isolated cases;

they never represent any trend. The general historical process is irreversible.

The need to minimise the significance of the Egyptian case is also reflected in the counterposing of what happened in Egypt to overall Soviet achievements in the Arab and Afro-Asian worlds. Besides Egypt, which is described as going backward, a long list of states are said to be on the right path of non-capitalist development;[20] Syria, Iraq and Algeria are quite often specifically mentioned as successful cases of revolutionary democracies[21] and the Arab world as a whole is depicted as an arena where the imperialist conspiracies have been defeated.[22]

Furthermore, the look-where-we-stood-twenty-years-ago-and-where-we-stand-now approach is used quite frequently and effectively. The Soviet writer compares the number of radical Soviet-oriented regimes in the Third World twenty, fifteen or even ten years ago, with the current state of affairs, and the undeniable conclusion is that in historical perspective the Soviet Union has done magnificently. The West has gone from one defeat to another; more and more states and political parties have adopted a socialist orientation.[23] For the Soviet leadership which started in the mid-fifties in the Arab world at zero point, this must be a very good argument to pursue in order to neutralise the effect and implications of the Egyptian case or any other setback.

Nevertheless, neither the apocalyptic confidence shown by the belief in the irreversibility of the historical process nor the boasting about the evident positive historical balance could have prevented the Egyptian case, along with the cumulative effect of the series of setbacks in the Arab-Israeli zone of the Middle East, from leaving their imprint on Soviet appraisals and expectations for the short run. It is quite clear from the post-1973 sources that much uncertainty about the immediate future, and a realisation that Arab as well as Third World politics in general are highly unpredictable, prevail today among Soviet experts. As stated by one of the sources, one should not talk of the assured victory of the revolution because it is impossible to determine the course of events in advance.[24] The conduct of these regimes is full of contradictions and inconsistencies — to use the language of other sources.[25] In other words, it is recognised that nothing should be taken for granted as far as the immediate practical policy level is concerned. A clear line is drawn between ceremonial statements about the future victory and operational assessments made for the sake of concrete decisions.

The Crisis of Rising Ideological Expectations

Since in the context of policy making short-run appraisals are far more significant than those for the long run, the admission by Soviet sources that the near future is unpredictable is an authentic reflection of a quandary in the minds of Soviet policy makers. That admission also reflects the fact that, two decades after the first Soviet breakthrough into the Arab world and other Third World countries, Soviet theory and practice have reached a point of crisis. The enormous ideological expectations regarding the future political development of the Arab and Afro-Asian world which have been constantly built up since the Twentieth Congress of the CPSU are the cause of that crisis one generation after the Congress. These progressively rising expectations have centred on one political stratum, known, in Soviet terminology, as the 'national bourgeoisie', which means, with specific reference to the Middle East, the Arab nationalist movements.

Of course, the Arab scene has not been without complications. The periodic eruptions of antagonism between the nationalist regimes and their indigenous communist parties frequently jeopardised Soviet achievements in some Arab countries, and consequently the Arab national bourgeoisie was occasionally depicted by Soviet theoreticians as an unstable, wavering, inconsistent political element. However, by and large in the overall Arab scene, the positive overwhelmed the negative and Soviet enthusiasm and hopes regarding the future were unshakable. Even the Six Day War, whose consequences generated so much Soviet anxiety about an imminent reversal of the trend in the Middle East, led in the years which followed to an increasingly radical atmosphere in the Arab world.

The theoretical elaborations on the developing opportunities in the Arab radical regimes began at a later stage to employ new concepts which would conform to these rising expectations. From the early sixties it was no longer the national bourgeoisie which ruled the radical Arab regimes but 'revolutionary democratic' elements which were neither bourgeois nor proletariat by their social origins but grew from the 'intermediate strata of society and assumed power due to the absence of strong and distinct bourgeois or proletarian classes.[26]

These revolutionary democratic parties — the Arab Socialist Union in Egypt, the FLN in Algeria, the Ba'th in Syria and Iraq — were said to have accomplished non-capitalistic and sometimes even socialist transformations in their own countries and were expected in the foreseeable future to transform themselves into Marxist-Leninist parties. Given these high hopes, an attempt was even made to cast doubt on the *raison d'être* of independent communist organisations of a traditional nature. The local communists in Egypt and Algeria were encouraged by Moscow to dissolve their parties and join individually the revolutionary democratic parties ruling their countries. There were, of course, quite a few sceptical voices less enthusiastic and more reserved about the political potentialities of the Arab and other revolutionary democrats,[27] but they were drowned in the ocean of optimism and jubilation about the radicalisation of the Arab nationalist movements.

Beginning, however, with the death of Nasir but more so after the showdown between Sadat and the pro-Soviet group in the Egyptian leadership, there seems to have been a change in the ratio between optimistic and reserved opinions emanating from Soviet sources. This de-escalation of Soviet hopes for the foreseeable future was accelerated even further by the July 1972 expulsion of Soviet advisers and technicians from Egypt, while after the October 1973 war there has been hardly an article on the subject which has not been in one way or another apologetic; the ideological expectations of the fifties and sixties were clearly frustrated in the march of the seventies, and Soviet scholarship was called upon to rationalise and explain how the non-capitalist or socialist-oriented revolutionary democrats had taken the wrong path.

The interpretations provided by the Soviet theoretical material are well anchored in a Marxist frame of reference. As in the sixties so in the present period the revolutionary democrats consist of the 'military-civilian intelligentsia' which represents the intermediate strata of society; they are said to have emerged as the dominant political power because neither bourgeoisie nor proletariat had been in existence as fully developed classes in those countries.[28] The class basis of the 'military-civilian intelligentsia' explains, according to Soviet sources, the contradictions and inconsistencies, in short the 'dual nature' of its behaviour.[29] As representatives of small-size capital accumulations, the revolutionary democrats fight the big bourgeoisie, but still regard themselves as standing above the proletariat in the social ladder; using socialist slogans they conduct a battle against big capital but simultaneously they cherish and defend small and medium-sized capital, guided by the principle of the sanctity of private property.[30]

Consequently, even the socialist orientation (*sotsorientatsiia*), which is pursued by the revolutionary democratic regimes in domestic economic policies, should not be confused, so claims the pertinent

Soviet material, with scientific socialism; it is rather a kind of
'subjective socialism' which is anti-capitalist in practice but not a
genuine socialism. Even if the official self-proclaimed title of the regime
concerned is that of 'scientific socialism', it is not necessarily so in
essence.[31] Also, there is no longer any expectation that socialist-
oriented regimes and parties will inevitably transform themselves into
Marxist-Leninist parties.[32]

To be sure, the anti-capitalist nature of these regimes is regarded as a
positive thing in itself, but the concepts and labels such as 'dual nature',
'inconsistency', 'contradictory behaviour', which in the fifties and
sixties had been reserved to describe the national bourgeoisie, are
employed presently also to depict the political character of the
revolutionary democrats, indicating the recent Soviet disappointment
with countries of the socialist orientation. Unlike the sixties, however,
when the Soviet theoreticians had been rather slow in awarding the title
of 'socialism' to non-Communist-led regimes,[33] that title is now
generously given to any radical regime which seeks to be so-called, on
the understanding that it is not co-extensive with the ultimate form of
scientific socialism.

The class character and policy of the revolutionary democratic
intelligentsia are clearly reflected in its conduct in the international
arena. On the one hand, the countries of the socialist orientation are
assisting in the struggle against imperialism, by strengthening their
friendly relations, solidarity and co-operation with the Soviet bloc.
That trend is explained by the fact that ideologically they are closer to
socialism than to imperialism.[34] On the other hand, these regimes are
not always consistent and from time to time, attempt 'to play on
contradictions between the Soviet Union and the People's Republic of
China' or 'contradictions between the socialist and the imperialist
countries'.[35] Furthermore, despite their alleged affinity with the Soviet
bloc these countries are often apprehensive about 'the growing might of
the Soviet Union';[36] the allusions to Soviet-Arab relations are evident.

One should add also that until the Twenty-Fifth Congress of the
CPSU in February 1976, Egypt was included, along with Algeria, Syria,
Iraq and the People's Democratic Republic of Yemen, in the list of
Arab countries of the socialist orientation.[37] However, after the
Congress, and perhaps also as a result of the cancellation of the Treaty
of Friendship and Co-operation between the two governments less than
a month later, Egypt has no longer been mentioned even as belonging
to that category of Third World nations.[38]

Thus Soviet theory admits that, and rationalises why, a trend towards radicalisation, which has progressively spread throughout the countries of the Third World — the Arab countries included — has not produced any guarantee against setbacks and retreats. Revolutionary democrats or national bourgeois — the situation remains as fluid and as unpredictable as it was two decades ago. Since the historical process has neither consolidated Soviet achievements nor provided stronger assurances against 'restorations' and 'deformations of socialist orientations' one is led to investigate whether the basic foundations of the Soviet policy of cultivating multilateral relations with the Arab and other client states have been re-examined and whether the Soviet theoreticians and practical decision makers have tried to work out or think about measures to prevent deterioration or at least make it less likely.

The Policy of Multiple Aid — Revisited

Reportedly, after October 1973 an 'undercurrent' opposing co-operation between the Soviet Union and the Third World countries developed inside the CPSU and the Soviet military establishment.[39] In addition to the strains and burden which such aid programmes evidently impose on the Soviet economy, the realisation that there has been no direct correlation between aid and influence and that Soviet investments in Egypt have not brought the Kremlin much influence, must have been prominent in the minds of those representing that 'undercurrent'. Evidently, the various questions of economic, technical and military assistance have undergone a thorough reappraisal in the period after October 1973 and the pertaining material deserves attention.

1. Economic Aid

Soviet policies of aiding Third World countries have always been justified in terms of enabling these countries 'to strengthen their economic and political independence'.[40] As far as economic aid is concerned, the declared aim has been the reduction as much as possible of economic ties, and even more so dependence, between a given Afro-Asian country and the capitalist nations to enable that country to pursue a genuinely 'independent' foreign policy, resisting the temptations and the pressures of neo-colonialism. As far as the radical socialist-oriented regimes are concerned, the declared objectives of Soviet economic aid are even farther-reaching: 'relying on world socialism the new nations are capable of accomplishing progressive reforms' which are in essence the elimination of the remnants of capitalist relationships in their societies.[41]

Inherent in these alleged operational objectives of the Soviet economic aid projects is the Marxist conviction that there is a direct correlation between domestic and foreign policies of regimes, or — to put it in the proper terminology — between the economic base and the policies of the superstructure. Therefore in the Soviet perception domestic economic policies are conceptually inseparable from foreign conduct; they are two aspects of the same reality. Nations which are pursuing a socialist orientation in their economy and cut themselves off from the world capitalist market are expected also to pursue a 'progressive' foreign policy of solidarity with the Soviet bloc.[42]

The post-1973 Egyptian scene, however, cast some serious doubts on this logical construction; it represented a case of a state which, with the help of the Soviet Union, had restructured its economic base according to a socialist model but was still able after that to reverse its political conduct on the national and international level. The questions raised in that context were: how it could happen and what could be done economically to prevent it. To put it in the Marxist language of R. N. Andreasian, a Middle Eastern expert who analysed recent developments in Egypt, the practical and theoretical questions are: Whether a socialist-oriented base does or does not enable (a state) to conduct a course of 'restoration'. What kind of economic base would be capable of reducing the chance of being manipulated by the superstructure?[43] Judging by the Soviet material analysing the Egyptian developments from an economic angle, it appears that there is no base which can restrain the superstructure from changing direction and generally very little can be done about it by the Soviet Union.

The Soviet analyses relate to two components of the Egyptian economy: the private sector and the state sector. Private property is the source of all political evil and therefore the Soviet material assistance given to Egypt and other countries for the accomplishment of 'progressive reforms' is aimed at the maximum expansion of the socialised state sector at the expense of the private sector. As mentioned above, however, due to their non-proletarian socialist conceptions, the Revolutionary Democrats are not eliminating private property entirely; they do away just with the big and foreign capital and leave the small, and sometimes medium-sized capital, untouched. By so doing, they maintain the seeds of evil in their own system. Consequently, despite the supremacy of the state sector and the reduced influence of Western capital in Egypt, small-sized capital has grown over the years into medium-sized capital[44] and currently fairly large capitalist enterprises exist in Egypt as well as in Algeria.[45]

The influence of the phenomenon can allegedly be detected in the policies of the Egyptian government, which simultaneously with the further development of the state sector, has embarked on the road of 'economic liberalisation' and an 'open door' policy aimed at the stimulation of private business. Accordingly, tax privileges were granted to small and medium-sized private enterprises, the sequester on some of the properties which had been nationalised in 1964 was cancelled and, worst of all, in May 1976 the government passed legislation which granted several tax and other privileges in order to encourage the ultimate evil – foreign capital investments. No wonder that foreign capital has been activated in this country as a result,[46] or that, furthermore, growing participation of the Egyptian bourgeoisie in the country's economic life has already been reflected in rightist and 'almost pro-imperialist' tendencies.[47]

Hostility towards the private sector is, of course, expected. Curiously enough, however, not all the blame is put on that sector. Soviet theoreticians have apparently concluded that even the socialised sector of the economy, whose expansion is deliberately encouraged by Soviet aid, cannot serve as a guarantee against political reversals. True, Soviet writers have always argued that a state sector is 'progressive' only if it is controlled by a 'progressive' regime; therefore a distinction has always been made between the state sector in Iran or Tunisia and that in the countries of the socialist orientation. Nevertheless, recent material has reflected severe disappointment with the economic and political elites which control the state sector of the socialist-oriented countries. The concepts reflecting that disappointment, which are in currency today in the pertinent Soviet material, are 'bureaucratic elite', 'bureaucratic bourgeoisie' or simply 'ruling elite'.[48] G. Mirskii, a long-time Soviet expert on Egypt, quoted an Arab Marxist as saying that 'new propertied groups' have developed even in those sectors of the economy which had undergone 'anti-imperialist' reforms and that this 'new bourgeoisie' of the 'socialist-oriented countries' is making the state sector its 'feeding-trough and breeding ground'.[49] The obvious lesson is, of course, that even the loyalty of those who run the socialist-oriented economy should not be taken for granted. The unstated general conclusion is that while Soviet economic aid is given in order to strengthen the independence of a country there is no security whatsoever against its misuse or abuse. Evidently, the Soviet theorists have resigned themselves to the fact that it does not reduce the element of unpredictability in the conduct of those nations.

2. Military Assistance

Strengthening the independence of the recipient countries is also the justification of the Soviet military aid projects. Moreover, as far as the radically prone regimes are concerned, military aid is also aimed at making the army 'an instrument of progressive social development'.[50] Inherent in that operational objective is the Soviet assessment and belief that the military is the most important political factor in the policies of the developing countries and that the convictions of the army officers prevail in most of the Third World regimes and guide their behaviour.

That attitude is certainly not new; it emerged in the late fifties, and in a more articulate form early in the sixties against the background of the Arab radical regimes in which the 'military intelligentsia', radical in its orientation, was indeed the dominant factor.[51] Cultivating relations with the national armies of these countries consequently became a top priority of Soviet regional policies. The Soviet military assistance was intended to align the national armies with the radical cause of their nations or, in other terms, make them the driving force of 'progressive social developments'.[52]

As stated already, 'progressive social development' has always been understood by Soviet theory in domestic as well as in foreign policy terms, i.e. it has been identical with the policy of economic independence from the West and 'solidarity' with the Soviet bloc. The Soviet Union believed that it could use military assistance to encourage the radicalisation of the national armies in two ways: first, military aid enhances the 'defence capability' of these countries by improving their 'peaceful and non-peaceful means' of defence.[53] In other words, Soviet offers of military aid accorded with the military priorities and perspectives of the recipient countries and were therefore attractive to the military elites of these countries. Second, by providing military assistance, in the form of arms and technological supplies as well as the training of military cadres, the Soviet Union helped the given army 'to overcome the legacy (*nasledie*) of neo-colonialism'.[54] More specifically, Soviet military assistance is intended to purge the national armies of the developing countries from Western military doctrines and conceptions as well as military equipment; the adoption of Soviet military thinking and the absorption of Soviet weapon systems by the national armies are expected to increase their desire for 'solidarity' with the Soviet bloc. Other considerations for providing military assistance, such as the expansion of the Soviet strategic infrastructure in various regions of the globe, are strongly denied and attributed only to the counter 'imperialist' military assistance; the Soviet motivation cannot appear anything but selfless.[55]

Nevertheless, in assessing the prospects and potentialities of the military in the developing nations the post-1973 Soviet sources do not seem to be so assured of its political quality. While it is recognised that 'the role of the military in the developing nations is not decreasing but is even increasing' it is also admitted that 'the danger of counter-revolutionary military action has remained and to a certain extent even increased'; the military may become, so it is claimed, instrumental in bringing about a 'temporary interruption of the revolutionary development'.[56]

The relative decline in positive Soviet expectations with regard to the military establishments of the developing nations is also reflected in the revision of some of the pertinent conceptions which were popular throughout the sixties. Unlike a decade ago, when Soviet articles referred to the radical military juntas in terms of selfless political powers accomplishing historical missions, which were reminiscent of the Marxist conception of the role of the proletariat,[57] the current Soviet material warns us against conceptualising the military as a 'subclass organism' and insists that it should be regarded as a reflection of the social and political 'correlation of forces' inside the society. Thus, the class structure of the society determines the orientation of its military and the political performance of the military may be 'progressive' as well as 'reactionary' depending on its social context.[58]

To be sure, the current Syrian and Iraqi military elites are favourably looked upon and no specific mention is made of a 'reactionary' role performed by the Egyptian military in 'interrupting temporarily the revolutionary development', but the overall spirit is of more scepticism and suspicion concerning the political role of the militaries in the developing nations, even the ones which for years have been nourished by Soviet material and organisational assistance. The specific feedback of the Arab case is easily recognisable. To sum up, while military assistance continues to be regarded as a means for furthering radical and pro-Soviet trends, its impact on the behaviour of the military elites is now looked upon as marginal, and as in the case of economic aid, unpredictable.

The 'National Fronts'

The realisation by the Soviet expert community that neither the socialised economic structure nor the Soviet-equipped and indoctrinated military establishment provides a guarantee against political reversals led to a limited rejuvenation of the more traditional Soviet thinking which has always been searching for securities against anti-Soviet trends in specific domestic political alignments, particularly in the promotion of different kinds of alliances between the indigenous communist parties and the incumbent revolutionary democratic regimes. The traditional thinking on the role of the communist parties inside radical non-communist regimes has undergone many changes since the Soviet breakthrough into the Middle East in the mid-fifties but it has always been guided by one major objective — to minimise, if not to eliminate entirely, the conflict between radical Arab nationalists and communists which was regarded as highly damaging to Soviet interests.

Late in the 1950s and early in the 1960s the effort focused on convincing, if not pressuring, the communists and the incumbent nationalists to form governing coalitions in which each of the parties would preserve its organisational independence. The communist parties were ordered to avoid any conflict with the nationalist regimes and to provide them with full political backing. This strategy was officially articulated by the Statement of the 81 Communist Parties in 1960 and by the Programme of the CPSU approved by the Twenty-Second Congress in 1961.[59] Nevertheless, in the reality of the Arab world this formula was not workable. Antagonism between domestic communism and nationalism continued, to the consternation of Moscow, and another kind of arrangement had to be thought of. Towards the mid-sixties, simultaneously with the emerging conception of revolutionary democracy, the idea of dissolving the communist parties and integrating individual communists into the ruling one-party regimes gained ground.[60] The declared intention was to make the individual communists influential inside the ruling parties and help them eventually to become genuine Marxist-Leninist parties.[61]

This strategy was implemented in Algeria and Egypt; it was not realised, mainly due to the resistance of the communists themselves, in Syria and Iraq.[62] As long as Nasir was alive, and despite the ousting of Ben Bella in Algeria, Moscow had no reason to regret the disintegration of the communist organisations in Egypt and Algeria. Only after Nasir's death, when the threat of Egypt's reorientation became real, did indications of some rethinking on that matter begin to show occasionally in Soviet material.[63] In the post-1973 theoretical discussions this revised frame of mind has become dominant.

The most conspicuous revival of an old attitude in the current thinking on the matter is that of the distrust towards military regimes which do not allow, in one way or another, the participation of communists in the government. These 'authoritarian' regimes, as they are called in the sources, are not trustworthy even if they embark on a radical path, because with the absence of 'popular initiatives' they are likely to make 'serious subjective mistakes'.[64] The Soviet insistence on the need to co-opt the communist parties into the ruling establishments is justified now, as in the past, in terms of 'expanding the mass base' of the regimes, thereby guaranteeing their continued radical character.[65] The belief that the revolutionary democrats' decision on the participation or non-participation of communists in the regime is, in the final analysis, the real criterion for their true intentions in foreign policy, is as strong today in Moscow as it was in the late 1950s and early 60s.[66]

Nonetheless, the specific form of dissolving the communist parties and the admission of individual communists into the ruling parties, as was the policy in Egypt and Algeria under Khrushchev and Brezhnev as well, are very severely criticised nowadays. The communists are expressly prohibited from uniting with any revolutionary democratic party whose programme is not genuinely Marxist-Leninist.[67] This kind of one (non-Marxist-Leninist) party system is evidently no longer to the liking of Moscow because in the reality of the Arab world it eventually led to the virtual disappearance of the communist factor from the scene, and when the moment of truth arrived and the one-party regime in Egypt reoriented itself there was no (communist) body powerful enough to prevent it. The re-formation of a communist organisation in Egypt in the summer of 1975 was a direct consequence of that mood of 'Communist renaissance' so apparent in the sources.

In contrast, the Syrian and Iraqi forms of communist participation in government in the framework of 'national fronts' are praised because the parties have been allowed to preserve their independent organisation and therefore, so it is argued, have maintained real influence on the thinking of the leaders of these regimes. According to the sources[68] that kind of alignment has proved its stability in recent Middle Eastern developments. However, on the basis of past experience, the communists are sternly reminded to be accommodating allies and to avoid any confrontation with the ruling revolutionary democrats.[69] All past attempts of Arab communist parties to assert themselves in radical regimes have led to their alienation from the regime and usually had disastrous consequences for the parties themselves as well as for Soviet relations with the countries concerned. The Soviet theoreticians reflect in their writings awareness of the delicacy of the situation; while communist participation is a kind of guarantee against reversals, it also involves great risks.

The 'Correlation of Forces'

While domestic politics have always been regarded by Soviet spokesmen as prime determinants of the foreign policy orientation of national regimes, international circumstances are said to have their impact as well. As mentioned above, the achievement of the independence by the post-colonial countries and in particular the radicalisation of their policies internally and externally are related by Soviet theory to the emergence of the Soviet Union as a world power on a par with the United States. This post-World War Two balance of power, or 'correlation of forces' to use the Soviet term, has made genuine national independence of Western domination a feasible option and determined the decision of many nations to opt for a non-capitalist road of development.[70]

1. The Energy Crisis

Within this growing favourable international environment a new positive phenomenon emerged after 1973 — a 'change in the correlation of forces between the Third World and the West', namely the realisation by these new nations of their bargaining power and its exploitation for political purposes as demonstrated by the policies of the oil-producing and exporting Arab countries.[71]

No wonder that the initial Soviet reaction to the oil boycott in 1973 and to the co-ordinated oil policy of OPEC which emerged since then was enthusiastic:[72] it affected the entire Soviet assessment of the more conservative regimes in the Middle East which were, in practice, the leading forces behind the new-found weapon of oil blackmail in international relations. At no point in the past did Soviet sources talk in such favourable terms about Saudi Arabia or Iran. Of course, these conservative regimes were not depicted as socialist oriented but they were described as countries where the national liberation revolution was already in its initial stages.[73] The inherent assumption here was that under specific circumstances even a tribal, or feudal, political structure could produce progressive foreign conduct.

This enthusiasm about the 'change in the correlation of forces' between the Third World and the West subsided after some time and some rethinking of the possible implications of the fantastic wealth accumulated by the oil-producing countries could be seen in Soviet sources. The recirculation of the petro-dollars in the form of investments in the economies of the Western countries led the Soviet sources to talk about the newly-developed 'oil aristocracy' and the danger of a 'spread of capitalist relations in the Third World'.[74] Evidently, the integration of the oil-producing countries into the

Western economic system is not welcomed by Moscow because of the anticipated political effect of such a development on the international conduct of these countries. Needless to say, the Saudi-American co-operation regarding the settlement of the Arab-Israeli dispute and the leverage exercised on Egyptian policy by Saudi Arabia and the Gulf oil states have confirmed that suspicion.

2. The Impact of American Diplomacy

Another aspect of the intensified Soviet concern about the international 'correlation of forces', reported indirectly by the sources, relates to the economic and political capability of the United States to buy off countries and regimes. Neocolonialism, despite its alleged disasters, is depicted as having a significant influence economically and politically.[75] The effect of the achievements of American diplomacy in arranging the Israeli–Egyptian and Israeli–Syrian disengagement agreements is evident. The American 'peace dove' is said to fly over the area 'carrying many millions of dollars'.[76] Needless to say any exclusively American-sponsored solution is negative by definition; the rightist forces of the Middle and Near East and elsewhere are interested in such a settlement of the Arab-Israeli dispute because it will strengthen the capitalist trends in the area.[77] This frame of mind is demonstrated also in some rethinking concerning the utility of regional conflicts from a Soviet point of view. Though it has never been explicitly admitted, since the mid-1950s almost any boiling regional situation in the Third World presented tempting opportunities to Soviet policy, almost any change of the status quo seemed likely to promote Soviet interest. There were, of course, several exceptions such as the Nasir-Qasim rivalry late in the fifties but the overall balance of regional flare-ups has been overwhelmingly positive. The post-1973 material contains for the first time some vague indications of a growing Soviet realisation that the tactic of crisis promotion may have exhausted itself and that regional conflicts might not necessarily, under any circumstances, work for the benefit of the USSR but the other way around.[78] Apparently, despite the 'disintegration of the colonial system of imperialism' and the change in the 'correlation of forces' between world socialism and the capitalist nations in favour of the former, neo-colonialism is by no means underestimated; on the contrary, it is recognised as powerful, influential and attractive economically and politically; its retreat is not anticipated in the near future.

Conclusions

Tracing evidence of a Soviet reassessment of operational and conceptual problems of influence was the purpose of this paper. We have found that the post-1973 theoretical material pertaining to that subject indicates preoccupation with these specific problems and an attempt at a thorough examination of past assumptions. It appears that at present, more than at any time in the past, there is doubt about the effectiveness and credibility of the factors and methods which have been traditionally regarded as promoting 'solidarity' and 'union' between the USSR and the National Liberation Movement. Recent experiences have tended to intensify Soviet scepticism about radical ruling elites as well as the effectiveness of such influence-promoting means as military and economic assistance; direct correlation between aid and influence is no longer expected. At the same time, some revival of old beliefs in the necessity of cultivating viable communist parties for the sake of co-operating with, not antagonising, the incumbent regimes, is evident. Nonetheless, there is no sign in the writings we have considered of an attempt to devise new ways to re-establish Soviet influence. At the beginning of the third decade of Soviet involvement in the Middle East, Soviet thinking on how to influence the politics of these countries has become, if not pessimistic, at least more sober and more inclined to avoid rigorous projections. Soviet thought has undergone a process of declining expectations.

Notes

1. The Institute of Latin America and the Institute of the Far East, as well as the Institute of Economics and the Institute of History and Philosophy of the USSR Academy of Sciences were also considered but naturally did not contribute very much to the Middle Eastern aspect.

2. See *Vestnik Moskovskogo universiteta; Vostokovedenie*, 1 (1974), p.108. The paper relating to the Arab world was presented by A. I. Stepanov and was entitled 'The Third Road of Colonel Qadhdhafi'.

3. *Narody Azii i Afriki*, 5 (1974), pp.238–9.

4. Ibid. 6 (1974), p.216.

5. 'Characteristics of the Social Structure and Role of the Bureaucracy in the Countries of the East', *Narody Azii i Afriki*, 1 (1975), p.69.

6. *Rabochii klass i sovremennyi mir*, 3 (1975), pp.3–18; 4 (1975), pp.149–50.

7. The 'constitutional' documents defining the basic concepts and the general framework are the Statement of the 81 Communist parties of 1960, the materials of the 20th–25th CPSU Party Congresses and the Statement of the Conference of the Communist parties of 1969. See note 59 below.

8. The Institute of Oriental Studies and the Africa Institute publish the bimonthly *Narody Azii i Afriki* (The Peoples of Asia and Africa); the IMEiMO publishes the monthly *Mirovaia ekonomika i mezhdunarodnye otnosheniia* (MEiMO) (World Economics and International Relations); *IMRD* publishes the bimonthly *Rabochii klass i sovremennyi mir*; the Institute of the Far East

publishes the quarterly *Problemy Dal'nego Vostoka* (Problems of the Far East); the Institute of the USA and Canada publishes the monthly *SSRA* (USA); the Institute of Latin America publishes the bi-monthly *Latinskaia Amerika* (Latin America); the Moscow State University publishes a twice-yearly series *Vostokovedenie* (Oriental Studies) as part of the *Vestnik Moskovskogo universiteta* (Herald of Moscow University); the Leningrad State University publishes a twice-yearly series *Ekonomika, filosofiia, pravo* (Economics, Philosophy and Law) as part of *Vestnik Leningradskogo universiteta* (Herald of Leningrad University); other sources, not directly involved but still of some relevance, were *Sovetskoe gosudarstvo i pravo* (Soviet State and Law) published by the Institute of State and Law of the USSR Academy of Sciences; *Mezhdunarodnoe rabochee dvizhenie* (The International Workers' Movement) published by IMRD; *Voprosy filosofii* (Problems of Philosophy) published by the Institute of Philosophy of the USSR Academy of Sciences. Of the non-academic theoretical journals *Kommunist* and *Kommunist vooruzhennykh sil* (Communist in the Armed Forces) were useful. In addition, three non-academic sources in the English language were useful: *International Affairs, New Times* and *Soviet Military Review. World Marxist Review* has been studied as well.

9. See A. Rubinstein (ed.), *Soviet and Chinese Influences in the Third World* (New York: Praeger Special Studies, 1975).

10. Polkovnik E. Dolgopolov, 'Armies of the Developing Countries and Politics', *Kommunist vooruzhennykh sil*, 6 (1975), p.76; G. Mirskii, 'The Developing Countries and World Capitalism', *MEiMO*, 3 (1976), p.37.

11. See for instance M. V. Igolkin, 'Towards a Methodology of Studying Nationalism in Developing Countries', *Narody Azii i Afriki*, 1 (1975), p.46; Mirskii, 'Developing Countries and World Capitalism', pp.43, 46.

12. See e.g. N. A. Simoiia, *On the Characteristics of National-Liberation Revolutions* (Moscow: Akademiia Nauk SSSR, Institut Narodov Azii, 1968) and V. F. Volianskii, 'The Role of the Subjective Factor in the Struggle for the Socialist Orientation of the Developing Countries of Africa', *Vostokovedenie: Vestnik Moskovskogo universiteta*, 3 (1971).

13. A. S. Kaufman, 'Problems of Theory of National Liberation Revolutions', *Narody Azii i Afriki*, 1 (1975), pp.64–5.

14. Igolkin, 'Towards a Methodology of Studying Nationalism', p.48.

15. R. N. Andreasian, 'Contradictions and Criteria of Non-Capitalist Development', *Narody Azii i Afriki*, 2 (1974), p.43.

16. 'New Manifestations in the Countries of the Socialist Orientation', *Rabochii klass i sovremennyi mir*, 3 (1976), pp.157–8.

17. E. Tarabrin, 'The Third World and Imperialism: a New Factor in the Correlation of Forces', *MEiMO*, 2 (1975), p.15.

18. A. I. Sobolev, 'The Proletariat of the Liberated Countries and Social Progress', *Rabochii klass i sovremennyi mir*, 3 (1975), p.12.

19. 'New Manifestations', p.158.

20. Ibid., p.156.

21. Kaufman, 'Non-Proletarian Theories of Socialism in the Liberated Countries', *Rabochii klass i sovremennyi mir*, 3 (1976), pp.43, 46.

22. Mirskii, 'Developing Countries and World Capitalism', p.36.

23. Mirskii, 'Developing Countries', p. 36; A. Kiva, 'On Certain Capitalist Developments in the Third World', *MEiMO*, 3 (1975), p.113; Tarabrin, 'Third World', p.13; *Narody Azii i Afriki*, 5 (1974), p.239.

24. Kaufman, 'Problems of Theory', p.63.

25. Andreasian, 'Contradictions and Criteria', pp.39, 46.

26. Secondary material on the evolution of Soviet theories on the National Liberation Movement during the fifties and sixties can be found in the following:

H. C. d'Encausse and S. R. Schram, *Marxism and Asia* (Penguin, 1966); K. London (ed.), *New Nations in a Divided World* (Praeger, 1963); J. H. Kautsky, *Communism and the Politics of Development* (Wiley, 1968); J. H. Kautsky, *Political Change in Underdeveloped Countries* (Wiley, 1967); W. Z. Laqueur, *Communism and Nationalism in the Middle East* (Praeger, 1961); R. Loewenthal, 'On National Democracy', *Survey*, 47 (April 1963); T. P. Thornton (ed.), *The Third World in Soviet Perspective* (Princeton Univ. Press, 1964); O. Eran, 'Soviet Perception of Arab Communism and its Political Role', in M. Confino and S. Shamir (eds.), *The USSR and the Middle East* (Israel Universities Press, 1973); *Mizan Newsletter* (Central Asia Research Centre, London); *Soviet Periodical Abstracts* (earlier title: *Selective Soviet Annotated Bibliographies*), *Asia, Africa and Latin America* (Slavic Languages Research Institute, Inc.).

27. See V. Tiagunenko, 'Current Problems of the Non-Capitalist Path of Development', *MEiMO*, 10 (1964), pp.13–25; Simoiia, 'National Liberation Revolutions'.

28. Andreasian, 'Contradictions and Criteria', p.38; Mirskii, 'Developing Countries and World Capitalism', p.28.

29. Ibid.

30. Andreasian, 'Contradictions and Criteria', p.40.

31. Igolkin, 'Towards a Methodology', p.47; Andreasian, 'Contradictions and Criteria', p.39; Sobolev, 'Proletariat of the Liberated Countries', pp.11–12. The only Arab country referred to specifically as having adopted scientific socialism is the People's Democratic Republic of Yemen.

32. 'Scientific Life', *Narody Azii i Afriki*, 5 (1974), p.239.

33. See Eran, 'Soviet Perception of Arab Communism'.

34. Andreasian, 'Contradictions and Criteria', pp.41–2, 46; Tarabrin, 'Third World', p.15.

35. Andreasian, 'Contradictions and Criteria', p.46.

36. Ibid., p.41.

37. O. Ul'rikh, 'The State Sector in the System of Social Relations of the Developing Countries', *MEiMO*, 4 (1975), p.141. See Kiva, 'On Certain Capitalist Developments', p.141.

38. G. Skorov, 'The Growth in the Role of the Liberated States in World Development', *MEiMO*, 4 (1976), p.44; Kaufman, 'Non-proletarian Theories of Socialism', p.43.

39. *Ruz al-Yusuf* (Egypt) 28 April 1975, p.3, reporting on the results of Foreign Minister Fahmi's visit to Moscow that month.

40. V. Bushuev, 'The Ideological Expansion of Imperialism in the Developing Countries', *Kommunist vooruzhennykh sil*, 13 (1975), p.77.

41. Tarabrin, 'Third World', pp.15, 18.

42. Kaufman, 'Non-Proletarian Theories of Socialism', p.48. The Soviet contention that these countries, led by revolutionary democrats, can bypass the capitalist stage of development and begin to build socialism with the help of the Soviet Union and despite the necessary domestic prerequisites for socialism (Igolkin, 'Towards a Methodology', p.44) is reminiscent of the Trotskyite conception of the 'permanent revolution' which contained the assumption that socialism could be built in Russia with the help of the industrialised socialist West.

43. 'New Manifestations', p.159.

44. Kiva, 'On Certain Capitalist Developments', p.118.

45. Andreasian, 'Contradictions and Criteria', p.39.

46. *Narody Azii i Afriki*, 6 (1974), p.235. The report is based on papers delivered on 23 April 1974 in a conference on 'The State Sector in the Countries of North Africa' held in the Africa Institute, Department for the Arab Countries.

47. *Narody Azii i Afriki*, p. 236; Sobolev, 'Proletariat of the Liberated

Countries', p.12.

48. 'Characteristics of the Social Structure', p.70; Mirskii, 'Developing Countries and World Capitalism', pp.38–9.

49. Mirskii, 'The Changing Face of the Third World', *Kommunist*, 2 (1976), p.111.

50. Dolgopolov, 'Armies of the Developing Countries', pp.80–1.

51. See Eran, 'Soviet Perception of Arab Communism'.

52. Dolgopolov, 'Armies of the Developing Countries', p.81.

53. Ibid., pp.80–1.

54. Ibid.

55. Ibid., p.80.

56. Ibid., pp.76–7.

57. See for instance G. Mirskii and T. Pokataieva, 'Classes and Class Struggle in the Developing Countries', *MEiMO*, 3 (1966), p.66.

58. Dolgopolov, 'Armies of the Developing Countries', p.77.

59. 'Statement of the Meeting of Representatives of the Communist and Workers' Parties, Nov. 1960', *World Marxist Review*, 12 (Dec. 1960); 'Programme of the Communist Party of the Soviet Union', *The Road to Communism, Documents of the 22nd Congress of the Soviet Union, 17–31 October 1961* (Moscow: Foreign Language Press, 1961).

60. See Akademiia Nauk SSSR, IMEiMO *The International Revolutionary Movement of the Working Class* (Moscow, 1964), p.314 (a second edition was published after Khrushchev's removal in 1965 but without any change in substance).

61. V. L. Tiagunenko, 'Socialist Doctrines on the Social Development of the Liberated Countries', *MEiMO*, 3 (1965), p.85.

62. See the writings of the Syrian Communist leader Khalid Bakdash in *World Marxist Review*, 8, 9 (1964).

63. See for instance Volianskii, 'Role of the Subjective Factor'.

64. Andreasian, 'Contradictions and Criteria', p.42.

65. Kaufman, 'Non-Proletarian Theories of Socialism', p.46.

66. See the statement to this effect in Igolkin, 'Towards a Methodology', p.47.

67. Kaufman, 'Non-Proletarian Theories of Socialism', p.46; Sobolev, 'Proletariat of the Liberated Countries', p.10; Dolgopolov, 'Armies of the Developing Countries', pp.79–80; Kaufman, 'Problems of Theory', pp.67–8; Sobolev, 'Role of the Proletariat of the Liberated Countries in the Social Progress of Society', *Narody Azii i Afriki*, 4 (1975), pp.229–30.

68. Dolgopolov, 'Armies of the Developing Countries', p.79; Sobolev, 'Proletariat of the Liberated Countries', p.9.

69. 'The Working Class of the Liberated Countries in the Struggle for Social Progress', *Rabochii klass i sovremennyi mir*, 4 (1975), p.158.

70. Dolgopolov, 'Armies of the Developing Countries', p.76; Mirskii, 'Developing Countries and World Capitalism', pp.35, 37.

71. Ibid., p.40; Tarabrin, 'Third World', pp.14, 22.

72. Ibid., p.20. Cf. Dina and Martin Spechler, 'The Soviet Union and the Oil Weapon: Benefits and Dilemmas', in this volume.

73. Kaufman, 'Problems of Theory', pp.61–2.

74. Mirskii, 'Changing Face of the Third World', pp.109–11.

75. Tarabrin, 'Third World', pp.12, 15.

76. Mirskii, 'Changing Face of the Third World', p.112.

77. Ibid., Skorov, 'Growth of the Role of the Liberated States', p.45; Tarabrin, 'Third World', p.22.

78. See. V. V. Zhurkin, 'Détente and the Politics of the USA in International Conflicts', *SShA*, 2 (1977), particularly p.8, discussing Secretary of State Kissinger's policy in the Middle East and Rhodesia; Tarabrin, 'Third World', p.22.

6 THE DOMESTIC IMAGE OF SOVIET INVOLVEMENT IN THE ARAB—ISRAELI CONFLICT

Theodore H. Friedgut

1. Introduction

A strong, almost mystical, respect for the power of the word, and a subsequent devotion of great energy and resources to the monopoly on communication has long been a prominent feature of the Soviet regime. Although public opinion in the broad sense of the word has never been known to inhibit Soviet decision makers,[1] Soviet leaders seek explicit public legitimation of their policies and therefore maintain a high level of social and political communication to the public. Such communication plays a part in both the domestic and external image projected by the regime, and it is therefore assumed by most students of the Soviet political system that the image or images projected are carefully formulated and that there is something to be learned of the values, goals and priorities of the regime through examination of the projection of any given issue.

If we study the Soviet presentation of the Arab—Israeli conflict as it appears in the principal press organs and journals in the period during and after the October 1973 War, we may be able to learn something of the perceptions which the Soviet leaders wish to induce in their reading public. In particular an attempt will be made to analyse the following points:

1. How is the dispute presented? What are the elements of conflict? What root causes are said to exist and what secondary conflicts grow out of these basic antagonisms?

2. What role is the USSR seen as playing in this conflict? Is it a disinterested great power conducting an even-handed policy? Is it a supporter, or even an ally of one side or the other?

3. What are the Soviet Union's motivations for its role and policies? Are these a discrete and distinct set of considerations, applicable only to the Arab—Israeli conflict, or do they form an integral part of the system of Soviet foreign policy evaluations?

4. In practical terms, what Soviet actions are taken in the Middle East and with what saliency and specificity are these actions presented to the Soviet public?

2. The Arab–Israeli Conflict and the Soviet Role In It

During the October 1973 War and in the months following, it was only
natural that the Arab–Israeli conflict was presented prominently (and
frequently) in the Soviet communications media, as indeed it was the
world over. The military conflict, the intense and complex negotiations
involving the UN, the great powers and the conflicting parties, the
international complications caused by the Arab oil boycott, all served
to bring the subject to the fore.

We may say at the outset that the Soviet communications media did
not seek to isolate or play down the subject, but on the contrary,
emphasised the connection between the Middle East conflict and
problems of international relations the world over. The interplay
between the events in the Middle East and such questions as détente,
Sino-Soviet relations, and in particular the tangled triangle of relations
between the emerging nations, the Soviet-led Communist countries and
the American-led non-Communist countries, all of these were discussed
in considerable detail for the edification of the Soviet citizen.

The Soviet media provided a platform for a broad range of bodies
expressing their views on the subject. Formal Soviet government
statements, the Soviet Trade Union Federation, the World Peace
Movement (which met in Moscow in October 1973), each of these and
many more occasions served for an exposition of Soviet perceptions
and proposals.[2] Reinforced by TASS reports of foreign responses to the
war consistent with those of the Soviet Union, this broad coverage
emphasised the Soviet position through constant repetition. The object
of such coverage appears to be the creation of an image of universal
unanimity – both domestic and foreign – in support of the Soviet
regime's policy. 'The Soviet Union, the socialist commonwealth and all
of progressive humanity . . .'[3] are firmly united on the pages of the
Soviet press, creating the same sort of confidence aimed at in 1939 by
the slogan 'Fifty million Frenchmen can't be wrong'.

The presentation of the elements of the Arab-Israeli conflict during
the period of fighting in October 1973 is, indeed, clear and consistent.
Perhaps the most comprehensive and detailed statement of the Soviet
position was given by the Chairman of the Soviet Council of Ministers,
Aleksei Kosygin, at a reception for the Danish Prime Minister.[4]

Kosygin presented as the basis of the conflict the aggressive policy of
Israel's ruling circles, with support and encouragement from abroad. He
quoted Brezhnev regarding the Soviet Union's interest in playing a part
in establishing a just and stable peace for all states and people in the
Middle East, and continued:

Solidarity with the peoples of Egypt and Syria and the other Arab states, defending their legitimate rights and interests in the struggle against the Israeli aggressor, and anxiety for the making of a just peace, this is the essence of [Soviet] policy in the Middle East.

The Soviet Union seeks nothing for itself in this region. All our actions there are aimed at helping the peoples of the Arab countries in liberating the territories seized by Israel, achieving a just political settlement, strengthening their independence, setting up a flourishing national economy and developing along the path of progress. Guided by this, we will further strengthen our solidarity with the Arab peoples and their righteous struggle.

Three main elements may be discerned in the presentation of the Arab—Israeli conflict in this and other authoritative Soviet statements during October 1973. The most prominent of these is Israel's aggression against the Arabs, resulting in seizure of their territories. Next in prominence is the definition of the conflict as the result of imperialist machinations against new nations struggling to be free. The third element, much less consistently presented at this time, is Israel's prevention of the self-determination of the Palestinian Arab nation.

The first, most prominent, and most repeated element is that of 'Israel's aggressive policy and seizure of Arab territories'. In Kosygin's speech above, in Brezhnev's speech at a reception for the Japanese Prime Minister[5] and in all the central speeches and commentaries reported at the time, the aggressive nature of Israel is presented as the main cause of the conflict.[6] Important here is the claim that a policy of aggression which is inherent in the Israeli regime's political nature is the real cause of the conflict, and the seizure of Arab territories is only a symptom.

At the time of the war, this was particularly emphasised by a commentator in *Krasnaia zvezda*, pointing out for the reader Israel's original sin and its continuity. The author writes: 'In 1948 the rulers of Tel Aviv added 7,000 square kilometres of territory to the 14,000 square kilometres belonging to them, evicting a million and a half Arabs from their native land'.[7] This element in the characterisation of the Arab—Israeli conflict returns frequently throughout the years, and is presented to the Soviet reader in numerous contexts. One prominent commentator writes: 'The Middle East crisis started with the Zionists' trampling of the legitimate rights of the Arab Palestinian people, frustrating the UN decision to set up an Arab state alongside the Jewish state in Palestine'.[8] The calling of early elections in Israel in 1977 was noted as 'a sign of bankruptcy of the entire aggressive course of Israel',[9] and a TASS dispatch reporting on sessions of the UN Human Rights Commission announced that 'many of the speakers emphasised that Israeli soldiers' trampling on the human rights and basic freedoms of the Arab population constitutes an integral part of Israel's foreign policy'.[10]

This attack on the fundamental nature of the Israeli state and its relations with the neighbouring Arab states is at times explained to the Soviet audience in an even broader context of the historical roots of Israel's outlook. In an attempt to clarify the Israeli mentality one Soviet author writes that with the help of thousands of hours of Bible study Israeli youth absorbs the historical and ideological justification of the expansionist aims of Zionism, of intolerance towards the Arabs, and of 'racist ravings about the exclusiveness of the Jews'.[11]

The audience is presented with the logical conclusion that the return of Arab lands seized by Israel (and definition of these lands as 'territories captured in 1967' or simply 'all Arab lands held by Israel' is inconsistent) is a *necessary* pre-condition to a peaceful settlement in the Middle East,[12] but whether the return of territories is *sufficient* to eliminate the conflict is unclear. Implicit in the description of Israel as inherently aggressive and hostile to her neighbours is the suggestion that in the Soviet view territory is not the root issue between Israel and the Arabs.

As regards the possibility that the Arabs may harbour ill-feeling towards Israel, and that there could be some danger to Israel from the Arabs, this receives only indirect confirmation in statements which emphasise Israel's right to security and international guarantees along with the other states and peoples of the Middle East. This equality of rights figures consistently in remarks of Brezhnev and Kosygin as well as in general Soviet proposals.[13] It is not, however, openly connected with any equality of culpability or equivalence of virtue. Indeed, when a certain Samuel Fox, representing Canada at the Congress of Peace-Loving Forces, 'voiced the accusation against the Arab countries as though they 'did not recognise the sovereignty of the State of Israel' and that this in his opinion was the root of the conflict', *Pravda* gave extensive and explicit coverage to the 'categorical repudiation' of the charge by Krishna Menon of India who blamed the conflict on the imperialist states and noted that it was impermissible to try to present aggressors as victims.[14]

Closely linked to the allegation of Israel's inherent aggressiveness is the Soviet view that the Arab—Israeli conflict is not a local matter of a dispute between two nations or nationalisms, but an integral and inevitable part of the world struggle between imperialism and the forces of national liberation. In this struggle, the Arabs in general are presented as playing an anti-imperialist role, while the Israelis are seen as firmly in the imperialist camp.

Izvestiia's commentator writes that the October War opened the eyes of those who considered the Middle East crisis as a regional problem concerning only the combatants themselves. It is well known, writes Kudriavtsev, that behind the Israeli aggressors stand powerful imperialist forces for whom the Middle East conflict is part of a world strategy.[15]

In all the Soviet leaders' speeches of the period, Israel's links with, and dependence on, imperialism are given emphasis, the emphasis varying according to the speaker. The Soviet government's statement of 8 October was distinguished by particularly strong language; it referred to 'foreign reactionary circles which consistently support Israel in its aggressive policies'. A *Pravda* commentator speaks of Israel's ties to 'imperialist forces and internal Arab reaction',[16] while Kudriavtsev in *Izvestiia* takes an extreme position, characterising Israel as 'an organic part of the system of imperialism', and writing:

> Under the leadership of its present rulers, Israel sees itself as a cog of the great imperialist countries ruled by the strong monopolies dictating expansionism as a foreign policy. This is even more so since the majority of Israeli monopolies are overseas branches of those large American companies which are controlled by Jewish capital.[17]

The expressions range between the one image of Israel as an independent actor willingly embracing and inspired by imperialism, and the alternative image of Israel as an obedient pawn wholly owned and controlled by reactionary monopoly imperialism. Despite this variation, the linking of Israel and imperialism occurs in almost every article and commentary on the Middle East.

As is the case with most of the images presented concerning the Arab—Israeli conflict, this theme did not originate with the 1973 crisis, for the CPSU's official stand on the 1967 war was that it resulted from 'a conspiracy of the most reactionary forces of international imperialism, and first and foremost the USA, directed against one of the units of the national liberation movement'.[18]

While the linkage of Israel and imperialism remains constant, the specific nature of imperialism and the identity of other allies or underlings aligned against 'the world of progress' shift with the change of circumstances. With détente high on the priority list, and the USSR anxious to reconvene the Geneva Conference, the United States was rarely singled out by name, though occasional references to 'American militarist circles' or to other American groupings distinct from the US government and people, are to be found.[19] This changed rather abruptly soon after President Carter's inauguration, when America *per se* became once more the central symbol of imperialism in the Soviet press. The context of this change, however, suggests that it had more to do with the human rights issue, prominent at the time, than with the Arab–Israeli conflict, in which no dramatic change could be noted in the first half of 1977.

The image of the 'imperialist camp' was enriched by the consistent addition of 'domestic Arab reaction' as Sadat's anti-Soviet policies developed, and as the Lebanese civil war progressed.[20] When the Syrians sent their troops into Lebanon the picture became even more complex, for the Syrians as protégés of the USSR could not be lumped in with 'imperialism, Zionism and domestic Arab reaction'. In intimating their disapproval of the Syrian intervention in Lebanon, the Soviet commentators had to create a 'right wing of the Arab national liberation movement', an essentially positive figure engaged in unwittingly negative acts, i.e. accommodating the interests of Zionism and imperialism by opposing what were styled the 'national patriotic forces' of Lebanon and their allies, 'the Palestine Resistance Movement'.[21] The clear and consistent image which we noted as characterising the presentation of the Arab–Israeli conflict during and immediately following the October 1973 War, becomes a more confusingly complex picture in 1976 and 1977. The perceptive Soviet citizen may deduce that this reflects with some degree of accuracy the falling fortunes of Soviet foreign policy in the Arab–Israeli arena at this time.

As hinted in some of V. Kudriavtsev's writings in *Izvestiia*, 'Jewish capital' or more frequently 'international Zionism' are pictured as more influential than Israel and distinct from it.[22] Thus the Soviet Trade Union Federation statement at the outbreak of the 1973 war referred to 'Israeli aggression supported by imperialist forces and by international Zionist circles'.[23] In this fashion, the Zionist movement can be accused of acting against Communism not only in the Middle East, but in Czechoslovakia and East Germany as well, and the Soviet citizen may be warned that 'international reaction, and one of its chief units, Zionism, are attempting to undermine the unity of the new

historic community of people – the Soviet Union'.[24] On the same
note, Israel's aid programmes in Africa are presented by Soviet
reporters as 'a Trojan horse for imperialist interests seeking to subvert
the national liberation movements there, and weakening the general
anti-imperialist front'.[25]

The logical extension of Israel's position as an ally or tool of
imperialism is the community of interest between the USSR and the
Arab states, based not only on 'sympathy for victims of aggression',[26]
but on 'the struggle against imperialism, fundamental to the very nature
of a socialist state'.[27] Joint communiqués of Soviet leaders with leaders
of Arab states emphasise this aspect of the Soviet–Arab alliance with
particular frequency.[28] In its ultimate development in the Soviet press
this formulation leads to identifying one side with all that should be
thought good, e.g. peace, independence, social progress, national
liberation; and the other side with all things which should be
condemned, e.g. imperialism, war, apartheid, Zionism, racism and
repression. The equating of disparate movements strips the reader's
world of any sophisticated ambivalence, reducing it to a
fundamentalist, two-camp simplicity in which it is easy to see on which
side the good citizen will be. In addition, as we will see, chains of
association are created for the reader, leading him to see the Arab–
Israeli conflict, which for a great many Soviet citizens may seem
distant, abstract and unimportant, in terms of more personal and
familiar phenomena.

It may, however, be of interest to note that when, at the time of the
October 1973 War, public meetings were called in factories, scientific
institutes or other places of employment, the reported resolutions kept
to the simplest possible formulations, concentrating on the demand for
an end to aggression and withdrawal of Israel's troops from Arab
territories.[29] Thus the Soviet regime preserves the traditional
distinction between propaganda, i.e. the comprehensive treatment of a
problem in its entirety, and agitation, i.e. the focusing of attention on a
single prominent aspect of a given problem.

There exists a third element in the definition of the Arab–Israeli
conflict by the Soviet media in the period of the October 1973 War.
This is the question of the rights of the Palestinian Arabs. It may seem
strange that this subject, so prominent in later Soviet writings and
becoming central by 1976 and 1977 – and certainly a sensitive element
in any projected settlement in the Middle East – should have been so
subdued during the war and in its immediate aftermath. Yet though this
element is undoubtedly present, it is the least emphasised and least

elaborated element in the Soviet presentation of the nature of the
Arab—Israeli conflict. In many of the authoritative statements, e.g. the
speeches of Brezhnev and Kosygin in the first week of the war, the
Palestinians are missing altogether. Even in a joint communiqué of the
Soviet and Syrian Communist Parties, the Palestinians are forgotten.[30]
In the programmatic documents which we have discussed, e.g. the
Soviet government's statement at the outbreak of hostilities, the
declaration of the Soviet Committee for Solidarity with the Countries
of Asia and Africa, or the declaration of the Soviet Trade Union
Federation, the question of the Palestinians is couched in terms of
ensuring 'the legitimate rights of the Arab people of Palestine', and is
given no specific content as to territory, statehood, representation or
any other aspects of the problem. In each of the above documents the
subject of ensuring the rights of the Palestinians is presented as an
elaboration of Brezhnev's formula of seeking a settlement which will
guarantee peace for all states and peoples of the area. At this point, the
Palestinians are presented amorphously and passively, while the Syrians
and Egyptians are clearly defined as actively fighting for their territory
and their domestic social and political achievements. This was the
pattern which had been followed immediately prior to the war.[31]

Beginning on 9 October, the Soviet reader was informed of
Palestinian 'partisan groups' actively operating in the rear of Israeli
forces, cutting railway lines, setting fire to fuel dumps, blowing up arms
factories and staging a rocket attack on an 'aircraft factory' in
Jerusalem.[32] Where attribution for the stories is given, the source is
generally a 'communiqué of Palestinian military representatives',
emanating from Beirut. Of particular interest is one TASS dispatch
datelined Algiers in which a clear distinction is made between attacks
carried out 'in Israel' and 'in the occupied Arab territories'.[33] This is a
rare distinction and, as previously noted, one not maintained
consistently or clearly. As noted, while there is occasionally distinction
between the territory of Israel and the 'occupied West Bank of the
Jordan', the Arab populations of both parts are almost always
considered Palestinians.[34] In discussions of the legitimate rights and
interests of the Palestinians in any eventual peace settlement, there is
no hint of any difference of status for Palestinians in different places,
nor is there any attempt to discuss whether there might be a difference
between Palestinians displaced as a result of the 1948 war and those
displaced in 1967. As was the case with the sufficiency of territorial
restitution as a basis for peace, ambiguity or silence as to the extent of
the Palestinians' rights is an important gap in the treatment of the

Arab—Israeli conflict by the Soviet media.

The clear Soviet definition of Israel's imperialist nature and the progressive essence of the Arab states as countries fighting a just war of liberation is reinforced in the Soviet media by a similar polar opposition in the description of each side's behaviour. While the Arab states are presented as showing 'great self-restraint and readiness to seek a political settlement of the conflict',[35] Israel is portrayed as a lawless state which 'uses piracy and violence as instruments of policy'.[36] This theme accompanies the fighting and the negotiations subsequent to the ceasefire. Israel's 'raising of tension', 'gross violations', 'provocations' are almost daily fare for the Soviet reader particularly during the negotiations after the ceasefire.[37] Even the comparison of Israel with the Nazis, so frequent in Soviet newspaper cartoons after the 1967 war, is briefly revived — though in a minor way.[38] Israel is portrayed as being beyond the pale — 'crudely violating elementary norms of international law and basic standards of human morality'.[39] In addition to portraying Israel as isolated from and condemned by the international community, the tenor of these attacks is such as to cast doubt on Israel's right to existence, or at least to imply that the destruction of Israel could, if circumstances took such a turn, be countenanced by the international community as involving just retribution.

Together with such accusations there is sometimes a hint of the possibility of direct Soviet involvement in the conflict to put an end to the above-described acts. Although the most publicised of such threats was that connected with the delay in putting the 22 October ceasefire resolution into effect,[40] similar statements were made from the outbreak of hostilities.[41] The threats, however, were always implicit, and Soviet commitment to the Arab cause, or against Israel, was never put in explicit terms of direct involvement of the Soviet armed forces. Indeed, any Soviet intention to take such steps was indignantly denied by official spokesmen in reaction to the American nuclear alert declared during the tension that accompanied the end of the fighting.[42]

The Arab—Israeli conflict is, however, put into a typology which does not exclude the possibility of such an involvement. One source writes:

> Just as Soviet might turned back Nazism thirty years ago, the USSR is honourably fulfilling its international duty, coming out in support of people fighting against imperialism and oppression . . . The USSR played an important role in turning back imperialist aggression in Korea, Vietnam and the Middle East.[43]

The linking of the Soviet Union's support of the Arab states against Israel to support of North Vietnam or North Korea is particularly interesting in that no distinction appears to be made between the latter cases, involving established Communist states, and the former, which are at best only in the category of states opting for a non-capitalist form of development.[44]

To sum up the image of the Arab–Israeli conflict, it is clear that it is not a limited local dispute over borders or between contending nationalisms with comparable claims and merits. The Soviet concept of the conflict is presented as running deeper and involving basic values of the Soviet state, legitimised through historical experience. The Arab–Israeli conflict is presented as an organic part of a world-wide, long-term struggle against imperialism, in defence of national liberation movements. It is a fundamental conflict between the 'sons of light and the sons of darkness'. In such a case the USSR is not only justified in taking sides, but is obliged by its principles to do so actively.[45]

While the nature of such active Soviet involvement is undefined, its basic motivation permits many forms and degrees in keeping with the circumstances in any given country, at any given moment. Soviet involvement may therefore be primarily diplomatic, or may involve military or economic aid in various forms or any combination of the above.

3. Soviet Support of the Arab Countries

If we take into account the presentation of the Arab–Israeli conflict as part of a world ideological and political contest — 'the struggle for men's minds' as many American sources were wont to characterise it in the 1950s — then we will not be surprised to find that political and economic aid features prominently in whatever is printed in the press regarding Soviet support for the Arab states, and that Soviet arms and military aid to the Arab countries are generally kept in low profile. In addition, it is made clear to the Soviet reader that while the immediate Arab–Israeli military conflict lends urgency and poignancy to Soviet ties with the Arab states, much of the economic, technical and even military aid is not a direct function of the conflict, but is extended to the Arabs because of the role which they play, actually or potentially, in the wider competition of world ideologies. Over and over again we can find statements in the Soviet press echoing or elaborating the latter part of Premier Kosygin's speech quoted at the beginning of our discussion.[46]

The scale and variety of Soviet foreign aid in the world at large has grown greatly since World War Two.[47] The change in the USSR's economic condition allows it to divert much larger quantities of manpower and resources than previously from domestic needs to serve the regime's foreign policy objectives, sending thousands of skilled technicians abroad as well as equipment and materials. Nevertheless, the limitations imposed by the basic economic law of scarcity must of necessity remain prominent in the consciousness of Soviet decision makers.

The political structure of the world has changed as well, with the emergence of a large bloc of newly independent states, open to influence as to the political and social philosophies which they will adopt. The Soviet Union, aspiring to, and capable of, global power status, must compete for influence over the political and military potential of the Third World, as well as for the geopolitical advantages offered in the form of military bases and natural resources such as oil, and the less tangible advantages of friendly co-operation on a cultural and technical level.

Global status, however, means that there are no small and far-off conflicts which can be ignored. Opinion, policy, implementation and explanation must be on tap whenever needed. The long and tortuous history of the Arab—Israeli conflict and the Soviet involvement in it can serve as an example of the resources demanded of a superpower, and the investment of energy needed to project the image of such involvement desired by the Soviet regime.

In institutional terms the USSR has adjusted to the growing importance of this part of foreign policy by establishing two high-level governmental bodies to deal with trade and aid in addition to the traditional Ministry of Foreign Trade. These are: (1) The Commission for Foreign Economic Relations of the Presidium of the Soviet Council of Ministers, chaired by Deputy Premier V. N. Novikov, and dealing mainly with questions of policy and co-ordination;[48] (2) The State Committee on Foreign Economic Relations, a ministerial-level body, headed since 1958 by S. A. Skachkov, a member of the Communist Party Central Committee.[49]

In addition, some Soviet technical institutions have been extremely active in drawing up plans and sending experts to various countries linked to the USSR by technical co-operation agreements. Moscow's 'Gidroproekt' Institute, for instance, has had specialists working in eighteen different countries, including Egypt, Syria and Iraq.[50]

Thus what was of necessity marginal in Soviet foreign policy implementation in earlier years has become a central instrument in the

USSR's relations with the developing countries, and among them, the Arab countries. A review of a collected edition of Brezhnev's foreign policy statements explicitly recognised the linkage between domestic issues and foreign policy operations by quoting Lenin on the necessity for applying all domestic resources to the development of revolutionary struggle, and linking this to the Soviet support for the Arab states.[51]

As the role played by the Soviet Union in the Arab—Israeli conflict grows and becomes more onerous, it must of necessity become the subject of more and more internal debates in which the allocation of resources and strategy alternatives are discussed. In addition, as mentioned at the outset, the legitimation of policy by public unanimity of support is a prominent feature of the Soviet political culture. This is true not only of the general public, but of specialised publics whose support may be sought by high echelon leaders should policy alternatives become a source of deep division. John A. Armstrong has noted that circles of middle-level officials and specialists may act as a sort of oligarchic surrogate for public opinion in influencing the development of policy and the manner in which policies are formulated.[52]

In the case of resources expended on aid to the Arab states, this could well apply not only to the growing numbers of returning experts but to the increasingly numerous privileged Soviet citizens who, as tourists or members of delegations, have the opportunity to witness something of Soviet activity in the Arab states, or have direct contact with Arab visitors and trainees in the USSR.

In the year 1973, 27,000 Soviet tourists visited Egypt alone, presumably in addition to advisers stationed there for comparatively long periods.[53] Arab, Asian and African students are prominent in numerous Soviet centres, and are often the object of xenophobic resentments among Soviet students and population. The Soviet population may well ask why its own needs are not met before those of foreigners, or alternatively may accept foreign aid as 'the Communist Man's Burden', concomitant with great power status. The latter opinion was voiced to the author more than once by Soviet citizens in Moscow, who noted that although the resources could surely be spent better at home, and that Egypt, in particular, had nothing of value to offer the USSR in return for aid, it was part of the Soviet Union's role as a world socialist power to offer aid to the Third World countries.[54] The questions are very much to the point and it would be unlike the Soviet authorities not to use the media to influence the doubting public on this point.

In urging the Soviet citizen to support the 'just national liberation struggle' of the Arab states, the Soviet media make no call for sacrifice, nor do they indicate that such aid may fall as a burden on the USSR. Rather, as we will see, mutual economic benefits are frequently emphasised.[55]

The entire presentation of Soviet material aid to the Arab states appears to be much less salient and specific than is the presentation of Soviet political support of the Arabs and condemnation of Israel. When a dozen former Soviet citizens, including former lecturers of the *Znanie* Society, which carries on a mass lecture programme for the Soviet public, and persons involved in journalism and publicity, were polled by the author as to how the subject of Soviet aid to the Arab countries was presented at such lectures, none could recall ever having heard a lecture on the subject, though much was said to have been made of such a specific subject as the importance of the Aswan Dam. In *Agitator*, a journal intended for individuals dealing with oral explanation of Soviet policies, the closest thing to the subject of aid is a topic appearing twenty-sixth on a list of twenty-nine topics recommended for presentation by lecturers and agitators — i.e. 'Broadening and deepening the friendly relations of the USSR with the developing countries of Asia, Africa and Latin America'.[56]

The lack of saliency accorded the subject is also reflected, however, in a frequent abstention from mentioning Soviet aid even in contexts within which it might be considered not only in order, but advantageous. A typical example is a report of a speech by the commander of the Syrian Air Force in 1974, which, although emphasising the excellence of Syrian air forces and anti-aircraft defences, makes no mention of the Soviet role in contributing to this excellence through training, advice and equipment.[57] It may be suggested that the newspaper is writing on a sensitive military subject for an audience for which the Talmudic injunction 'A hint is sufficient for a wise man' might apply, yet we find similar omission of the mention of Soviet aid on civilian subjects as well, and in other media.[58] Even analytical articles in periodicals often appear to underplay the potential and actualities of a direct Soviet role in such important subjects as the oil crisis[59] or the role of armies in developing societies.[60] In the first-mentioned article, only the ending hints that the USSR might have any interest or role in Middle East oil politics, stating that 'the USSR proposes a clear and positive programme of economic co-operation on a basis of equality and mutual respect'. The second-mentioned essay gives a full political analysis of the role of the military in new states – emphasising the army's influence in domestic and foreign affairs and the importance of ideological education and 'proper' social origins in determining the army's character. No direct discussion is offered of the USSR's experience in this field. Once again, however, the summary paragraph deals with the subject:

> The USSR and other socialist countries, true to their international obligations, engage in extensive co-operation to strengthen the defensive capacities of the young national states which are taking the path of non-capitalist development. This aid evokes a high evaluation from the revolutionary democratic leadership and leading public figures in countries of socialist orientation. It gives these countries the possibility of overcoming fully the legacy of colonialism, strengthens their economy and defensive power and makes possible social progress.

The ideological and moral elements are emphasised here, as is the benefit to the USSR's standing in the developing world, but the reader learns little of what co-operation actually involves or of how extensive and how expensive it has been. Even sources which recite the achievements of the Soviet aid programme in the Arab countries give only a partial and general picture.[61]

One knowledgeable observer of the Soviet Union has stated that foreign aid given by the USSR is one of the subjects on the Index of the censorship, thus accounting for the spottiness of factual treatment.[62] Even a well-connected and sympathetic author such as Alexander Werth notes that he was unable to obtain any comprehensive statistics on Soviet foreign aid programmes.[63]

If there appears to be a general reluctance to give prominence and specificity to the discussion of material aid to the Arab states, this is incomparably more so regarding military aid. The immorality of the arms business is traditional stock-in-trade for moral crusaders such as the Soviet Union sets itself up to be, and the last thing the Soviet regime would want to do is to denounce American capital's export of weapons, and then confuse the Soviet citizen by giving details of similar Soviet transactions. The general pattern is to limit any note of Soviet arms deliveries to the vague formula used by Sumbatian (see note 60 above), referring only to 'strengthening the defensive capacities of young national states', while publicising in great detail each specific purchase and delivery of military equipment from non-Soviet sources. Rare is the blunt public statement such as Brezhnev made to the 25th

Congress of the CPSU: 'Our country has helped — and as the 1973 war showed — effectively helped strengthen the military potential of . . . Egypt, Syria and Iraq'.[64] Generally the Soviet reader learns of the efficacy of Soviet arms aid through quoted statements of foreign observers. Meanwhile, a standard headline 'Deliveries and Purchases' (*postavki, zakupki*) in the Soviet army newspaper *Krasnaia zvezda* lists the non-Communist world's arms deals.[65] Half a dozen times during 1975 in connection with Middle Eastern events, this newspaper reminded its readers that the United States is reputed to be the world's largest exporter of military supplies. The Soviet reader thus lives in a world in which Israel's aggressive aims are encouraged by a flood of American arms as part of the profit-making schemes of a military-industrial complex bent on creating tension the world over, while the Arab states enjoy some 'military co-operation' with the Soviet Union, but without mention of arms *sales* to states involved in conflict, much less to other parts of the world such as Peru, Kuwait or Iran.

This reticence about direct reference to arms supplies broke down only slowly even under the impact of the October 1973 War. While the Soviet media gave great coverage to the achievements of the Arab armies and the efficacy, indeed the superiority, of their weapons, it was only on the tenth day of the fighting, on 15 October, that the Soviet origin of these weapons was explicitly acknowledged. In the interim, even as the fighting raged, an *Izvestiia* correspondent surveying the political and military background of the conflict contrasted Israeli 'aggressive militarism' to the devotion to peaceful construction of the Egyptians who 'with the friendly assistance of the Soviet Union have constructed the giant Aswan Dam . . . [while] the Syrian people have tamed the wild Euphrates'.[66]

In discussions of the battles, Israeli aircraft were identified as Skyhawks, Phantoms and Mirages, names long familiar to the Soviet reader from the Vietnam War or earlier stories of Israeli military activity.[67] Israeli tanks are specified as 'largely of English and American manufacture'[68] or more specifically as 'American-made Pattons'.[69]

Until 15 October, the Soviet media did not reveal to its public the secret of the widely-noted superiority of the Arab equipment. Then a quotation from Israel's Premier Golda Meir was used to explain that the course of the fighting was influenced by the quality of the Soviet arms used by the Arab armies as well as by the fact that Soviet military experts helped in training these armies.[70]

Even then, although the Soviet origin of Arab arms was mentioned freely and with understandable satisfaction during this period, the Soviet media avoided details of individual weapons. The *New York Times* was quoted as discussing the effectiveness of Soviet anti-aircraft missiles, but only much later was the SAM-7 missile specifically named in the Soviet press as having given particularly effective cover to the Suez Canal crossing.[71] In an interview with a Syrian tank commander a Soviet correspondent tells how the tank's crew (the correspondent refers to it as 'our tank') destroyed four Centurions, thus proving the machine's superiority.[72] Similarly, the MiG-21 is reported as being better than the Phantom.[73]

From the end of the first week of the war, by which time it was clear that the Egyptian and Syrian offensives had been turned back, the Soviet media reported airlifts of American supplies to Israel, increasing the detailed treatment of these as time went by.[74] It took two and a half years before the Soviet public found out that the USSR had operated a similar airlift to Egypt.[75]

One could suggest that publication of certain details regarding the effectiveness of Soviet weapons may have had a specific domestic audience in mind as well as general considerations of Soviet prestige. *Komsomol'skaia pravda*, a newspaper catering for Soviet youth and young adults (pre-army and army age), quoted British and Egyptian sources on the effectiveness of Soviet weapons and stated:

> The course of combat action has dealt a crushing blow to the campaign pursued by Israel and the US, who have tried to instil in the Egyptian soldier that the weapons of the Egyptian army allegedly do not meet the requirements of the times and are much inferior to the weapons with which the US has equipped Israel.[76]

Surely the Egyptian soldier was not the only one meant to be reassured.

In the context of the dispute with Egypt, the Soviet press revealed a number of previously undisclosed aspects of the nature and extent of Soviet involvement in the Arab—Israeli conflict. In addition to the revelation of involvement of Soviet personnel in military action (see note 42 above), an anonymous Soviet critic of Sadat's published memoirs told his audience that an 'aerial bridge' was formed to supply Egypt at the time of the 1973 war, and that 'nearly all the weapons in the Egyptian army are Soviet'.[77] The greatest detail on the scale of Soviet arms supply to Egypt was, however, given in an article published in *Krasnaia zvezda*, in response to a reader's letter asking why Sadat had abrogated the Soviet—Egyptian Friendship Treaty. Quoting the

Washington Star News, the author of the article informs his reader that if Western arms are to be substituted for the Soviet arms which were supplied to the Egyptian army, it will involve supplying weapons for 332,500 soldiers, 450 warplanes, 2,000 tanks and 1,700 cannon – 'a matter of many billions of dollars'.[78]

In Soviet treatment of the delicate question of military aid to the Arab countries we can see an effort to maintain an image consistent with that presented regarding the fundamental nature of the Arab–Israeli conflict. The conflict provides an urgent and intense focus for Soviet aid to the Arab countries, an opportunity for the USSR to prove that as a 'friend in need' the Soviet Union is 'a friend indeed' to the Arabs. At the same time, the military conflict with Israel is presented as only a particular manifestation of a general phenomenon – i.e. the threat of 'imperialism and domestic reaction' against the developing countries. In this situation the USSR offers itself as a source of support and a guarantor of the new nations' independence. Such a guarantee involves arms supply, but goes far beyond into every sphere of technical and economic support.

4. The Functions of Soviet Aid

The scope of the Soviet aid programme to the Arab countries is far broader than military aid, and as noted, although the Arab–Israeli conflict serves as a convenient focus, justifying a Soviet presence and even Soviet influence, Soviet activity in the Arab countries is presented as proceeding from a much more universal and ideological motivation.

While the weight of heavy industrial projects which dominate Soviet foreign aid programmes is emphasised in a manner familiar to the Soviet citizen from his domestic surroundings, the media take note of everything from ballet stars and chefs to health, sciences, art and youth exchange programmes.[79] The Soviet citizen can understand from this that his government is carrying on a comprehensive and complex programme of foreign relations, as befits a world power.

The image of Soviet aid to the Arab countries has other goals in addition to stimulating the patriotic pride of a great power's citizens: (1) as noted in the characterisation of the Arab–Israeli conflict, there is the political-ideological element represented by references to the internationalist traditions of the Communist party and its role in anti-imperialism; (2) perhaps of greatest interest and significance is a revolutionary transformational aspect, explaining that Soviet aid is intended to create a hospitable environment for socialist development in the Arab states, through the encouragement of a dominant state sector in the economy, and the creation of a numerous proletariat and technical intelligentisa.

The first element, that referring to ideological tradition, to the duty of internationalist solidarity and anti-imperialism, is often placed in the context of time-honoured symbols of the Bolshevik Revolution.[80] 'Leninist principles', 'a historical process of uniting our peoples in the common struggle against imperialism', 'a practical enrichment of the principles of proletarian internationalism',[81] are some|of the phrases quoted from Soviet, or even more frequently from foreign sources. Such language indicates that however pragmatic the Soviet leadership may be in its own face-to-face meetings with other powers, the image in which it seeks to mould the consciousness of the Soviet and foreign public is somewhat different. It is the fundamentally positive and legitimate stance of faithfulness to principle bequeathed to the regime by the founders of its class ideology.

Relatively rarely do we find the ideological duty supplanted by reference to the more national 'great-power' duty. When this substitution occurs it is generally within the context of questions of a settlement of the Arab—Israeli conflict. Thus, Sadat in late 1973 is quoted as approving the Soviet Union's policies 'as a great power sensible to the responsibility of keeping the peace. . .',[82] and Soviet activity in the Middle East in seeking a political settlement or restoring war damage is linked to a respect for general human values.[83]

By maintaining this distinct separation between the rights and duties of the great powers in the political sphere and the rights and duties emanating from proletarian internationalism, the Soviet Union avoids placing the contending great powers on a basis of overall equality and legitimacy. In the area of political rights in which the USSR, particularly since the 1973 war, has been struggling to maintain a threatened position, great power equality is claimed. Here the instrumental character of the Arab—Israeli conflict and its usefulness to the USSR become clear. The Soviet Union's recognised status as co-chairman of the Geneva Conference, embodying recognition of the legitimacy of Soviet interests in the Middle East, is repeatedly pointed out as a basis for the legitimacy and necessity of Soviet participation in any proposals for a settlement.[84] When it comes to a discussion of general foreign aid to the Arab countries, the Soviet press contrasts Soviet support of 'liberation and independence' to 'enslavement by imperialist monopolies' and combats any tendency towards an objective comparison of advantage between socialist and capitalist aid programmes.[85]

In presenting Soviet policy as the embodiment of anti-imperialist internationalism, the Soviet media also maintain the assumption that there is a natural tendency towards Soviet values within all the Arab states and that economic and political ties with the USSR can only strengthen such a tendency. 'Fighting counter-revolutionary forces from within and imperialist forces from without strengthens the progressive outlook of the ruling party, and its members' desire to strengthen their ties with other similar forces on the international scene'.[86]

The call for unity, so prominent in Soviet diplomacy among the Arab states, is based on the expectation that such latent tendencies will become dominant through example and contact. While Soviet aid is not presented as conditional or self-seeking, the development of relations is predicated on the blossoming of a radical community of interest between the USSR and the Arab world. A *Pravda* columnist explains: 'Soviet relations with Syria, Iraq and Egypt are not of a chance character. They are based on general principles of joint struggle against imperialism, colonialism and Zionism'.[87] A review of Brezhnev's foreign policy speeches over the past decade comes to the following conclusion: 'The success of the anti-imperialist struggle depends in great measure on how close and stable is the militant solidarity between the socialist countries, the international working class and the national liberation movement'.[88]

Here again, the Arab—Israeli conflict has instrumental utility for the Soviet presentation of its case. As an enemy common to all the Arab countries, whatever their political orientation, Israel can be presented as proof of the non-Communist world's hostility to the Arabs. This image can be used not only for external diplomatic purposes of convincing non-radical Arab regimes that the USSR is the true friend of the Arabs, but for domestic purposes as well. The repeated resolutions of African, Asian and Arab conferences denouncing 'imperialism, colonialism, neo-colonialism, Zionism, and racial and religious discrimination in all forms',[89] serve to tell the Soviet citizen that he is in harmony with the majority of mankind, and that this majority looks to the USSR as its model.

When, in the eyes of the Soviet regime, a government backslides, as did Sadat in the wake of the October War, official communications become programmatic recitals of the consistent and ideologically principled behaviour of the USSR, and the future benefits to be derived from such virtue. The telegram sent by the Soviet leadership on the 1975 anniversary of the Egyptian revolution makes the following points:

1. Nasir's revolution put Egypt on the path of national independence, anti-imperialism and progressive social and economic reforms.

2. The progress of the revolution is organically linked with the creating and strengthening of close friendship and comprehensive co-operation between the USSR and Egypt based on a common interest in the fight against imperialism.

3. The USSR has consistently supported Egypt against Israeli aggression and imperialist attempts to recoup lost positions. This is an immutable principle of Soviet policy fulfilling both the letter and the spirit of the Soviet–Egyptian Treaty of Friendship and Co-operation.[90] Having created a clear image of ideological principle, the Soviet media can then present this as the yardstick by which the conduct of each side should be measured.

The disappointment of the Soviet regime at its setback in Egypt is understandable, for it represents a failure of what is probably the central effort of the whole Soviet aid programme, i.e. initiating the transformation of the Arab countries into proletarian societies with socialist economies. The exposition of this goal to the public is a distinct element of the publicity given to the Soviet aid programme in the Soviet press. Three points are emphasised: the hastening of socio-economic transformation; the guaranteeing to the developing country of the political and economic independence necessary to effect this transformation, and the creation of the indigenous social classes regarded as most efficacious in carrying on the social struggle.[91] All three of these are closely interrelated.

The foundation of socio-economic transformation as explained in the Soviet press is the development of basic economic projects in the state sector. Though Soviet aid is not restricted only to such projects – just as it is not restricted solely to countries of socialist orientation – it is the heavy, state-sponsored projects, the Aswans, Hilwans, Rumaylas and such, which are given priority. While it may be claimed that these make the most attractive news stories, the Soviet media give an additional, and for them immeasurably more important, explanation. Hilwan and similar projects are the key to developing heavy industry, 'the only road to social progress'.[92] Noting the technical and economic projects sponsored by the USSR and the socialist countries, Aziz Muhammad, Secretary of the Iraqi Communist Party, claims in *Kommunist* that they democratise Iraq, pushing the country towards eventual socialism.[93] Similar statements can be found both in Soviet ideological propaganda and in interviews with officials in the Arab countries.[94]

The approach to development expressed here is not only of a cumulative economic effect, with the Hilwan and Naj Hamadi projects benefiting from Aswan electricity, but with these projects creating a nucleus of strength for social and political transformation.[95]

Such transformation, however, is far from automatic, and whatever natural tendencies there may be towards socialism appear to be in spite of the small numbers of the proletariat and technical or cultural intelligentsia.[96] These are the classes which in Marxist theory are expected to lead the movement towards socialism. They provide the core of self-interest, theoretical understanding and organisational ability around which the revolutionary movement can be organised. The absence of a developed proletariat and technical intelligentsia in revolutionary Russia leaves its mark on that country and its regime to this day. But Russia in 1917 was far ahead of contemporary Iraq or Algeria. The expectation expressed by one of the leading Soviet Middle East experts is that as the numbers of the working class and organised agricultural labourers grow there will be increasing institutionalised left-wing influence to combat domestic reaction.[97]

Until such a time as the organised masses begin to exert their influence, other classes determine the course of the Arab countries' development, and, as Beliaev sees it, using the terminology and conceptual framework made famous by Milovan Djilas' critique of Communism, Egypt under Sadat has become the victim of a 'new class', a 'bureaucratic bourgeoisie'.[98] A similar, if more conventional explanation of the difficulties on the road of socialist transformation notes the strength of 'petty bourgeois nationalism' in developing countries. Subscribers to this outlook are largely of the middle class and intelligentsia. They are willing to participate in the fight against colonial rule, and mistrusting those who were associated with the colonial powers turn to the USSR as a model, but they shy away from any close identification with the USSR because they are 'apprehensive of the growing power of the socialist camp'.[99]

Unlike Demchenko, who considers it a great achievement that millions of Arabs march under the slogan of socialism, although 'one may argue as to how different political leaders understand and implement socialist concepts',[100] Andreasian concludes that 'non-capitalist development' is a fragile reed to lean on, and that it can only grow into socialist revolution under the aegis of 'a party guided by scientific socialism'.[101] In these two views we have a representation of one of the fundamental ideological disputes within the Soviet regime, a dispute which began in Lenin's time and continues to this day.[102] However, while the argument goes on, the Soviet aid programme is working to provide the Soviet worker with an Arab class comrade.

It is when this 'grand march of historical development' breaks down, as so frequently happens, in the unstable and unpredictable Middle East, that the picture drawn for the Soviet audience must be changed. While Iraq and Algeria continue to be portrayed in the Soviet press as lands of optimistic striving and social progress, the reporting on Egypt deals less and less with magnificent construction, and turns to the dark and negative portrayal which characterises Soviet reporting of Israel. Corruption, scandal, drugs, violence and decay[103] — these are the background against which is portrayed Sadat's adherence to reaction and treacherous compromise with Israel and imperialism at the expense of the Palestinians.[104] The role of Israel as aggressor in the Arab—Israeli conflict is portrayed less, and the elements of world imperialism and the social conflicts in the Arab world, which formerly lay in the background, now move to the fore.

'The rupture of Arab solidarity by the forces of imperialism and internal reaction, as is known, brought about the fratricidal war in Lebanon', states one Soviet reporter.[105] 'The Middle East is the crossroads of many interests and influences. . . the Lebanese crisis was profitable to imperialists, Israeli aggressors and Arab domestic reaction in diverting attention from the main problem', says another.[106] 'Arab reaction' intends to go to Geneva only to make a deal with imperialism against the Palestine Liberation Organisation, says this same author,[107] steadily raising the harshness of his tone. As the debate proceeds, the image projected becomes more and more of political and ideological analysis based on the two-camp view of a world in conflict, in which warring classes struggle for material and political advantages. As the 'anti-imperialist unity' so cherished by the Soviet media fades from the foreground, so does the element of international conflict within the Middle East, and the Arab—Israeli conflict gives way to a description of general class struggle.

5. Conclusions

What emerges from all the parts of our analysis is that the Soviet involvement with the Arab countries is far more fundamental and immanent than is its interest in the Arab—Israeli conflict. In the Soviet view the importance of the conflict appears to be instrumental rather than intrinsic. It provided an avenue of entrance for the Soviet Union into the Middle East at a time when the United States had successfully closed off Turkey, Iran and Greece to Soviet influence. The Arab—Israeli conflict provides a focus for Soviet policy, an arguing point as to the benefits of close relations between the Arab world and the Soviet Union.

But what the Soviet Union presents to its public as the basis of Soviet activity in the Middle East is not merely an analysis of the justice of one side in the conflict and the irredeemable wickedness of the other, in a national and territorial conflict, but a comprehensive justification for the promotion of a socio-political model of development. The Soviet model of development, presented in the newspapers and journals, is one of rapid transformation, the injection of newly activated masses into the political system, destroying and removing old ruling classes and political structures.

In this perspective, the Arab—Israeli conflict and the prospects for a peace settlement take on a different look. The Soviet interest in a settlement becomes a function of its success in transforming one or more of the leading countries of the Arab world into reliable Soviet allies and imitators. If this is achieved, then it may be suggested that a Soviet interest in an Arab—Israeli settlement would grow, on the premise that any military conflict might be aimed at destroying states which are undergoing socialist transformation, as indeed the Soviet Union claimed was the case in 1956, 1967 and 1973. In a situation in which its influence is marginal or declining, instability in the Middle East might well hold out more temptation to the Soviet Union, despite the evident dangers of conflict on a global scale.

What is clear from the material we have reviewed is that the Soviet Union has invested considerable efforts in trying to fulfil its expectations, and has gone to considerable lengths to convince its public that on both principled and pragmatic grounds, such efforts are fully justified.

Notes

1. For a discussion of this point see Alexander Dallin, 'Soviet Foreign Policy and Domestic Politics', in Erik P. Hoffman and Frederic Fleron Jr, *The Conduct of Soviet Foreign Policy* (Chicago: Aldine-Atherton, 1971), pp.36—49.

2. The Soviet government's formal statement on the outbreak of hostilities was published in *Pravda*, 8 October 1973, and was widely reprinted in other leading Soviet newspapers. The deliberations of the Congress of the World Peace Movement (the International Congress of Peace-Loving Forces) were presented in detail. The highlights of this coverage were Brezhnev's speech to the Congress, reported in ibid., 27 October 1973 and the resolutions of the Congress, ibid., 4 November 1973.

3. See, for instance, such a formulation by V. Pustov, *Krasnaia zvezda*, 13 October 1973. Also Iu. Glukhov, *Pravda*, 2 January 1977.

4. *Izvestiia*, 17 October 1973.

5. *Pravda*, 9 October 1973.

6. See also Brezhnev's speech to the Peace Congress, ibid., 27 October 1973; the official Soviet government statement, ibid., 8 October 1973; commentaries by V. Kudriavtsev, *Izvestiia*, 23 November 1973 and Colonel A. Leont'ev, *Krasnaia zvezda*, 20 October 1973.

Slogan number 53 of the sixty-one slogans for the anniversary of the October Revolution, published in the main Soviet newspapers on 14 October 1973, reads: 'Peoples of the world! Demand a cessation of Israel's aggression against the Arab states, and liberation of all Arab lands seized by the Israeli aggressor. . .'

7. Colonel A. Leont'ev. 'When the Mirage Dissolves', *Krasnaia zvezda*, 20 October 1973. Later Soviet commentaries give the numbers of Arabs displaced by the 1948 war as 400,000 — see I. D. Zviagel'skaia and G. I. Starchenkov, 'Israel: Army and State', *Narody Azii i Afriki*, 4 (1974) — or simply as 'hundreds of thousands', see Iurii Glukhov, *Pravda*, 31 December 1976, who adds that 'As a result of perennial Israeli aggression . . . a people numbering today three million, is scattered in many countries'.

8. V. Kudriavtsev, *Izvestiia*, 5 April 1977.

9. G. Ratiiani, *Pravda*, 26 December 1976. See also Iu. Glukhov, ibid., 22 December 1976.

10. *Trud* and *Izvestiia*, 16 February 1977. See also Iu. Tsaplin, *Pravda*, 21 March 1977, who writes that terror and repression as practised by 'Tel Aviv's ruling circles' are nothing less than 'the practical embodiment of Zionism'.

11. L. Korneev, 'Garrison State', *Krasnaia zvezda*, 19 February 1977.

12. See, for instance, *Izvestiia*, 24 October 1973.

13. *Pravda*, 19 January 1977, reporting Brezhnev's speech in Tula or Kosygin's speech at a meeting with Saddam Husayn of Iraq in ibid., 2 February 1977.

14. Ibid., 30 October 1973.

15. V. Kudriavtsev, 'The Middle East: The Way to Settlement', *Izvestiia*, 23 November 1973. Much the same argument is presented in M. A. Pavlov, 'The Socialist International and the Middle East', in *Narody Azii i Afriki*, 5 (1973), pp.23–4. Pavlov writes that the majority of the International supports Israel as 'the chief barrier to Communism in the Middle East', and refuses to recognise the anti-imperialist struggle of the Arabs.

16. 'Observer', *Pravda*, 12 October 1973.

17. V. Kudriavtsev, *Izvestiia*, 19 October 1973.

18. *KPSS v rezoliutsiiakh i resheniiakh s"ezdov, konferentsii i plenumov tsentral'nogo komiteta* (Moscow, 1972), pp.283–4. A similar evaluation of Israel's war aims is expressed by L. Koriavin, *Izvestiia*, 17 October 1973, linking 1967 and 1973 explicitly.

19. See the general formulations of 'Imperialism, relying on Zionism. . .', *Pravda*, 29 December 1976, or 'Israel and its patrons', *Pravda*, 23 January 1977, or 'imperialist circles supported by the American military', *Izvestiia*, 18 January 1977.

20. See, for instance, the statement of the Arab Communist and Workers' Parties, published in *Pravda*, 29 December 1976.

21. V. Kudriavtsev, 'In Whose Interests?', *Izvestiia*, 26 February 1977, in which he writes: 'Now imperialism operates not only through its own strength and that of its Israeli allies, but with the help of domestic Arab reaction and right-wing forces in the national liberation movement'.

22. See note 17. V. Kudriavtsev, political observer for *Izvestiia*, writes frequently and is perhaps the most extreme in his condemnation of Israel and his support for the Palestine Liberation Organisation. Whether he is the same person as Vladimir L. Kudriavtsev, the 75-year-old Deputy Chairman of the Soviet Committee for Solidarity with the Countries of Asia and Africa, and also listed as

a political commentator in *Izvestiia* – see *Prominent Soviet Personalities* (Metuchen, New Jersey: Scarecrow Press, 1968), p.330 – is not totally clear, though the style and outlook seem similar. Another V. Kudriavtsev, also dealing in Middle East affairs, died in 1975.

23. *Pravda*, 9 October 1973. A similar formulation appears in the widely reprinted declaration of the Soviet Committee for Solidarity with the Countries of Asia and Africa – ibid., 8 October 1973. See also B. Krotkov in *Krasnaia zvezda*, 17 November 1973.

24. *Izvestiia*, 24 December 1976.

25. V. Solodovnikov, *Izvestiia*, 27 December 1973.

26. Brezhnev, in *Pravda*, 9 October 1973.

27. B. Gafurov *et al.* (eds.), *Vneshniaia politika Sovetskogo Soiuza*, (Moscow: Mezhdunarodnye Otnosheniia, 1973), p.151.

28. See the Soviet–Egyptian communiqué in *Pravda*, 6 March 1974, which speaks of the joint struggle against imperialism, colonialism and aggression, and the Soviet–Syrian communiqué, ibid., 7 March 1974, which speaks of 'common aims in the struggle against imperialism, Zionism, and colonialism'. (Note once again the equivalent usage of 'Zionism' and 'aggression'.)

29. See the reports in *Pravda* and *Trud*, 18 October 1973, *Krasnaia zvezda*, 13 October 1973 and *Pravda*, 21 October 1973.

30. *Pravda*, 9 October 1973. The communiqué was reprinted in at least six other central papers.

31. For example, the Soviet–Yugoslav communiqué at the end of Kosygin's visit to Belgrade, *Pravda*, 2 October 1973.

32. See *Pravda* and *Krasnaia zvezda*, 9 October 1973, and *Izvestiia*, 13 and 16 October 1973. Many of these 'actions' in fact never took place at all.

33. *Izvestiia*, 14 October 1973. Another instance of this distinction being preserved is to be found in the report of A. Vasil'ev, 'A Rebuff to the Occupiers', *Pravda*, 3 April 1977, in which he distinguishes carefully between Arab demonstrations within Israel and Arab demonstrations on 'the occupied West Bank of the Jordan', though he calls all the demonstrating Arabs 'Palestinians'.

34. In addition to the preceding note, see Iu. Glukhov, *Pravda*, 31 December 1976, who writes of 450,000 Palestinians living in Israel within its 1967 borders.

35. The Soviet government declaration, *Pravda*, 9 October 1973, repeated frequently in other contexts.

36. Ibid.

37. From mid-November to mid-December 1973, *Izvestiia* has seventeen such references and *Krasnaia zvezda* twelve.

38. A. Leont'ev in *Krasnaia zvezda*, 16 October 1973, compares Israel's bombing of the Arab countries to the Nazis' bombing of the USSR and England in World War Two. However, no cartoons in *Izvestiia* in the months October–December 1973 use the theme of comparing Israel and the Nazis. For use of such cartoons during the period 1967–72 see Yeshayahu Nir, *The Israel–Arab Conflict in Soviet Caricatures, 1967–1973* (Tel Aviv: Tcherikover, 1975), pp.80–3.

39. *Izvestiia*, 14 October 1973. See also V. Vinogradov, in *Krasnaia zvezda*, 19 October 1973.

40. *Pravda*, 24 October 1973. 'The Soviet government warns the government of Israel of the most serious consequences which will result from a continuation of aggression against the Arab Republic of Egypt and the Syrian Arab Republic'.

41. Examples are: The Declaration of the Soviet government, *Pravda*, 8 October 1973 and the TASS statement on the sinking of the Soviet freighter *Il'ia Mechnikoff* in the Syrian port of Tartus, *Pravda*, 13 October 1973, reprinted in numerous central newspapers. Similar and even more explicit threats were made by the Soviet authorities in the context of the fighting in 1956 and 1967.

42. *Pravda*, 28 October 1973. There is to the author's knowledge, only one reference acknowledging that Soviet military personnel actually fought on behalf of the Arabs (except for references to Soviet advisers killed by Israeli action in the 1969–70 War of Attrition). This came in the context of the revelations spurred by worsening Soviet–Egyptian relations, discussed in detail below. In *Pravda*, 19 February 1977, an article attacking Sadat states that Soviet personnel took upon themselves the defence of Egyptian air space – putting an end to Israeli incursions. No date of reference is given with this statement, but it would seem to refer to the War of Attrition in 1970.

43. *Krasnaia zvezda*, 16 April 1975. Additional, similar references are made by Iraqi Communists and Algerian trade unionists who note the USSR as the country remembered for saving humanity by defeating Nazism – an image that would appear to be closer to a Soviet self-image than to one used by representatives of Arab or African countries among whom anti-colonial associations might be expected to be more prominent.

44. See discussions in E. Fedorov, 'Progress and Peace – Indivisible', *Izvestiia*, 6 November 1973, and B. Gafurov, *Vneshniaia politika Sovetskogo Soiuza*, p.158.

45. For a discussion of the development of this attitude in Russian and Soviet Communist thought from Zinoviev's 1915 essay defining 'just' wars, up to the 1968 explication of the Brezhnev Doctrine, see William Korey, 'The Comintern and the Geneology of the "Brezhnev Doctrine" ', *Problems of Communism*, XVIII, 3 (May–June 1969), pp.52–8.

46. See note 4. For additional examples see V. Kudriavtsev, 'In Whose Interests?', *Izvestiia*, 26 February 1977, and TASS report from Baghdad, quoting the Iraqi newspaper *al-Ba'th* published in *Pravda*, 15 March 1977.

47. O. M. Gorbanov and L. Ia. Cherkaskii, *Sotrudnichestvo SSSR so stranami Arabskogo vostoka i Afriki* (Moscow: Nauka, 1973), p.70, write: 'Before World War Two, for objective reasons, the USSR's support of the peoples of the Arab and African countries was primarily of a moral and political character'.

48. See *Soviet Economy in a New Perspective* (Washington: Government Printing Office, 1976), foldout following p.16, and Jack Brougher, 'USSR Foreign Trade', in above, p.686, for discussion of this body.

49. The biography of Semen A. Skachkov is to be found in the 1966 yearbook of the *Bol'shaia Sovetskaia Entsiklopediia* (Moscow: Sovetskaia Entsiklopediia, 1966), p.611.

50. *R. Moscow*, 9 October 1973/*FBIS III*, 10 October 1973.

51. 'A Leninist Course in the International Arena', *Kommunist*, 1 (1974), pp.39–53. See particularly pp.41, 47.

52. John A. Armstrong, 'The Domestic Roots of Soviet Foreign Policy', in Hoffman and Heron, *The Conduct of Soviet Foreign Policy*, pp.50–60.

53. *Trud*, 21 August 1974.

54. A similar analysis, but an opposite conclusion, i.e. that the USSR is being bled of good money for the 'ignorant, unwashed masses' of the underdeveloped countries, who live 'even worse, pardon me, than do our own folks', is expressed by Alexander Galich's apocryphal Soviet Everyman, Klim Petrovich Kolomiitsev, in the song, 'How K. P. Stood Up Against Economic Aid to Underdeveloped Countries', in A. Galich, *Pokolenie obrechennykh* (Frankfurt: Posev, 1972), pp.269–71. Alexander Werth, *Russia: Hopes and Fears* (New York: Simon and Schuster, 1970), p.232, cites 'What's the good of wasting money on these people?' as a common reaction in the USSR, where he claims, 'Charity begins at home moods are strong'.

55. Baruch A. Hazan, *Soviet Propaganda* (New York: Wiley, 1976), p.197, notes a *Radio Moscow* broadcast in Arabic intended for foreign audiences in 1972 as declaring 'The Soviet people . . . are also helping the Arab peoples, consciously

denying themselves material things'. No such theme is presented to the Soviet public by the media, though it is quite clear that Soviet citizens understand the existence of such a problem.

56. *Agitator*, 2 (1975), p.2.

57. *Krasnaia zvezda*, 17 October 1974. The same phenomenon may be observed a year later on the following Syrian Air Force Day, in ibid., 17 October 1975.

58. *Pravda*, 24 November 1973, reporting on Syrian reconstruction of war damaged facilities, says nothing of Soviet aid.

59. See *Kommunist*, 5 (March 1974), pp.100–10.

60. Iu. Sumbatian, 'Armies in the Political Structure of Countries with a Socialist Orientation', *Aziia i Afrika segodnia*, 4 (1974), pp.17–19.

61. See the article by Semen Skachkov, 'Economic Co-operation of the USSR with the Developing Countries', *Kommunist*, 12 (1973), pp.41–52, or E. Mukhin, *Krasnaia zvezda*, 16 August 1975, who states that all the socialist states together have granted the developing countries 11 billion rubles in credits, but gives no framework of time.

62. Hedrick Smith, *The Russians* (New York: Quadrangle, 1976), p.373.

63. Werth, *Russia*, p.232. See also Adam Ulam, *Expansion and Coexistence* (New York: Praeger, 2nd edn., 1974), p.760: 'It is almost impossible for the Soviet consumer to arrive at a precise calculation of how far his privations are related to the expense his government incurs in arming the progressive Arab states'.

64. *Pravda*, 25 February 1976.

65. See, for instance, *Krasnaia zvezda*, 22 and 24 April and 5 and 13 May 1977.

66. L. Koriavin, *Izvestiia*, 9 October 1973. See also Iu. Trushin's TASS dispatch, 18 October 1973, *R. Moscow* in English, 18 October 1973/*FBIS III*, 19 October 1973.

67. *Krasnaia zvezda*, 10 October 1973; *Izvestiia*, 13 October 1973. The names of Phantoms and Mirages often appeared both literally and as puns in the Soviet press. See, for instance, Nir, *Caricatures*, pp.57, 63, 92 and Colonel A. Leont'ev, 'When the Mirage Dissolves', *Krasnaia zvezda*, 20 October 1973.

68. V. Pustov, *Krasnaia zvezda*, 13 October 1973.

69. *Izvestiia*, 14 October 1973.

70. *Pravda*, 15 October 1973; *Izvestiia*, 16 October 1973.

71. *Krasnaia zvezda*, 7 December 1973; in an interview with the then chief of the Egyptian general staff, Lieutenant-General Shazali. The interview is reprinted in condensed form from the Egyptian press.

72. M. Sagatelian, in *Izvestiia*, 31 October 1973.

73. *Izvestiia*, 31 October 1973, and B. Orekhov, *Pravda*, 1 November 1973.

74. *Izvestiia*, 12 and 14 October 1973, *Pravda*, 14 and 16 October 1973. *Izvestiia*, 20 October 1973, specifies that American planes were taking the supplies to Israel. In almost every case these were TASS dispatches quoting American press sources.

75. V. Vinogradov, 'Harming National Interests', *Krasnaia zvezda*, 10 April 1976, writes of the USSR sending 'air and sea supplies to Egypt in her hour of trouble'. The only hint of this during the war itself was by TASS correspondent Leonid Latyshev in an English language broadcast, *R. Moscow*, 17 October 1973/*FBIS III*, 17 October 1973, who stated: 'The public of Arab countries directly link the growth of the fighting efficiency of the Egyptian and Syrian armies with the military aid which has been rendered and is rendered by the Soviet Union'.

76. Andrei Krushinskii, *Komsomol'skaia pravda*, 21 October 1973.

77. *Pravda*, 19 February 1977. The commentary concludes that in playing down the importance of Soviet military aid, Sadat is serving the cause of 'imperialism and reaction'.

78. V. Vinogradov, 'Harming National Interests', *Krasnaia zvezda*, 10 April 1976.

79. See *Trud*, 12 January 1974, *Krasnaia zvezda*, 17 May 1975, and *Trud*, 12 October 1975, for references to some of these very varied programmes.

80. *Pravda*, 9 April 1974, traces Soviet foreign aid activities back to Lenin's November 1917 Decree on Peace.

81. A Somali newspaper quoted in *Krasnaia zvezda*, 8 November 1975; Arab Socialist Union Secretary Rif'at al Mahjub, opening Soviet–Egyptian friendship week, quoted in *Pravda*, 24 December 1974; L. N. Lebedinskaia, reporting to a conference on the working class of the developing countries in *Aziia i Afrika segodnia*, 7 (1975), p.5.

82. A Sadat press conference as reported in *Pravda* and *Trud*, 1 November 1973.

83. See Iu. Tiunkov, *Literaturnaia gazeta*, 6 November 1974, and a *Krasnaia zvezda* preview of an Arabic language translation of Marshal Konev's memoirs for references to Soviet devotion to universal humanist values.

84. See, for instance, Brezhnev's Tula speech, *Pravda*, 19 January 1977, or V. Kudriavtsev in *Izvestiia*, 8 February 1977, or the quotations from the Egyptian press in *Pravda*, 11 January 1977.

85. See the many criticisms of Sadat's 'open door policy', e.g. K. Geivandov, in ibid., 8 February 1977.

86. K. Truevtsev, 'Iraq, Striving Towards the Future', *Aziia i Afrika segodnia*, 3 (1974), pp.28–30. See also *Pravda*, 14 October 1973, with regard to the People's Democratic Republic of Yemen.

87. V. Mikhailov, *Pravda*, 3 March 1974.

88. *Agitator*, 21 (1973), p.5.

89. A. Vasil'ev's report on the Cairo conference of heads of African and Arab states, *Pravda*, 10 March 1977.

90. *Trud* and *Krasnaia zvezda*, 26 July 1975.

91. Semen Skachkov, 'Economic Co-operation', *Kommunist*, 12 (1973), p.48 is explicit on this point, stating: 'Economic and technical co-operation of the USSR with the developing countries exercises a beneficial influence not only on [the recipients'] economies, but has specific social consequences as well'.

92. Iu. Glukhov, *Pravda*, 7 January 1974.

93. Aziz Muhammad, 'Lenin and the National Liberation Movement', *Kommunist*, 1 (1974), p.75.

94. See Iu. Sumbatian, 'Countries of Socialist Orientation', *Agitator*, 1 (1975), pp.40–3, or the statement of Rashid Urar, Chairman of the Algerian Union of Food Industry Workers, in *Trud*, 10 March 1976.

95. See items by B. Orekhov in *Pravda*, 25 February 1974, re Iraq, and Iu. Glukhov, ibid., 7 January 1974 re Egypt.

96. P. Demchenko, 'The Arab East: A Time of Great Change', *Pravda*, 28 December 1974, points this out but nevertheless lays claim to advances by socialism in the Arab world.

97. I. Beliaev, 'Egypt: Stages of Revolution', *Aziia i Afrika segodnia*, 7 (1975), pp.2–4.

98. Ibid., cf. Oded Eran, 'The Soviet Perception of Influence: The Case of the Middle East', this volume, p.138.

99. R. N. Andreasian, 'Contradictions and Criteria of Non-Capitalist Development', *Narody Azii i Afriki*, 2 (1974), pp.38–49.

100. Demchenko, 'Arab East', *Pravda*, 28 December 1974.

101. Andreasian, 'Contradictions', p.49.

102. Alexander Dallin, 'Soviet Foreign Policy and Domestic Politics: A Framework for Analysis', in Hoffman and Fleron, *The Conduct of Soviet Foreign Policy*, p.46.

103. For corruption see *Trud*, 29 January 1977. A tale of feudal bandits terrorising the Egyptian countryside can be found in *Sovetskaia Rossiia*, 15 January 1977, and the breakdown of Egyptian transport and communications is lamented in *Krasnaia zvezda*, 7 January 1977.

104. Sadat's 'betrayal' of the Arab national liberation movement, and in particular the charge that he is selling out the Palestinians in return for American support has grown steadily as a theme in the Soviet press since the September 1975 separation of forces agreement. See for example *Pravda*, 20 February 1977, *Trud*, 1 January 1977, and in particular the reporting on Sadat's April 1977 visit to Washington in which he is accused by the Soviet press of accepting less than a total withdrawal of Israeli forces from all occupied territories, and of accepting President Carter's formula of a 'homeland for the Palestinians' which is interpreted as less than an independent Palestinian state. *Pravda*, 7 and 8 April 1977; *Trud*, 7 April 1977.

105. *Izvestiia*, 2 February 1977.

106. V. Kudriavtsev, ibid., 8 February 1977.

107. V. Kudriavtsev, ibid., 26 February 1977.

PART 4   THE CONFLICT ARENA

7 THE SOVIET UNION AND EGYPT: THE CONSTRAINTS OF A POWER-CLIENT RELATIONSHIP

Yaacov Ro'i

For many years Egypt was the focus of Soviet attention in the Middle East and the relationship with Egypt the linchpin of Moscow's interests in the region. After Anwar al-Sadat's accession to the presidency in October 1970 and particularly his successes in overcoming his domestic opponents, Soviet—Egyptian relations began to show signs of serious strain.

Indeed, the Treaty of Friendship and Co-operation concluded at the end of May 1971 was, paradoxically, evidence of Soviet conviction of the need to regularise and formalise the relationship following Secretary of State William Rogers' visit to Egypt at the beginning of the month and the ousting of Ali Sabri and the other 'Nasirite' key figures who joined him in a plot against Sadat.[1] The first major crisis came in July 1972 with the ending of the Soviet military presence in Egypt, and after October 1973 relations between Moscow and Cairo deteriorated still further. This paper traces the causes of this development up to the abrogation of the Treaty of Friendship and Co-operation in March 1976. In particular, it considers whether the main factor in this deterioration was the Arab—Israeli conflict or whether the key lay rather in the Egyptian domestic situation, which dictated an orientation towards the West, combined with the Soviet Union's unwillingness to condone some sort of balance between the two superpowers as Egypt's joint mentors and allies.

It has been frequently suggested that one of the reasons for the initial rapprochement in the 1950s and 1960s was the major role Egypt played in what has perhaps been the Middle East's most important and most permanent dispute, the Arab—Israeli conflict. Whether this was in fact the case, a *sine qua non* for the viability of the Soviet—Egyptian rapprochement was the co-ordination of positions regarding the conduct of the conflict. Indeed, from the very early stages, the USSR demonstrated a many-sided support for the Arab, and particularly the Egyptian, position on the conflict despite conceptual divergences over its very essence and purpose. Before 1967, for example, the Arabs saw the conflict as a means to destroy Israel physically, while Moscow regarded Israel as a reality and believed that any attempt to annihilate it would evoke an undesirable international confrontation; the USSR preferred to attribute its own hostility to Israel to the latter's alleged role as Western imperialism's main instrument in its struggle against the Arab national liberation movement. Nevertheless, the Soviet Union supplied the Arabs with the weaponry they required to fight Israel and trained them in the use of these arms. The convergence of purpose and interest following the Six Day War, when both sides agreed on the need for a reversal of the war's outcome, facilitated co-operation in 'eliminating the consequences of the aggression'. Yet even then the USSR was not always in total agreement with the methods suggested by Cairo. Dissensions came to a head when Sadat became president, and although not confined to the Arab—Israeli conflict, centred on what Sadat regarded as the crucial test of his leadership — the restoration of Egyptian prestige on the battlefield. Even the *modus operandi* achieved early in 1973, that led to the renewal of arms supplies and enabled the October War to be launched, in no way mitigated Soviet—Egyptian differences.[2] On the contrary, after the war, having achieved what he believed to be the maximum success military action could bring in the recovery of the lands lost in 1967, the Egyptian President found himself at last able to participate in the diplomatic process from a position of equality. He thereupon turned to the USA as the sole power able to apply effective pressures on Israel in order to follow up his military achievement.

Yet a short digression into Egypt's goals, policies and orientations in the domestic and international arenas after October 1973 demonstrates that not all the strains of the Soviet—Egyptian relationship emanated from Egypt's shift of emphasis from military to diplomatic action *vis-à-vis* Israel or from the implications of Cairo's partnerships in the realm of power politics in the context of the conflict with Israel.[3] Other processes hitherto overshadowed by the predominant goal of a war to recover Egypt's prestige now came to the fore as Sadat, strengthened by his military achievement, was able to pay increasing attention to urgent internal problems. Prominent among these processes were: the 'open-door' economic policy; the call for a 'technological revolution'; the encouragement of the private sector;[4] the reduction of the role of the Arab Socialist Union in Egyptian politics; the increasing estrangement from the more radical Arab regimes in favour of the conservative, wealthy oil producers;[5] and a general desire to replace military, economic and political dependence on the Communist world by maximum manoeuvrability among the major international power centres, i.e. in addition to the superpowers and the Arab oil producers, Western Europe and the non-aligned countries.

Each of these tendencies had an adverse affect on the Soviet–Egyptian relationship, which had traditionally been based on: (1) arms supplies intended to meet Egypt's principal needs in its conflict with Israel; (2) Soviet and East European dominance of the Egyptian economy, in which those branches that the USSR was able and willing to develop were stressed and the public sector systematically nurtured. This was a prerequisite for a government system that would be *a priori* inclined towards reliance upon Soviet and East European aid and guidance; (3) collaboration and co-ordination in the fields of party work, local government, the secret police, education and propaganda, all of which had played major roles in implementing Nasirite Arab Socialism; and (4) a maximum manipulation of inter-Arab politics in which Egypt and the other regimes with which Moscow had close relationships were destined to play the dominant role – simply towing along the conservative states among which the USSR had little or no sway.

In this way some of the very same factors that reduced the conflict orientation of the Egyptian leadership – the new economic policy, the partnership with Washington and the growing dependence on the Arab oil states[6] – operated against Egyptian–Soviet collaboration. While the student must beware of drawing hasty conclusions from this pattern, he can clearly not ignore it.

The complexities of Soviet–US relations must also be borne in mind in order to gain a correct perspective. From the Egyptian point of view the rapprochement with the USA may not necessarily have precluded a continued positive relationship with the USSR. Sadat probably meant what he said when he insisted that it was a strategic error for Egypt to be at loggerheads with either great power. Indeed, in theory at least he sought to preserve the military option, which meant leaving the door open to a return to the Soviet fold until Western weaponry was delivered. (Even in optimal conditions, approximately three years would presumably be needed for Egypt to change its major weapon systems. In the circumstances, particularly given Egypt's economic constraints, the time factor was an unpredictable variable.) The circumstances of the Soviet–US relationship, however, were such that despite the sincere desire of both sides to avoid a military confrontation, neither was prepared to concede *a priori* any of the means available within the rather flexible framework of détente, of gaining political advantage at the expense of the other.[7] This was true of the world arena as a whole and within it of the Middle East, and in particular Egypt as an obvious key to regional trends.

This then is the general context of the Soviet–Egyptian relationship in the period under question. It encompasses developments inside Egypt, in Soviet and Egyptian foreign policy and in the Arab–Israeli conflict,[8] and certain trends in international and particularly Middle Eastern politics as well as in the Soviet Union, especially given the considerable commitment of the Brezhnev leadership to Egypt before October 1973.[9] It is only by taking all these factors into consideration that Soviet–Egyptian relations can be comprehended.

Relations between Moscow and Cairo included all the major spheres which comprise ties between partners in the international arena, particularly between superpowers and medium-sized, technologically backward 'client' states. From the Soviet point of view these relations were satisfactorily defined by the May 1971 Treaty of Friendship and Co-operation which contained both general declarations and specific references to political, military, economic and other aspects of the relationship. While Cairo did not officially reject this framework until March 1976, it was clearly calling for a Soviet reevaluation some time before.[10] Moscow's failure – or refusal – to reappraise either the conceptual or practical guidelines of its Egyptian policy brought to the fore the fundamental nature of the disagreement between the two states after October 1973.

For the first three months after the war, Moscow and Cairo maintained contacts at a medium and lower level only. The first senior-level contact was Egyptian Foreign Minister Isma'il Fahmi's visit to the Soviet Union from 21 to 24 January 1974, immediately after the signature of the first Egyptian–Israeli disengagement agreement. Both sides talked of the time-tested effectiveness of Soviet–Egyptian co-ordination and co-operation, of the economic and military aid extended by the USSR to Egypt, and of the need to 'develop and strengthen' the friendship between the two countries. Gromyko stressed Brezhnev's personal interest in strengthening Soviet–Egyptian relations – the secretary-general himself met Fahmi for a four-hour talk – and said that their concerted action would further the work started at Geneva a month before and continued by the disengagement of forces agreement. The ultimate aim of this collaboration was to solve 'the radical questions' of a Middle East settlement on the basis of the Security Council's 'well-known resolutions'. That the USSR desired to prevent a rift at this stage and to smooth over its exclusion from the disengagement negotiations could be seen in Gromyko's sympathetic allusion to the agreement without mentioning that it was inspired by the US.[11] Fahmi, for his part, stressed the gratitude of all Egyptians for the constant Soviet assistance in developing Egypt's economy and enhancing its defence potential.[12] The communiqué at the end of the visit noted that Soviet–Egyptian co-operation rested on 'long-term foundations of principle', and that the events of October 1973 had 'reaffirmed the strength and desirability of Soviet–Egyptian friendship'. It said too that 'the firm and long-term basis' of the May 1971 treaty would continue to be the criterion for developing mutual relations. As to the settlement of the Middle East 'crisis', the sides agreed that the disengagement agreement had 'a positive significance, taking into account that it is to be followed up by a radical settlement in the Middle East on the basis of full implementation' of Resolutions 242 and 338. Moscow and Cairo agreed that a 'lasting and just peace' necessitated the withdrawal of Israeli troops 'from all Arab territories occupied in 1967' and 'respect for [the] legitimate rights of the Arab people of Palestine', whose representatives must have 'equal participation' in the work of the Geneva Conference 'in the nearest future'. Finally, the communiqué stressed the importance 'in the struggle for a just settlement' of 'close co-ordination of actions of the Soviet Union and Egypt at all stages', as well as 'the importance and usefulness . . . of maintaining . . . regular contacts [and] exchange of opinion . . . at all levels on questions of bilateral Soviet–Egyptian relations and the international situation'.[13]

Egyptian comment on Fahmi's visit to Moscow noted that while the USSR felt itself excluded from the centre of action, although it was a friendly party with a direct interest in developments, it had welcomed the Egyptian foreign minister with ostentatious ceremony. The success of the visit – Fahmi described his talks with Brezhnev and Gromyko as having been conducted in complete understanding – meant the continuation and cultivation of the friendly relations between the two countries during the transition from war to peace. It was understood from Fahmi, the Moscow correspondent of *Ruz al-Yusuf* reported, that Brezhnev had expressed full support for Egypt's latest consultations and contacts, notably those relating to the separation of forces agreement.[14] According to *al-Ahram*, however, the Soviet leadership had insinuated that Egypt would have achieved more had the USSR been a party to them and would achieve more in the future with Soviet participation at all stages of the negotiations leading to a just and lasting peace. The future consultations the two sides agreed upon were said to concern a Syrian–Israeli separation of forces agreement and the participation in the Geneva Conference of both Syria and the Palestinians.[15]

Less than six weeks after Fahmi's visit, Gromyko visited Cairo (1–5 March) where he met Sadat and Fahmi. The Soviet media presented this visit as part of the USSR's effort to achieve a settlement. Indeed, the Soviet foreign minister arrived in the area during one of Kissinger's visits: he came to Cairo from Damascus and then returned to the Syrian capital for talks on the projected Syrian–Israeli disengagement agreement. While in Cairo he met Yasir Arafat and the head of the PLO political department, Faruq Qaddumi. The talks between Gromyko and his hosts, conducted 'in a cordial and constructive atmosphere', covered both the Middle Eastern situation, in particular the Geneva Conference, and bilateral relations.[16] The Soviet media mostly claimed that the visit was a further manifestation of Soviet–Egyptian co-operation. The two sides once more 'expressed their united view about the necessary participation of the Soviet Union in all stages of the settlement', and the visit also 'resulted in Egypt receiving the agreement in principle of the Soviet Union to take part in the work of clearing the Suez Canal . . . proof of the unwavering nature of Soviet–Egyptian co-operation'. But some sources criticised those in Egypt who were casting aspersions on its relations with the USSR, notably an article by Ihsan Abd al-Quddus in *Akhbar al-Yawm* on the day Gromyko arrived in Cairo which denied that the Treaty of Friendship and Co-operation had political value for Egypt.[17]

March 1974 also saw in Egypt an intensive propaganda campaign against the memory of Jamal Abd al-Nasir, followed by criticism of this 'de-Nasirisation' in the Soviet media;[18] and in inter-Arab politics the end of the oil embargo, an achievement in which Sadat played a leading role.[19]

Before the Syrian–Israeli agreement was reached, Sadat himself made a series of statements on Egypt's relations with Moscow. There was some doubt, which Sadat seemed determined to encourage, whether his remarks were aimed primarily at the USSR – in order to stimulate a change in Soviet policies – or at the USA, perhaps to help the Nixon administration overcome potential sceptics or opponents of an Egyptian rapprochement. Whatever the motive, in a speech before students in Alexandria on 3 April, the Egyptian president revealed new details of the deterioration in relations in 1971–2 and blamed the two superpowers for impeding, at the 1972 and 1973 summit talks, any remedy for the impasse in which the relations with Israel had been prior to October.[20] At a joint session of the A.S.U. Central Committee and

the People's Assembly on 18 April, Sadat announced that Egypt was
terminating its reliance on Soviet weaponry and turning to other
sources. Since November he had approached the Soviet Union four
times with requests for certain items of military equipment, requests
that Sadat described as being neither extraordinary nor impossible, and
he had twice been told that his requests were being considered.
However, judging that this reply was unreasonable and that it would be
irresponsible to leave Egypt's armed forces without the necessary means
of defence, he had not only decided to diversify their sources of arms
but actually taken action. Continuing his discourse on the
'misunderstanding' prevailing between Moscow and Cairo, in particular
Soviet remarks that Egypt had abandoned socialism, Sadat reminded
the USSR that Egypt had chosen the socialism that accorded with its
own needs and circumstances. Egypt could not consent to criticism by
a foreign power of its basic policies, including its 'economic openness'
and its improved relationship with the USA. Noting that détente had
brought together the opposing ideologies of capitalism and
communism, Sadat hoped that the USSR would come to realise that
Egypt wanted good relations with the leading representative of each
and had no desire to replace one world power or camp by the other. He
hoped, too, that Egypt and the USSR would once more sit together as
friends, so that the USSR could become convinced of his balanced
policy towards the two superpowers, just as in February 1973 the
Kremlin had finally been persuaded that the July 1972 expulsion had
not been undertaken in collaboration with the USA.[21] Still in April, in
an interview with an ABC correspondent, Sadat said that although his
relations with the USA and Kissinger's activities and successes had caused
tension in Egypt's relations with Moscow and had aroused Soviet
sensitivities, he would continue to pursue a policy of equilibrium
between the two superpowers, as both were guarantors of the ceasefire
and the implementation of Security Council Resolution 242.[22]

Meanwhile, in another interview, the Egyptian president disclosed
further information on the difficulties Moscow had placed in his — and
Nasir's — path in the pre-1973 period.[23] Early in May, the Egyptian
Akhir Sa'a wrote that Sadat's exposure of the Soviet abuse of arms
supplies to exert political pressure showed how history had come full
circle. Egypt's position *vis-à-vis* the USSR had come to resemble the
subservience to the West's arms supplies to the area that had led to the
original liaison with Moscow in the form of the Czechoslovak—Egyptian
arms deal. The Egyptian leadership appreciated that its sole reliance on
the USSR obstructed the free exercise and implementation of the

national will and placed the armed forces in a position of dependence. The *Akhir Sa'a* article concluded with the Soviet evasion of Sadat's request for arms, noting in contrast that Moscow had decided to supply Syria with MiG-23s, SAM-9s and other sophisticated weaponry.[24]

The official Soviet stand continued, outwardly at least, to assume that a relationship of friendship and understanding still existed. The new Soviet ambassador to Cairo, Vladimir Poliakov, brought Sadat a Note from Brezhnev in mid-May which was said to call for a 'more positive' relationship.[25] The considerable attention paid by Soviet media to the anniversary of the Friendship and Co-operation Treaty stood in sharp contrast to Egypt's silence on the same occasion.

In June Cairo gave President Nixon red-carpet treatment and a tumultuous welcome on the first visit of a US president to the area since Franklin Roosevelt had met Ibn Saud on his return from Yalta in 1945. Sadat was frankly pleased by this prestigious visit and was well aware of the political value of the agreements concluded with Washington during and after it. Yet, while he continued to insist that his economic policy was essential for Egypt's development and reiterated that he had begun to diversify his sources of weaponry (in Europe), he still called for an end to the 'misunderstanding' that had arisen between Egypt and the USSR, specifically for top-level talks between himself and Brezhnev in Cairo. The Soviet leadership, Sadat noted, had told Algerian president Houari Boumedienne that it was angry with the Egyptians, *inter alia* because of their decision to purchase arms elsewhere; yet, the Egyptian president was adamant, he had no choice. Moscow's attitude to Egypt, he insisted, was based on erroneous analyses and a failure to alter its outmoded approach. He had reminded Moscow, through Bulgarian Party Secretary Todor Zhivkov, that it was he himself who had renewed the agreement by which the USSR continued to enjoy the naval facilities accorded it in recognition of Soviet support in 1967, although this arrangement violated Egyptian sovereignty.[26] Later in the summer, in one of his recurrent statements on Soviet–Egyptian relations, Sadat reiterated his accusations that Moscow was failing to supply arms. At the same time he admitted that ample tangible evidence of the friendship between the two states existed in the form of the Aswan High Dam, the Hilwan iron and steel complex and the arms supplied since 1955; Moscow had merely to appreciate that the relationship must be based on equality.[27] This last remark may well have referred to Sadat's insistence that Brezhnev come to Cairo.

The day after Sadat's speech on the anniversary of the revolution, yet without referring to the passage in which Sadat had declared his desire to improve Soviet–Egyptian relations, a high-ranking Soviet commentator published a fierce attack on the Egyptian government for its rapprochement with Washington on the issues of the Arab–Israeli conflict and economic aid. *Izvestiia's* editor-in-chief, Lev Tolkunov, accused the Egyptian president of negotiating with the USA behind the USSR's back. Even though the argument that Moscow had delayed supplies of offensive weaponry so as to prevent an Arab victory over Israel had been discredited, anti-Sovietism in Egypt continued. Rumours were being spread about 'the uneconomic nature' of industrial plants built with Soviet help and the inferiority of Soviet to Western enterprises and equipment. Tolkunov claimed that these stories were intended to prepare the ground for the penetration of Western capital and the 'liberation of Egypt from economic dependence on the Soviet Union'. In Cairo, however, 'progressive circles' were asking whether the West was able or wanted to promote the country's public sector and industry or improve the population's living standard.[28]

The USSR was thus charging the West, in particular the USA – and indirectly also Sadat – with endeavouring to create a barrier between the Soviet Union and Egypt and to split the Arab world, which had shown such outstanding unity both in the October War itself and in the use of the oil weapon. The ultimate aim was to pressure Egypt and the other Arab states to abandon their hard-won achievements in the economic, social and political spheres.

Sadat's call for a summit meeting with Brezhnev had bred two Notes from the CPSU secretary-general.[29] Yet, as Sadat made clear, only an actual visit by Brezhnev to Cairo – for which he had been calling since July 1972 as a prerequisite for mending relations and re-establishing them on a 'new' basis – could remove the 'misunderstanding' that prevailed.[30] By early September the visit had been officially announced and a date set (in October) for Fahmi to go to the Soviet Union to prepare the agenda.[31] Expectations in Egypt that Brezhnev's visit would turn 'a new leaf' in the relationship were considerable. While not retracting his accusations, Sadat inserted a note of optimism into his references to the USSR that were obviously intended for Soviet ears. Despite the decision to diversify the sources of Egypt's arms supplies, he told a Kuwaiti newspaper, he was aware that there was no substitute for the USSR in this field.[32] He even admitted to Egyptian newspapermen, within less than three weeks after the announcement that Brezhnev intended to visit Egypt, that understanding was increasing and relations improving.[33] After Fahmi's visit to Moscow, during which Brezhnev's trip to Cairo was scheduled for January 1975, Sadat told a press conference (in Rabat) that relations were now good and that 'other matters' would be clarified when Brezhnev arrived in Egypt.[34]

Soviet officials and sources carefully fostered Egyptian hopes regarding Brezhnev's visit. A senior Soviet Middle East expert, Igor Beliaev, said that the two leaders would be discussing co-operation in the military field ('the strengthening of Egypt's defence capabilities') as well as economic and other questions. In an interview to the Lebanese *an-Nahar* he made clear, too, that Moscow still considered Cairo the main bulwark of the Palestinians and the natural centre for their political activity.[35] Late in December another senior commentator, Pavel Demchenko, wrote that although the private sector had been reactivated and measures were being taken to attract financial assistance from the capitalist countries, there could be no rejection of the progressive path Egypt had taken in recent years. The political atmosphere in Egypt and indeed throughout the Arab world was favourable to all-round co-operation with the USSR.[36] Throughout December the Egyptian press applauded the USSR and its policy in the Middle East, while Sadat reiterated that the new relationship with the USA was not to be at the expense of Cairo's relations with Moscow. If Kissinger's step-by-step diplomacy proved unsuccessful, Cairo would adhere to the Soviet policy of an immediate reconvening of the Geneva Conference.[37]

Meanwhile, a number of indications denoted an improvement also on the level of practical politics. Some of the long-delayed Soviet arms were said to be reaching Egypt.[38] From 12 to 17 December, Soviet naval units paid an 'official, friendly visit' to Alexandria for the first time since July 1972.[39] Although on the very eve of Brezhnev's planned visit Fahmi and War Minister Abd al-Ghani al-Jamasi were invited to Moscow only to be told of its postponement,[40] the atmosphere surrounding their talks seemed to indicate a new mutual understanding.

An expression of this goodwill was Sadat's statement early in January that he was convinced that the reasons for the postponement were justified,[41] in other words that they were irrelevant to considerations of Soviet–Egyptian relations: whether they were connected with Brezhnev's health or other matters such as problems within the Soviet leadership does not concern us here. The Egyptian president also admitted that the two sides agreed during Jamasi's visit to Moscow in December that the USSR would supply some of the weaponry Cairo was demanding, although the equipment agreed upon compensated neither for all the arms lost in the October War nor for the development of the Israeli arsenal since then, but rather reactivated agreements made before October 1973. All the matériel that had reached Egypt from the USSR between 22 October 1973 and January 1975, Sadat pointed out, was the small quantity paid for by Algerian President Houari Boumedienne during the war and small amounts of ammunition and spare parts.[42] Nonetheless in January and February 1975 — despite Sadat's visit to France in late January, reported to be a first step in a five-year plan to re-equip the Egyptian armed forces with Western arms — major items of Soviet weaponry, including MiG-23s, arrived in Egypt.[43]

Gromyko's visit to Cairo of 3–5 February seemed, however, to mark a return to the situation in the months before the announcement of Brezhnev's visit, although both Sadat and Gromyko still publicly asserted that the visit would take place. Even before Gromyko's arrival Sadat had been criticising the Soviet Union for the postponement of Brezhnev's visit. He had insisted that the questions outstanding — military aid, trade agreements, repayment of the Egyptian debt to the USSR, a Soviet nuclear reactor — would be settled when Brezhnev finally came to Egypt.[44] Meanwhile, he alluded to the possibility of Soviet involvement in domestic unrest in Egypt — Marxist students had been arrested in demonstrations at Cairo University on 2–4 January 1975 — and expressed doubts whether Soviet arms supplies to Egypt would indeed be renewed, especially in view of Moscow's past refusal to supply weaponry, and showed his irritation at the refusal to grant a moratorium on Egypt's debt to Moscow. Sadat even said he could not rule out the possibility of abrogating the Friendship and Co-operation Treaty, yet this had to be examined from the point of view of Egyptian interests and especially military dependence on the Soviet Union. By the end of January too, Sadat was saying that during Fahmi's and Jamasi's visit to Moscow in December — which he had earlier described as opening a new page in relations with the USSR — the Soviet leadership had shown no understanding of Egyptian policies, particularly regarding the Geneva Conference.[45] Now, during his visit to Cairo, Gromyko was reported to have protested against the misrepresentation of Soviet aims and attitudes by both 'high political levels . . . and . . . Egyptian information elements well known for their links with America and historically hostile to Egyptian–Soviet relations'. Gromyko was said to have told his hosts that Moscow had actually resolved to postpone the payment of the Egyptian debt, but had changed its mind in view of Egypt's purchase of arms from Britain, not only at a higher cost than Soviet arms but also in hard currency. Moreover, Gromyko insisted that the Soviet Union had the right to reprove Egypt for these Western arms purchases, as it had to be consulted (by virtue of the Treaty) on Cairo's major foreign policy measures, even though Egypt was an independent state. As a friend, the Soviet Union considered it had a duty to warn Cairo against US plans in the area. Gromyko denied any 'fundamental difference' in the view of the two sides on the US role, although Egypt was counting on a 'new, more flexible and more objective understanding on the part of the United States', and the USSR was convinced that despite its declarations Washington still considered that Israel's task was to implement America's political objectives in the Middle East, as evidenced by 'increasing military and financial support for Israel'. The US step-by-step diplomacy, moreover, contradicted Arab interests, as it was intended to destroy Arab solidarity and isolate the Arabs 'from their friends in the world, and first and foremost from the USSR'. The USA, Gromyko was said to have told Cairo, was not exerting pressure on Israel to make a total withdrawal but helping it to evade solving the basic problems and separating the Sinai from the Golan Front. Moscow still considered that in the long run the Soviet Union and Egypt were 'in the same trench in confrontation with Israel and America' and that their relationship was essentially one of 'strategic friendship' that should not be 'reduced to the level of mere tactics', i.e. seen merely in the light of US initiatives. The Soviet foreign minister assured his hosts that his government was 'prepared to discuss all economic and military problems'.

Egypt, for its part, according to 'informed diplomatic sources' in Cairo, was ambivalent about its own path. The military was thought to be pressing for Soviet military equipment, doubting the viability of the 'diversification' of arms supplies for a country in a state of war, since the USSR alone could ensure the air bridge that was vital when hostilities broke out. At the same time, the civilian leadership sought to give Kissinger another three or four months to 'obtain something reasonable' through bilateral negotiations before calling for a renewal of the Geneva Conference.[46]

Sadat explained the connection between his stand on the Geneva Conference and his demand for arms in a lengthy interview with *al-Hawadith*'s chief editor, Salim al-Lawzi. Just as he — and Nasir before him — had demanded large quantities of sophisticated weaponry to enable Egypt not only to go to war but also to proceed towards a peaceful settlement of the Middle East crisis from a position of strength, so now he wanted Egypt's stockpiles to be replenished as a *sine qua non* for going to Geneva. The Egyptian president denied that he desired to eject the USSR from the region; on the contrary, Egypt needed a Soviet presence to prevent a return to a US monopoly in the handling of Middle Eastern affairs. He had indeed sought to terminate the situation that had arisen after the Six Day War in which Egypt had authorised Moscow to represent it at the superpower level, specifically in the USSR–US talks on the settlement of the crisis, and as a result of which the Soviet Union had become Egypt's patron in the international arena. Yet the fact that he had neither abrogated the Treaty of Friendship and Co-operation, despite Soviet violations of some of its stipulations,[47] nor retracted the Soviet naval facilities, showed that he did not desire the USSR's departure from the area. All Sadat wished was to return to the pre-1967 relationship in which Egypt had been an independent partner and had carefully preserved its neutrality regarding East and West alike. The Soviet Union's fabrications that he sought to eject it from the area, that socialism no longer existed in Egypt and that Saudi Arabia demanded the abolition of socialism and the ASU were simply the USSR's reaction to his repudiation of its patronage.[48]

The failure of the Kissinger mission at the end of March 1975 to achieve a second Egyptian–Israeli agreement seemed to tilt the balance once more in favour of an improvement of the Soviet–Egyptian relationship. Sadat was quick to reassert that the Egyptian–Soviet relationship was 'one of principle, not one of seizing opportunities or an ephemeral friendship'; he hoped, too, that this was Moscow's attitude.[49] He told an NBC correspondent that he still hoped to meet Brezhnev in Cairo to discuss the entire range of their relationship.[50]

Although the USSR's diplomatic activity in the weeks following Kissinger's failure showed it was fully aware of the opportunities presented to it, it was unwilling or unable to meet Cairo's requirements. This applied particularly to the moratorium on the Egyptian debt. During his Moscow visit in April, Fahmi told his hosts that Egypt, because of its economic circumstances, was unable to pay its debts. Cairo could not pay instalments in 1975 of the order it had paid in the past – not even 1974. The Egyptian foreign minister was told that his government's request had been rejected as an attempt to impose conditions on the USSR.[51] Sadat pointed out that this was merely accepted practice for war-stricken countries; the Soviet Union itself had paid only a symbolic sum of its debt to the USA for aid received in World War Two under Lend-Lease. Nor could he understand why Syria had been granted a moratorium. Asked whether he could not use funds from the oil-producing Arab states to repay his debts, he said this money was earmarked for economic development which would eventually contribute to this end, but could not be so used directly.[52]

The entire question of Egypt's debt to the USSR and its repayment has not yet been systematically analysed. There can, however, be little doubt that estimates such as 8, 6, or even 4 billion dollars include both the economic and military debts accumulated over the years. Many of the contacts between Egypt and the Soviet Union since October 1973 have centred on how much of the debt Egypt would repay and how quickly. The haggling that has preceded the annual trade agreements has shown the importance Moscow attributes to receiving the payments due to it both because of its need for the actual returns on its investments and because of the political pressure involved, especially given Egypt's strained economy. The greater amount of Egyptian exports in the years beginning 1974 reflects these repayments. The sums involved have clearly exceeded the interest due on the economic debt, i.e. have covered either the interest or part of the principal on the military debt as well. (Although the USSR has continued to include in these arrangements some $50 million worth of aid, the Egyptian export figure has exceeded that of the Soviets by approximately $200 million.[53])

Soviet efforts to promote a Middle East settlement, specifically by reconvening the Geneva Conference, were likewise futile. Meanwhile, the US administration 'reassessed' its Middle Eastern policies, which, together with preparations for President Ford's meeting with Sadat in Salzburg in June, brought about a new spate of Egyptian–US goodwill. The renovated rapprochement between Cairo and Washington demonstrated at Salzburg and after[54] resulted in a further deterioration of the Moscow–Cairo relationship. However, while *Pravda* published another stringent attack on the Egyptian press for distorting Soviet policy in the Middle East so as to arouse anti-Soviet sentiment in the Arab world,[55] the Soviet government invited a high-ranking Egyptian economic delegation to the USSR for negotiations on the Egyptian debt.[56] Sadat said the invitation had been motivated by rumours that he was intending to abrogate the Treaty of Friendship and Co-operation and added that in his opinion there had been no substantial change in the Soviet–Egyptian relationship since July 1972, apart from 'tactical manoeuvring'.[57]

Presumably, moreover, the renewal of Kissinger's mission had the most negative impact on the Soviet–Egyptian discussions of a possible reconsolidation of the Egyptian debt. As a CPSU Central Committee paper pointed out in an article entitled 'The Struggle for the New Egypt', describing Egypt's economic achievements in the wake of Soviet and East European aid: 'It is not only a matter of how much and what Egypt is producing today with the aid of co-operation with the Soviet Union and the other socialist countries. The main thing is what political purpose this co-operation serves'.[58]

The Secretary of State arrived in the Middle East on 21 August and remained until after the signature of the second Egyptian–Israeli disengagement agreement on 1 September. Indeed, this agreement infuriated the Soviet leadership, as expressed in a vicious offensive in the Soviet media. Not only was it – like its predecessor – the result of a diplomatic process which excluded the USSR; it also provided for US observation devices and brought US technicians to man them. Moreover, the second agreement led to official statements by the US administration on a certain commitment to giving military aid to Egypt[59] and in October, to an official visit by Sadat to the USA.

Throughout September, Sadat described the USSR's stand on the interim agreement as 'an open provocation' and an attempt to split Arab ranks. He again surveyed the historical background of the 'misunderstanding' and blamed the current crisis on the Kremlin: the efforts he was prepared to make for the sake of friendship with Moscow – it was only for that reason that he had gone to Geneva in December 1973 – were not being reciprocated.[60] A few days before his trip to the USA, the Egyptian president repeated his interest in maintaining 'balanced relations' with the USSR, the USA and 'everybody else'. He called upon Moscow to prove its understanding of this 'balanced' position instead of seeing it as a pro-American stand.[61]

The Soviet Union was not sympathetic. On the very eve of Sadat's departure for Washington, *Pravda* published – under the authoritative signature of 'Observer' – one of the most vehement attacks on the Egyptian government and press that had as yet appeared in the Soviet media. The CPSU daily stressed that the 'diversified' political, economic and military support the USSR had extended to Egypt since the 1952 revolution had been vital to that country's political and economic independence. *Pravda* insisted that the main economic achievements of revolutionary Egypt had been made possible by Soviet economic aid (the Aswan High Dam, the Hilwan metallurgical plant, land reclamation, etc.), while Soviet military aid enabled these gains to be protected from the 'imperialist machinations of the former colonial powers', the struggle against which 'was closely interwoven with the exceptionally complicated interrelationships of the states situated in the Middle East area . . . Israel's expansionist ambitions enjoyed the support of the forces of international imperialism and Zionism'. This had been shown in 1956, 1967 and 1973; since the October War too, 'the Soviet Union has been consistently pursuing the course of promoting friendly co-operation with Egypt in the military field under the existing agreement. But . . . co-operation cannot develop if one of the sides follows the line of undermining it'. As to the Treaty, 'the main political document which determines the character of Soviet–Egyptian relations', *Pravda* denied that it had been arbitrarily imposed on Cairo by the Kremlin, as Sadat had constantly claimed.

'Observer' also considered the question of a Middle East settlement, to achieve which 'a relevant international mechanism' had been set up. While he did not reject partial or intermediate measures, provided they constituted 'a component, organic part of an all-embracing settlement' and were 'worked out and adopted within the framework of the Geneva Conference', he opposed using Geneva as 'a smokescreen for approving steps undertaken to obviate the Conference'. Herein lay 'the fundamental difference' between the Soviet position and that of those who 'under cover of the step-by-step policy, actually led to freezing the situation . . . and perpetuating the Israeli occupation of Arab lands'. The recent agreement 'blunted the urgency' of liberating both the rest of Sinai and the territories of other Arab countries and dealt a blow at efforts to ensure the legitimate, inalienable rights of the Palestinian Arab people. The introduction of US personnel, moreover, was a development which, as the Vietnam precedent had demonstrated, was 'fraught with far-reaching and dangerous consequences'. It also undermined Arab unity, as against Soviet emphasis on 'the importance of the cohesion of the Arab states and the strengthening of their united action in the struggle against continued Israeli aggression'.

The USSR, 'Observer' concluded, still sought to preserve 'all the good things achieved' through Soviet–Egyptian friendship and even to 'deepen and enrich [it] further . . . on the basis of the community of interests in the struggle against intrigues by the forces of imperialism and aggression and for peace and the independence and social progress of nations'.[62]

Towards the end of the year discussion on the Egyptian debt was reopened as part of talks on the 1976 trade protocol. Cairo maintained it was doing its best not to sever relations with the USSR.[63] Yet Sadat made it clear that he was being sorely tried. Moscow, he said, had indeed exerted pressures on Egypt and was continuing to do so. Before, it had desired to prevent Egypt from going to war; now, it sought preferential status and the repayment of Egypt's military as well as its economic debts. Early in the new year (1976) in an interview with the Kuwaiti *as-Siyasa* Sadat again raised the issues of the Egyptian military and economic debts and of the weaponry losses which the USSR had refused to replenish even though Cairo was prepared to pay.[64]

Those traditionally associated with a pro-Soviet position in the Egyptian media and in debates on Egypt's orientation in both the domestic and international arenas seemed in the early weeks of 1976 to be making a last, rather unconvincing stand. *Ruz al-Yusuf* stressed the importance for both sides of co-operation as well as their common interests and stands on basic issues and accused the USSR of strengthening by its short-sighted policies precisely those in Egypt who sought to undermine its position there.[65] Lutfi al-Khuli, one of the prominent figures of the Egyptian Left, published a lengthy article after a visit to the Soviet Union during which he had discovered that the Soviet–Egyptian relationship was being publicly debated there, too. Journalists and friends in Soviet party circles and research institutes of the Academy of Sciences had told Khuli that Moscow sought continuation and development of the Egyptian revolution which it still regarded as being of vital importance in the Middle East. The Soviet Establishment appreciated that Nasir had chosen Sadat as his deputy, and that Sadat was not only one of the architects of the revolution but had the power to further it — together with the Egyptian masses. Moreover, despite Soviet appreciation of the progressive social and economic measures Nasir had taken, these had not been considered as making Egypt socialist but rather as advancing the country on an anti-capitalist path. It followed that Soviet circles did not consider Sadat's coming to power a reactionary development. At the same time Egypt was still a class society, which meant inevitable contradictions of interest and a struggle over the country's development; yet this was Egypt's own affair and the Soviet Union would respect the choice of its people. The USSR's continued faith in Egypt under Sadat even after the events of May 1971 had resulted in the Treaty of |Friendship and Co-operation.

As to Egypt's rapprochement with the USA, this was a vital and natural tendency in a world of co-existence. The Soviet objection was to the balance Cairo sought between the two superpowers. The USSR was a socialist power which did not strive to impose monopolist interests or opportunist investments and had helped Egypt in time of both war and peace to develop its economy and strengthen its armed forces. Reciprocity and mutual interest must determine the nature of relationships between states and not attempt to reach an equilibrium; the USSR did not place its own friendship with Egypt on the same level as its friendship with Western states.[66]

Another article, appearing in *Ruz al-Yusuf*, also noted that the state of Soviet–Egyptian relations attracted considerable attention in the USSR. The Soviet media had been instructed not to publish any material antagonistic to Egypt, although it was known that in Egypt the media were printing anti-Soviet articles. The basic sympathy for Egypt had not changed. The article stressed that Soviet officials as well as the man in the street pointed out the traditional friendship between the two countries, which had been a symbol of the relations between the socialist camp and the newly independent states and had made its mark in the international arena. People in the USSR did not think it feasible that relations could deteriorate so considerably as a result of disagreement over the Egyptian debt and arms supplies since, in their opinion, the relationship was deeper and more comprehensive. The *Ruz al-Yusuf* correspondent agreed that the main complaint heard in Moscow about Egypt was that it had ungratefully and unjustifiably deprived Moscow of the fruits of the October War and was co-operating with the USA to reach a settlement without the USSR, thus weakening the Soviet position in the entire region. He disagreed, however, with Lutfi al-Khuli on the Soviet view of Egyptian socialism, saying that it was widely considered in the USSR that Egypt had been socialist under Nasir, which made doubts about current 'openness' and encouragement of Western capital all the more poignant. As to the Egyptian debt, his Soviet acquaintances pointed out that the Soviet Union itself was in considerable economic difficulties; moreover, if Moscow made far-reaching concessions to Egypt, other developing countries would demand the same.[67] This argument did not, of course, answer Sadat's query why the USSR had agreed to a moratorium on the Syrian debt.

Even Sadat appeared to be associating himself with the adherents of Egypt's traditional pro-Soviet tendencies. Early in February, in a statement published in a Lebanese newspaper on the problem of relations with the USSR, he said he had decided for the moment to mitigate his attacks on the Soviet Union in order to examine the possibility of renewing the dialogue with the Kremlin.[68] This may have meant that he was considering suggestions for improving relations or at least waiting for the 25th CPSU Congress at the end of the month. It may also have been a final attempt to secure a concession on his debts, or even a tactical position in the domestic situation: after new demonstrations by students and other groupings, Sadat retreated from an earlier proposal to permit the establishment of political parties and announced instead the forming of 'theoretical platforms' within the ASU,[69] declaring in the process that the regime was moving towards freedom of the press and political organisation.[70]

However, towards the end of February on the eve of his departure for Jidda to secure large credits from Saudi Arabia and then from the other oil-producing Arab states to help extricate Egypt from its economic difficulties, Sadat again attacked Moscow — this time in an interview with the Saudi newspaper '*Ukaz*. The Soviet Union had failed to replenish war material lost in October 1973; it had rejected requests for a moratorium on the military debt and to reschedule payments on the economic debt for 10—15 years; it had sought to prevent the 1973 war and had sold Egypt second-rate military equipment; and it had incited Arab states and regimes against one another (Syria against Egypt, Syria against Iraq, Egypt against Libya).[71] It was later stated that on his tour of the Arab Persian Gulf states Sadat had complained of the limitations imposed upon him by the USSR and the difficulties inherent in his relations with Moscow. There was said to have been agreement on the need to abrogate the treaty for two reasons: that Arab policy necessitated avoiding international axes so as to ensure maximum manoeuvrability and that no state could maintain an agreement that did not bring it at least as much benefit as disadvantage.[72]

A storm was, indeed, brewing, although the Soviet leadership seemed to have no inkling of its implications or severity. True, Brezhnev in his address to the 25th CPSU Congress put Egypt last on the list of Arab states singled out for special mention. Yet his description of the role played by the 1971 Treaty was ample indication that he did not take Sadat's rantings seriously. After stressing continuous Soviet support of the Arabs and attacking those who were 'using the escalation of a partial agreement to put back the time of real decisions', the secretary-general said:

Certain forces have made persistent attempts to undermine Soviet—Egyptian relations. As far as the USSR is concerned, we remain true to the principled line of strengthening them. This is reflected in the treaty of friendship and co-operation . . . which we see as a long-term basis of relations meeting both the interests of our countries and the entire world.[73]

It is possible that Moscow got wind of what was in store only at the very last minute; it was later reported that the USSR suddenly offered Sadat all the sophisticated weaponry and spare parts he needed — but the offer was rejected: it had come too late.[74]

Two weeks after the CPSU Congress events came full circle. It seems that Sadat's decision to abrogate the Treaty unilaterally was a function not only of Washington's demonstration of goodwill but also of its ability to implement its commitments: in addition to increasing economic contacts, the Ford administration had overcome congressional opposition to the supply of military equipment — at this stage C-130 transport aircraft. Perhaps the Egyptian president's step reflected that he too had overcome domestic opposition: he announced, simultaneously with the abrogation, that no far-reaching changes would take place within the existing socio-political order. He attributed the abrogation to Soviet political interference in Egypt's domestic affairs, such as a statement by the Soviet leadership to Sami ash-Sharaf as early as March 1971 that Sadat was liquidating the Egyptian revolution,[75] and to the intolerable economic and political pressures which Moscow had placed on Egypt since Nasir's time. Indeed, the last straw had been Moscow's prohibition of Indian help for Egypt in the very sensitive sphere of aircraft maintenance.[76] It was clear, Sadat said, that the USSR intended to bring Egypt to its knees by exacerbating the country's economic crisis and making its military equipment unusable. The exploitation of 'the fact that the Soviet Union is the stronger party', either to implement and honour the Treaty or to ignore it, according to Soviet interests, left Sadat no alternative but to abrogate it.[77]

Speaking to officers and men of his Second Field Army, Sadat said the Treaty had caused the relationship to become abnormal, as it had enabled the USSR to violate Egypt's sovereign rights as an independent state. Sadat took exception to Brezhnev's speech at the CPSU Congress in which he had split the Arab world into blocs, with his comrades — Syria, Iraq, Algeria and the Palestinian Resistance — on one side and Egypt on the other.[78] The Egyptian president pointed out that since July 1972 the relationship had been tense, with only brief interludes of relaxation. He had repeatedly told Moscow that Egypt took pride in its independence and the exercise of its national will and opposed any attempt at patronage. Yet the Soviet Union had interfered openly in Egypt's domestic affairs and accused Cairo of throwing away the achievements of its revolution. Moscow had criticised Sadat's decisions to diversify his sources of military equipment, although this had been made necessary by the Soviet refusal to replenish matériel lost in the October War, and open up his country economically, socially and politically, although this was essential for Egypt's development. Sadat noted on the occasion the sharp distinctions the Kremlin had drawn between Egypt and Syria on the question of military supplies.[79] He also pointed out that the Soviet Union itself had concluded agreements with the West, notably the USA and Germany, to purchase the most advanced technological knowhow and equipment in agriculture and industry and insisted that Egypt's openness had not meant alignment with the West — just as before Egypt had not been aligned with the East.[80]

The debate on the abrogation of the Treaty in the Foreign Affairs Committee of the People's Assembly raised a number of new points concerning the relationship. Some reservations were even expressed about the abrogation. Muhammad Abd as-Salam az-Zayyat, chairman of the Egypt–USSR Friendship Society, feared it would have an adverse effect on the USSR's economic projects in Egypt, adding that entire cities subsisted on this co-operation. A representative of the Left, Yusuf Abu Sayf, chief editor of *at-Talia*, said he would vote against the abrogation, since until recently the USSR had been Egypt's principal source of arms. Good relations should be pursued with Moscow because future relations with the USA and the West were uncertain; he reminded the committee that Israel still held Sinai.

On the other hand, Mahmud Abu Wafiya of the centre — the Arab Socialist Platform of Egypt — said that the Treaty's abrogation would make no difference to Egypt's economy. The Soviet Union would not take any drastic economic measures against Egypt for fear of minimising chances of reducing the Egyptian debt and perhaps endangering the country. Moreover, economic pressure was already being exerted. For example, he pointed out, only three turbines were operating at the High Dam, the others being paralysed for lack of spare parts. The USSR refused to repair these turbines and even demanded interest on Egypt's military debts. Foreign Minister Fahmi said Sadat had considered all the aspects of the situation, the main ones being Soviet violations of the Treaty. These included attempts to intervene in Egypt's domestic affairs, pretensions to patronage over the Egyptian revolution, permission to Soviet Jews to emigrate to Israel as a condition of Moscow's trade agreement with the USA, a grinding insistence on repayment of debts, a disregard of Sadat's Notes, and failure to meet commitments concerning enterprises Moscow had helped to set up.[81]

Despite indications of opposition, the ASU Central Committee not surprisingly endorsed the abrogation. Its announcement censured the Soviet leadership for appealing to the Egyptian people in a futile attempt to maintain a dialogue with it. Sadat, the announcement pointed out, always spoke for the people of Egypt and expressed its will.[82] The increasing references to Soviet interference in Egyptian domestic affairs and especially to the Soviet appeal to the Egyptian people over the heads of the country's leadership may well have been allusions to the re-formation in July 1975 of the Egyptian Communist Party which sought to lead a popular struggle against the regime's policies. Just as the disbandment of the party eleven years before had been a function of the Soviet–Egyptian rapprochement, so its renewal should, or perhaps even must, be seen as a reflection of the Soviet – Egyptian crisis.[83] In the context of Communist activities in Egypt, People's Assembly Speaker Sayyid Mar'i in fact accused the USSR of attempting to sabotage the Egyptian domestic front. Communist material had been confiscated that announced the creation of the Communist Party Organisation with the aim of reuniting workers and students and unifying the Marxist groupings in Egypt so as to be able to change the regime.[84]

The abrogation of the treaty was followed by the annulment of the naval facilities the USSR retained in Egyptian ports. [85]

In distinction to the July 1972 decrees which Soviet officialdom – and Western commentators – made out to have been desired by the Kremlin at least *post factum*, there was now no attempt to pretend that the abrogation was of any benefit to the Soviet Union. On the contrary, Moscow took up the cudgels. Sadat's decision seemed irrevocable and left Moscow with nothing to lose. On 15 March, TASS put out an official statement according to which:

This action by the President of Egypt is a new demonstration of the unfriendly policy towards the Soviet Union which he has been pursuing in practice for a long time. This puts a legal seal on a situation in which this policy has, in fact, paralysed the operation of the . . . Treaty . . . TASS is authorised to state that the responsibility for the consequences of the Egyptian leadership's policy as a whole towards the Soviet Union in recent years, and for the abrogation of the . . . Treaty . . . rests entirely with the Egyptian side. The Soviet Union has pursued and will continue to pursue a principled, consistent policy designed to develop friendly relations with the Arab Republic of Egypt and with the Egyptian people.[86]

A massive offensive was now unleashed in the Soviet media against Sadat's Egypt. One of *Izvestiia*'s senior commentators, Viktor Kudriavtsev, explained the abrogation of the Treaty — Soviet sources were understandably reticent on the issue of naval facilities — as designed to pave the way for Egyptian arms purchases in the USA and Western Europe and Egypt's inclusion in the Western sphere of influence. He claimed that relations with Moscow had been deteriorating since Sadat had become president and opened the Egyptian economy to private enterprise and international capitalism; Saudi Arabia, moreover, had given considerable economic assistance to Egypt on the condition that it adopted an anti-Communist and anti-Soviet policy. He denied that Cairo's current orientations and measures would help it overcome its economic difficulties. Finally, he again accused Egypt of conducting an anti-Arab policy by abandoning the struggle against imperialism and Zionism, as evidenced by the second separation of forces agreement.[87]

The Soviet provincial press listed the economic and military salvation the USSR had brought Egypt over a long period of time and even took up some of Sadat's charges, denying in particular that Moscow had ever interfered in Egyptian domestic affairs. It accused Sadat of actually creating enormous economic difficulties for his country and weakening its military potential. It was stressed that those Egyptians who still hoped for good relations, suggesting that the Treaty's abrogation changed little in the relationship, were not being realistic.[88]

True, Soviet officialdom sought to convey that in the sphere of economic relations, notably of technical co-operation (the construction and equipment of industrial enterprises in Egypt), no change had occurred. Moreover, it continued to appreciate Egypt's significance as the most important Arab state and the axis of relations between the Arab world and the USSR. Yet it seemed that as long as Sadat's regime remained there was no future for the Soviet–Egyptian relationship. As ex-ambassador to Moscow Hafiz Ismail was reported to have said, this relationship had been damaged both by objective circumstances and emotions which would impede any effort to improve it. Soviet experts were quoted as saying that the only precedent of a similar nature was the Nazi abrogation of the Soviet–German Treaty of 1939.[89]

The relationship between the Soviet Union and Egypt had been intense and many-sided for over fifteen years when Nasir died in September 1970. It had been one of the major factors of Middle East politics and perhaps the most important factor of Egyptian foreign policy. The vitality and flexibility of this relationship had been especially apparent after the Six Day War when the USSR penetrated the main fields of Egyptian life: political, economic, military and social. In so doing it formed direct ties not only with Nasir but also with most of the important figures in his entourage, especially those who were connected with the main centres of power, the various intelligence services and police agencies which controlled Nasir's Egypt.

Nasir's death and the ensuing struggle for power between Sadat and the Nasirite leaders of the different power centres, which led to the ousting of the latter, were a rude shock to Moscow. In order to ensure continuing Soviet influence in this key country, the Kremlin decided to formalise the relationship in a comprehensive Treaty of Friendship and Co-operation. Yet regional developments combined with domestic constraints made Sadat unable and unwilling to play the game according to the rules which Nasir had abided by. He was determined to show that he was capable of restoring what his predecessor had lost in 1967 and he was not prepared to accept Nasir's axiom — after the latter had felt himself slighted by Washington — that the only major power with which Egypt could co-ordinate its policies was the Soviet Union. It could be argued that the personal factor which largely determined Nasir's ultimate dependence on the Soviet Union (his wounded pride because of American treatment) also shaped Sadat's pro-American orientation. Sadat seems to have felt insulted by the Kremlin's apparently low estimation of his leadership on the Egyptian, inter-Arab and international levels. The personal factor was highlighted in constant demands that Brezhnev come to Cairo, references to Soviet disregard for his Notes and his insistence that Moscow had been no more considerate towards Nasir. It may also account for what often seems like his provocative goading of the Soviet leadership.

Even before October 1973 Sadat had begun making overtures to the West, and especially the USA, concerning negotiations over an Arab—Israeli settlement and economic aid. In the former sphere there seemed little room for co-operation, given Egypt's position of inferiority after the Six Day War that necessarily limited its ability to progress towards a settlement on anything like its own terms. In the economic sphere, however, Sadat and his advisers considered that much could be gained from Western entrepreneurship. Indeed, they attributed Egypt's economic difficulties largely to Soviet economic aid and its concomitants and thought that a complete conceptual breakthrough in the country's economic management was necessary to end Egypt's technological and economic backwardness.

After the October War, rapprochement with the USA was considerably facilitated. The recovery of some of the territory lost in 1967 and the military achievement at the beginning of the war gave Sadat the prestige necessary to enter into negotiations as an equal. The USA, for its part, was more than willing to play the role of arbitrator, and a period of a new tie between Cairo and Washington began.

The USSR, already on the defensive following Sadat's decisions of July 1972, was not prepared to be allotted its role by the president of Egypt. It rejected Sadat's right to choose the partner to help him implement his policies, in particular when the choice fell on its major competitor both in the realm of a political settlement of the conflict, in which Moscow insisted that the Soviet Union must be a full and equal partner, and in the restoration of the Egyptian economy. The USSR held a number of trump cards which it proceeded to display. In the first place the Soviet Union had been appointed co-chairman — with the USA — of the Geneva Conference that was to supervise the advance from the ceasefire to a settlement. Secondly, it was the sole supplier of sophisticated weaponry to Egypt (and Syria), its airlift during the war having proved to the Arabs the unreserved Soviet commitment to their cause. Thirdly, in the economic sphere, the Soviet Union had not only built numerous plants which had still to repay their construction costs, but was still active in the establishment of several major industrial undertakings. Finally, the USSR had considerable influence in the entire economic sector which had been largely developed for two decades according to Soviet conceptions and criteria.

Moscow began to apply pressure. It was least successful in the attempt to settle the Arab–Israeli conflict. Yet, although blatantly unable to prove indispensability at all stages of the peacemaking process, the USSR sought to demonstrate its potential as troublemaker by inciting other Arab elements to see Egypt's steps towards a settlement as betrayal of the Arab cause, and by supporting the Palestinian organisations, for which the Soviet Union remained the sole powerful protector. It also sought to bring home to Cairo the benefits to Syria of Soviet participation in the negotiations that led to the Syrian–Israeli disengagement agreement. In the realm of military aid its pressures were more obviously effective although hardly more successful in the long run. It almost suspended military aid which, although not as crucial as before the October War, when Sadat had urgently needed large quantities of the best equipment at maximum speed, was still important, especially given the losses in the war, the futility of having weaponry without spare parts and maintenance requirements, and American arms supplies to Israel. In the economic field, too, Moscow enjoyed considerable leverage and delayed some of the economic and technical aid which Egypt was expecting. Even more serious was its refusal to put a moratorium on the Egyptian debt and its adamancy in getting its pound of flesh. In view of the size of this debt, and Egypt's desire to manifest credibility as it wooed Western investors, this was a very powerful weapon. Finally, there were indications of Soviet support, even if indirect, for Sadat's domestic opponents, as well as outright encouragement of his adversaries in inter-Arab politics. The leftist forces that persistently emphasised Egypt's need of a continued Soviet alliance were in constant contact with Moscow. Asad, Arafat and Qadhdhafi at various periods enjoyed greater and more open support.

In this way Soviet–Egyptian relations deteriorated steadily from October 1973 to March 1976, apart from a few months late in 1974 and a few weeks in the spring of 1975. From an analysis of these developments it can be seen that while the issue of a settlement of the Arab–Israeli conflict was a major cause of dispute between Cairo and Moscow, given Egypt's increasing connection with Washington on this very score, it was surely not the sole one and cannot be considered separately. The growing American orientation of the Sadat administration, which was the central point of controversy, seems primarily the result of domestic trends and of the belief held by Sadat and his closest advisers that the evils of Nasir's rule and the troubles their country was suffering emanated from the Soviet connection and presence. At first Sadat seemed to have hoped to preserve a balance between the USA and the USSR and to benefit from the support and aid of both superpowers. Moscow, however, was not willing to concede its status as traditional and closest ally, apparently assuming that it had sufficient hold on Egypt to prevent Sadat from cutting the Gordian knot. But Sadat was not prepared to accept Soviet conditions and dictates. The outcome was his abrogation of the Treaty of Friendship and Co-operation and annulment of Soviet port facilities. Thus Moscow lost its dominance in the Middle Eastern country where it had done most to ensure its influence and power. The superpower/client relationship between the USSR and Egypt, so carefully and systematically built up, had been demolished.

Notes

1. For the conclusion of the May 1971 Treaty see Yaacov Ro'i, *From Encroachment to Involvement. A Documentary Study of Soviet Policy in the Middle East, 1948–1973* (Jerusalem: Israel Universities Press, 1974), pp.548–52. For the domestic Egyptian context of the signing of the Treaty, see P. J.

Vatikiotis, 'Egypt's Politics of Conspiracy', *Survey*, XVII, 2 (83) (Spring 1972), pp.83–99.

2. See Ro'i, 'The USSR and Egypt in the Wake of Sadat's "July Decisions" ', *Slavic and Soviet Series* (Tel Aviv), 1 (September 1975).

3. For the Egyptian situation and Sadat's policies and options in the post-October War period, see Shimon Shamir, 'Egypt after the Yom Kippur War: A Provisional Balance Sheet', *The Wiener Library Bulletin*, XXVIII, New Series, 35/36 (1975), pp.57–64. Sadat laid down his new course in the 'October Paper' presented to a joint meeting of the ASU Central Committee and the Egyptian People's Assembly on 18 April 1974. See e.g. *R. Cairo*, 1 May 1974/*SWB IV*, 3 May 1974.

4. The state or public sector was not, of course, abolished, but was now shown to be a practical necessity rather than an ideological dictate. Indeed, there does not seem to have been any significant shift in practice towards the domestic private sector. Most private sector investment is foreign. See Eliyahu Kanovsky, 'Recent Economic Developments in the Middle East', *Occasional Papers* of The Shiloah Centre for Middle Eastern and African Studies, Tel Aviv University (June 1977), p.11.

5. The oil producers' great wealth had suddenly become highlighted and their political impact enhanced by their use of the oil weapon; see Dina and Martin Spechler, 'The Soviet Union and the Oil Weapon: Benefits and Dilemmas', in this volume.

6. In the short run the first and third of these factors might have precisely the opposite effect, i.e. of dragging Egypt into a war with Israel. However, any serious attempt to grapple with the economic situation can be presumed to operate against such a tendency; so too must the inevitable apprehension that a growing militancy, let alone an actual military confrontation with Israel, would increase Cairo's dependence on other Arab states.

7. See Galia Golan, 'The Arab–Israeli Conflict in Soviet–US Relations', in this volume.

8. Notably (i) the 11 November 1973 Egyptian–Israeli six-point agreement, including the exchange of prisoners (in which the USSR played no role); (ii) the opening of the Geneva Conference on 21 December 1973 under joint Soviet–US chairmanship in accordance with Security Council Resolution 338; (iii) the Egyptian–Israeli disengagement agreement of 17 January 1974 (in which the USSR again played no role); (iv) the Syrian–Israeli disengagement agreement of 29 May 1974; (v) Kissinger's failure on 28 March 1975 (in the effort to achieve a further Egyptian–Israeli agreement); (vi) the second Egyptian–Israeli disengagement agreement of 1 September 1975 (in which again the USSR played no role).

9. Both the existence and the degree of this commitment were made manifest in January 1970 and October 1973.

10. *Al-Ahram*, for example, on 3 April 1974 called for relations to be reconstituted on a new basis.

11. Sadat revealed later that Fahmi had twice contacted Moscow during the negotiations that led to the agreement (*R. Cairo*, 14 March 1976/*FBIS V*, 16 March 1976) presumably to show the USSR that Egypt still considered it a partner in implementing its policies.

12. TASS in English, 22 January 1974/*FBIS III*, 23 January 1974.

13. TASS in English, 24 January 1974/*FBIS*, 25 January 1975.

14. *Ruz al-Yusuf*, 28 January 1974.

15. *Al-Ahram*, 26 January 1974.

16. Joint statement on the talks – *R. Cairo*, 5 March 1974/*FBIS V*, 6 March 1974. For Gromyko's meeting with Arafat, see Baruch Gurevitz, 'The Soviet Union and the Palestinian Organisations', in this volume, p.259.

17. *R. Moscow* in Arabic, 2, 4 and 6 March 1974/*SWB I*, 5, 6 and 8 March 1974. In fact, the negotiations and agreements with the USSR on participation in clearing the Canal and rebuilding the Canal Zone and its devastated cities revealed both Soviet eagerness to be party to these processes and Egyptian preferences for the Western, notably the American, contribution to them.

18. The Egyptian debunking of Sadat's predecessor followed a purge of the Egyptian media and the reinstatement in prominent positions in the information services of men who had been ousted by Nasir, notably the Amin brothers. For the Soviet reaction, see *R. Moscow* in Arabic, 14 March 1974/*SWB I*, 18 March 1974. As the Egyptian media's criticism of Nasir intensified, especially in the last months of 1975, the Soviet media responded with an increasing *apologia* for the deceased president.

19. If hostility to Israel was the permanent major factor cementing the Arab countries, the principal instrument of implementing this unity *vis-à-vis* Israel's 'imperialist protectors' was the oil weapon. Its use had indeed brought the Soviet Union considerable political, as well as some economic, advantage and Moscow accordingly expressed great dissatisfaction at the indiscriminate renewal of the flow of Arab oil to the West. See Dina and Martin Spechler, 'The Soviet Union and the Oil Weapon', in this volume.

20. *R. Cairo*, 3 April 1974/*SWB IV*, 5 April 1974.

21. *R. Cairo*, 18 April 1974/*SWB IV*, 20 April 1974.

22. *R. Cairo*, 28 April 1974/*FBIS V*, 29 April 1974.

23. *Al-Hawadith*, 24 April 1974.

24. *Akhir Sa'a*, 1 May 1974. Hafiz al-Asad's Moscow visit of 11 to 16 April – intended in part to strengthen Syria's hand in the negotiations over its disengagement agreement with Israel and to emphasise that Syria was so strengthened as a result of its co-operation with the USSR – was indeed marked by a new arms deal and a long-term economic aid agreement.

25. Poliakov arrived in Egypt on 14 May and presented his credentials on the following day. Cf. Amnon Sella, 'Changes in Soviet Political-Military Policy in the Middle East after 1973', in this volume, pp.38–9.

26. *R. Cairo*, 22 and 26 June and 23 and 27 July 1974, and *MENA* 19 July 1974/*FBIS V*, 24 and 27 June 1974 and *SWB IV*, 25 July 1974.

27. *Ruz al-Yusuf*, 23 September 1974.

28. *Izvestiia*, 24 July 1974.

29. Brezhnev's first Note had presumably suggested that the summit take place in Moscow and the second, brought by Ambassador Poliakov (see above p.188) – following Sadat's rejection of a fifth trip to Moscow before Brezhnev came to Cairo at all – suggested preliminary talks to prepare the ground for the summit. A proposed visit to Moscow by Fahmi in July had been postponed, yet this was presumably the outcome of circumstances irrelevant to Soviet–Egyptian relations since a number of other visits of foreign ministers were put off at the same time.

30. Sadat told CBS chief commentator Walter Cronkite that Brezhnev would be coming to Egypt 'because I have visited the USSR four times' – *MENA*, 22 June 1974/*FBIS V*, 24 June 1974. For his July 1972 statement in which he called for 'an Egyptian–Soviet meeting at a level to be agreed upon, for consultations regarding the coming stage', see Ro'i, *From Encroachment to Involvement*, p.575. Sadat had renewed his invitation to Brezhnev when Gromyko visited Cairo early in March.

31. *R. Cairo*, 6 September 1974/*FBIS*, 9 September 1974; *al-Hawadith*, 11 September 1974. It was later announced that Brezhnev was due to go to Damascus and Baghdad as well.

32. *As-Siyasa*, 19 September 1974.

33. *Ruz al-Yusuf*, 23 September 1974. Previous references to relations being frozen – on 26 and 28 August – may well have referred not only to military and economic aid, but also to the Kremlin's hedging on Brezhnev's visit to Egypt.

34. *Al-Ahram*, 31 October 1974. Although the absence of any communiqué on the conclusion of the Fahmi visit was interpreted by observers to indicate the persistence of basic disagreements, it probably reflected Sadat's desire to leave fundamental questions to his own talks with Brezhnev. Egypt's rapprochement with the PLO late in September may have facilitated the improvement of its relations with Moscow, yet it was surely not a principal factor in this development.

35. *An-Nahar*, 4 November 1974.

36. *Pravda*, 28 December 1974.

37. *Voice of the Arabs*, 17 December 1974/*FBIS V*, 18 December 1974.

38. For Soviet arms supplies to Egypt, see Sella, 'Changes in Soviet Political-Military Policy', in this volume.

39. For the visit, see *Krasnaia zvezda*, 13 December 1974, and *R. Moscow* in Arabic, 18 December 1974/*SWB I*, 20 December 1974.

40. The two ministers visited Moscow from 27 to 30 December. In addition to talks with their respective counterparts, they were received by Brezhnev in 'a Moscow suburb' – *Voice of the Arabs*, 29 December 1974/*SWB I*, 30 December 1974.

41. *R. Cairo*, 2 January 1975/*SWB IV*, 4 January 1975.

42. In a later statement Sadat said the sole weaponry Egypt had received during these 14 months was within the framework of 'a tank deal' agreed upon 'earlier' and for part of which Boumedienne had paid during the war – *R. Cairo*, 1 May 1975/*SWB IV*, 3 May 1975.

43. *Al-Anwar*, 8 January 1975; *Le Figaro*, quoted by *MENA*, 24 January 1975; and *Ruz al-Yusuf*, 3 February 1975.

44. *Al-Hawadith*, 18 March 1975; for part of the story of Soviet arms supplies cf. Roger F. Pajak, 'Soviet Arms and Egypt', *Survival*, July–August 1975, pp.165–73.

45. *Al-Anwar*, 8 January 1975; *al-Bayrak*, 9 January 1975; *Le Monde*, 27 January 1975. The statement on the possibility of abrogating the Treaty, made to *Le Monde* just prior to Sadat's French visit, was presumably intended to give additional weight to his arguments in Paris.

46. *Journal of Palestine Studies*, IV, 3 (Spring 1975), pp.137–9, quoting *al-Balagh*, 10 February 1975.

47. While Sadat did not explain his accusations, a Lebanese newspaper had written almost a year before that Cairo interpreted the USSR's failure to consult with it either before or after Soviet–US summit meetings and its rejection of Egyptian proposals for a Brezhnev–Sadat meeting as violations of the May 1971 Treaty – *al-Usbu al-Arabi*, 29 July 1974.

48. *MENA*, 19 March 1975/*FBIS V*, 21 March 1975.

49. *R. Cairo*, 29 March 1975/*FBIS V*, 31 March 1975.

50. *R. Cairo*, 6 April 1975/*FBIS V*, 7 April 1975.

51. One Egyptian comment on Fahmi's visit described it as an attempt to salvage a relationship that was important to both partners. The Egyptians, it said, had been disturbed by the Soviet Union's withholding of economic aid (including industrial equipment and spare parts) and arms supplies and by its rejection of a moratorium; the USSR had been disturbed by the Egyptian domestic situation that it interpreted as hesitancy about the socialist option, by Egyptian collaboration with the USA in Kissinger's step-by-step diplomacy without even consulting Moscow, and by attacks on the USSR in the Egyptian media. The same source said that while Fahmi had failed to achieve any Soviet concession on the

moratorium, he had persuaded Moscow to review its economic assistance and reached a compromise formula regarding negotiations on an Arab–Israeli settlement that recognised the possibility of working towards a solution outside Geneva provided this were part of a general solution. It was also suggested that the reference to the May 1971 Treaty in the joint statement on the visit meant that the question of arms supplies had been satisfactorily solved – *Ruz al-Yusuf*, 28 April 1975.

52. *R. Cairo*, 1 May and *MENA*, 14 May 1975/*FBIS V*, 2 and 14 May 1975. For the Syrian moratorium, see Galia Golan and Itamar Rabinovich, 'The Soviet Union and Syria: the Limits of Co-operation', in this volume, p.219.

53. For further discussion of Soviet aid to Egypt, see Gur Ofer, 'Economic Aspects of Soviet Involvement in the Middle East', in this volume. It is perhaps of interest that Egypt has apparently not paid the entire sum laid down in the agreements; cf. *Ruz al-Yusuf*, 21 March 1977.

54. The Salzburg meeting was followed – still in June – by the appearance of the Sixth Fleet flagship in the Suez Canal on the day it opened to shipping and a subsequent visit to Alexandria; a State Department announcement that Washington had agreed to sell Egypt military vehicles and was considering the training of Egyptian officers; and new economic agreements covering US aid to Egypt.

55. *Pravda*, 15 July 1975.

56. The Egyptian delegation led by Finance Minister Ahmad Abu Ismail was in Moscow from 22 July to 2 August. The Egyptian side suggested fixing a period of grace in which no instalments on the Egyptian debt to the USSR would be paid and then drawing up a new schedule for repayment, taking the Egyptian economic situation into consideration. The Egyptian proposal seemed, however, to have been left pending. The Soviet side headed by First Deputy Minister of Foreign Trade Mikhail Kuz'min suggested for its part that Moscow continue participating in Egypt's economic and social development plans. It was agreed that Cairo would submit a list of projects to which the USSR would contribute. The topic would then be taken up again by the two sides and a date would be fixed for Kuz'min to visit Cairo – *MENA*, 23, 24, 25 and 30 July and 1 and 2 August 1975; *R. Cairo*, 1 August 1975/*FBIS III*, 25, 28 and 31 July and 1 and 4 August 1975. Soviet sources that mentioned the talks were silent on the issue of the rescheduling of payments – TASS in English, 2 August 1975/*FBIS III*, 4 August 1975.

57. *Al-Hawadith,* 21 August 1975.

58. *Sotsialisticheskaia industriia*, 23 July 1975.

59. For example, President Ford to *Los Angeles Times*, 25 September 1975.

60. *R. Cairo*, 4, 15 and 28 September 1975/*SWB IV*, 6, 17 and 30 September 1975; also *as-Siyasa*, 8 September 1975.

61. Sadat made one such statement to the Kuwaiti *al-Qabas, R. Cairo* 22 October 1975/*FBIS V*, 23 October 1975; also to *al-Hawadith*, which published the interview with him only on 31 October 1975.

62. *Pravda*, 25 October 1975.

63. *As-Siyasa*, 22 December 1975.

64. *R. Cairo*, 7 January 1976/*FBIS V*, 9 January 1976.

65. *Ruz al-Yusuf*, 12 January 1976.

66. *Al-Ahram,* 14 January 1976. The distinction the USSR admitted (even if unofficially) that it made between different categories of states with which it had bilateral relations is instructive to the western student of Soviet foreign policy. Lutfi al-Khuli wrote again on Soviet–Egyptian relations, with suggestions for their improvement, in *al-Ahram*, 21 and 28 January, 4 and 11 February 1976. In these articles, Khuli argued that the two countries had identical or at least

overlapping strategic interests which had to be the basis of their ties, and that their relationship was disturbed by technical obstacles, namely the lack of a common language, and problems not intrinsic to it, namely the attitude to the Geneva Conference and US step-by-step diplomacy.

67. *Ruz al-Yusuf*, 5 January 1976.

68. *Al-Hawadith*, 3 February 1976.

69. These were to give expression to the entire range of opinions in Egypt. Three platforms were indeed established in March 1976. The main, centre, one was called the Arab Socialist Platform of Egypt; the left-wing one – the Platform of the National Progressive Unionist Rally; and the right-wing one – the Socialist Liberal Platform. In November 1976 these platforms became separate parties (the word party being substituted for platform in their names), and the Arab Socialist Union was dissolved.

70. *R. Cairo*, 25 January 1976.

71. Ibid., 21 February 1976/*FBIS V*, 23 February 1976.

72. *As-Sayyad*, 29 April 1976.

73. TASS in English, 24 February 1976/*FBIS III*, 25 February 1976.

74. *Al-Watan* (Kuwait), 16 April 1976.

75. Sharaf had been one of the group that had sought to oust Sadat in May 1971 and with which Sadat had accused the Kremlin of collaborating.

76. After continuing Soviet refusals either to supply spare parts for Egypt's MiG-21s or to undertake the recurrent overhauling of the MiG engines, without which the planes would become 'scrap metal', Sadat had approached New Delhi, which had its own enterprises for the construction of MiG-21s. In February, 1976 four months after he had made his request, the Indians had told him that Moscow had forbidden them to supply spare parts or check the Egyptian engines – *R. Cairo*, 14 March 1976/*FBIS V*, 16 March 1976. Sadat had made a similar request to the Yugoslavs and the Chinese, but they did not have all the equipment he needed – *ANSA* (Rome) in English, 25 March 1976 and *MENA* in English, 26 March 1976 (quoting a Sadat interview with *Der Spiegel*)/*FBIS V*, 26 and 31 March 1976.

77. *R. Cairo*, 14 March 1976/*FBIS V*, 16 March 1976.

78. No such remarks, or remarks that could be so interpreted, appeared in the official text of Brezhnev's speech.

79. On different occasions, Sadat had expressed satisfaction at Soviet supplies to Syria, saying these strengthened the entire Arab potential. The very comparison, however, between Moscow's policy towards Syria and Egypt stressed discrimination against the latter.

80. *R. Cairo*, 22 March 1974/*FBIS V*, 23 March 1976.

81. *al-Akhbar*, 16 March 1976.

82. Ibid., 29 March 1976.

83. The party announced its re-formation in a 'political report' put out in July 1975 by its secretariat and published in August in the Lebanese press – *as-Safir*, 4 August 1975 and *al-Hurriya*, 11 August 1975. This document declared the party's intention to lead the day-to-day struggle of the proletariat, fallahin and working masses and to strengthen 'the national and progressive forces' so as to build 'a front of popular forces'. For the disbandment of the party in 1964 see Ro'i, *From Encroachment to Involvement*, pp.377–8. Cf. Oded Eran, 'The Soviet Perception of Influence: the Case of the Middle East', in this volume, p.142.

84. *MENA*, 30 March 1976/*FBIS V*, 1 April 1976.

85. *R. Cairo*, 4 April 1976/*FBIS V*, 5 April 1976. The USSR's naval units in fact left Alexandria on 15 April, the day fixed for the termination of facilities – *al-Ahram*, 16 April 1976. For the earlier termination of rights in Marsa Matruh, see Sella, 'Changes in Soviet Political-Military Policy', in this volume, p.64, n.93.

86. TASS in Russian for abroad and in English, 15 March 1976/*SWB I*, 17 March 1976.

87. *Izvestiia*, 4 April 1976.

88. E.g. *Sovetskaia Moldaviia*, 7 April 1976.

89. *Ruz al-Yusuf*, 28 June 1976.

8 THE SOVIET UNION AND SYRIA: THE LIMITS OF CO-OPERATION

Galia Golan and Itamar Rabinovich

Within a comparatively brief span, October 1973 to the spring of 1977, Syrian—Soviet relations completed what appeared to be an almost complete circle. The close co-operation of the October War and its aftermath was replaced by a period of tension which culminated in the latter half of 1976 but which was again replaced by renewed co-operation. A closer look at that relationship though, reveals that the differences between the three phases and the transition from one to the other were not all that marked. Relations between Syria and the Soviet Union were not free of problems during the first phase; tension between them was controlled, and their rapprochement has been qualified.

In addition to the intrinsic interest in Soviet—Syrian relations and the changes they have undergone, the course of this relationship in recent years raises a number of questions: Were the changes described above a product of the October War and its consequences or were they the result of earlier processes accelerated by the war? What was the interplay among Syria's domestic politics, its regional policy and international orientation? What explains the Soviet Union's cautious response to the changes in Syrian policy and what accounts for the course Syria's relations with the Soviet Union have taken as distinct from Egyptian—Soviet relations? What was Syria's place in the context of broader Soviet considerations? A detailed analysis of the period October 1973—December 1976 offers at least partial answers to these questions.

Soviet—Syrian relations in the period under review are the latest chapter in a long and often misconstrued relationship which goes back to the mid-1950s. The earlier phases of this relationship are only remotely linked to recent and current developments, but the first ten years of Ba'thi rule in Syria (1963—73) and particularly the years 1970—3 had a more direct impact on this period. Three characteristics of the USSR's relationship with Ba'thi Syria seem to have crystallised during the years 1963—70: (1) from its first days, the Ba'thi regime conducted an 'anti-Western' policy, and from 1965 it drew closer to the Soviet Union, but a stable consistent relationship failed to develop

between Syria and the USSR. Rather, relations between the two
countries were subject to sharp changes within comparatively short
periods; (2) in periods of co-operation relations could be very close and
intimate, but even during such periods the Syrians jealously guarded the
independence of their decision-making process; (3) comparatively little
reliable information has become available about Soviet—Syrian relations
during this period, probably due to the secretive nature of both
political systems.

The first three years of President Hafiz al-Asad's regime did not
bring far-reaching changes in Soviet-Syrian relations. Asad did not seem
to be disturbed by the fact that in the internecine Ba'thi struggles of
the years 1969—70 the Soviets and the Syrian Communists had lent
their support to his rivals. When Asad finally won in November 1970
and established his regime, he formulated his foreign policy according
to perceived interests rather than sentiments. The Soviet Union was
Syria's major source of external support in the conflict with Israel, as
well as its major arms supplier. Moreover, co-operation with the Soviet
Union suited the image that the Asad regime sought to project.

While Asad was interested in continued co-operation, the Soviets
were anxious to consolidate their position. They pressured Syria to sign
a treaty of friendship like the ones signed by Egypt (in 1971) and Iraq
(in 1972) and later by Somalia and others. But Asad insisted on the
appearances as well as on the essence of independence and rebuffed
Moscow's proposals. Still, relations continued to develop, and in 1972
they seemed to assume a greater importance with the expulsion of
Soviet military advisers from Egypt and the signing of a large Soviet—
Syrian arms deal. With the decline of the Soviet Union's position in
Egypt — and the loss of Soviet air bases there — Syria was to move into
a more significant position in Soviet strategic considerations. Syria had
generally played a secondary role in Soviet policy in the Middle East,
Egypt and Iraq having been of greater strategic and political importance.
Whilst Moscow may well have been planning to enlarge its facilities and
role in Syria as part of its overall effort to strengthen its position in the
Middle East, the troubles with Egypt — apparent at least as early as 1971 —
most likely prompted the Soviets to develop Syria as an alternative,
even if temporary, to Egypt. Hence the 1972 arms deal, the beginning
of Soviet military expansion in Syria in the form of the project to
enlarge Syrian ports so as to accommodate Soviet ships, and the
building of air bases, particularly in north-east Syria. While the major
purpose was Moscow's own strategic interests (facilities and air support
for its Mediterranean squadron), these undertakings, as well as
economic and political contacts, were implemented with a degree of

publicity designed to counter the negative conclusions which might be drawn regarding Soviet—Arab relations in the wake of the Soviet—Egyptian difficulties.

At the same time these strategic benefits carried a political price: good relations with the ruling party tended to be at the expense of the local Communist movement. This type of problem had long been characteristic of Soviet policy in the Third World in general, and had often appeared in Soviet relations with the Syrian Communist Party in particular.[1] In the 1970s the principal issue was the local Communist Party's opposition to joining a national front with the Syrian Ba'th, primarily because such an alliance clearly marked the Communists as *junior* partners and in fact limited them to a large degree. The Soviets prevailed, however, and, despite splits and arguments within the Syrian Communist Party, the latter joined such a national front in 1972. The party's internal problems over Moscow's dictates persisted, however, and were aggravated by the opposition of some to the Soviets' line regarding the Arab—Israeli conflict as well.[2]

War and Disengagement: October 1973—June 1974

The composite nature of the Soviet Union's relations with Syria was illustrated by the events of the period immediately preceding the October War. There were several reports of complaints and disagreements, the details of which have not been confirmed, though it is quite clear that some friction between the two countries arose in September 1973.[3] The theory that these apparent strains were part of a well-planned disinformation effort was belied by Soviet behaviour at the time and seems most unlikely.[4] The most significant facts are that, like the Egyptians, the Syrians informed the Soviets of their war plans only a few days before the event, probably on 4 October, so that the Soviet Union saw no alternative but to go along with plans in the preparation of which it had not directly participated.[5]

During the war the Soviet Union was quick and generous in resupplying the Syrian army. But as far as major strategic decisions were concerned the Syrians painfully realised that their interests were subordinated to those of Egypt. Reportedly, the Soviet Union had agreed prior to the war to a Syrian request that it respond with a ceasefire proposal forty-eight hours after the outbreak of war.[6] The Soviets did in fact make such a proposal to the Egyptians some six hours after hostilities had begun and again the following day, with the claim that Syria had so requested. While the Syrians have yet to confirm, deny or elucidate their part in those early Soviet ceasefire bids, they did complain when the ceasefire was actually arranged on 21 October 1973. Purportedly planning a counterattack together with Iraq, Asad complained in a speech on 29 October 1973 that the Soviet–American proposal had caught him by surprise.[7] Moreover, the ceasefire resolution was based on Security Council Resolution 242 which until this time Syria had not explicitly accepted.[8] Although he may have been kept informed of Moscow's proposals to Egypt during the war, Asad does not appear to have been as direct a party to Soviet steps in those days as Sadat, who apparently played a much more important role in Soviet calculations at the time.

The tensions produced in Syrian–Soviet relations by the course of the October War were soon overshadowed by the far more significant political developments which followed it. The beginning of negotiations towards a settlement of the problems created by the October War, the efforts to settle the Arab–Israeli conflict and the assumption of an active and prominent role in these matters by the United States all had diverse repercussions on the Soviet–Syrian relationship. The Soviet Union and Syria were brought closer together by their common suspicion of the United States and of Egypt's motives and conduct. Moscow was concerned over the American role, the prospective rise in American influence and the expected further drift of Egypt – and possibly other Arab states – into the American orbit. Damascus for its part was particularly worried lest Egypt be the sole Arab beneficiary of Washington's initiatives. It suspected that Egypt's commitment to its wartime ally might weaken or even disappear once Egypt's own demands were met.

At the same time, however, Syria did not dispute the soundness of Egyptian policy. If it were proved that Washington was able and willing to bring about Israeli withdrawals, Syria was not opposed to regaining Israeli-held territories through American mediation. While Syria was unwilling to follow Egypt in dissociating itself from the Soviet Union and did not show the same diplomatic flexibility, it was ready to deal with the United States, through Egypt or directly. This was clearly manifested when, during Secretary of State Kissinger's visit to Damascus in December, agreement was reached for the opening of interest sections between the United States and Syria. It was a first step towards renewed diplomatic relations and a significant indication that Syria's position between the two superpowers was amenable to change.

During the last months of 1973 and the first half of 1974 Soviet–Syrian relations were governed by two specific issues: the Geneva Peace Conference and the Syrian–Israeli disengagement agreement. Moscow and Damascus were divided on the issue of Syria's participation in the Geneva Conference. The Soviet Union, for its part, vigorously pursued the idea of a peace conference in the wake of the war — a conference to be based on Security Council Resolutions 338 and 242. Its motivation was simple and obvious — it was a co-chairman of the Geneva Conference and as such was interested in promoting this theatre of activity to the detriment of the United States' and Kissinger's active single-handed role. Syria's outlook, however, was different in two respects. Damascus did acquiesce in the general Arab line formulated at the Algiers summit conference and accepted the notion of an Arab—Israeli peace conference in principle. But it was determined not to attend the conference before it was reassured that Egypt was not making a separate deal with Israel and that Syria was not to be confronted with *faits accomplis* unacceptable to it. Throughout November and December 1973 the Soviet Union continued its efforts to allay Syrian fears and urge it to participate in the Geneva Conference. These efforts were to no avail, however, and the Soviets even seemed to have been poorly informed of Syria's intentions. As late as 15 and 17 December the Soviet media were reporting Syria's intention to participate, only to carry on 18 December Syria's announcement of its refusal to do so.[9]

The differences of opinion between the two were to continue even after the conference opened. At this stage they were caused not so much by Syria's suspicions of Egypt as by its objections even to the minor concessions which participation in a peace conference seemed to entail. The differences between the Soviet and Syrian perspectives in this matter were manifested on several occasions throughout the late winter and early spring of 1974. Thus, during Asad's important visit to the Soviet Union in April, Leonid Brezhnev, despite Syrian reticence, cited the Geneva Conference as the 'authoritative forum' for negotiations.[10] He went on to add, in the same context, a demand for 'reliable guarantees for security for all the countries of the Middle East' and a few lines later 'ensurance of *security and sovereignty for all the states* in the area' — phrases which were usually designed to reassure Israel with regard to the more radical Arab demands.[11]

Persistent as these differences of opinion were, they were overshadowed in the months of February to May 1974 by Soviet—Syrian co-operation in an effort to secure an advantageous disengagement agreement for Syria. The stage for this phase was set by the signing of the Egyptian—Israeli disengagement agreement in January. Syria's turn came next and Moscow saw both the need and the opportunity to play an active role and to demonstrate that its client fared at least as well, possibly better, than the friends of the United States. These aims were to be achieved in a number of ways. The Soviets obviously decided that the negotiations for a Syrian—Israeli disengagement would not follow the pattern of the Egyptian—Israeli agreement from the point of view of exclusive American mediation. Thus they sought to have these negotiations in Geneva or, failing this, to ensure that the Soviet Union at least *appeared* to be playing a role, primarily by means of an unprecedented dovetailing of Soviet Foreign Minister Gromyko's visits to the area with those of Kissinger. Just how much of a role Moscow actually would play and what type of role this would be, i.e. for, against, obstructive, etc., was another matter. In the early period of negotiations the Soviet Union seemed willing enough to credit Kissinger with efforts to gain disengagement, reserving for Gromyko's journeys the task of seeking a genuine settlement of which disengagement was said to be only a minor, albeit constructive part — so long as it was not substituted for a settlement itself, as Israel and America were liable to attempt.[12] Thus belittling Kissinger's efforts — without, however, objecting to them — Soviet domestic and foreign propaganda argued that the Arabs had and could achieve progress towards fulfilment of their demands not because of a change in Israeli or even American thinking but because of the firm support received from the Soviet Union. This was not a new argument, but it was intensified in the spring of 1974 as Moscow directly responded to what it called imperialist (or Western, Zionist or Chinese) slanders that the Soviet Union was not taking an active part in the search for a settlement, thereby abandoning the Arabs' cause in the interests of détente with the United States or some other superpower objective.[13] This was primarily a tactic whereby the Soviets increasingly supported the more radical wing of the Arab world, mainly Syria but also the PLO for example, both so as to offer something the Americans could not or would not offer, and to bring pressure upon Egypt as the rift between Moscow and that country grew.

Moscow's preferential support of Syria and its policy manifested itself in two major ways. One was an endorsement of Syria's hard-line position at a time when Syria was launching its war of attrition on the Golan Heights. Gromyko's speeches during his visits to Damascus were definitely more militant than his statements in Cairo, as was the communiqué that was published at the close of his second visit to Damascus in March 1974. The communiqué insisted on the need for a timetable of Israeli withdrawal and on the Arabs' right to use 'any means', namely force, in order to regain their rights.[14] More importantly and concretely, the Soviets ostentatiously delivered large quantities of weapons and equipment to Syria in April 1974 — including the coveted MiG-23s and at that time reportedly granted Syria a twelve-year moratorium on repayment of its military debt.[15] Moscow's prominent display of its good relations with Syria was capped by an official visit by Asad to the Soviet Union on 11–16 April 1974 which was hailed both then and much later as a significant step in the relationship. During this visit, the Soviets publicly referred to the arms deal and to Soviet military aid in general, at the same time delivering the strongest attacks to date on Kissinger's 'partial settlements' (Brezhnev called them 'ersatz plans').[16] While this could hardly be construed as Soviet encouragement of Syria to agree to disengagement, it might have been meant as opposition to the agreement offered (ostentatiously and exclusively by Kissinger) at that time, i.e. Israeli agreement to withdrawal from the territory taken in the 1973 war only. The Egyptian disengagement agreement suggested that this was probably merely a starting point on Israel's part, to be followed by larger concessions, so that the Soviets may have felt safe in criticising the present proposal, relatively confident that a better deal would be forthcoming, for which they could claim credit.[17]

In the event, the Soviet Union's strategy certainly worked to Syria's advantage. It reinforced the other assets which Syria possessed during the negotiations and enabled it to emerge from them with achievements that were comparatively more impressive than those of Egypt. From the Soviet Union's own point of view the results were mixed. Moscow's participation in and impact on the process of negotiations were at least more salient than in the Egyptian case. Thus, Gromyko and Kissinger met in Geneva on 28–29 April just prior to the arrival in the Middle East of both foreign ministers on 4 and 5 May respectively. The two ministers met again in Cyprus on 7 May, as Gromyko returned home from Syria, and once more on 28 May after his arrival in Syria on the 27th — immediately before the announcement of the disengagement agreement. Whatever co-ordination had existed between the Soviets and the Syrians throughout May, however, apparently did not last until the final phases of the negotiations. The completion of the talks and final agreement were achieved in a manner which played into the hands of Kissinger, who again appeared as the architect of disengagement. The only concession to the Soviets was the signing of the agreement in Geneva and, indeed, Brezhnev was to emphasise the need to return to the Geneva framework even as he welcomed the achievement of disengagement (attempting, of course, to claim a share of the credit for its successful conclusion).[18]

Transition to a New Syrian Policy: June 1974   September 1975

Many of the decisions and moves of the period October 1973—May 1974 were made in a rather hasty fashion. The unclear outcome of the war, the danger of renewed warfare, the pressures on the Egyptian and Syrian regimes to regain freshly lost vital territories as well as other factors led to the adoption of a series of measures which later had to be rationalised and placed in the context of a broader policy. In Syria's case the formal adoption of a new policy was done at a rather late stage, at the Twelfth National Congress of the Ba'th Party. The Congress was held in July 1974, and a communiqué containing some of the resolutions and referring to others was published in August.[19] While the Congress reaffirmed the fundamental principles of Syria's position in the Arab—Israeli conflict, it also formulated a 'transitional policy' which could facilitate the Syrian government's participation in negotiations for agreements, partial or more comprehensive, with the United States and Israel. The Syrian decision to continue with the step-by-step diplomacy under American auspices was taken primarily in the context of the Arab—Israeli conflict. Syria's leaders saw no reason to object to a modality which, they well realised, could lead to further Israeli withdrawals in return for minor concessions. But in the event, this new policy affected Syria's international orientation as well. It entailed closer relations with the United States and, consequently, a measure of strain in Syrian—Soviet relations.

This became apparent during the first few weeks which followed the signing of the Syrian—Israeli disengagement agreement. Thus the Soviet Union watched with growing concern President Nixon's visit to Syria, the resulting renewal of US—Syrian diplomatic relations and, in August, the visit to Washington by Foreign Minister Khaddam. Accompanying this was President Asad's assertion of Syria's right to modify its policy, when he referred in an interview to 'differences between friends and to his country's right to enter into other friendships in the world'.[20] The Soviet Union, in turn, emphasised its contribution to the achievement of the disengagement agreement and any progress towards a settlement as well as the solid long-term nature of Soviet—Syrian friendship. In a sterner manner the Syrians were frequently advised 'to discern the existing dangers and to distinguish between friends and foes'.[21]

It was not, however, Soviet opposition which obstructed or restrained Syria's rapprochement with the United States but rather the course which American diplomacy in the Middle East took in the summer of 1974. Early in the summer Washington decided, in co-ordination with Jerusalem, Cairo and Amman, that the next round of negotiations was to consist of an Israeli–Egyptian agreement followed by an Israeli–Jordanian one. Syria's turn was to come only later. The Americans probably reasoned that the difficulties involved in arranging a second agreement on the Golan were likely to delay, possibly even obstruct, the whole negotiating process. It was also felt that by bringing about a Jordanian–Israeli agreement with Egypt's implicit blessing, Jordan's position as 'the state concerned' with regard to the West Bank could be assured. All of this was unacceptable to Syria. Together with the PLO Damascus forced Egypt to change its position in August, and then won a greater victory when its position was adopted by the Rabat summit conference in October. These developments also suited the interests of the Soviet Union, but they were accomplished by the Syrians who effectively manipulated inter-Arab relations without much recourse to Soviet aid.

The resolutions adopted at the Rabat summit conference delayed and hindered the American efforts to bring about a second Egyptian–Israeli agreement. But the efforts continued all the same and for almost a year, from October 1974 to September 1975, they provided the main focus of diplomatic activity associated with the Middle East conflict Both the Soviet Union and Syria followed the course of these diplomatic efforts with suspicion. This proximity of outlook brought the two countries closer together as did their common support of the PLO. But full co-ordination of policies did not occur and symptoms of strain as well as differences of opinion over the nature of a general settlement with Israel and the Geneva conference remained evident

One instance of Soviet–Syrian Co-operation occasioned by a congruence of interests concerned the renewal of the United Nations observers' force (UNDOF) mandate in November 1974. Possibly the joint strategy was worked out during Asad's talks in Moscow on 26–27 September and 3 October 1974 on his way to a from North Korea. Presumably the Soviets agreed to support a Syrian policy which sought to create uncertainty and tension with regard to Syria's willingness to renew the mandate. The Soviet Union reinforced Syria's activity in a number of ways. Soviet propaganda included comments on the need for Syria to raise its combat readiness and for it friends, such as the Soviet Union, to be prepared to repel Israeli aggression. The Soviets continued arms deliveries and still more provocatively sent a naval contingent on an official visit to Latakia

(20–25 November).[22]

Yet the Soviet Union's past behaviour when hostilities were expected suggested that it did *not* in fact take its own alarmist reports seriously.[23] Rather, its policy seems to have sought to exploit the convergence of the Vladivostok Soviet–American Summit and the UNDOF mandate's renewal date. The atmosphere of tension, maintained until the Syrians announced the renewal of UNDOF two days after the Vladivostok talks, could be used to underscore the urgent need for an overall settlement and the essential role of the Soviet Union in pressing the United States for this.[24]

Soviet and Syrian outlooks and policies were less compatible in other instances. Thus, when Foreign Minister Khaddam visited Moscow in April 1975, the Soviets apparently sought to gain agreement on their three-pronged 'basis' for a settlement, i.e. Israeli withdrawal, Palestinian rights and guarantees for all states in the area. The first and the third of these were the problematic points with Syria, including as they did implicit recognition of Israel (at the very least), thereby ruling out only any aspirations Syria might have for a Greater Syria (the concept which saw Palestine including present-day Israel as southern Syria), but also, apparently, territorial ambitions that went beyond the 1949–67 borders of Israel. The fact that the Soviets sought to convince the Syrians specifically on the issue of Israel's right to exist was demonstrated by the particular emphasis given in Gromyko's speech honouring Khaddam. Gromyko not only included the third clause, i.e. the guaranteed existence of all countries, but even went so far as to specify Soviet willingness to provide 'strictest guarantees' to Israel itself.[25] While this was not a new position from the Soviet point of view, its emphasis on this occasion indicated the Soviets' intention to have their position understood by the dissenting Syrians. That the Syrians were in fact dissenting was indicated by the absence of any reference whatsoever to the third clause from the final communiqué issued with Khaddam.[26]

Moscow apparently also made it clear to the Syrians that it saw the territories occupied in 1967 as the limits of Arab demands, for although Gromyko himself spoke only more generally of Israeli withdrawal from territories 'of other countries' and 'of others', the communiqué on Khaddam's talk with Brezhnev did specify the 1967 territories. More significantly, both the Soviet media and the Arabs themselves were to explain Gromyko's comments as a commitment to an Israel within its 1949–67 borders. For example, *Izvestiia* commentator Matveev gave this interpretation in a long Moscow radio discussion of Gromyko's remarks, and George Habash's paper *al-Hadaf* referred critically to the speech as a declaration by the Arabs' 'ally to guarantee the borders of Israel, as defined by the 1967 frontiers'.[27] The Soviets' position on Israel's borders (1949–67 lines or the 1947 partition plan lines) was and has remained unclear; indeed, even as Brezhnev and Gromyko were making the above statements, a series of articles appeared in *Izvestiia* referring to the 1947 lines.[28] Yet the official presentation by Brezhnev and Gromyko to visiting Arab officials (and rumoured to have been presented to the Israelis as well)[29] would indicate Moscow's *preference*, at least, as the basis for approaching a renewed conference – a preference sufficiently strong to dictate this difference of opinion with Syria (and the Palestinians).[30]

Less visible at the time but of greater significance for the future were the two countries' responses to Egypt's separate dealings with the United States. The Soviet Union's response was varied: efforts to pressure and tempt Egypt, a shift of attention to alternative clients in the area and an emphasis on an overall settlement and the Geneva Conference. Syria, for its part, sought to build a power position that would be based on three foundations: the development of Syria's military potential; the promotion of military co-ordination on the Eastern Front under Syria's hegemony; and the acquisition of political influence over two of Syria's Arab neighbours – Jordan and Lebanon – as well as over the PLO.

This power position was to free Syria from its dependence on Egypt – so painfully manifested in 1973 and 1974 – and to enable it to take military and diplomatic initiatives of its own. The development of a military potential entailed a continuation of good relations with the Soviet Union, but seen from a broader perspective the whole process signified a further Syrian drift out of the Soviet orbit. The diplomatic initiatives which Syria's rulers had in mind were oriented towards the United States, which had already demonstrated its ability to bring about Israeli concessions. These trends were given further impetus by the signing of the second Sinai agreement in September 1975 and by the turn of events in the Lebanese civil war early in 1976.

Syrian–Soviet Relations: September 1975–December 1976

Developments in the final quarter of 1975 and during the first few weeks of 1976 followed what had by then become a familiar pattern: common Soviet and Syrian denunciation of a separate Egyptian–Israeli agreement reached under American auspices, followed by a divergence in diplomatic strategy and further Syrian drift away from the Soviet Union. The common denunciation of the Sinai Agreement and the anxiety about its potential impact on the respective interests of the Soviet Union and Syria brought Asad for an unexpected visit to Moscow on 9–10 October 1975. Not much is known about the visit, which was of a practical rather than a ceremonial nature. The joint communiqué published at its close was singularly uncommunicative. But subsequent developments would indicate that the visit failed to produce a co-ordination of policies.

A divergence in diplomatic strategy soon became apparent when Syria initiated a discussion of the Palestinian issue at the Security Council (which eventually took place in January 1976). Essentially this initiative was a repetition of the tactics employed successfully in the summer of 1974; the very raising of the issue of the Arab–Israeli conflict at the UN, which US step-by-step diplomacy was seeking to avoid, confronted Washington with a major dilemma. The Soviet Union took no exception to the blow thus dealt to American diplomacy and Egyptian policy nor did it object to the promotion of the PLO's interests. The Soviets were wary, however, of the prospect that the Syrian manoeuvres, by shifting the focus to the UN, would undermine the Geneva Conference as the framework for negotiations. Similar considerations led it to object to Syrian and Palestinian plans to amend Security Council Resolution 242 upon which the Geneva Conference was based.[31] Indeed, during the Security Council debate, even as Syria was criticising Egypt's position at the UN for opposing any change in Resolution 242, *Pravda* went so far as to praise the Egyptians for supporting the Soviet proposal for reconvening Geneva.[32] The Soviet Union refrained from supporting (or even reporting) the Syrian bid to amend Resolution 242, while trying to accommodate the Syrian–Palestinian demands by a proposal for a new resolution containing mutual recognition of Israel and Palestinian rights.[33] Presumably this Soviet stand was dictated not by some basic commitment to Israel, but by purely pragmatic, or what the Soviets considered 'realistic' considerations. The most obvious was that the United States was likely to veto any amendment to Resolution 242 or anything too binding on the PLO issue: more basically, however, the Soviet Union was probably acutely aware of how difficult it had been to obtain Resolution 242 originally, i.e. a framework open to different interpretations but potentially sufficient to bring the various parties to negotiations. Therefore it feared any tampering with that resolution and, in this connection, any formal preconditions *vis-à-vis* Geneva at this time.

But perhaps most disconcerting from Moscow's point of view was the motivation behind the Syrian denunciation of the Sinai Agreement and the subsequent efforts to undermine it. The Syrians were offended by Cairo's readiness to make another separate agreement with Israel as well as Washington's assumption that it was best to deal with the Arab world primarily through Cairo. It was precisely in order to refute such notions that Syria had been building its power position in its immediate environment. From this point of view it became essential to discredit the Sinai Agreement. Hence Syria's political offensive in September and October which was designed to isolate Egypt in the Arab world. Such isolation was to undermine the Sinai Agreement and to impress upon the United States that it was best to deal *directly* with Syria, which conclusion could hardly be welcomed by Moscow. In addition, Syria initiated a discussion of the Palestinian issue before the Security Council, a measure which won the surprising support of the USA. Thus Syria succeeded in appearing, in contradistinction to Egypt, as the supporter of the Palestinian cause by bringing this core issue back on to the centre of the stage. Moscow must have realised that this Syrian policy was essentially directed towards the USA; nonetheless, since the Palestinian issue was involved, the Soviet Union obviously saw no option but to support it.

This slight shift in the direction of US–Syrian co-operation became much more ominous, from the Soviet point of view, in January 1976 with developments related to Lebanon. The Lebanese civil war had broken out in April 1975 and during its first seven months there were a number of common elements in the Soviet Union's and Syria's policies towards it. Both countries supported the Muslim–Leftist–Palestinian coalition, opposed partition and sought stabilisation. But Syria's direct intervention in the Lebanese civil war in January 1976 and the direction of its policy assumed during late winter and spring 1976 were most disturbing from Moscow's point of view. The Lebanese civil war provided the Asad regime with an opportunity to demonstrate that it was Syria rather than Egypt that could exercise effective influence in Lebanon. While this, as such, need not have disturbed Moscow, the target of this Syrian policy appeared to be the United States. And, indeed, Syrian policy with regard to Lebanon was not only directed, apparently, towards Washington, but was the basis for actual Syrian–American co-ordination. Moreover, when the Syrian effort to impose a settlement of the Lebanese civil war failed, the Syrian government decided that the vital interests and important goals involved in its Lebanese policy necessitated a forceful intervention against the Lebanese Left and the PLO. The Soviet Union thus had to face the situation of one Soviet client battering – for the wrong purposes – other Soviet clients, such as Kamal Jumblatt and Yasir Arafat, who were in turn being supported by Iraq and Libya (as well as to some extent by Egypt).

Apparently, it was largely in an effort to steer Soviet policy in the Middle East out of this impasse that Aleksei Kosygin went to Iraq and Syria at the end of May and the beginning of June 1976. The joint Soviet–Iraqi communiqué published on 31 May included an implicit criticism of Syrian intervention in Lebanon, stressing that 'the right solution to the Lebanese crisis can be reached by the Lebanese people themselves'.[34] But Soviet efforts to deter the Syrians from continued intervention in Lebanon and to persuade them to cease their pressure on the Palestinians and the Left were rebuffed. On the eve of Kosygin's arrival in Damascus he was confronted with an insulting *fait accompli*. Regular Syrian army units crossed the border into Lebanon during the night of 31 May–1 June and launched an offensive designed to subdue the PLO and the Lebanese Left. The timing of the invasion may not have been chosen in order to spite and embarrass the Soviet leadership, but the Syrian leaders were not willing even to soften the effect by changing the date. The explanation seems to lie in the great importance Hafiz al-Asad attached to the sovereignty of the decision-making process in his political system. Indeed, this is what he – and other Syrian spokesmen – said, in somewhat different language, when they were asked about the tension in their relations with the Soviet Union.[35]

The tension lasted throughout the latter half of 1976 and manifested itself in a number of ways. Soviet – and Syrian Communist – criticism of Syrian policy in Lebanon became explicit and frequent in the summer, while Soviet military supplies to Syria reportedly were affected.[36] In response, towards the end of 1976, the Syrians appeared to be considering cancellation of the port services accorded the Soviets in Tartus although they refrained from responding directly to Soviet criticism so as to avoid fully-fledged propaganda warfare with the Soviet Union. The Soviet decision to risk a crisis with Damascus cannot have been an easy one (and indeed, there may have been differences of opinion within the Kremlin on it, for generally speaking, *Izvestiia* did *not* join in the direct criticism of Syria). Having lost Egypt (which had abrogated its friendship treaty with Moscow in March), Moscow had only Syria as a 'client' amongst the confrontation states of the Arab–Israeli conflict. While the Soviets were steadily working to improve their relations with Jordan – indeed, King Husayn paid an apparently successful visit to the Soviet Union even as the Soviet–Syrian crisis was in full swing – they were still far from wooing Jordan away from the Americans.[37]

Moreover, Jordan was by now allied with Syria (which move had received Soviet approbation over the past year – probably in hopes that such an alliance would eventually sway Jordan to Syria's more radical pro-Soviet orientation rather than Syria to|Jordan's pro-West direction), and King Husayn supported Syria's policy in Lebanon. The Soviets were striving to strengthen their position with the more radical 'rejection front' of the Arab world, e.g. Iraq and Libya, both of which had long opposed Syria's efforts in Lebanon, but this option posed problems for Soviet aspirations regarding the Arab–Israeli conflict inasmuch as the 'rejection front' opposed Moscow's position on a settlement.[38] This is not to say that the Soviets did not hope to gain some points with these states by their anti-Syrian position, but it is unlikely that they saw such a trade-off as a wholly fruitful one on a long-term basis.

As to the PLO itself, here too Moscow's moves were almost inexplicable, for there was nothing in the Soviet–PLO relationship to suggest that Moscow saw this group as a more important, effective or even dependable ally than Syria. Indeed, there had been many signs that the last thing Moscow wanted was to be left with only the PLO, as distinct from the Arab states, in the context of the Arab–Israeli conflict – and the Soviet–American competition in this context. A plausible explanation of the Soviet move was Moscow's overriding concern over Syria's growing independence and possible collusion with the United States. Such concern was apparent also in the Soviets' efforts to dissuade the Syrians from participating in the |Riyadh Quadripartite Conference in late June 1976 which, the Soviets feared, might lead to a Syrian–Egyptian rapprochement. Nonetheless, the Soviets, like the Syrians, sought to limit the Moscow–Damascus dispute by refraining from any high-level criticism – a June 1976 announcement by TASS being the most official criticism beyond that expressed by the press or lower-ranking Soviet officials abroad.

This period of strain in Soviet–Syrian relations caused by the Lebanese war ended early in 1977. The tension was gradually alleviated, port services in Tartus remained unhampered, and a process of at least partial rapprochement began, which culminated in Asad's visit to the Soviet Union in April 1977. A number of factors contributed to this development, the most important of which was the fact that the temporary settlement of the Lebanese crisis and the political ceasefire

between Syria and the PLO–Lebanese Left removed the major
immediate source of friction in Soviet–Syrian relations. The Syrian
Ba'thi regime was interested, both for domestic and external reasons,
in ending the tension in its relations with the Soviets. Domestically, the
regime came under criticism from radical Ba'thi elements tied to Iraq
who accused Asad of adopting an increasingly conservative policy. It
was important for him to refute this charge. Externally, a continued
conflict with the Soviet Union ran against the grain of his foreign
policy. The Soviets, too, saw no benefits accruing to their Middle
Eastern policy from continued tension with Syria, particularly given the
renewed efforts by the Americans to achieve a Middle East settlement
with the advent of the Carter administration in Washington. The
rapprochement was not, however, total for the underlying problem of
Syrian independence, as well as the ongoing differences of opinion
regarding the nature of – and means of achieving – a Middle East
settlement remained.

Conclusions

The Syrian drift away from the Soviet Union since the October War was
determined by factors similar to those responsible for the sharper
westward turn of Egypt, i.e. Soviet infringements on national
sovereignty and Soviet inability to produce satisfactory results in the
context of the Arab–Israeli conflict. Syria, whose relations with the
Soviet Union, position on the Arab–Israeli conflict and domestic
political circumstances were different from those of Egypt, was
touched but not seriously affected by the same developments before
the October War. But as shown above, the October War, its outcome
and consequences, and the new conditions created in the Middle East in
its aftermath induced the Asad regime to reduce his country's
dependence on the Soviet Union.

Nonetheless, two major factors served to restrain the shift in Syria's
policy: (1) the Ba'thi regime's self view and the image it sought to
project prevented too close a rapprochement with the United States
and too dramatic a rift with the Soviet Union; and (2) the lesson
derived from Egypt's experience since 1972 indicated that it was more
advantageous to maintain relations with both superpowers. Thus Syrian
policy towards the Soviet Union during the three years under study was
conducted on two levels. The major trend was the steady movement
towards a more independent position, the pace of which was largely
determined by the course of the Arab–Israeli conflict and inter-Arab
relations. At the same time, Syria continued her co-operation and

co-ordination with the Soviet Union when there was a congruence of the interests of the two countries as, for example, at the time of the Israeli–Egyptian Interim Agreement.

Soviet interests in Syria tended to grow with the deterioration of Soviet–Egyptian relations, as the Soviets sought to replace Egypt as a strategic asset, as well as to bring pressure on it by means of augmented support for and involvement with Syria. Yet the Soviets too appeared to have been governed by certain restraints, inasmuch as Moscow was unwilling (as was the case, even more so, in Soviet–Egyptian relations) to make those concessions necessary to a continued close relationship, such as support for Syria's policy in Lebanon, and, at the same time unable to find suitable leverage even in the field of arms supplies, to limit Syrian independence (or to control Syrian decision making).

As for Moscow's strategic interests, these were moving somewhat beyond the immediate area of the Arab–Israeli conflict (e.g. to the Indian Ocean or even westward in the Mediterranean area); it is possible that the Soviet Union was beginning to view its stake in Syria as somewhat less important. Therefore, just as Moscow was unwilling to pay the price demanded by the Arabs for returning to Egypt or entrenching itself in Jordan, it may have been willing to risk severe problems with Syria when other, even tactical, considerations appeared to be more important. Nonetheless, the Soviet effort to limit – in time to end – the crisis with Syria suggested that Moscow still sought a foothold in the confrontation states, hoping still to play a role in the moves for a settlement of the Arab–Israeli conflict and thereby regain some active Soviet role in the area rather than forfeit it to the United States.

Notes

1. See John Cooley, 'The Shifting Sands of Arab Communism', *Problems of Communism*, XXIV, 2 (1975), pp.32, 33; Robert Freedman, 'The Soviet Union and the Communist Parties of the Middle East: An Uncertain Relationship', in Roger E. Kanet and Donna Bahoy (eds.), *Soviet Economic and Political Relations with the Developing World* (New York: Praeger, 1975); also Oded Eran, 'The Soviet Perception of Influence: The Case of the Middle East', in this volume.

2. Freedman, 'The Soviet Union and the Communist Parties of the Middle East', and 'Special Documents – The Soviet Attitude to the Palestinian Problem', *Journal of Palestine Studies*, II, 1 (1973), pp.187–212, in which the Syrian Communist Party was reprimanded for too positive an attitude towards the Palestinians.

3. *R. Damascus*, 5 December 1972/*SWB IV*, 7 December 1972 (Asad interview), *al-Jadid* (Beirut), 9 November 1973, cited by Moshe Maoz, *Syria Under Hafiz al-Asad: New Domestic and Foreign Policies* (Jerusalem Peace Papers,

1975), and *Le Monde*, 22, 23–24 September 1973. For this period in Soviet–Syrian relations see Galia Golan, *Yom Kippur and After: The Soviet Union and the Middle East Crisis* (London: Cambridge University Press, 1977), pp.21–73.

4. At the time the Soviets denied the existence of any problem, thus ignoring the Arabs' disinformation campaign if such indeed existed. *An-Nahar* (Beirut), 1 March, 1974; TASS, 3 October 1973.

5. *an-Nahar*, 1 March 1974 (Sadat interview); *R. Cairo*, 15 September 1975/*FBIS V*, 16 September 1975 (Sadat speech); *Ma'ariv* (Tel Aviv), 15 May 1975; Mohamed Heikal, *Road to Ramadan.*

6. *R. Cairo*, 15 and 28 September 1975/*FBIS V*, 16 and 29 September 1975 (Sadat's speeches); *Ma'ariv*, 15 May 1975; and alleged talk by Soviet Amabassador to Egypt Vinogradov, *as-Safir* (Beirut), 16 April 1974.

7. *R. Damascus*, 29 October 1973/*SWB IV*, 31 October 1973 (Asad's speech); *Le Monde*, 31 October 1973.

8. *R. Moscow*, 22 October 1973/*FBIS III*, 23 October 1973, quoted the Syrian ambassador in Moscow as announcing Syria's acceptance of Resolution 242.

9. *Pravda*, 15 December 1973; *R. Moscow* in Arabic, 17 December 1973/*FBIS III*, 18 December 1973; TASS, 18 December 1973/*FBIS III* 19 December 1973.

10. *Pravda*, 12 April 1974.

11. Ibid. See also Yaacov Ro'i, 'The Soviet Attitude to the Existence of Israel', in this volume.

12. Primakov on *R. Moscow*, 3 March 1974/*FBIS III*, 4 March 1974; *R. Moscow* in Arabic, 6, 7 March 1974/*FBIS III*, 7, 8 March 1974. See also editorial, 'For a Just Peace', *New Times*, 10 (1974), p.1 and 'Disengagement in Sinai', p.10; *Pravda*, 3 March 1974; *Sovetskaia Rossiia*, 27 February 1974; *R. Moscow*, 2 March 1974/*FBIS III*, 4 March 1974; *R. Peace and Progress*, 27, 28 February 1974/*FBIS III*, 28 February, 2 March 1974.

13. *Pravda*, 28 February 1974; *R. Moscow* in Arabic, 28 February 1974, 6, 8 March 1974/*FBIS III*, 1, 7, 11 March 1974.

14. *Pravda*, 8 March 1974. Asad said in a speech after Gromyko's departure that Syria would accept Resolution 242 if two conditions were fulfilled: total Israeli withdrawal and full recognition of the Palestinians' rights. He also said, however, that Palestine, including the present State of Israel, 'is a basic part of Southern Syria'. *R. Damascus*, 8 March 1974/*SWB IV*, 11 March 1974.

15. *INA*, 26 May 1974.

16. *Pravda*, 12 April 1974.

17. Soviet Middle East commentators **Igor' Beliaev** and **Pavel Demchenko** were to offer explanations of the term 'ersatz plans' which supported this interpretation. Demchenko explained that Israel was refusing to agree to a withdrawal from all the territories occupied both in 1973 and 1967 but was instead offering to withdraw only from the area occupied in 1973 – which offer he described as 'ersatz plans'. *Pravda*, 27 April 1974; See also P. Demchenko, 'The Middle East: From War to Peace', *Mezhdunarodnaia zhizn'*, 4 (1974), pp.85–8.

18. *Pravda*, 30 and 31 May 1974.

19. The communiqué is analysed in detail in I. Rabinovich 'Phases in Syria's Policy Toward Israel Since 1973', in A. Hareven (ed.) *Between War and Settlements* (Hebrew edition), Tel Aviv, 1977, pp.41–53.

20. *Al-Ahram*, 5 July 1974 in *Journal of Palestine Studies*, IV, 1 (Autumn 1974), pp.191–2.

21. R. Vasilyev, 'New Horizons of Soviet–Syrian Friendship', *International Affairs* (Moscow), 7 (1974), pp.85–8; see also V. Alexandrov, 'Middle East: A New Step Towards Peace', *International Affairs* (Moscow), 8 (1974), pp.86–8.

22. *R. Moscow* in Arabic, 18, 20 November 1974/*FBIS III*, 19, 21 November

1974. For arms deliveries see *New York Times*, 16 November 1974.

23. When hostilities appeared imminent, e.g. in 1967 and 1973, the Soviets usually moved their forces away from the area.

24. An interview with a Syrian CP leader (a staunch Soviet supporter) even held the implied threat that war would break out if the Geneva Conference were *not* reconvened. *R. Moscow* in Arabic, 18 November 1974/*FBIS III*, 19 November 1974.

25. *Pravda*, 24 April 1975.

26. Ibid., 27 April 1975.

27. *Al-Hadaf* (Beirut), 17 May 1975, quoted in *Journal of Palestine Studies*, IV, 4 (1975), p.146, and the Palestinian interpretation of the speech on p.145. Also *R. Moscow*, 27 April 1975/*FBIS III*, 28 April 1975.

28. *Izvestiia*, 12 and 15 April 1975.

29. *Le Monde*, 12 April 1975.

30. The Soviet position on the 4 June 1967 lines as Israel's legal borders was laid down after the October War by Gromyko at the Geneva Conference opening and repeated in an October 1974 article in *Mezhdunarodnaia zhizn'*. It was repeated by the same journal in February 1975 and again in March 1975 (all of these were also carried in the English-language version of the journal, *International Affairs*), and in a *R. Peace and Progress* broadcast in Arabic, 6 March 1975. The line in these articles was that Israel was missing an opportunity to have these boundaries recognised as the final legal borders. See Galia Golan, 'The Soviet Union and the PLO', *Adelphi Papers*, 131 (1977) and Ro'i, 'The Soviet Attitude to the Existence of Israel', in this volume, pp. 236–8.

31. The PLO demanded an amendment to Resolution 242 so that its attendance at Geneva could be accommodated by a change in the Geneva framework itself (to include a discussion of the Palestinian problem as one of national political rights rather than as a refugee problem, which was the 242 formulation). The Soviets had been opposing this PLO demand, see Baruch Gurevitz, 'The Soviet Union and the Palestinian Organisations', in this volume.

32. *Pravda*, 15 January, 1976.

33. *As-Siyasa*, 12 January 1976.

34. *Pravda*, 1 June 1976.

35. See, for instance, President Asad's interview with *Events* (London), 1 October 1976.

36. For criticism of Syria see e.g. *Pravda*, 10, 11, 12, 13 June 1976; *Izvestiia*, 12 June 1976; *Krasnaia zvezda*, 10 June 1976; *Trud*, 23 June 1976; TASS, 16 June 1976; Y. Tyunkov, 'The Lebanese Knot', *New Times*, 25 (1976), pp.14–15; Yuri Potomov, 'The Lebanon Crisis: Who Stands to Gain?' *New Times*, 26 (1976), pp.8–9. For an account of Brezhnev's letter to Asad, see *Ruz al-Yusuf*, 26 July 1976.

37. Indeed, the Soviets did not appear to be willing to pay the price necessary for such a success, for they reportedly demanded cash payments and the presence of Soviet technicians as part of the SAM defence system deal offered to Jordan.

38. There were chronic problems for Moscow in Iraq, not unlike those with Syria, some of which at various times were even connected with the Soviets' effort to juggle friendship with both Syria and Iraq. Soviet interests in Iraq, however, like those with Libya, were guided by other, strategic considerations rather than those of the Arab–Israeli conflict.

9 THE SOVIET ATTITUDE TO THE EXISTENCE OF ISRAEL*

Yaacov Ro'i

Soviet leaders and other officials have on numerous occasions claimed that their government recognises the Israeli state's right to exist as an independent and sovereign political entity. Moscow has, indeed, repeatedly insisted that neither the act of severing diplomatic relations with Israel on 10 June 1967 nor the refusal to renew them implies any reservations regarding this right of existence. Yet the fact remains that the USSR has not renewed relations with Israel at the time of writing (mid-1978). Moreover, it has been in the forefront of a political and diplomatic anti-Israel offensive that has intensified since the October 1973 War. It bears no small responsibility for Israel's virtual isolation in the international arena; it has given considerable support to the Palestine Liberation Organisation's campaign for legitimacy and international recognition and its demand for a Palestinian state, although refusing to endorse officially the PLO's call to replace Israel with a secular, democratic state encompassing all of Palestine; finally, Moscow has filled the Arab arsenals with large quantities of sophisticated weaponry for the declared purpose of war against Israel.[1]

The co-existence of two seemingly contradictory attitudes – the formal acceptance of Israel's existence side by side with the political and military support for Israel's enemies, some of whom deny Israel's right to exist, and seek to undermine its very existence – demands examination. In this paper I hope to clarify the intentions underlying these attitudes and so contribute to an understanding of the Soviet Union's policy towards Israel.

1. The USSR's Declared Position

Less than two months after the October 1973 War, Soviet Foreign Minister Andrei Gromyko told the opening session of the Geneva Conference of which the USSR and the USA were the official co-sponsors: 'Any document adopted by this conference must contain clear-cut commitments by Israel to withdraw from all territories occupied in 1967'. At the same time, 'it is necessary to ensure respect

* I should like to thank Mr Yossie Goldstein for help in organising the material on which this essay is based.

for and recognition of the sovereignty, territorial integrity and political independence of all states of the Middle East and their right to live in peace. This also refers to Israel'. Israel's right to exist, Gromyko went on, 'was recognised by the very fact of the formation of that state on the decision of the United Nations. It was confirmed by the fact that many states, including the Soviet Union, established diplomatic relations with Israel in the past'.

However, Gromyko immediately qualified this statement:

'This right cannot be unilateral. It is unthinkable without respect for sovereign rights of other states and peoples . . . This fully refers to the principle of inviolability of the frontiers . . . It is only the legitimate frontier recognised by those who are on its both sides that is really safe. In the specific Middle East situation such are the demarcation lines that existed on 4 June 1967 . . .

The Soviet Union is not hostile to the State of Israel as such. It is Israel's policy of annexation, of trampling on the norms of international law and UN resolutions that has caused the general, including the Soviet Union's condemnation.[2]

Israel's right to exist has indeed been frequently reasserted and has become part of the official Soviet line. Gromyko told the UN General Assembly in September 1974 that while Moscow supported 'the legitimate demands of the Arabs', it favoured Israel's existence and development as an 'independent sovereign state'.[3] In April 1975 the USSR's permanent ambassador to the UN, Iakov Malik, told the Security Council that the 'lasting and just peace in the Middle East' which his Government favoured meant both 'to satisfy the lawful rights of the Arab people of Palestine, including its right to the creation of its own State and to grant to all States in the region the possibility of free existence and development'.[4] CPSU general secretary Leonid Brezhnev made a similar statement at the 25th CPSU Congress in February 1976,[5] while the Soviet government statement on the Middle East issued in late April again stressed that one of the elements of the 'radical political settlement of the Middle East conflict' which the Soviet Union favoured was 'international guarantees for the security and inviolability of the frontiers of all the Middle Eastern states and their right to independent existence and development'.[6] Early in 1977 Brezhnev, at an official ceremony in Tula, again underlined this point. 'The Near East needs a lasting and just settlement, which will not infringe upon the vital interests of a single state or a single people. Israel has, of course, the right of sovereign independence and a secure existence. But the Arab people of Palestine have the same right.'[7]

The Soviet Union has declared that it is willing, even eager, to participate in guaranteeing Israel's existence. Western commentators have laid considerable emphasis on such statements, interpreting them as indicating Soviet goodwill towards Israel. But this explanation ignores the context in which the declarations have been made and the fact that the USSR has constantly sought some form of co-operation with the USA in guaranteeing the Arab—Israeli status quo and in implementing UN resolutions to this end. Soviet diplomatic efforts in 1948, 1956 and recurrently since 1967 have demonstrated in practice the Kremlin's conception that ensuring its own status as a great or super power has meant *inter alia* actively participating in the settlement of international crises, specifically by being included among its guarantors.[8] True, this position has required a certain *a priori* moderation, but the Soviet Union has mostly been prepared to make concessions in order to achieve what it considers a more important objective: the act of guaranteeing takes precedence over what is guaranteed.

The October 1973 War was no exception to the rule. Speaking to the World Peace Congress in Moscow at the end of October, Brezhnev said that 'in the cause of normalising the situation in the Near East', the USSR was prepared to 'co-operate with all countries concerned . . . to take part in providing appropriate guarantees' that would ensure 'all States and peoples in the Near East . . . peace, security and inviolable frontiers'.[9]

At first, the Soviet intention was presumably to provide guarantees for an imposed settlement through the agency of a UN peacekeeping force in which it hoped (as in 1948 and 1956) to take an active part. However, even after Moscow's attempt to send its own contingent to this force had been frustrated, the USSR continued to indicate willingness to give guarantees. In April 1975, when Syrian Foreign Minister Abd al-Halim Khaddam visited Moscow, Gromyko said that if the Israeli leadership had

a real desire to ensure peaceful conditions for the existence and development of the Israeli State . . . it would only have to abandon its plans to annex other peoples' territories, to pull out from them and to take the road of peace with the Arab States. Israel may get, if it wishes to, the strictest guarantees with the participation — under an appropriate agreement — of the Soviet Union too. These guarantees would ensure peaceful conditions for the existence and development of all States of the Middle East.[10]

Addressing the 25th CPSU Congress in February 1976, Brezhnev reiterated Soviet readiness 'to participate in international guarantees for the security and the inviolability of the borders of all countries in the Near East either within the UN framework or on a different basis'.[11]

Despite indications of a new, more flexible attitude towards Israel at Geneva, moderate statements made in particular during meetings with Western statesmen,[12] and the positive attitude implied in the very willingness to give guarantees, the Soviet communications media continued to denounce Israel as obstructing a settlement, violating ceasefire lines and arrangements, threatening the Arab states and preparing a new war, as well as perpetrating acts of barbarous cruelty against the Arab population of the territories it had captured in 1967 and inflaming, if not actually causing, the Lebanese civil war.

Official Soviet statements actually included threats to Israel. Some of these were specific, others more veiled. That most of them were merely the vituperative upbraidings of a frustrated and ineffective superpower and did not have great practical significance did not detract from their implications; there can be little doubt that these pronouncements were intended as threats. The October War had ended on the note of a Soviet warning to Israel that its 'flagrant flouting' of the cease fire laid down in Security Council Resolution 338 would lead to 'the gravest consequences'.[13] Nearly a year later, presumably with an eye to the approaching Arab Rabat conference and Brezhnev's announced intention of visiting the Middle East, the Soviet Union warned more explicitly that the Arab countries would neither be intimidated by Israel's receipt of American arms nor sit idly by while Israel made preparations for war. There was an obvious limit to the Arab peoples' patience as their desire to achieve the speediest possible 'liquidation of the consequences of Israel's aggression' was legitimate and justified.[14] In the autumn of 1974, on the anniversary of the October Revolution, Gromyko made a similar claim that 'Israel's chauvinist intoxication' had led it to 'rely on force of arms. But this is a gross miscalculation, which is fraught with danger, not least for Israel itself'.[15]

In 1975 the Soviet radio continued to dwell upon the risks to Israel's security inherent in the policy of establishing new settlements in 'the occupied territories'; in its obstructionism over the issue of a peace settlement — Israel could not hope to win wars for ever given the Arabs'

increasing wealth and strength and must therefore strive to attain a
peace settlement quickly; and in its purchase of strategic weaponry. In
view of Israel's size and population the purchase of Pershing missiles,
for example, was likely to lead to an indescribable disaster for the
Israelis themselves.[16]

On a different level, but with a similar intention, Israel was described
as undergoing the worst crisis in its history, the October War having
brought about a radical change in the country's mood as well as general
confusion in the population's basic conceptions.[17] The Soviet media
devoted considerable space to the dangers to Israel's welfare inherent in
the domestic upheaval — economic difficulties and political and social
unrest — that had hit the country immediately after the war. More
than ever in the past, these sources maintained, Israelis themselves were
doubting the future of the State. According to one broadcast, the
primary reason for these doubts was the allegedly dwindling economic
support from Jewish organisations abroad.[18] (This statement was
particularly interesting in that it stressed the link between Israel and
world Jewry; it is also perhaps not fortuitous that organisations
normally described as 'Zionist' when singled out for the support they
gave Israel were described by the much less pejorative 'Jewish' when
that support was not forthcoming.)

The Soviet government statement of April 1976 also contained a
veiled warning to Israel. It not only spoke of Israel's 'cruel occupation
policy' and of 'racial discrimination and oppression' and made the
unsolved Arab—Israeli conflict the progenitor of the Lebanese civil war,
but also referred to the 'serious responsibility' which governments that
continued to obstruct the resumption of the Geneva Conference must
'naturally assume'.

The statement, moreover, noted the confirmation by the UN of the
Palestinians' 'right to create their own state on the territory of
Palestine'. This was obviously a reference to UN General Assembly
Resolution 3376 of November 1975 which (reiterating Resolution 3236
of November 1974) had reaffirmed the rights of the Palestinian people
to 'national independence and sovereignty' amd 'self-determination'.
The Soviet statement, like the UN resolutions, made no attempt to
define the borders of the Palestinian state: yet UN Resolution 3236,
which recalled 'the relevant resolutions which affirm the right of the
Palestinian people to self-determination', referred implicitly to the
Palestine partition resolution of 29 November 1947, support for which
Moscow has never abandoned.[19]

Indeed, the entire question of the frontiers which the USSR

considers legitimate for Israel is central to an understanding of Moscow's conception of Israel's existence. True, the Soviet media tended to ridicule Israel's demand for secure frontiers. Forgetting, or simply ignoring, similar Soviet demands during and after World War Two, *Pravda* insisted that the entire idea of secure borders was a propaganda stunt that was merely intended to deceive world opinion; the notion had no relevance to reality for no boundary was secure.[20] The issue actually caused disagreement with the French Socialist Party delegation led by François Mitterand that visited Moscow on 24–25 April 1975: the French side wanted the official communiqué on the visit to refer specifically to Israel as one of the Middle Eastern states that was to be promised 'safe and secure borders'. while the Soviet side rejected the request.[21]

None the less, over the past three decades, during which Moscow devoted considerable attention to 'the Palestine question', it had ample opportunity to apprehend the precise significance which each of the various territorial suggestions put forward in the international arena has for Israel's existence. In discussing the question of Israel's internationally recognised borders therefore, the Soviet Union considered which borders were to be regarded as legitimate. While it seemed intent to show support for Israel's existence within the frontiers of 4 June 1967, as in Gromyko's Geneva declaration in December 1973, it was occasionally carefully ambiguous about its intentions and sometimes – even prior to the April 1976 statement – clearly supported a return to the frontiers suggested in the 1947 partition resolution. Thus, although Soviet officials and media agreed that Israel's withdrawal to the boundaries of 4 June 1967 was a *sine qua non* or 'basis' for any settlement (cf. above),[22] it was not always clear that this withdrawal was regarded by Moscow as sufficient to guarantee Israel's existence. From the autumn of 1974, with the Soviet acknowledgement of the Palestinians' right to set up their own state, Moscow's doubts on this soon began to be voiced. *Kommunist*, perhaps the most authoritative of all official written sources, revealed a new sophistication in the Soviet position. In an article on the Middle East crisis, it distinguished between Israel's territory as originally stipulated by the 1947 partition resolution that formed the basis for the establishment of the Jewish State, its 'actual frontiers' – i.e. those of 4 June 1967, and the 'occupied territories' which gave Israel control of 'more than three times its territory [already] illegally augmented in 1948'.[23]

In the spring of 1975, some Soviet sources became more explicit –

and more extremist. In April a senior member of *Izvestiia's* editorial
staff wrote:

> History shows that the Near East crisis began with the aggressive
> policy of the Israeli state from its very establishment. Already then
> its leaders disregarded the decisions of the UN and demonstrated a
> racist approach to the Arab population of Palestine. It is relevant in
> this connection to recall the UN decision of 29 November 1947 that
> stipulated the partition of Palestine into two states — an Arab and a
> Jewish one.

The Soviet government organ then went on to show how the additions
made in 1948–9 by the Israeli State to the territory allotted to it in
November 1947 together with Transjordan's annexation of the West
Bank had prevented the establishment of the Arab State.[24] Towards
the end of May 1975, on the eve of President Ford's European tour and
meeting with Sadat in Salzburg, Soviet circles in Washington suggested
that if Israel did not agree to return to the borders of 4 June 1967,
those who demanded its withdrawal to the partition resolution lines
would get the upper hand.[25] In addition, the Soviet monthly
International Affairs made several similar statements in this period that
Israel was forgoing the opportunity to have the Armistice Agreement
demarcation lines recognised as its final legal boundaries.[26] As to
Soviet maps, they invariably give the 1947 boundaries as the official
ones dividing Palestine into an Israeli and an Arab state, with the 1949
borders marked merely as ceasefire lines.

The USSR, moreover, was well aware that even the return to the
1947 boundary and the establishment of a Palestinian Arab state as
stipulated by the partition resolution were not tantamount to
satisfaction of Palestinian–Arab national demands. The April 1976
statement spoke of the establishment of such a state as part of the
process of satisfying these demands. The other part was presumably the
return of the Arab refugees to their lands so that even in what remained
of the state of Israel a process of 'de-Zionisation' would begin. In the
first stage it would become a binational state in which the Arab
population would have equal national rights, and when — as the
demographic trends of the two populations indicated — the Arabs
became a majority, the process would be completed.[27] The return of
the refugees was obviously what was meant by the constant harping on
the need for a settlement conforming to unspecified 'UN resolutions'
as against specific references to Security Council Resolutions 242, 338

and 339 or General Assemby Resolutions 3236 and 3376. It was pointed out, moreover, that Resolution 3236 adopted at the 29th Session of the General Assembly 'confirmed the inalienable right of the Palestinian people to self-determination without any outside interference, to national independence and sovereignty and their right to return to their property and homes from which they had been evicted'.[28]

The Soviet attitude towards Israel's existence, as expressed in official statements and commentaries, was thus carefully defined. It comprised an unequivocal recognition of the state of Israel's right of existence, even including declarations that the USSR was prepared to offer its services as guarantor of that right. However, Soviet statesmen and public media alike suggested from time to time that Israel's existence was being threatened by the policies adopted and implemented by its own government, warnings that seemed tantamount to an admission that the existence of Israel was not a foregone conclusion or even a postulate of international affairs but rather something that depended upon the nature of Israeli policy. The occasional but always meaningful allusions to the 1947 partition resolution boundaries as Israel's lawful frontiers gave these admonitions a rather sinister connotation, since it was generally accepted in Israel — as it had been by the USSR itself in 1948 — that such frontiers made nonsense of any recognition of Israel's existence.

2. The Soviet Attitude in Practice: The Bilateral Level

The Soviet Union has, it is true, refrained from resuming diplomatic relations with Israel. It has, however, maintained numerous contacts with Israeli officials and diplomats at various levels and in various parts of the world. These contacts existed before October 1973 but became more frequent afterwards in direct proportion to the growing need to use the threat of renewing relations with Israel as a means of political leverage *vis-à-vis* the Arabs. Whereas Cairo and Damascus have both resumed diplomatic relations with the USA (in November 1973 and June 1974 respectively), giving Washington access to both sides to the conflict, Moscow has presumably reasoned that until the Geneva Conference begins and creates an operative framework for elaborating a peace settlement, it can anticipate no practical advantage from resuming relations with Israel. Then perhaps, when the peacemaking process is underway, within a framework which presupposes full Soviet participation, the USSR will desire to show that it too has direct communication with both sides, to give the impression of adopting an even-handed and responsible position towards both parties, to be able to counterbalance the enhanced US influence in the Middle East, and possibly even to create at least an option of applying pressure on Israel.

At the opening of the Geneva Conference in December 1973, Gromyko met his Israeli counterpart, Abba Eban, for a first meeting at ministerial level since the severance of diplomatic relations. Soviet sources did not mention the event at all; Eban for his part said that it reflected the Soviet resolve to transform the atmosphere that had dominated Soviet–Israeli relations since 1967. Moscow, he maintained, realised that without Israel no Middle East settlement could be achieved and considered it desirable to try to influence the Israeli position by a serious, matter-of-fact clarification of the issues under dispute between the two governments. Eban clamed that his conversation with Gromyko had been friendly and useful. He also reported the two ministers' agreement that this meeting was not to remain a solitary contact, and that the Soviet and Israeli missions to Geneva would continue to hold talks within the framework of the conference.[29] Over a year later Eban disclosed that Gromyko had stated at their meeting that the USSR had been one of the first states to recognise Israel and would not retract that recognition 'whichever Arab nation asks us to'.[30]

A further meeting at foreign minister level was held on 24 September 1975 between Gromyko and Yigal Allon, who succeeded Eban in 1974, at the offices of the Soviet UN delegation in New York. While the content of their talk was kept confidential, it was reported that the two ministers discussed the nature of the relationship between their governments and again agreed on principle that further contacts be maintained. Gromyko, moreover, was said to have stated that Moscow would not alter its position on the resumption of full diplomatic relations given Israel's refusal to withdraw to the borders of 4 June 1967 and recognise Palestinian suzerainty on the West Bank.[31] The speed with which the Soviet side responded to the Israeli suggestion for a meeting and the fact that it lasted three hours were, however, considered to indicate Soviet interest in a dialogue.[32]

The UN was the scene of a number of meetings. Early in April 1974 Soviet UN Ambassador Iakov Malik received Yosef Teko'a, his Israeli counterpart, to discuss the renewal of the UNDOF (United Nations Disengagement Observation Force) mandate and the Soviet draft resolution condemning Israel for discriminating against certain national units in this force and among the observers. (The reference was to Israel's refusal to allow soldiers and observers of states that had severed relations with it, including Poland and the USSR, to enter its territory.)

This was the first time since June 1967 that a Soviet–Israeli meeting had taken place in the headquarters of the Soviet delegation to the UN.[33]

In May 1976 a further contact was established at the UN – this time between Malik and Teko'a's successor, Chaim Herzog. The meeting between the two ambassadors was held on Herzog's initiative resulting from his appraisal that the Soviet government's declaration on the Middle East (see p. 233) indicated a more moderate line towards Israel; Foreign Minister Allon told the Israeli government that this evaluation was disproved in the course of the conversation.[34]

In Washington too, Anatolii Dobrynin and Simha Dinitz, the Soviet and Israeli amabassadors there, were said to have held several meetings – initiated by the Soviet side – beginning April 1974. Unofficial meetings at a lower level were also held between Israeli and Soviet diplomats posted to Western Europe.[35] The Soviet Union seemed intent on keeping open a channel of direct communication with Israel.

Early in April 1975 two Soviet envoys were actually sent on a clandestine official mission to Israel for talks with Prime Minister Yitzhak Rabin and Foreign and Defence Ministers Yigal Allon and Shimon Peres. This initiative by the Soviet government was apparently a result of the failure of the Kissinger mission of March 1975 and the ensuing difficulties between Washington and Jerusalem. It was reported that the Soviet envoys mainly discussed the Geneva Conference, as the chances of its reconvening had been considerably increased by the Secretary of State's failure. The two Soviet officials were said to have maintained that the US step-by-step diplomacy and policy of partial settlements had proved ineffective. They told the Israelis that the USSR was ready to re-establish diplomatic ties once meaningful progress towards a settlement had been made, and to guarantee Israel's security within the 1967 borders after a settlement had been reached.[36]

The Soviet government also maintained indirect contacts with Israel. For example Sargent Shriver, US Democratic presidential aspirant, was said to have served as an intermediary between the two sides.[37]

In addition, a number of non-governmental delegations travelled in both directions. In each of the three years following the October War, Soviet delegations visited Israel for the anniversary of Victory Day in Europe – at the invitation of the Israel–USSR Friendship Movement. Each of these delegations comprised three members, among them presidium members of the Union of Societies for Friendship and Cultural Relations with Foreign Countries, academicians and on two occasions women pilots of World War Two fame. The first such delegation pointed out that the aim of Soviet policy on the Middle East conflict was to guarantee peace and security to all the states and peoples of the region. The delegation also expressed a desire to exchange visits of Soviet and Israeli delegations and for the speedy resumption of relations in all fields. One of its members declared that neither the Soviet government nor people was hostile to the state of Israel despite disagreement with its policies and that 'diplomatic relations will be resumed and relations of friendship will develop in all fields between the USSR and Israel as soon as the obstacles that caused the severance are removed'. Another delegation member said: 'I think most people want normal relations between our two states, with informational, cultural, scientific and commercial exchanges. People must live and let live. We can help achieve this'.[38] The 1975 delegation also noted the prevalence in Israel of a general and genuine desire for peace and a renewal of relations with the USSR. At the same time, it accused Israel's communications media of being hostile to the Soviet Union. It also declared that if Israel condemned the severance of relations, it had simply to remove the reasons for the severance in order for peace to be established and relations renewed.[39]

Israeli delegations which visited the Soviet Union included a delegation of members of the Israel—USSR Friendship Movement, individually selected by its host, the Union of Societies for Friendship and Cultural Relations with Foreign Countries. The delegation visited Moscow, Leningrad and Volgograd and had talks with a variety of Soviet officials, public figures and Middle East experts. Although their visit was accompanied by a few minor gestures of friendship, as well as some indications of differences of opinion within the Soviet establishment on issues relating to Israel and the Palestinians, the general feeling among delegation members was that conditions were unfavourable to a renewal of diplomatic relations.[40] The central media made only the barest reference to the visit, in a laconic announcement of the delegation's departure.[41] Other Israelis visited the USSR for international conferences and sports events; some of these reported that the Soviet authorities had made every effort to give them favourable treatment, others ran into various kinds of difficulties, while a third group was actually prevented from entering the Soviet Union.[42]

The various contacts, gestures and assiduously noncommittal hints by the USSR that it might be interested in resuming diplomatic relations with Israel were largely belied by the actions and statements of the Soviet leadership and government. These blatantly contradicted Western anticipation of such a development: both before and after the opening session of the Geneva Conference, Washington sources were busy forecasting the renewal of relations, reporting that the Kremlin was moving in just such a direction.[43] The Soviet position was also in sharp contrast with that of the Israeli government which did not conceal its desire to renew relations. Yigal Allon said at the end of 1974: 'If I believed an Israeli approach could encourage Moscow and subsequently also the states of Eastern Europe to resume their ties with Israel, I would not hesitate to make one'.[44] Allon reiterated Israel's willingness to renew relations in an interview with the Italian Communist *Paesa Sera* early in 1975, adding that he did not understand why Moscow discriminated against Israel, especially as this meant limiting its ability to take part in the peacemaking process in the Middle East.[45]

Thus the Soviet government took no steps towards a renewal of relations, although during one short period Moscow too seemed to be considering taking advantage of a potential coincidence of interests of the Soviet and Israeli governments to enhance its manoeuvrability *vis-à-vis* the Arabs and Washington respectively. In the weeks following the Syrian–Israeli separation of forces agreement in May 1974 and the concomitant improvement of US–Syrian relations, the Soviet delegation at the Geneva Conference indicated that the improved atmosphere surrounding Arab–Israeli relations enabled or perhaps even obligated the USSR to resume relations with Israel. Otherwise all initiatives would remain in American hands during the expected intensification of activity in the peacemaking process following the Syrian–Israeli agreement. Moreover, the delegation considered, relations with Israel would give the Soviet side more bargaining leverage with the Arab states.[46] At about the same time, a TASS correspondent was reported to have told an Israeli journalist that the severance of relations had been a mistake. When the Israeli expressed his doubts about the credibility of rumours that relations would soon be re-established, as this would not bring Moscow any advantage and would merely annoy the Arabs, he was told simply that Egypt had renewed relations with the USA.[47]

On the whole, however, Moscow insisted that any change on this score depended on yet further progress in resolving the Arab–Israeli conflict. Speaking at the 29th Session of the UN General Assembly, Gromyko denied that the Soviet position was 'one-sided'. The Soviet Foreign Minister declared: 'real, not illusory, progress towards a Middle East settlement will create prerequisites for the development of relations between the Soviet Union and all states of the Middle East.

including Israel'.[48]

Although in the early summer of 1975 'Communist sources in Washington' were alleged to have stated that discussions were being held in Moscow on the possibility of renewing diplomatic ties with Israel,[49] there seemed actually to be a certain regression in the Soviet position during 1975. Indeed, the second Israeli–Egyptian disengagement agreement of late summer 1975 could hardly appear to Moscow as 'real progress'.[50] The stand taken in June 1974, or even by the two clandestine envoys to Israel in April 1975, stood in sharp contrast to Gromyko's reported position in September of that year taken presumably in the context of the anti-Israel atmosphere engendered by the UN anti-Zionist campaign (see below). Rumours leaked by East European sources at the very close of 1975, that Poland had been assigned as the first Soviet bloc state to renew diplomatic ties with Israel – a leakage that was considered preparatory to the resumption of relations by Moscow[51] – proved unfounded, or at least premature. Even when Brezhnev in his speech at the 25th CPSU Congress in February 1976 tried (against the background this time of a growing impasse in Soviet–Arab relations) to create an impression of potential goodwill, he used the most noncommittal terms. He said: 'We favour the creation of conditions for the development of our relations with all countries in the Near East. We do not have any prejudices against any of them.'[52] For those who might have had any illusions regarding the sympathetic connotations of this lack of prejudice, the April 1976 statement made clear that it referred to Israel 'if [it] drops its policy of aggression and takes the road of peace and good-neighbourly relations with the Arabs'.

As given practical expression on the level of bilateral relations, the USSR's attitude to Israel's existence was, then, no less double-edged than in the sphere of its declared position. On the one hand the Soviet government was unwilling to renew diplomatic relations; on the other, it sought to maintain direct and indirect contact with Israeli representatives and repeatedly stressed that in certain circumstances it would indeed resume relations. The issue was clearly not one of principle but rather of tactics, in which Moscow sought to take advantage of the absence of full direct ties to apply pressures and score points on a maximum number of political and diplomatic fronts.

3. The Soviet Attitude in Practice: The International Arena

The protracted severance of diplomatic relations by the USSR and the East European states was a major factor in Israel's increasing isolation

in the international arena. There have even been indications that
Moscow played an encouraging role in the severance of relations with
Israel by a considerable number of African states, beginning with Idi
Amin's Uganda, a process that gathered momentum during 1973.[53]
When, towards the end of 1974, the Arabs began to press for Israel's
exclusion from the UN the USSR was again in the forefront of the
anti-Israel offensive.

Soviet UN representatives had long been calling for sanctions against
Israel in Security Council discussions of the Arab—Israeli conflict,
but their demands had not previously been of operative significance. In
a speech at the Council in April 1974 Malik had again asked it not to
content itself once more with a mere condemnation, but rather to 'take
effective measures to call a halt to the acts of aggression and the
brigandage of the Israeli militarists'. Addressing Israeli Ambassador
Teko'a, Malik said: 'You and your country have been condemned. You
are isolated and alone. You are supported by only one major Power and
by no one else.'[54]

It was therefore not surprising that the Soviet Union associated itself
with Arab efforts to oust Israel from the UN and its affiliated
organisations. The first UN committee to decide on sanctions against
Israel was UNESCO: in November 1974 the 18th session of its General
Conference resolved to terminate assistance to Israel and exclude it
from UNESCO's activities and regional groups. The resolution,
proposed by the Arab states, was supported by the USSR and the other
Soviet bloc states.

By mid-1975 Soviet sources were stressing that the demand was
being heard throughout the world to expel Israel from the UN because
of its unwillingness to respect the decisions and principles of that
organisation. 'UN circles' and even Western diplomats were said to be
talking in these terms as well as such forums as the Jidda Conference of
Muslim foreign ministers and the approaching Lima Conference of
non-aligned countries. The activities of the US Senate in favour of Israel
were said only to weaken the Israeli position given the persistent
rumours that American senators were being bribed by Zionist
organisations.[55]

Officially, however, Moscow refrained from declaring its support of
Israel's expulsion. In this way, the very adoption of a stand on a
potential issue became a matter of negotiation, giving the Soviet Union
maximum manoeuvrability and every likelihood of political or
diplomatic advantage and achievements. Danish Foreign Minister Knud
Andersen who met his Soviet counterpart on 28 May told journalists

that according to Gromyko the USSR would not support any suggestion to eject Israel from the UN.[56] 'Observers' too were said to believe that the Soviet Union had no interest in supporting Israel's expulsion but would try to exploit the threat to put pressure on Israel. Meanwhile, the USA requested the Soviet government to exert its influence on Third World states to retract the support of many of them for Israel's expulsion.[57] In fact, the Lima Conference (25–30 August), like the Kampala Conference of the Organisation of African Unity a month before, did not raise the issue publicly although its political declaration 'most severely condemned Zionism as a threat to world peace and security'. (The Kampala Conference too had passed a resolution that attributed 'the racist regimes in occupied Palestine and . . . Zimbabwe [to] a common imperialist origin'.) It was thus not surprising that in the period following Lima Soviet sources reported that the USSR had decided against supporting any suggestion affecting Israel's UN membership,[58] even before Arab efforts to oust Israel from the UN finally petered out. The last such endeavour was a somewhat lame attempt by Arab representatives at the UN Credentials Commission to prevent Israel's acceptance to the 30th Session of the General Assembly.[59]

In view of the failure of the campaign on behalf of Israel's expulsion on the one hand, and the condemnation of Zionism at a number of international forums and occasions on the other, the discussion of Israeli and Palestinian questions in the General Assembly primarily took the form of an attack on Zionism.

While this was of less immediate practical significance than the issue of Israel's UN membership it did cast doubt on Israel's actual *raison d'être*. The USSR had in the past given vociferous expression to its fundamentally negative attitude to Zionism for a wide variety of reasons, particularly of a domestic nature, that had no direct bearing on Soviet foreign policy. Indeed, this stand had formerly been largely irrelevant both to the actual politics of Soviet–Israeli relations and to Moscow's views on the existence of the Israeli state. This now changed; first with the increasing attention paid in the international arena to the PLO, an organisation which embodied the demand for Israel's annihilation as a separate, independent political entity, and then with the intensified international campaign against Zionism. These two developments gave the USSR's hostility to Zionism a new, practical significance.

One of the reasons why Soviet propaganda had long coupled Zionism and imperialism had been to prove to the Arabs that an alliance with the Soviet Union was essential given the inevitable co-operation between the USA and Israel. The realities of US–Arab relations after the October 1973 War had not led to any mitigation of the USSR's anti-Zionist propaganda; it had if anything merely caused even more extreme formulations, including descriptions of Zionism which the USA could in no way accept. This, incidentally, is an instructive example of the adaptability of Soviet propaganda to international trends.

In late summer 1975, in the immediate aftermath of the Lima Conference's condemnation of Zionism, the Soviet media described the 'strategy of Zionism' as 'a policy of genocide and the intention to drive out by force and to wipe from the face of the Near East soil a whole people – the Palestinian Arabs'.[60] Finally, just over two months later, on 10 November, the Soviet bloc duly supported the General Assembly resolution that denounced Zionism as 'a form of racism and racial discrimination'.[61]

Jewish emigration from the USSR to Israel was another field in which the Soviet stand on Zionism had an obvious practical connection with the USSR's conception of the existence of the Jewish state. Although at the time of Israel's establishment in 1948, the Soviet Union had conceded that its *raison d'être* was the need for a refuge for the Jewish people inhabiting capitalist countries, it had never officially accepted Israel's claim to be the national home of the entire Jewish people. Moscow had, however, at different times assisted, even encouraged, the emigration to Israel of Jews from the East European people's democracies and permitted a small emigration from the Soviet Union on the basis of 'reunification of families'. While the problems connected with this issue are beyond the scope of this essay, it is relevant to note that there has often been an inverse relationship between Moscow's declared attitude to Israel and the extent of Jewish emigration to Israel from its own confines.[62] This has largely been the consequence of numerous factors extraneous to the practical gesture of official recognition to Israel as a Jewish state – Soviet domestic circumstances and the USSR's global and Middle Eastern policies: particularly Soviet–US and Soviet–Arab relations.[63] Moscow has always hinted that the possibilities it has given Jews to emigrate must be attributed to either US pressures[64] or the civil rights which its own constitution confers on Soviet citizens. It has, however, virtually claimed credit for using this emigration to aggravate Israel's internal crisis and exacerbate social dissension and economic problems (housing, unemployment, etc.). It might even be maintained that the Soviet Union has sought to show

how, through Soviet Jewish emigration to Israel, it has dealt a fatal blow to Israel's claim to be the state of the entire Jewish people. On the one hand, Soviet officials and communications media alike have consistently maintained that the vast majority of Soviet Jewry has no desire to go to Israel; most do not apply to emigrate at all and even of those that do increasing numbers (from 1975 to 1978) never reach Israel. On the other hand, of those who reach Israel, large numbers have insurmountable difficulties in adapting to Israeli life that demonstrate the absurdity of Israel's claim to be capable of gathering in even a small portion of the Jewish Diaspora and have led to a massive emigration from Israel itself, both of Soviet Jews and many others. Soviet Jewry's contentment with conditions in the USSR and absorption problems in Israel are also said to be the sole reasons for the drastic decline in Soviet Jewish emigration since 1973.[65]

The practical implications of the Soviet attitude to Israel's existence in the international arena have thus been various. While Soviet representatives have been violently anti-Israel on the polemical level, they and their government have been careful not to commit themselves to measures — such as Israel's expulsion from the UN — at least until such time as these acquire practical significance. Once, however, an anti-Israel procedure has become a question of actual politics, the USSR has been a natural proponent of it. Here, too the interrelationship between the attitude to Israel's existence and Moscow's relations with other states has been manifest: thus, although the granting or withholding of exit permits is in no way connected with the former, the USSR has been eager to claim credit for the difficulties caused to Israel by Soviet Jewish emigration and also by the decrease in both the emigration itself and the numbers of emigrants arriving in Israel.

Conclusion

I have suggested that the USSR has been following a dual policy on the existence of Israel. Since the question of whether to endorse Israel's continued existence or actually further its annihilation has not yet acquired practical political significance in the period since October 1973, Moscow has been able to avoid adopting any stand that might commit it should this basic circumstance change. It is doubtful whether the decision-making bodies or institutions have even posed the question what they would resolve in such an event. Until the issue becomes pertinent, the Kremlin will presumably persist in leaving all options open. This lack of decision by the Soviet leadership presumably also accounts for the different nuances of opinion expressed by the various media, institutions and commentators on the issues we have discussed, which cannot be explained only by the continual fluctuations in Soviet relations with, and intentions regarding, the USA and other factors in the Middle East situation.[66] Until the Kremlin is forced by circumstances to take a policy decision, a certain leeway evidently exists for the airing of different attitudes. The basis *leitmotif* of ambiguity expresses itself in: formal acceptance of Israel's right to exist together with actions and behaviour that invalidate Israel's sovereign, independent existence; a consistent refusal to re-establish official diplomatic relations together with occasional gestures and contacts at varying levels in the USSR or Israel or on neutral territory; a vociferous attack on Zionism in terms which are tantamount to rejecting Israel's *raison d'être* and calls to 'de-Zionise' Israel reminiscent of the PLO's slogan of a democratic secular state, together with the permission given to a certain number of Jews to emigrate to Israel, and so on.

The logic behind the ambiguity is fairly clear. Moscow has little chance of gaining much by outright commitment to Israel's continued existence; the USA's record of such a commitment has frequently shown over three decades the considerable disadvantages which this position has had in the regional area[67]. At the same time, the USSR's various threats implying hostility to the existence of the State of Israel serve to intimidate the Israeli government, which cannot be absolutely confident that they will in no case be implemented; to persuade the Arabs of the advantages of a certain measure of partnership with Moscow; and to demonstrate to the USA that chances of a settlement without US–Soviet co-operation are inevitably limited. If, however, the USSR opts for outright hostility to Israel, it is in danger of losing certain advantages – possibly even inviting a military confrontation with its rival superpower. All this is quite apart from the USSR's semi-mystical conception of the existence and power of the Jewish people which must make any decision actually to destroy Israel seem very difficult, if not impossible, to implement. Another factor on a very different level is the presumed apprehension that the removal of Israel would endanger the entire regional balance of forces, the consequences of which are impossible to anticipate.

An in-between position, therefore, can probably enable the Soviet Union both to have and to eat as much of the cake as it can, particularly today when it is engaged in an uneven struggle to recover its position in the Middle East and to repair its image in the West. In this situation its attitude to the tiny state of Israel cannot be separated from either its regional or its global considerations and strategies.

Notes

1. For details of the Soviet–Palestinian relationship, see Baruch Gurevitz, 'The Soviet Union and the Palestinian Organisations', in this volume. Although the USSR rejected Israel's 'false propaganda contentions' that 'the Palestinian struggle for independence' threatened its existence (*RPP* in Hebrew, 30 October 1974/*IMB*, 8 November 1974), it was well aware of the significance of the PLO's demand for its own state and for the establishment in all Palestine of a democratic, secular state.

2. TASS in English, 21 December 1973/*FBIS III*, 26 December 1973.

3. GA OR, A/PV. 2240, 24 September 1974.

4. S/PV 1822, 28 May 1975.

5. TASS in English, 29 February 1976/*FBIS III*, 25 February 1976.

6. TASS in English, 28 April 1976/*SWB I*, 30 April 1976.

7. *Pravda*, 19 January 1977.

8. That this was one of the implications of the post-World War Two division of the world into two camps, the one headed by the USSR and the other by the USA, was highlighted by Soviet collaboration with the USA in preparing the ground for the UN Partition Resolution on Palestine in October–November 1947, less than one month after Stalin's second-in-command Andrei Zhdanov had announced the tenet of the two camps at the founding conference of the Cominform. Still under Stalin, with the Korean War underway, Georgii Malenkov, secretary of the Soviet Party's Central Committee, told the CPSU's 19th Congress that the USSR was 'ready for co-operation' with the Western Powers, 'having in mind the observance of peaceful international standards and the guaranteeing of a stable and lasting peace' – quoted in Myron Rush (ed.), *The International Situation and Soviet Foreign Policy* (Columbus, Ohio: Charles E. Merrill, 1970), p.151.

9. *R. Moscow*, 26 October 1973/*SWB I*, 29 October 1973. A similar statement was made in the joint communiqué that marked the conclusion of Tito's Soviet visit a few weeks later – *Pravda*, 16 November 1973.

10. TASS in English, 23 April 1975/*SWB I*, 25 April 1975.

11. TASS in English, 24 February 1976/*FBIS III*, 25 February 1976.

12. For example, a French Socialist Party delegation led by François Mitterand that visited the USSR in April 1975 (see below); a delegation of fourteen US senators that visited the USSR in the autumn of the same year; and US Democratic Party presidential aspirant Sargent Shriver who was in Moscow about the same time – *Ha'aretz*, 18 May, 3 October and 3 November 1975.

13. TASS in English, 23 October 1973/*FBIS III*, 24 October 1973.

14 *RPP* in Hebrew, 16 September 1974/*IMB*, 20 September 1974. For the Rabat Conference, see pp. 17 and 47; for Brezhnev's intended Middle Eastern tour, see pp.189–90.

15. *R. Moscow*, 6 November 1974/*SWB I*, 8 November 1974.

16. *RPP* in Hebrew, 30 January, 22 August and 1 October 1975/*IMB*, 5 February, 22 August and 6 October 1975.

17. *R. Moscow,*, 30 December 1973/*IMB*, 31 December 1973.

18. *R. Moscow*, 3 July 1975/*IMB*, 8 July 1975.

19. All other UN resolutions had spoken only of the Palestinians' rights to compensation and to return to their homes. For the statement itself, see note 6 above.

20. *Pravda*, 23 November 1973. One month later, at Geneva, Gromyko was himself speaking of safe boundaries, see above. Defending the Soviet attack on Finland early in the war a Soviet government statement of 13 November 1941 said: 'The USSR's policy towards Finland was naturally determined by consideration of security for the borders, vital centres and communications of the USSR . . . and by awareness that aggressive enemies of the USSR . . . were

prepared to convert Finland into a base of operations for an attack on the Soviet Union' – *USSR Information Bulletin*, 110 (21 November 1941); at the Tehran Big Three Conference of November 1943, Stalin justified his terms for peace with Finland, including cession of Finnish territory near Leningrad 'as not over reaching or too harsh. He argued that the territorial acquisitions were necessary for Russian security' – Herbert Feis, *Churchill, Roosevelt and Stalin* (Princeton, 1957), p.209.

21. *Ha'aretz*, 18 May 1975.

22. *Pravda*, 6 November 1967, even justified the October War by the Syrians' and Egyptians' desire to liberate the lands which Israel had occupied in 1967.

23. L. Tolkunov, 'The Near East: Sources of the Crisis and Ways of Settling It', *Kommunist*, 13 (1974), pp.97–105.

24. *Izvestiia*, 12 April 1975. The *Izvestiia* statement states exactly the opposite of what Iakov Malik told the Security Council in March 1949, namely that Israel carefully fulfilled UN decisions, although the violation attributed to Israel by *Izvestiia* preceded March 1949.

25. *Ha'aretz*, 29 May 1975.

26. *International Affairs* (Moscow), November 1974, March and April 1975. The last of these statements read:

> The Israeli expansionists should not forget that their refusal to withdraw their troops from all the Arab territories occupied in 1967 deprives the State of Israel of any chance of having the Arab States recognise its existence within the boundaries which existed prior to June 5, 1967, that is, of confirming the territorial demarcation between the Arab countries and Israel which resulted from the Palestine War of 1948–1949 and which has not yet been formally endorsed by anyone anywhere.

27. The struggle for equal rights for Israel's Arabs was the main theme of a long article by *Izvestiia* 'political observer' Vikentii Matveev (10 June 1976) who visited Israel in May 1976.

28. *International Affairs* (Moscow), April 1975.

29. *Ma'ariv*, 28 December 1973.

30. *Ma'ariv*, 18 April 1975.

31. *Ha'aretz*, 26 and 29 September and 15 October 1975; *Ma'ariv*, 26 September 1975. Despite the general impression conveyed by the press that there was little sign of change, Allon was reportedly optimistic, seeing in his talk indications of a possible renewal of diplomatic relations and future political contacts on the Arab–Israeli conflict – *Ha'aretz*, 19 October 1975.

32. *NYT*, 26 September 1975.

33. *Ma'ariv*, 5 April 1974. Once again, the Soviet central press which covered Gromyko's meetings in New York omitted any reference to his talk with his Israeli counterpart.

34. *Ha'aretz*, 17 May 1976.

35. *NYT*, 12 April 1975; *Ma'ariv*, 9 May 1975.

36. The Israeli press even reported that the envoys implied that Moscow would not insist on Israel's withdrawal to the borders of 4 June 1967 in every instance, but would be satisfied with the evacuation of the great majority of the territories occupied during the Six Day War – *Ha'aretz*, 11, 13 and 14 April and 4 September 1975; and *NYT*, 12 April 1975. In an interview with *Ma'ariv*, 18 April 1975, Rabin referred to the 'exaggerated' publicity given to 'inaccurate information' on the Soviet visit.

37. *Ha'aretz*, 26 November 1975.

38. *Ha'aretz*, 12 and 13 May 1974.

39. *Ha'aretz*, 12 May 1975.

40. *Ha'aretz*, 26 and 29 September and 1 October 1975. Apart from one Rakah (New Communist List, i.e. Communist Party) member, the delegation was composed of members of left-wing Zionist parties.

41. The announcement read:

A group of Israeli public figures, who are in favour of settling the Near East problem on the basis of the UN Security Council resolutions and who favour an improvement of relations between Israel's peace-loving forces and the Soviet community, has been visiting the Soviet Union from 22 September to 1 October at the invitation of the Soviet Peace Committee. During their stay the visitors acquainted themselves with the life and work of Soviet people, the part they play in the struggle for peace and security of the people, and toured the country. Members of the group met representatives of the Soviet community. *R. Moscow*, 1 October 1975/*FBIS III*, 1 October 1975.

42. *Ha'aretz*, 29 August 1975; *Ma'ariv*, 3 October 1975. *Ha'Universita* (Tel Aviv University magazine), 25 December 1975.

43. Quoted in *Ha'aretz*, 21 and 23 December 1973 and 25 January and 3 March 1974.

44. *Ma'ariv*, 27 December 1974.

45. *Ha'aretz*, 6 February 1975.

46. *Ha'aretz*, 6 June 1974.

47. *Ha'aretz*, 25 June 1974.

48. GA OR, A/PV. 2240, 24 September 1974.

49. *Ha'aretz*, 10 June 1975.

50. This agreement, with its stipulation to bring US technicians to Sinai, aroused violent Soviet censure and could only be interpreted as a relapse or retreat when compared with the official Geneva Conference framework.

51. *Ha'aretz*, 24 December 1975.

52. TASS in English, 24 February 1976/*FBIS III*, 25 February 1976.

53. The Soviet press not only reported with open satisfaction each African state that severed relations with Israel before, during and after the October War; it also published several commentaries analysing the process. Some of these seemed to insinuate a not disinterested Soviet role. *Pravda*, on 1 November 1973, in an article entitled 'Israel's Isolation', wrote, for example: 'When in March 1972 the government of Uganda severed relations with Israel and proposed that the so-called "experts" from Tel Aviv leave the country, few people could assume that an active chain reaction would quickly follow'. *Pravda* went on: 'It is a question not only of Israel's further isolation, but also of the collapse of the "African strategy" of influential imperialist circles which hoped with Israel's help to weaken the national liberation movement in Africa. . .' On 22 November the same paper wrote: 'The severance of relations with Israel on the part of the black African states and the strengthening of [their] solidarity with the Arab countries have demonstrated the political maturity of the young African states. . . . The consequences of these actions will demonstrate in the most favourable fashion the growth and strengthening of the anti-imperialist forces in Africa'.

54. S/PV. 1767, 14 April 1974.

55. *R. Moscow*, 3 July 1975 and *RPP* in Hebrew, 21 July 1975/*IMB*, 8 and 25 July 1975. The reference to US Senate activity is presumably to the May 1975 letter to President Ford signed by 76 Senators.

56. *Ha'aretz*, 9 June 1975.

57. This was the meaning of US Ambassador Walter Stoessel's request for a meeting with Gromyko on 25 July 1975 to present him with a detailed account of Kissinger's Milwaukee speech of 14 July in which the Secretary of State had emphasised Washington's opposition to any attempts to expel UN member

nations from either the General Assembly or specialised agencies – *Ha'aretz*, 28 July 1975.

58. *Ha'aretz*, 17 September 1975.

59. *NYT*, 30 September 1975.

60. *R. Moscow*, 30 August 1975/*SWB I*, 3 September 1975.

61. The resolution, passed by 72 votes to 35, with 32 abstentions, recalled *inter alia* the General Assembly's Resolution 3151 (XXVIII) of 14 December 1973 which 'condemned the unholy alliance between South African racism and Zionism'; and both the Kampala resolution of the Organisation of African Unity and the Lima political declaration.

62. In 1948, in the heyday of this relationship, no Jews were allowed to leave the USSR for Israel. On the other hand, in the periods 1954–6 and 1964–7 when Moscow was openly supporting the Arabs in the conflict, Jews were permitted to emigrate to Israel; see my article, 'The USSR's Stand on the Emigration of Soviet Jews to Israel as a Factor in its Policy Towards the Arab–Israel Conflict, 1954–1967'. *Behinot* (Jerusalem) 5 (1974), pp.25–41.

63. The question of Soviet Jewish emigration has long been a topic raised in Soviet–Arab discussions. Late in 1974 the Soviet government was reported to have assured Arab representatives that it would channel Jewish emigration to the West rather than to Israel – *Ha'aretz*, 17 December 1974.

64. This was implied, for example, in Gromyko's message to Kissinger on 26 October 1974 rejecting attempts 'to ascribe to the elucidations furnished by us the nature of assurances of some sort and quasi obligations on our part regarding the departure of Soviet citizens from the USSR – TASS in Russian for abroad, 18 December 1974/*SWB I*, 20 December 1974.

65. Cf., for example, *Pravda*, 6 July 1975; TASS in Russian for abroad, 4 September 1975/*SWB I*, 6 September 1975. Of course the numerous Soviet comments on the issue of Jewish emigration also have other motivations such as the USSR's extreme sensitivity about the 'success' of its experiment in building a multinational society and therefore its interest in stressing its Jews' satisfaction with Soviet conditions; and the need to dwell upon those who have opted to go to other Western countries besides Israel, both to show the Arabs that not all – or even most – emigrants go to Israel and the need to condemn the preference of these Jews for capitalism. In this way the Jewish emigration is made to appear as a movement of traitors to the Soviet Union and its way of life rather than as a national revival.

66. There can be little doubt that a number of groupings in the Soviet establishment are more intensely anti-Zionist than others: the secret police which is battling with emigration, ideologues who hope perhaps, in spite of all setbacks, to achieve a viable Arab socialism in certain Arab states, or propagandists who need to vilify Zionism for domestic ends; yet this division of labour and interest seems to be of very little significance on the operational level.

67. True, the circumstance has changed in the post-1973 period, but the new trend is, at the time of writing, still of somewhat questionable political significance and it is still early to draw conclusions as to the lessons to be learned from it.

10 THE SOVIET UNION AND THE PALESTINIAN ORGANISATIONS*

Baruch Gurevitz

This paper examines the Soviet Union's attitude to the Palestinian people and the Palestinian organisations within the overall framework of Soviet policy in the Middle East and, more specifically, in the context of the USSR's insistence on a political solution to the Arab–Israeli conflict.[1] If, before the October War, the Soviet Union worked towards this aim chiefly through Egypt, since that date the increasing American initiatives in the area and Sadat's pro-Western orientation have made the USSR seek to strengthen its position elsewhere.[2] In this context, the Palestinians provided an obvious target of Soviet interest: on the one hand, their demands gained unprecedented attention in the post-October 1973 period in both the Arab world and the international community, while on the other, the USA refrained from espousing their cause or opening direct channels of communication with them.

Nonetheless, the Soviet Union has not found the Palestinians and their organised representatives an easy partner in fulfilling Soviet aims in the Middle East. This paper intends to examine Moscow's attempts to establish influence over the Palestinian organisations and the difficulties encountered by Soviet policy because of the Palestinians' radicalism, internal dissensions and reluctance to submit to Soviet patronage.

Although the Palestinian problem has existed as a recognised international issue since 1947–8, the Soviets did not pay much attention to it prior to 1967. The Six Day War brought the problem to the forefront of world attention and made it more acute: as a result of the war Israel occupied territories administered by Jordan and Egypt which in 1947 had been intended to form the nucleus of a Palestinian Arab state adjacent to the Jewish one[3] and which in 1967 had a population of close to one million Palestinian Arabs. Immediately after the war the Arab states demanded a return to the territorial status quo ante bellum. Security Council Resolution 242 of November 1967 in

*I would like to thank Dr Galia Golan and Dr Yaacov Ro'i for their assistance in writing this paper.

254

which their demand was expressed also declared the right of the states of the area to secure and recognised boundaries; since Israel, however, was given no clear assurance of such borders, it considered itself unable to withdraw from the territories it had occupied during the war. Moreover, as the resolution referred to the Palestinians as a refugee, and not a national, problem it was unacceptable to the Palestinians.

This new situation, in which areas densely populated by Palestinians were occupied and their political future unclear, politicised the Palestinian problem as never before. The Palestine Liberation Organisation (PLO, founded in 1964) acting as the representative of the Palestinians, therefore became an increasingly important political factor in the region.

From the spring of 1968 signs could be detected in the Soviet mass media of increasing interest in the PLO and Palestinian terrorist activities within Israeli-occupied territory.[4] The PLO was defined as a legitimate resistance movement with modest political goals, the implication being that it was demanding a return to the status quo before June 1967. From time to time the liquidation of Israel was presented as an objective of the radical factions within the Palestinian movement and not of the movement as a whole.[5] It seems that the Soviet mass media portrayed the PLO in this manner not only because of the increasing prestige of that organisation in the Arab world, but especially because Egypt, which was at that time the cornerstone of Soviet involvement in the Middle East, was the patron of the PLO and as of mid-1968 acted as middleman between it and the Soviet Union. It was only in 1972 that any intensive relationship developed between the Soviet Union and the PLO as a direct consequence of the deterioration in the relations between the Soviet Union and Egypt. The change in the political constellation in the Middle East following the expulsion of Soviet military personnel from Egypt in July of that year turned the Soviet Union's attention to the PLO in its search for alternatives to Egypt and in an attempt to increase its popularity among the radical Arab states, Syria and Iraq. A major *Pravda* article following Yasir Arafat's much publicised visit to Moscow in late July 1972 emphasised the change the Palestinian resistance movement had undergone and the USSR's own sympathy to it 'as an ally of the liberation struggle of the Arab peoples'.[6]

Indeed, Soviet support of the Palestinian organisations now took the form of practical help — particularly shipments of light weapons from the Soviet Union to the PLO through Syria.[7] Although Soviet policy still maintained that the terrorist methods introduced by the radical segments of the Black September group did not serve the Palestinian national cause,[8] the Soviet mass media seemed to be trying in the ensuing period to portray the PLO as a popular national movement by showing the close ties between it and the Palestinian people living in the occupied territories, thus stressing the organisation's broad national base.

In the October War itself, when the armies were confronting one. another and the two superpowers were trying both to stop the fighting and to make political capital out of the situation, no special attention was paid to the Palestinian problem. In fact, the Palestinians, lacking a strong army, played no active role in the war and there are indications that to a certain extent they disappointed the Arab states and possibly even the Soviet Union by failing to create a serious passive resistance movement.[9] They had apparently not prepared for the possibility of war and were unable to promote sabotage activities in the occupied territories.

When the ceasefire was finally declared the Palestinian problem and the PLO once again came to the fore, their value increasing in the eyes of the Soviet Union and the radical Arab states as American involvement and political initiatives in the area intensified. The Soviet reaction to the political changes occurring in the Middle East was based on the desire to rebut American activity by revealing it as basically Israel-oriented and by showing the considerable benefit the Arabs could reap from continued collaboration with the USSR.

Indeed, official Soviet policy now began to insist that any political resolution to the conflict must include the fulfilment of the 'national legitimate rights of the Palestinians', as opposed to the rights of the Palestinians merely as refugees, implying that after a total withdrawal of Israeli forces from the occupied territories, as demanded since 1967, some form of Palestinian sovereignty would be established on the West Bank and the Gaza Strip. Such a settlement, to which, as was incessantly repeated in Soviet statements, the Soviet Union and the USA would be co-guarantors, would not only legitimise Soviet involvement in the Middle East but also make it a political necessity since only the USSR would have leverage with the Palestinian organisations.

The Kremlin therefore proceeded on two levels. It sought increasingly to prove the indispensability of the PLO in any Arab–Israeli settlement and to demonstrate its own leverage with that organisation. Immediately after the October War, the Soviet Union demanded, with apparent success, that the PLO stop its terrorist activities on the Lebanese border so as not to jeopardise the ceasefire and the possibility of a peace conference.[10] At the same time the Soviet Union strove to assist the PLO in its efforts to attain political strength and significance: on 15 November, in a joint communiqué with Yugoslavia, the Soviet Union made a first official statement of support for the Palestinians' demands for a 'national entity'.[11]

Despite these signs of a Soviet–Palestinian rapprochement which would be of benefit to both parties there was disagreement on a number of crucial issues, on which there was no consensus among the various Palestinian groups themselves.

One of these was the use of terror. The USSR has on numerous specific occasions tried to justify the use of terror by the PLO. This has been particularly true of the deeds perpetrated by the Palestine National Front whose activities on the West Bank were considered an expression of the struggle for national liberation.[12] Soviet sources have pointed in the process to Israeli policy in the occupied territories and the Palestinians' resulting sense of hopelessness and alienation which makes them resort to terrorist activities.[13] *Izvestiia*'s chief editor, Lev Tolkunov, writing in July 1974, conceded that the Palestinian movement had a right to use military tactics if these were directed against military objects, but argued that the Palestinians should not justify

> reckless acts like Munich and hijacking by claiming that they were a product of the dead-end life in the refugee camps and terrorist activities of Israel's military . . . The main thing in the Palestine movement is the struggle of the masses to liberate the lands seized by Israel and to return to their rightful birthplace. Since Israel refuses to give up the land it seized the Palestinians are waging an armed struggle. The essential issue is to choose correctly the form of this struggle and make it more effective.[14]

In general, however, the Soviet position on terror has been negative. Moscow has persistently claimed that the Palestinian movement as a whole does not support the use of terrorism. Such activities are supposedly undertaken by opposition groups within the movement or outside it, defined in the Soviet mass media as 'pseudo-partisans'.[15] In accordance with this line, the Soviet Union has insisted that the PLO is a force struggling for the liberation of its land and has denied that the use of terror is part of its programme. This attempt to dissociate the PLO from terrorist activity led to a statement following the attack on

schoolchildren in the Israeli town of Ma'alot in May 1974 that 'the PLO
condemned the incident'.[16] The Kremlin has tried to convince the
Palestinians that terrorism does not serve their interests on tactical
grounds as it has alienated the Palestinian movement from world
opinion. Moscow has therefore suggested that the PLO condemn the
radical elements that use terrorism on the grounds that it obstructs the
fulfilment of the national goals of the Palestinian movement.[17]
Accordingly, the Soviet Union has repeatedly condemned terrorist
activities, in particular the hijacking of planes, the dispatching of letter
and parcel bombs and attacks on the civilian population.[18]

The use of terror, however, is a relatively minor issue in Soviet–
Palestinian relations. Far more troublesome is the Soviet Union's
interest in achieving Palestinian agreement to participate in a peace
conference. The Palestinians would be an asset to the Soviet contention
that the USSR was indispensable to peace talks; moreover, they could
be used to terminate the negotiations if these turned out not to be in
the best interests of the Soviet Union (or the PLO). Therefore, at the
beginning of November 1973 in an attempt to establish a common
political platform, the Soviet Union sent a memorandum to the leaders
of the PLO – Yasir Arafat, the official leader of the PLO, Georges
Habash, the leader of the Popular Front for the Liberation of Palestine
– a movement which defines itself *inter alia* as Marxist–Leninist, and
Naif Hawatima who split from the Popular Front in 1969 and founded
the Democratic Popular Front for the Liberation of Palestine – in
which each was asked to define the goals of the Palestinian cause.[19]
Later in November Arafat and the leaders of the Popular Front for the
Liberation of Palestine and the Iraqi-backed Arab Liberation Front met
in Moscow on the initiative of the Soviet Union to discuss the
possibility of a united policy towards a peace conference.

The Soviet mass media made very little reference to the visit itself
and to the issues which were discussed. However, some details were
made public in Beirut: the Palestinian delegation met Boris Ponomarev,
Politburo candidate member and secretary of the Central Committee of
the Communist Party, and other Soviet leaders and discussed a number
of central issues. On the issue of a peace conference, those in favour,
led by Hawatima, maintained that the new political developments in
the Middle East created a situation which could be exploited for
recognition by the international community of a Palestinian national
entity and even for the foundation of a Palestinian state. Those who
opposed this view, led by Habash, claimed that participation of the
PLO in a peace conference would be interpreted as a *de facto*

recognition of the State of Israel and as such, a betrayal of the
Palestinian national ideal.[20] Moreover, there was an important legal
argument against PLO participation at Geneva. UN Resolution 338,
which had made provision for the convening of the Geneva Peace
Conference, had given it the task of implementing UN Resolution 242
which, as mentioned above, had never been accepted by the PLO.

In the ensuing period the Soviet Union continued to favour the
PLO's participation in the Geneva Conference as the representative of
the Palestinian people. It was in this context particularly that the Soviet
Union considered it essential that the PLO should present a united
front, able to put forward a national political platform, which would
be demonstrated in the formation of a Palestinian government-in-exile
with leaders drawn from the West Bank and the Gaza Strip.[21]
Accordingly, the Soviet Union was very careful not to favour officially
any one of the Palestinian organisations, emphasising rather the
Palestinian issue as a whole and possible political resolutions.

Hardly less troublesome in the Soviet–Palestinian relationship was
the definition of the future Palestinian state and its boundaries, the
main issue being whether this could be based on the West Bank and
Gaza Strip territories occupied by Israel – what the Palestinians refer to
as a 'mini-state' and the Soviet Union officially favours.

These then were the points at issue in Soviet–Palestinian contacts
which became increasingly frequent. Following the November meeting
in Moscow, Gromyko met Yasir Arafat on two occasions during his visit
to the Middle East in March 1974, in Cairo and Damascus. According to
a source close to the Palestinians, the Lebanese *al-Muharrir*, a promise
was made to Arafat by both Gromyko and the Egyptian government
that no part of Palestine would be returned to Jordan. Other PLO
spokesmen claimed that the Soviet Union promised to recognise the
Palestinian state on the West Bank and the Gaza Strip as soon as it
might be established.[22] No Soviet source published any details of
Gromyko's talks with Arafat, apart from the issuing of an official
invitation to Moscow by the Soviet government (previously Arafat's
visits to Moscow had been under the aegis of the Soviet Committee for
Solidarity with the Countries of Asia and Africa). This invitation was at
one and the same time an important step towards full recognition of
the PLO and proof that Soviet policy, fighting a rearguard action to
preserve its leverage regarding a Middle East settlement, would
emphasise the Palestinian issue in any political negotiations and come
out in defence of the Palestinian people by attracting the attention of
the international community to their plight.

In June 1974, the Palestine National Council decided to found a ruling authority on the West Bank and the Gaza Strip — although the term 'state' was not mentioned so that there would be no misunderstanding that a 'mini-state' was being considered.[23] In the same month Soviet sources stated clearly for the first time that the 'national legitimate rights of the Palestinians' which Moscow supported in fact meant an independent state.[24] The Soviet sources now claimed that immediately after the war Arafat did indeed accept the idea of a Palestinian state on the West Bank and the Gaza Strip and tried to direct PLO policy in that direction. Just before the Rabat conference in October even Brezhnev spoke unambiguously about a Palestinian state.[25] At the same time official Soviet statements were on the whole studiously noncommittal on the question of boundaries. The assumption must be that Moscow would agree to any such state that might come into existence between Jordan and Israel, either on the West Bank and the Gaza Strip (the areas occupied by Israel since June 1967) or in the entire area allotted to the Arab state by the Partition Resolution of 29 November 1947;[26] as we shall see below there have been indications that the growing political awareness of Israel's own Arab population is likely to lead to an unequivocal preference for the latter. The question of the Palestinian state's eastern border with Jordan is always carefully skirted in public deliberations or comments.

Soviet support for the idea of a Palestinian mini-state was in fact fraught with problems in Moscow's relationships with the splinter groups of the PLO, mainly with Habash. In September 1974, Habash resigned from the executive committee of the PLO in demonstration of his opposition to what he defined as the PLO's 'moderate line'. His group, along with the PFLP—General Command, the Arab Liberation Front and the Popular Struggle Front, forms what is known as the Rejection Front within the PLO, which refuses to agree to any negotiations with Israel. On the other hand Moscow considered Naif Hawatima to be a realistic leader who 'understood the processes of history' and claimed that he agreed to the concept of a Palestinian state on the West Bank and the Gaza Strip,[27] although in fact Hawatima made it clear that this was merely an intermediate and temporary step on the way to complete national fulfilment.

Despite reservations regarding the Ma'alot incident (see above) which was carried out by Hawatima's followers, Moscow continued to emphasise Hawatima's 'moderate approach' and his tendency to a realistic solution with regard for the pragmatic needs of the situation, in contrast to the unrealistic demands of the more radical elements among the Palestinians and continued formal relations with the Democratic Popular Front.[28]

While Hawatima's tactical acceptance of the idea of a mini-state suited the USSR, Arafat's approach was more ambiguous and therefore less convenient for Soviet purposes. Indeed, Arafat never made any public statement in favour of a mini-state. The Soviet Union explained this by the negative influences of the radical Palestinian elements of the Rejection Front which, in its view, undermined all decision making and all movement towards constructive solutions to the Palestine problem. The uncompromising attitude of these groupings hindered Arafat's ability to manoeuvre towards a political solution, although from time to time, Moscow claimed, the PLO was able to overcome the splintering factions in the disputes and to present a united front. This claim would be made when the relations between the Soviet Union and the PLO were improved, as a result, according to the Soviet press, of 'the growing maturity' of the PLO.[29]

The Soviet Union persistently sought to encourage this 'maturity', as can be seen from the numerous discussions between Soviet and Palestinian leaders. When Arafat visited Moscow between 30 July and 4 August 1974, he headed a Palestinian delegation consisting of Zuhayr Muhsin, the secretary of as-Saiqa (the Vanguard of the Popular Liberation War) which is under Syrian influence; Yasir Abd-Rabuh from Hawatima's Democratic Front; Taysir Qubah from Habash's Popular Front: Abu-Mayzar, the spokesman of the PLO; and Faruq Qaddumi, head of the PLO's Political Department. This coalition delegation was intended to demonstrate the united/front which existed in the Palestinian organisations. The arrival of the delegation in Moscow was the occasion for Tolkunov's above-mentioned article in *Izvestiia* (30 July). In it the Palestinians were asked to explain their platform and define their tactical and strategic goals. The article condemned radical Palestinian elements for being 'unrealistic' and at the same time praised the three main leaders — Arafat, Habash and Hawatima — for realising the importance of Soviet support and the need for a realistic and practical platform. It referred to a joint Egyptian—Jordan statement, made at the end of July, in which it was stated that the PLO did not represent the Palestinians living in Jordan, to prove that the USSR, together with the radical Arab states — Libya, Syria and Iraq — were the mainstay and support of the PLO, as against the 'Arab reactionaries', Egypt, Jordan and Saudi Arabia, who were supported by and collaborated with American imperialism.[30] At the end of the visit a joint communiqué was issued. The three operative paragraphs said:

(a) The sides noted with satisfaction the importance of the decision taken at the conference of the heads of the Arab states in Algiers (November 1973) and the conference of Muslim states in Lahore (February 1974) on the recognition of the PLO as the sole legitimate representative of the Arab people of Palestine.

(b) The Soviet Union expressed its support of the participation of the Palestine Liberation Organisation in the Geneva Conference and exercising equal rights with other participants.

and

(c) In answer to the request of the Palestine Liberation Organisation executive committee, the Soviet side gave consent to the opening of a PLO representation in Moscow.[31]

In this statement the Soviet Union thus drew yet closer to full recognition of the PLO. Moscow expressed its fundamental approach, which has been reiterated many times, that the PLO should be an equal and active participant in the Geneva Peace Conference. This is an important tactical gesture but obviously problematic given both Israel's consistent opposition to this demand and the disunity and bickering within the Palestinian organisations over the same issue.

In the context of its efforts to achieve Palestinian participation at Geneva, the Soviet Union realised that a new interpretation should be found of Resolution 242, more amenable to the Palestinians. The *Izvestiia* article said, for example, that the Geneva Peace Conference would convene with the participation of the PLO only on condition that the Palestinian question be defined 'as a political question, as a question of securing the lawful national rights of the Arab people of Palestine, and is not confined to the refugee problem'.[32]

Soviet recognition of the PLO as the sole representative of the Palestinians was, however, clearly qualified, since on this point the statement referred specifically to the Lahore and Algiers conferences. The Soviet Union was not ready to commit itself to an unambiguous formula in regard to a subject on which there was no clear consensus among either the Palestinians or the Arab states (the visit took place prior to the Rabat Conference of October 1974). Only after the Rabat Conference did the Soviet Union support UN General Assembly Resolution 3236 of 22 November 1974, which recognised the Palestinian problem as a political, national one, and indirectly recognised the PLO as the sole representative of the Palestinian people.

The discussion during a further Arafat visit to Moscow (from 25 to 30 November 1974) was influenced by the Rabat Conference. It was during this visit that Arafat for the first time officially met Prime

Minister Kosygin and the Soviet mass media gave wide coverage to the visit and to the political achievements of the PLO. The TASS announcement of the meeting between Kosygin and Arafat was worded as if this were the meeting between two heads of state.[33] The joint communiqué issued at the end of the visit, pledging the Soviet Union's continued support for 'the struggle of the Arab people of Palestine for their legitimate rights, including their inalienable rights to self-determination and creation of their own national home up to the formation of their statehood', approved the Rabat decisions.[34]

Throughout the next year, when the PLO was a centre of attention at the UN, the Soviet Union considered itself the patron of the PLO. These discussions at the UN, in which the Palestinian entity was recognised *de facto* by the international community, served to highlight the Soviet achievement of emphasising the Palestinian issue as the heart of the conflict in the Middle East. This fact placed the United States under very heavy pressure, as was manifested when it was compelled to use its veto in the Security Council in January 1976 (against a resolution calling for the establishment of a Palestinian state and the right of the refugees to return to their old homes) and to stand alone in its support of Israel.

The Soviet Union, however, was unable to translate its apparent victory at the UN into meaningful political successes in the Middle East. It made tremendous efforts to regain some of the initiative in the Middle East, seeking to use the PLO to block Kissinger's attempts to reach interim agreements between Israel and the confrontation states. Aleksandr Soldatov, an important diplomatic figure, was appointed Soviet ambassador to the Lebanon in September 1974, apparently because PLO headquarters were centred in Beirut.[35] Diplomatic contacts between Moscow and the PLO in the period increased significantly and in addition to the visits by Hawatima and Arafat to Moscow in November 1974, on 2 February 1975 Gromyko met Arafat in Damascus as also did Vladimir Vinogradov, Soviet Ambassador to the Geneva Conference, on his Middle East tour in March. Between 28 April and 4 May Arafat led yet another PLO delegation to Moscow where he met Gromyko. This visit concluded a round of meetings that Moscow had initiated with the Arab foreign ministers in an attempt to exploit Kissinger's failure to reach an interim agreement between Israel and Egypt in March 1975.[36] It seems that during this visit a certain amount of progress was made in convincing the PLO to participate at Geneva, as indicated in the joint statement issued in Moscow on the conclusion of the visit in which the two sides 'stressed the importance of the participation of the representatives of the Palestinian Arab people, with equal rights with other interested sides in an effort towards a Middle East settlement, a Geneva Peace Conference on the Middle East included'.[37] From Palestinian comments after the visit, it seems that Resolution 242 was discussed in Moscow, yet no mention was made of it in Soviet statements on the visit. However, the PLO delegation, which from Moscow went to Prague and Sofia, insisted that the Geneva Conference must convene only on the basis of General Assembly Resolution 3236 which the PLO regarded as an amendment to Security Council Resolution 242. For its part the Soviet Union avoided even mentioning this Resolution in its constant demands to reconvene the Geneva Conference so as not to create unnecessary difficulties. Only after the signing of the second interim agreement between Egypt and Israel in September 1975 and after a new bout of discussions of the Palestinian issue at the UN, did the Soviet Union link the convening of the conference in Geneva to UN Resolution 3236 in addition to Resolution 338.[38] The Soviet Union considered the Geneva Peace Conference as the most suitable framework through which a final settlement could be reached and was of the opinion that the PLO had to participate as an equal partner in the conference. This could be achieved only if the basis for discussion were Resolution 3236. Since then the Soviet Union has not referred to any particular resolution, preferring such general statements as 'appropriate UN decisions'.[39]

For a Soviet political initiative to have reasonable chances of success Moscow needed the PLO to imply, even in the most indirect manner, *de facto* recognition of the state of Israel and thus enable the Soviet Union, through the United States, to bring pressure to bear on Israel to recognise the PLO. This recognition was vital because the Soviet Union has always stressed its willingness to participate in international guarantees to Israel within an overall settlement.[40] However, during discussions with Arafat no progress was made in this direction. Against this background of deadlock Arafat returned to Moscow on 25–30 November 1975. Just prior to this visit, on 9 November, Gromyko had sent a memorandum to Kissinger seeking to initiate the reconvening of the Geneva Conference.[41] The joint communiqué issued at the end of Arafat's visit included his express support of this Soviet initiative.[42] Indeed, Gromyko and Ponomarev succeeded in convincing Arafat that the PLO delegation would be able to raise any matter it wished at Geneva, specifically 'the satisfaction of the legitimate national rights of the Arab people of Palestine, including its right to create a national state of its own on Palestinian territory in accordance with UN resolutions'.[43]

At a press conference on 27 November Arafat explained that the Palestinians' agreement to participate in the Geneva Conference was based on international law as defined in UN Resolution 3236 in which the PLO was recognised as the sole representative of the Arab people of Palestine. He emphasised once more the importance of the Soviet initiative in convening the Geneva Peace Conference.[44] It should be noted too that in the joint communiqué the Soviet Union had made certain concessions to the PLO such as omitting any reference to guarantees of the security of the existing states in the Middle East and, in the paragraph on the Israeli withdrawal, refraining from specific mention of 'territories occupied in 1967'.

In the joint communiqué the Soviet Union confirmed the Palestinians' right to fulfil their legitimate national rights on Palestinian territory 'according to UN resolutions'. It seems that this formula was the most that both sides could agree upon, since in subsequent interpretations it was evident that no real progress had been made towards reaching a common policy. The formula could be interpreted as *de facto* recognition of the existence of a Jewish state, which is also based on UN resolutions. Yet, while *New Times* reiterated the usual Soviet position on a political solution to the Middle East conflict at the time that the joint statement with Arafat was published,[45] the PLO declared unequivocally that the joint statement should not be interpreted as recognition of Israel. Faruq Qaddumi said in Italy 'many people want us to recognise Israel. What sort of recognition can we give if we do not represent a state? In order to recognise someone you have yourself to be someone'.[46]

The general impression gained after Arafat's November visit was that the disagreements between the Soviet Union and the PLO had not been solved. The Soviet mass media played down the visit and the PLO's spokesman stated that another PLO delegation would come to Moscow in the near future in order to discuss the opening of the PLO office in Moscow that had been agreed upon over a year earlier.[47] This issue was in fact an interesting indication of the differences between the PLO and the Soviet Union. East Germany had agreed to the opening of an office in Berlin in August 1973, previous to the October War; a PLO office had opened in Bulgaria in August 1974, in Czechoslovakia in May 1975, and in Hungary in September 1975. Yet the Soviet Union lagged behind: the office in Moscow was opened only in June 1976 and then without full diplomatic recognition but merely as representing the PLO to the Soviet Committee of Solidarity with the countries of Asia and Africa. One may perhaps infer that, once again, the Soviet Union was trying to keep all the options open and not to commit itself to any definite position.[48]

From November 1975 it became obvious that the Soviet political initiative was unable to get off the ground mainly because of the inflexible policy of the PLO and, during 1976, because of the added complication of the civil war in Lebanon. Syria's role in the civil war is discussed elsewhere in this volume. What concerns us here is the dilemma which the USSR faced when two of its allies in the region — Syria and the Palestinians — began to fight each other.[49] Since the outbreak of the Lebanese War, the USSR had supported the Leftist elements in Lebanon, including the PLO, accusing the Right of undertaking provocations against the 'progressive elements' and of causing the civil war with the agreement and support of the Arab reactionary states and American imperialism.[50] However, the Syrian armed intervention and attempt to impose a ceasefire which would maintain Syrian influence in Lebanon soon led to conflict between Damascus and the Palestinians. The dissension between its two protégés prevented the Soviet Union from maintaining a clearly defined position on the war in Lebanon and particularly on the Syrian involvement, although, as we shall see below, it seemed in practice to prefer its relations with the Syrian government, even at the risk of possibly jeopardising its ties with the Left and the PLO. However, this preference was not clearly expressed in public statements and in the mass media.

The Soviet dilemma was highlighted when Kosygin visited Syria at the beginning of June 1976. The joint communiqué at the end of the visit reaffirmed that a just and lasting peace in the Middle East could be reached only if all the territories occupied by Israel in 1967 were liberated and the national rights of the Palestinians to self-determination and 'a national home' were fulfilled.[51] The replacement of the Palestinian state by a 'national home' was obviously initiated by the Syrians because Kosygin, in his address to Syrian Prime Minister Mahmud al-Ayyubi, referred explicity to a Palestinian state. On the other hand, the Syrian prime minister spoke on the same occasion in very general and vague terms, referring to the Palestinians' right to self-determination.[52] Presumably the federation that was to emerge as a result of Syria's recent alignment with Jordan[53] would include a 'national home' for the Palestinians. A commentary which appeared in *Pravda* after the visit actually stated that 'the representatives of the Palestinian people' should participate in the Geneva Peace Conference, without reference to the PLO.[54] Thus, having to choose whether to support Syria (which had become the focus of Soviet strategy with regard to the Arab–Israeli conflict) or to lose its foothold in that country, the Soviet Union preferred the former option, especially given the weakening of Soviet influence in the Middle East as a result of the cancellation of the Treaty of Friendship and Co-operation with Egypt and the improved relations between the United States and Syria itself. At first, the Soviet Union continued supporting Syria. Nonetheless, as the Syrian involvement in Lebanon became more complicated, Soviet criticism of Syria gradually increased. The PLO and the radical Arab states, Algeria, Iraq and Libya, meanwhile demanded that the Soviet Union condemn and even take action against Syria. Moscow preferred giving moral support and sympathetic propaganda coverage to the PLO to placing real pressure on Syria and it was as part of this scenario that the PLO office was opened in Moscow (see above). Tension between Syria and the Soviet Union mounted at the beginning of July. When Foreign Minister Abd al-Halim Khaddam went to Moscow to find out whether the Soviet Union had reneged on its original stand of support for Syria and more specifically to ensure that arms shipments and other aid would continue, Moscow appears to have warned Syria not to over-step the mark in its attacks on the PLO. At the same time the Soviet Committee of Solidarity with the Countries of Asia and Africa sent out a call to all 'peace-loving forces' to support the PLO and the 'progressive elements' in Lebanon and emphasised that the conflict in Lebanon should be terminated without 'interference from foreign countries'.[55]

As Syrian pressure on the PLO grew and the organisation's situation became extremely grave, the PLO increased its demands on the Soviet Union to take up an active political stance against Syria. In mid-July Brezhnev sent President Asad a memorandum, apparently asking for a ceasefire.[56] When, on 29 July, a ceasefire agreement between Syria and the PLO was signed, TASS published the Syrian Communist Party's declaration supporting it.[57] This declaration completely ignored the subject of Syrian withdrawal from Lebanon, but emphasised the patriotic duty of 'the Arab national forces' and the PLO to make an effort to liberate the 'occupied territories' and to guarantee 'the national rights of the Arab people of Palestine'. It explained, moreover, that the crisis in Lebanon had come about as a result of a conspiracy between the USA, Israel and international Zionism with the intention of spilling the blood of both Syria and the PLO. Finally, it maintained that the agreement of Syria and the PLO strengthened the friendly relations and collaboration of the Soviet Union with them.

The Soviet press expressed the optimistic approach that the ceasefire agreement would last and would lead to the end of the conflict. The ceasefire was defined as a significant step towards the normalisation of relations between Syria and the PLO.[58] At the same time the Soviet Union continued to state its opposition to the partition of Lebanon. It also gave much publicity to the Israeli 'naval blockade'[59] which enabled the Soviet Union to take diplomatic steps on an issue that would not harm its relations either with Syria or the PLO. On 13 August Moscow sent a telegram to Washington asking the USA to interfere and break the Israeli blockade. This was a manifest demonstration of Soviet support of the PLO which was not at the expense of Syria.[60]

When the fighting was renewed shortly afterwards, some criticism of the Syrian role in Lebanon appeared in the Soviet press.[61] However, soon an attack appeared on 'leftist elements among the Palestinians' for sabotaging any attempt to end the crisis in Lebanon. For the first time the Soviet Union was openly accusing the Palestinian radical elements of being the direct cause of the continuation of the crisis in Lebanon, which served the interests neither of the PLO, the Syrians, nor the Soviet Union.[62] This statement brought into the open the Soviet criticism of the PLO and its preference for Syria.

The Lebanese Civil War thus showed that the PLO, in spite of its increasing political importance, was regarded by the Soviets as a secondary force *vis-à-vis* the local Arab governments; its significance has been only tactical.

The main question arising in the light of the various constraints of Soviet—PLO relations which we have so far discussed is whether the Soviet Union contemplated seeking an alternative to the PLO and what measures it used to influence the PLO to behave in accordance with Soviet interests. There is naturally no documentation upon which to base an unequivocal answer. A clue, however, may perhaps be found in Soviet comment on developments in the Israeli-occupied territories and trends among their population. According to the Soviet conception of a national resistance movement, by which the oppressed population must be the core of the national revolution, a Palestinian resistance movement should be a mass movement against Israeli occupation, imperialism and colonialism.[63] Such a movement was expected to express the interests of the masses and unite all progressive and national elements. However, reality on the West Bank and the Gaza Strip was completely different and was no less a disappointment to the Soviet Union than was the PLO. This sentiment was expressed in *New Times*: 'The guerrilla action sprang and developed largely spontaneously without any political platform, without any definite outlook . . . [The guerrillas] embarked upon adventurism and terror . . . which prevented them from founding a strong mass base in the occupied Arab territory'.[64]

The Soviet Union had attempted from 1969 to activate a mass Palestinian movement through the Jordanian Communist Party whose members on the West Bank incited the population to demonstrations and strikes, opposing the use of terror. Some Communist cells meanwhile accumulated weapons for a future stage when the national opposition would pass from passive organised resistance to political activity led by a popular front, and finally to military opposition. In March 1970 the Arab Communists on the West Bank founded an underground organisation, al-Ansar, the objective of which was to create a firm political base in the Palestinian movement and which was a Communist attempt to influence and maybe control the Palestinian resistance movement.[65] However, it remained a relatively small movement till the Palestine National Front (PNF) was established in August 1973.

In May 1973 the Jordanian Communist Party published a memorandum calling for the foundation of a Palestinian national front. It stated that the Communist Party was doing its best to unite and strengthen the Palestinian national movement and to consolidate the ties between the Arab national liberation movement with the world revolutionary movement under the leadership of the Soviet Union and the socialist countries.[66] The Jordanian Communist Party suggested that the resistance movement and the PLO should:

1. Unite their various factions on the basis of a realistic platform.
2. Unite all the Palestinian elements in the occupied territories and thus enable representation from all strata of the population. The new PLO council would then elect an executive committee which would be the legal representative of the Palestinian people and direct its struggle.
3. Re-evaluate the existing platform of the PLO and prepare a new platform based on (a) a new approach to the UN resolutions dealing with the Palestinian issue; and (b) a confirmation of the belief that the Palestinian national movement is part of the liberation movement of the Arab nation.
4. Define its main goal at the present stage, which should be the liquidation of the Israeli imperialist aggression from 1967, and struggle for the fulfilment of UN Resolution 242, which included

the withdrawal of the Israeli forces from all the Arab-occupied
territories and guaranteed the legitimate rights of the Palestinian
Arab people and their right to define their future.

5. Support by all means the foundation of a broad national front in
the occupied territories to oppose Israel's occupation and the policy
of settling Jews on Arab land and of forcing Arab emigration from
the West Bank.

6. Found a military resistance movement in the occupied territories.

7. Actively support the return of the PLO to Jordan.

This call on the part of the Jordanian Communist Party emphasised
the political solution to the Palestinian problem. It demanded that the
main impetus behind the struggle for its implementation come from the
Palestinian people living in the occupied territories while the Palestine
National Front become the political cornerstone of this Palestinian
resistance movement.[67]

The PNF, whose platform was based on this memorandum, included
the Communist party, socialists, ex-Ba'thi members, individuals from
groups opposing King Husayn on the West Bank, trade unions and
representatives of the free professions. Its platform emphasised that the
PNF regarded itself as an integral part of the PLO even though
demanding a revision of its policy.[68] The foundation of the PNF was
viewed by its leaders as a turning point which transformed the
Palestinian movement into a fully-fledged national movement with a
political and organisational framework embracing all the national
organisations. The different social strata represented in the various
political organisations that had existed heretofore now met in the PNF
as a result of a common interest and with the object of fulfilling a
common goal, namely the liberation of Palestinian territory from Israeli
occupation and the implementation of the Palestinian right to
self-determination.

Hardly any information is available on how the PNF operates or is
organised. Till the end of 1974 its activities were kept well concealed.
When arrested its members would admit to membership of the Front
and stress that their activities were solely political, having nothing to do
with questions of security. The Israeli security forces for their part did
not necessarily see membership of the PNF as a reason for punitive
measures.[69]

At the end of 1974 and the beginning of 1975, as reported by
foreign correspondents in Beirut relying on information from PLO
sources, a number of Palestinian activists brought to trial by the Israeli

authorities admitted that they had undergone military and ideological training in the Soviet Union and that they were members of the PNF. Those of its members who had been in Moscow for training were active in leftist circles and were in touch with members of the Jordanian Communist Party.[70] At the trial of Muhammad Yasin, an engineer from Nablus and member of the PNF, the judge, Lieutenant-Colonel Gershon Orion, stated that the Soviet Union ran a special training camp on Soviet territory for recruits from the West Bank who reached it secretly, carrying false documents. Yasin confessed to being a PNF member and said he had gone to Jordan on 4 November 1974. There he had been introduced to a number of people in the Amman clinic of Dr Yaqub Ziya ad-Din, the well-known Communist leader, and had then been transferred to the Soviet Embassy in Damascus where he had received a visa to the Soviet Union on 13 November and flown directly to Moscow. In the USSR he had received a new identity card under the name of Qasim Rashid and begun to study philosophy, economics, first aid and the use of weapons. During the trial an Israeli security representative explained that the aim of the PNF was to incite to demonstrate, to distribute pamphlets and slogans and carry out sabotage; he added that Yasin's training had not been organised through regular PLO channels.[71]

The PNF was represented in the Palestinian National Council, its delegation including people who had been expelled from the West Bank. Abd al-Jawad Salih, the ex-mayor of El-Bira who was expelled in 1974, actually headed the delegation; it was his view that since the leaders of the PNF had gone underground in the occupied territories, only those who had been expelled could participate in the Council.

At the end of 1975 and in early 1976, the existence of an active national movement became apparent. This movement attempted to channel the dissatisfaction of the Palestinian people into political activity and indeed succeeded in organising massive protest against the Israeli occupation. The discussion of the UN Security Council on the Palestinian issue on 12 January 1976 — with the participation of a PLO representative (and in the absence of the Israeli representative) — was not only the source of much satisfaction in the occupied territories; it also led to a new wave of demonstrations and disorders in protest against the US veto.[72] Radio Moscow emphasised the significant role of the PNF in organising these activities and described the history of this organisation and the important contribution of Communist participation in the PNF.[73]

The establishment of a Jewish settlement at Qaddum on the West

Bank by Gush Emmunim — a radical national-religious organisation —
incited a new wave of demonstrations and protests. The attempt of
Betar (the youth movement of the Israeli radical right-wing Herut
party) to pray on the Temple Mount in Jerusalem at the beginning of
March was also followed by an outcry. Unrest, in the form of student
demonstrations, a business shutdown, the resignation of seven mayors
on the West Bank and numerous political meetings, reached its peak at
the time of the elections to the municipal councils on 12 April 1976.[74]
In these elections the PNF played a significant role, the East Jerusalem
al-Fajr appealing to the population to participate in them as a national
duty. It was explained that they would be used to frustrate the Israeli
intention to set up Arab administrative autonomy in the occupied
territories.[75]

In order to demonstrate a united front between the PNF and PLO
the dividing line between them was blurred in the election campaign.
Radio Moscow however, in explaining developments on the West Bank,
characterised the new dynamics as one of struggle against the
occupation, which had increased after the formation of the PNF. The
Palestinian struggle, it claimed, was being fought at this stage on a
political front which took the form of mass demonstrations, public
protests, strikes and business shutdowns. In this manner, Radio Moscow
went on, the population was showing its strength and its readiness to
draw closer to the PLO and Arab progressive elements, as well as to the
'Arabs inhabiting Israel'.[76]

Just before the elections, a PNF delegation, headed by Abd al-Jawad
Salih, arrived in Moscow for a week's stay (from 5 to 12 April). The
visit had been initiated by the Soviet Union, apparently following a
decision to establish direct contacts with the representatives of the
Palestinian population on the West Bank as a result of political
developments there; the Soviet search for ways to demonstrate its
sympathy and support for those Palestinians not connected with the
conflict in Lebanon; and the need to find a possible alternative to the
PLO as representative of the Palestinian cause at the Geneva
Conference.

The TASS announcement which described the visit said the
delegation reported to the Soviet Union on the massive demonstrations
of the Palestinian population and the important PNF contribution to
organising Palestinian political resistance. The delegation was said to
have made it clear that the PNF considered itself a part of the PLO.[77]

Indeed, the PNF and Soviet approaches on the need for a political
solution to the Arab—Israeli conflict were co-ordinated both

ideologically and politically. The PNF, moreover, suited the Soviet concept of a national movement based on the masses.[78] It could be expected that at a certain stage Moscow might suggest that the PNF represent the demands of the local population for a Palestinian national state at the Geneva Peace Conference.

The outcome of the elections strengthened the status of the PNF. In the key cities of Nablus, Tulkarem, Hebron and Ramallah the national blocs founded on PNF initiative gained an overwhelming victory. Most of the 150 new faces on the city councils were young academicians or free professionals with strong national tendencies, many of whom had sympathies with the PNF.[79] Although the role of the local municipalities is limited to municipal problems, daily contacts with the Israeli military administration and attempts to raise money from Jordan, the elections crystallised the political and social changes afoot on the West Bank. These changes brought to light a new leadership which not only sought to demonstrate greater efficiency at the municipal level but was committed to a Palestinian national ideology to be expressed in the future. The Soviet Union for its part was highly satisfied with the results of the elections and considered them a victory for the PNF.[80]

At the same time important developments were taking place among the Israeli Arabs. While the entire subject of the Israeli Arabs is beyond the scope of this paper, it is necessary to stress the manner in which the Soviet Union links developments among them to the Palestinian cause. Moreover, in the Israeli Communist Party (Rakah), the USSR has an instrument similar to the Jordanian Communist Party-initiated PNF. Since the October War a process of radicalisation has taken place among the Israeli Arabs as expressed in the elections to the municipal council of Nazareth in December 1975, where Rakah won by a wide margin, and in the 'Day of the Land' demonstrations on 30 March 1976.[81] There is indeed a correlation between the national awakening of the Israeli Arab minority and the PLO and West Bank Arab attitude to this population. The Palestine National Council, at its eighth conference in Cairo in 1971, had already co-opted three Israeli Arabs as representatives of the Palestinian Arabs 'under Israeli occupation since 1948'.[82] In the political programme adopted by the Palestine National Council in Cairo in 1972, clear goals were defined in regard to the Israeli Arabs.

> . . . to strengthen the national unity between our citizens of the occupied territories since 1948 with those of the West Bank and

those who are outside our occupied country . . . to protect our citizens in the occupied territories since 1948 and support their struggle to preserve their Arab national identity; to adopt their problems and assist them in uniting in the struggle for liberation.[83]

These resolutions were expressed in PLO propaganda on the eve of the elections in Nazareth. The PLO appealed to the citizens of Nazareth to vote for the Democratic Front under Rakah leadership. The demonstrations on the 'Day of the Land', which underlined the process of radicalisation prevalent among the Israeli Arabs, were organised officially by the Committee for the Protection of Arab Lands, in which Rakah played a dominant role, as the Soviet press pointed out. To all intents and purposes Rakah became the mouthpiece for the cry against government appropriation of Arab lands in the Galilee and won great popularity among the Israeli Arabs.

Rakah has been consistently loyal to the Soviet stand on the Middle East both ideologically and politically and has maintained good relations with the Communists both in the Gaza Strip and, particularly, on the West Bank.[84] It considers the Palestinian resistance movement an anti-imperialist nationalist movement fighting against occupation and for the fulfilment of the political rights of the Palestinian people. While it recognises the PLO as the sole representative of the Palestinian people, it does not support the idea of a 'Palestinian national secular state'. Rather, it mirrors and represents the Soviet conception of a Palestinian state adjacent to the Israeli one within its June 1967 borders.[85] However, Rakah Knesset member Tawfiq Ziyyad said on the 1st of May celebration in 1976 that if the Israeli Arabs were not given full equality they would 'publicise in the press the need for a new state which will accept them together with their lands'.[86] This statement suits the Soviet conception of the need to keep the subject of the demarcation lines open. One may assume that should the question of the Israeli Arabs reach crisis proportions, Rakah would support their secession to an adjacent Palestinian Arab state together with their lands, maybe even considering a compromise between the borders of 1947 and these of 1967.

At its 18th Congress in December 1976 in Haifa Rakah followed exactly the Soviet approach to a settlement in the Middle East. A peace programme was adopted, emphasising the collaboration of Jewish and Palestinian Communists and 'progressive elements'.[87] During 1977 this programme of collaboration was indeed implemented. At the beginning of March Rakah and a number of small Jewish and Arab leftist organisations decided to put up a single list of candidates for the forthcoming general elections in Israel (May 1977). The new alliance was named The Democratic Front for Peace and Equality (Haddash).[88]

Thus a front was set up in Israel parallel to the PNF, and its foundation was duly welcomed by the Soviet government.[89] The PLO also indicated its approval: the Palestine National Council which met in Cairo on 14–21 March 1977 stressed 'the importance of the relations with progressive democratic Jewish forces in the occupied patria and abroad, forces which are fighting Zionism as an ideology and practice'.[90]

Immediately after the session of the Palestine National Council in which a major attempt was made to demonstrate a more moderate approach and a Palestinian consensus, Arafat led a large delegation of representatives from the different organisations to Moscow (4–8 April). It was his first visit since November 1975 and indicated a new search for a closer relationship between the USSR and the PLO. Moscow made great efforts to welcome the delegation, and for the first time Arafat was received by Leonid Brezhnev. Nonetheless, it seems that the two sides could not reach an agreement beyond the usual statements and therefore no joint official communiqué was issued at the end of the visit.

TASS, however, published a very interesting commentary after the visit which emphasised that

> Leonid Brezhnev reiterated the principled course of the CPSU and the Soviet state aimed at attaining an all-embracing Middle East settlement, of which ensuring the national rights of the Palestine Arab people, its right to self-determination, including the creation of an independent Palestine state must be an integral element.

The TASS commentator noted that Arafat too 'expressed deep satisfaction' with the 'excellent' Soviet–Palestinian relations. Although no specific issues were mentioned, it is of interest to note that this statement expressed the Soviet Union's ideological support for the PLO as a national liberation movement and an active anti-imperialist force:

> The Palestine resistance movement has traversed a hard road of courageous armed struggle, of growing national consciousness and political maturity, uninterrupted efforts to strengthen the movement's ranks. Today the Palestine resistance movement, which scored considerable successes in the matter of upholding the

legitimate rights of the Palestinians, has become one of the avanguard [*sic*] detachments of the Arab national liberation movement, and assumed a well pronounced anti-imperialist orientation. The Palestine liberation organisation has become a recognised and tested leader of the Palestinian struggle, the sole legitimate representative of the Palestine people.

The statement concluded by welcoming the resolutions of the Palestine National Council

'aimed at strengthening the unity of the Palestinian ranks and which elaborated a concrete action programme'. 'It also said that the 'most important decisions' included attaining unity in the military sphere, reiterating the right of the PLO to participation at every international forum where the Palestine problem and the Arab—Israel conflict are being discussed, confirming the course towards developing co-operation with socialist countries'.[91]

A month later, at the beginning of May, the PLO held a first official meeting with representatives of Rakah.[92] The Soviet mass media paid great attention to this meeting, describing it as 'a historic event and a major contribution to peace and the independence of peoples, as well as the anti-imperialist struggle in the Middle East'.[93] The Rakah—PLO meeting was presented as a significant step in the Soviet initiative for peace in the area.

Thus, after the crisis of 1976, the relations between the Soviet Union and the Palestinians improved formally, if not in substance. However, the international position of the Palestinians was beginning to change: President Carter's statement in favour of a Palestinian homeland[94] may well have opened up a new American political initiative in which the Soviet Union will have to react to US initiatives even on the Palestinian issue.

Conclusion

Since the October War Soviet—Palestinian relations have come a long way. The Palestinian issue became a cornerstone of Soviet policy in the Middle East. Nonetheless, whereas in 1973—4 the Soviet Union was able to use the Palestinians to obstruct American policy in the Middle East by encouraging a radical Arab position, the Palestinians turned out to be too independent to accept all-out Soviet patronage and dictates. As a result, the Soviet Union found itself reacting to developments in the area, unable to take a political initiative based on the special Soviet–PLO relationship.

We have seen, for example, how the Lebanese crisis complicated Soviet–Palestinian relations even further. On the one hand, it was in the Soviet interest for the PLO to take a certain amount of punishment from the Syrians to make it more dependent on the Soviet Union. On the other hand, the punishment should not be so severe as to make the PLO wholly dependent on an Arab state. After the Lebanese civil war, because of its dissatisfaction with Soviet–PLO relations, the Soviet Union turned its attention to the Palestinians of the West Bank, who were undergoing a process of political and social change. The Soviet Union tried to build a direct bridge to the local population in the Israeli-occupied territories in order to put pressure on the PLO. It therefore emphasised the role of the PNF as an organiser of a popular Palestinian mass resistance movement, and as an indication of the political evolution of the local population. Nonetheless, although the PNF might indeed have eventually become an alternative to the PLO, it was presented by the Soviet media as an organic part of the PLO, probably in order not to antagonise the latter.

To conclude, it seems that the prospects for Soviet success in the Middle East are quite limited even concerning the Palestinian issue. The Soviet Union is in a very delicate position in which it has little room for political manoeuvring. Even though its consistent support of the Palestinians in the international arena and contacts with the PLO have given it a definite advantage in its attempt to establish its influence in the Middle East, this advantage is by no means certain. The USA itself has sought an approach to the Palestinians, as evidenced by several statements made by President Carter in the first months of his administration. The continued internal disputes in the PLO and its inability to reach a minimally moderate course that might pave the way to participation in the process of a negotiated settlement seem, however, to make it less and less satisfactory as a viable representative of the Palestinian people. The Soviet Union may, therefore, lose the political advantage it has created through its consistent support of the Palestinian issue.

Notes

1. See Robert O. Freedman, 'The Soviet Conception of a Middle East Peace Settlement', in this volume.
2. For Egypt see Yaacov Ro'i, 'The Soviet Union and Egypt: the Constraints of a Power-Client Relationship', in this volume.
3. On 29 November 1947 the United Nations decided to partition Palestine

into a Jewish and an Arab state. The Jews accepted this resolution and declared their independence on 14 May 1948. The Arabs rejected the idea of partition and preferred to go to war. As a result the Arab state did not come into existence; the West Bank was annexed by Jordan in 1950 and the Gaza Strip became a military zone under Egyptian control.

4. V. Kudriavtsev, 'The Plot Against Jordan', *New Times*, 14 (April 1968).

5. *Pravda*, 19 November 1969.

6. Ibid., 29 August 1972.

7. M. Maoz, *The Soviet and Chinese Relations With the Palestinian Guerrilla Movement* (Jerusalem: Davis Institute, 1974), p.11. It is almost impossible to document from public sources precise information on armament supplies.

8. *New Times*, 35 (Auguest 1973). The Black September group is a radical terrorist organisation named after September 1970 when the Jordanian Army routed the Palestinians in Jordan and the Palestinian organisations were outlawed in that country.

9. When Syria and Egypt began the war, the PLO could in theory have assisted the Arab effort by creating a passive resistance movement on the West Bank and Gaza Strip and thus diverting Israeli forces from the other two fronts. In Soviet military writing great emphasis is always laid on the importance of guerrilla warfare. For Soviet anticipation of some such behaviour, see Theodore Friedgut, 'The Domestic Image of Soviet Involvement in the Arab–Israeli Conflict', in this volume, p.156 and n.32.

10. *The Guardian*, 6 November 1973.

11. TASS, 15 November 1973/*FBIS III*, 16 November 1973.

12. *Pravda*, 31 January 1969. For the Palestine National Front, see below.

13. TASS, 20 May 1974/*FBIS III*, 25 May 1974. See Galia Golan, 'The Soviet Union and the PLO', *Adelphi Papers*, 131 (1977), pp.19–21.

14. *Izvestiia*, 30 July 1974.

15. *R. Moscow*, 15 November 1976/*SWB I*, 16 November 1976.

16. *New Times*, 21 (May 1974).

17. V. Terekhov, 'International Terrorism and the Fight Against It', *New Times*, 11 and 21 (March and May 1974).

18. *Izvestiia*, 30 July 1974 and *Aziia i Afrika segodnia*, 6 (June 1975), p.15.

19. *an-Nahar*, 25 November 1973. See also Golan, 'The Soviet Union and the PLO', *Adelphi Papers*, 131 (1977), pp.11, 15–19.

20. *an-Nahar*, 18 August 1974.

21. Ibid., 4 November 1974.

22. *Al-Muharrir*, 13 March 1974.

23. N. Bukharov, 'Palestine National Council Session', *New Times*, 25 (June 1974).

24. *R. Moscow*, 4 June 1974/*FBIS III*, 5 June 1974.

25. *Pravda*, 12 October 1974.

26. See Yaacov Ro'i, 'The Soviet Attitude to the Existence of Israel', in this volume.

27. *Izvestiia*, 30 July 1974.

28. It is of interest that Hawatima has usually visited Moscow before, during or after Arafat's visits: he preceded Arafat in November 1974 and later participated in the PLO delegation led by Arafat that month. In December 1975 he made a much publicised visit on his own that ended in a joint communiqué, a custom usually reserved for heads of states or important organisations. His latest visit (at time of writing, mid-1977) was in June to July 1977, a month after Arafat when he met Politburo member Boris Ponomarev, See *FBIS III*, 27 June 1977.

29. *Izvestiia*, 30 July 1974.

30. Cf. Galia Golan and Itamar Rabinovich, 'The Soviet Union and Syria: the Limits of Co-operation', in this volume, p.221.

31. TASS, 4 August 1974/*FBIS III*, 5 August 1974.

32. *Izvestiia*, 30 July 1974. See also Golan, 'The Soviet Union and the PLO', *Adelphi Papers*, 131 (1977), pp.10–15.

33. TASS, 27 November 1974/*FBIS III*, 29 November 1974.

34. TASS, 30 November 1974/*FBIS III*, 2 December 1974.

35. Soldatov had been Ambassador to London from 1960–6, Deputy Foreign Minister 1966–8, Ambassador to Cuba 1971–4, and from February to September 1974 Director of the Institute for Foreign Relations (in the Foreign Ministry). In addition he was concurrently twice a member of the Auditing Commission of the Central Committee of the Soviet Communist Party.

36. See Ro'i, 'The Soviet Union and Egypt', p.193; and Golan and Rabinovich, The Soviet Union and Syria', p.222 (all in this volume).

37. TASS, 5 May 1975/*FBIS III*, 6 May 1975.

38. Ibid., 9 November 1975 and *Izvestiia*, 13 November 1975.

39. *Sovetskaia Rossiia*, 19 November 1975. See also Golan, 'The Soviet Union and the PLO', *Adelphi Papers*, p.13.

40. *Pravda*, 24 November 1975. See Ro'i, 'The Soviet Attitude to the Existence of Israel', and Freedman, 'The Soviet Conception of a Middle East Peace Settlement', in this volume.

41. TASS, 9 November 1975/*FBIS III, II*, November 1975. See Freedman, 'The Soviet Conception of a Middle East Peace Settlement', in this volume, p.304.

42. Ibid., 28 November 1975/*FBIS III*, 1 December 1975.

43. Ibid.

44. *R. Moscow* in Arabic, 27 November 1975/*FBIS III*, 28 November 1975; and TASS, 27 November 1975.

45. *New Times*, 48 (November 1975); *FBIS III*, December 1975.

46. *Davar*, 8 December 1975, based on *Corriere Della Sera*, 7 December 1975.

47. *al-Ittihad*, 1 December 1975.

48. B. Hazan, 'Involvement by Proxy', unpublished paper prepared for the Conference on the Palestinians and the Middle East Conflict held at Haifa University, 1975.

49. For a discussion of the Syrian role in Lebanon see Galia Golan and Itamar Rabinovich, 'The Soviet Union and Syria: the Limits of Co-operation', in this volume.

50. E.g. *Pravda*, 18 March 1976.

51. *Izvestiia*, 5 June 1976.

52. *Ath-Thawra*, 4 June 1976.

53. See Golan and Rabinovich, 'The Soviet Union and Syria', in this volume, p.227.

54. *Pravda*, 6 June 1976.

55. TASS, 10 July 1976/*FBIS III*, 12 July 1976.

56. *Le Monde*, 20 July 1976.

57. TASS, 2 August 1976/*FBIS III*, 6 August 1976; also *Pravda*, 3 August 1976. Although the connection between the agreement and Brezhnev's memorandum cannot be proved, we can assume that it had a certain impact on the Syrian president.

58. *Pravda*, 4 August 1976.

59. The Palestinians continued to receive shipments of armaments from the radical Arab countries like Iraq and Libya. This blockade was supposedly directed against shipments from Libya.

60. *New York Times*, 14 August 1976.

61. See statement of Afro–Asian Solidarity Committee in *Pravda*, 26 August 1976; also ibid., 28 August 1976.

62. *Pravda*, 8 September 1976.

63. See R. Landa, 'From the History of the Palestine Resistance Movement (1967–1971)', *Narody Azii i Afriki*, 4 (1976) and 'The Contemporary Stage of the Struggle of the Palestine Resistance Movement', *Narody Azii i Afriki*, 5 (1976).

64. A. Kornilov, 'Meeting with the Fedayeen', *New Times,* 42 (October 1972).

65. Kh. Bagdash, 'Lenin and the Struggle Against Opportunism and Revisionism in the National Liberation Movement', *World Marxist Review*, 4 (April 1970).

66. *Al-Ittihad*, 18 August 1973.

67. *An-Nahar*, 30 May 1974. The entire programme was supported by the Israeli Communist Party, see *Zo Haderekh*, 28 July 1976.

68. *Al-Ittihad*, 7 September 1973; also F. Qaddumi, A. Maizar, 'The Crux of the Middle East Crisis', *World Marxist Review*, 7 (July 1976). Exact information on the composition of the PNF is not known.

69. This was once noted by an Israeli judge at the trial of a certain Dr Muhammad al Walidi from Ramallah who admitted belonging to the Front and claimed that the mayor of Ramallah, Karim Khalaf, as well as other well-known West Bank leaders, were also members. The judge queried why only Dr Muhammad al Walidi had been brought to trial. See *Davar*, 27 September 1976.

70. *Ha'aretz*, 30 September 1976.

71. *Ma'ariv*, 24 January 1975.

72. Based on a paper prepared by Elie Rekhess of the Shiloah Centre for Middle Eastern and African Studies, Tel Aviv University, 'Aravyei Hashtakhim' (The Arab Population of the Occupied Territories), January–July 1976.

73. *R. Moscow* in Arabic, 8 February 1976/*SWB I*, 11 February 1976. al-Watan, the underground newspaper of the PNF, published in January 1976 an article urging collaboration with the Soviet Union and calling for the PLO to participate in the Geneva Peace Conference. It was also published in *al-Ittihad*, 27 January 1976.

74. Prior to the elections on the West Bank, the Arabs there expressed their solidarity with the Israeli Arabs on the 'Day of the Land', which was a major demonstration held on 30 March 1976 against the government policy of confiscating lands for regional development.

75. *Al-Fajr*, 25 January 1976.

76. *R. Moscow* in Arabic, 8 April 1976/*SWB I*, 10 April 1976.

77. TASS, 6 to 14 April 1976/*FBIS III*, 8, 13, 19 and 20 April 1976.

78. *Pravda*, 13 April 1976 and *Izvestiia*, 14 April 1976.

79. As the PNF is an underground organisation, none of those elected openly identified himself as a member of it.

80. *Pravda* and *Izvestiia*, 15 April 1976.

81. Elie Rekhes, 'Aravyei Yisrael Le'ahar 1967' (The Israeli Arabs After 1967), *Skirot*, Shiloah Centre (June 1976). See note 74 above.

82. The members are Sabri Jiryis, Habib Qahwaji, Mahmud Darwish.

83. Y. Harkabi (ed.), *The Resolutions of the Palestinian National Councils*, 3–4 (Truman Institute, Hebrew University, 1975), pp.160, 181.

84. E.g. *Zo Haderekh*, 28 July 1976.

85. This was clearly stated at the Rakah Conference in December 1976, *Zo Haderekh*, 22 December 1976.

86. Copy of the speech can be found in the Shiloah Centre Library.

87. *Zo Haderekh*, 22 December 1976.

88. Among these groups were a fraction of the Israeli Black Panthers led by Charlie Biton and a few Arab groups which had come into existence in March 1976 in connection with the 'Day of the Land' demonstrations.

89. *New Times*, 11 (March 1977).

90. *Davar*, 21 March 1977, quoting the Council's resolution. Arafat had wanted to include in the resolution a call for collaboration with the Council for Peace between Israel and the Palestinians, which includes left-wing Zionists such as Matti Peled and Aryeh Eliav. However, the radical Palestinian elements limited the appeal to anti-Zionist forces.

91. TASS, 8 April 1977/*FBIS III*, 11 April 1977.

92. The PLO delegation was composed of the following members of the Central Council of the PLO: Majid Abu Sharar, General Secretary of the Revolutionary Council of Fatah; Assam Abd al-Latif, member of the Executive Committee of the Democratic Front; Abdullah Hurani, PLO General Director for Information and Culture; and Arabi Awad, member of the Central Committee of the Communist Party of Jordan. The Rakah delegation was composed of Wolf Ehrlich, Chairman of the Central Control Commission; Emile Tumah, member of the Politburo; Uzi Burstein, member of the Politburo; Ali Ashur, member of the Central Committee. *R. Moscow*, 4 May 1977/*SWB I*, 6 May 1977.

93. *R. Moscow*, 5 and 16 May 1977/*SWB I*, 7 and 20 May 1977.

94. *New York Times*, 17 March 1977.

11 THE SOVIET CONCEPTION OF A MIDDLE EAST PEACE SETTLEMENT

Robert O. Freedman

Introduction

Some of the most complex problems confronting observers of Middle Eastern events since the October 1973 war relate to Soviet intentions regarding an Arab—Israeli peace settlement. Is the USSR genuinely interested in a peace settlement? If not, why has it been so active in trying to achieve some sort of settlement? If it does want a settlement, what are the features of the settlement it desires? Does it care which borders are established and does it have definite conceptions concerning other aspects of the content of the settlement, or is the only thing that matters to the Kremlin that it be a party to achieving and guaranteeing the settlement? In other words, does Soviet insistence on being included in the peacemaking process have any significance for the Soviet leadership beyond that of its competition with the USA for influence in the Arab world — a competition that it views as being of the zero-sum game variety?

Traditionally, the Soviet Union has seized upon the Arab—Israeli conflict and tried to create an 'anti-imperialist' Arab unity directed against Israel and its primary Western supporter, the United States, as a major vehicle for increasing its influence in the Middle East. In this way it has sought to circumvent the inter-Arab, and inter- and intra-state rivalries with which this very volatile area has been seared to promote Soviet strategic goals. While, however, this tactic had some success in the period in which the various Arab states were moving towards a new round of fighting, it has proved much less successful in a period in which the main momentum has focused on the peacemaking process. This has perhaps been the major Soviet dilemma in the Middle East since 1973.

These, then, are some of the problems and questions to which this paper will address itself. It will do so by looking into the series of peace plans which the Soviet leadership has proposed since the 1973 war; Soviet efforts to co-ordinate Arab strategy on a possible peace settlement; Soviet reactions to American and other peace initiatives; and a variety of Soviet activities that may be considered as facilitating or obstructing a Middle East peace settlement.

The numerous peace plans launched by both regional and extra-regional parties to the Arab–Israeli conflict since October 1973 had as their starting point UN Security Council Resolution 338. This was, in effect, a ceasefire resolution aimed at ending the 1973 Arab–Israeli war. It called upon the parties to implement UN Resolution 242 'in all of its parts' immediately after the ceasefire came into effect and called for negotiations between the parties to the conflict.[1] Unlike the situation after the 1967 war, however, all the parties to the conflict (except the PLO and, initially, Syria) were now prepared to meet in face-to-face negotiations, and the first Arab–Israeli peace conference since 1949 was held in Geneva in December 1973. A discussion of the peace conference and its consequences will be presented in the next section of the paper; before moving to it, however, it is necessary to present the two central peace concepts which have been discussed since 1973, since much of the deliberations among the central parties to the conflict (Egypt, Syria, Jordan and Israel) have tended to revolve around them and even the PLO, whose charter (at the time of writing – August 1977) continues to call for the destruction of Israel, has exhibited a great deal of concern that one or the other form of settlement will be imposed upon it. Essentially, the two peace plan models, which shall be called here Model I and Model II, have the following central characteristics. The model I peace agreement calls for the return by Israel of all or almost all of the land it captured in the 1967 war and the establishment of the status quo ante bellum in relations between Israel and its Arab neighbours. This is, essentially, a continuation of the armistice agreement that existed between 1949 and 1967 with no diplomatic, economic or cultural relationships between Israel and its Arab neighbours. The only difference between such a peace plan and the 1949–67 situation would be that demilitarised zones would be emplaced in border areas and that the Arab states would formally forswear their previous plans to destroy Israel, while for its part Israel would promise not to go to war against them. Variations of the Model I peace concept provide for the passage of Israeli shipping through the Straits of Tiran and through the Suez Canal. In addition, since the 1973 war, increasing numbers of the proponents of the Model I plan have also called for the establishment of a Palestinian state or entity in the West Bank and Gaza Strip areas after their evacuation by Israel, although there have been sharp differences of opinion as to whether such a Palestinian state or entity would be linked with Jordan, and whether it would have to commit itself permanently to live in peace with Israel. The main supporters of the Model I peace plan since the

1973 war have been Egypt and Syria, with Jordan reluctantly going along with the concept of an independent Palestinian entity. Support for such a plan has also come from some quarters in the State Department of the United States, which sees in it much of the defunct Rogers Plan, and some of the West European states.

The Model II peace plan differs from the Model I peace plan primarily in the situation which is to result after the withdrawal of Israeli forces from the bulk of, it not all of, the territories it captured in 1967. The proponents of the Model II plan call for the establishment of diplomatic, trade and cultural relations between Israel and its Arab neighbours as part of any peace agreement, and argue that only in this way can Israel be assured that the Arab states have finally 'accepted' it as a legitimate entity in the Middle East. Not surprisingly, the main proponents of this peace plan are found in Israel, although it also has many supporters in the United States, including a number of influential Congressmen and Senators and President Jimmy Carter. The supporters of the Model II peace plan tend to be divided on the desirability of establishing a Palestinian state on the West Bank and Gaza Strip: those in Israel primarily favour a strong link between any such entity and Jordan, if not a return of the West Bank directly to Jordan, while a number of Americans are more sympathetic to an independent Palestinian state, albeit one pledged to live in peace with Israel.[2] Following his November 1977 visit to Israel, Sadat apparently also endorsed the Model II peace plan.

The next section of this paper will trace the policies of the Soviet Union towards these two peace models against the background of Middle Eastern political developments following the end of the October 1973 Arab–Israeli war.

The Evolution of Soviet Policy towards an Arab–Israeli Settlement following the October 1973 Arab–Israeli War

1. From the End of the War to the First Egyptian–Israeli Disengagement Agreement

At the conclusion of the war, Soviet policy makers were able to point to a number of gains in their Middle East and world position. Perhaps the main Soviet gain was the creation of the 'anti-imperialist' Arab unity they had advocated for so long, and the concomitant apparent isolation of the United States from its erstwhile allies in the region. Not only had Syria, Iraq, Egypt, Jordan, Algeria, Kuwait and Morocco actually employed their forces against Israel, but even such staunch one-time allies of the United States as the conservative regimes of

Kuwait and Saudi Arabia, in addition to sending troops to the front, had declared an oil embargo against the United States, while the tiny Persian Gulf sheikhdom of Bahrein had ordered the United States to get out of the naval base it maintained there.

On the strategic level, the Soviet world position was greatly enhanced by the war. NATO faced its biggest crisis since the Suez War of 1956 because of West European opposition to the supplying of Israel from US bases in Europe. Differences over policy towards the oil embargo exacerbated the strains within the alliance still further. Meanwhile, the Common Market was split by the failure of Britain, France, Italy and West Germany to come to the aid of fellow EEC member Holland, which like the US was also hit by a total oil embargo. Thus, although Soviet–American détente had suffered a major blow, with large numbers of Americans both inside and outside the government now openly opposing Nixon's détente policy towards the Soviet Union and the trade and strategic arms policies that went with it, the Soviet Union's position in the world, and particularly in the Middle East, had been greatly improved by the war. Indeed, at the end of the war, it appeared as if the USSR had won a major victory in its 'zero-sum game' competition with the United States for influence in the Middle East. Most of the Soviet gains, however, were to prove ephemeral, and the United States was soon able to improve its position in the region while that of the USSR began to worsen rapidly.

The first problem faced by the Soviet leadership in the postwar period was the disintegration of the Arab unity which had been created by the war, as both Iraq and Libya rejected the Soviet-supported ceasefire agreement. A far more serious problem for the Soviet leaders after the war lay in Egypt, where Soviet influence, partially restored by massive shipments of military equipment, had again begun to erode. By the end of the war the primary alignment in the Arab world was the Egyptian–Saudi Arabian alliance, with the Egyptians supplying the military power and the Saudi Arabians the oil leverage. Secretary of State Henry Kissinger clearly recognised this, and remembering Sadat's past efforts to improve relations with the West and his evident dislike of the Russians, whom he had openly opposed on a number of occasions since becoming Egypt's president in October 1970, realised that he had a unique opportunity to win over Egypt – and perhaps the rest of the Arab world as well. This realisation must have played a major role in motivating US efforts to work out an exchange of prisoners (7 November) and finally a complete disengagement agreement (18 January), which resulted in Israel's withdrawal not only from its salient near Cairo, but also from the east bank of the Suez Canal, enabling the Egyptians to control both banks of the canal for the first time since 1967.

As might be expected, the Soviet leadership was far from happy with these developments, from which it had been excluded.[3] As American influence in Egypt began to rise despite the Soviet warnings, Moscow sought to counter this in part by deepening its relationship with the Palestine Liberation Organisation — one of the most anti-settlement and anti-American forces in the Middle East — by floating a 'trial balloon' for the establishment of a Palestinian state.[4] It would appear that the USSR worked for the establishment of a Palestinian state in part at least — i.e. in addition to the declared aim of defusing 'the Middle East crisis' — to secure another area in the Middle East where it could exercise influence, along with South Yemen, Iraq and Syria. This was to be a central element in Soviet strategy over the next three years.

The first major Soviet peace proposal following the 1973 was delivered at the Geneva Peace Conference in late December. Representing the Soviet Union was Soviet Foreign Minister Andrei Gromyko whose speech set forth a number of points which the Soviet leadership claimed were basic to an Arab—Israeli peace settlement. These comprised a number of apparent gestures to Israel, including recognition of the need for the parties to the conflict themselves to work out a peace settlement (direct negotiations had long been an Israeli demand). Gromyko also raised the possibility of establishing demilitarised zones on the basis of reciprocity, and the temporary stationing of international personnel in certain areas — if such an arrangement were to be decided 'on a basis mutually acceptable to the parties concerned'.

Gromyko did not stress the Palestinian issue in his presentation; this was to be one of the main differences between his December 1973 peace proposal and subsequent Soviet peace pronouncements, particularly those of 1976 and 1977. He did emphasise, however, the need for ensuring 'justice' with respect to the Arab people of Palestine and for safeguarding their 'legitimate rights' (although he did not stipulate what those rights were). He also stated the necessity for the participation of representatives of the Arab people of Palestine in solving the Palestinian problem.

All in all, Gromyko's presentation at the Geneva Peace Conference may be considered as fitting into the Model I peace plan described above which called essentially for a return to the status quo ante of 4 June 1967, with mutual pledges not to resort to war. As far as Israel's claims to anything more than this from the Arabs, were concerned, Gromyko stated:

Israel's Arab neighbours have declared their readiness to reach
agreement on a settlement on the basis of the well-known Security
Council Resolutions which clearly express the principle that all
states involved in the conflict have the right to exist.[5]

This was hardly the reassurance that Israeli leaders were looking for,
although it appeared to be all the USSR was willing to propose at the
time.

The Geneva Conference brought the Soviet Union as one of its
co-chairmen into the centre of Middle East diplomacy. Yet the Geneva
Conference soon adjourned and was not quickly or easily to be
reconvened. In place of multilateral discussions on a general peace
settlement, American Secretary of State Henry Kissinger seized the
diplomatic initiative for his country by negotiating partial agreements
with the eventual goal of creating the basis and atmosphere for a
general settlement. In doing so, he established the USA as the mediator
between Israel and its Arab neighbours, gained a great deal of prestige
in the Arab world for the USA (particularly since he was able to secure
some Israeli territorial withdrawals) and continued to leave the Soviet
Union, diplomatically, out in the cold. Indeed, the Soviet leaders were
apparently caught by surprise by the first Kissinger-arranged Israeli–
Egyptian disengagement agreement on 18 January. When Egyptian
Foreign Minister Ismail Fahmi made a hurried visit to Moscow
immediately afterwards to explain the Egyptian action, *Pravda* wrote of
his talks there:

It was stressed that an important factor in the struggle for a just
settlement in the Near East is the close co-ordination of the actions
of the Soviet Union and Egypt at all stages of this struggle including
the work of the Near East Peace Conference and all the working
groups which come out of it.[6]

The Soviet leadership probably put this assertion in the description
of Fahmi's visit because Soviet–Egyptian co-ordination was anything
but close at this point. In a feature article on 30 January 1974 *Pravda*
warned against the disengagement agreement on the grounds that it
would lead only to a partial settlement of the Arab–Israeli conflict and
weaken the unity of the Arab countries. This was to be a consistent
Soviet theme over the next few years as Kissinger continued his shuttle
efforts.

2. From the Egyptian–Israeli Disengagement Agreement to the Soviet–American Summit in Moscow

Following the signing of the Egyptian–Israeli disengagement agreement, the momentum of Middle Eastern events seemed to favour the United States. Even the decision by the US to hold a conference of energy-consuming nations in mid-February did not serve to arrest the slow splintering of Arab unity on the oil embargo. Indeed, by this time it appeared to be only a matter of time until the oil embargo was lifted, because now Saudi Arabia's oil minister, Sheikh Ahmed Yamani, as well as Sadat, talked openly about lifting it. In this atmosphere Kissinger made yet another journey to the Middle East at the end of February, shuttling back and forth between Damascus and Jerusalem and procuring from the Syrian leaders the list of Israeli prisoners-of-war which the Israelis had demanded as a precondition to disengagement talks with Syria. At this point it appeared that once again Kissinger would be able to pull off another diplomatic coup. This, apparently, was too much for Moscow. Consequently, Foreign Minister Gromyko followed Kissinger to Damascus. The Soviet–Syrian communiqué issued upon Gromyko's departure demanded a fixed timetable for Israeli withdrawal from all occupied territory, threatening a 'new eruption' of war that would bring about a 'threat to peace and security in the Middle East and throughout the world' if Arab demands were not met.[7] Strengthened by new shipments of Soviet arms, and encouraged by Soviet support, the Syrian regime of Hafiz Asad, less willing to make peace with Israel than Egypt, thereupon begun a war of attrition against Israeli positions on the Golan Heights.

Apparently, the Soviet and Syrian leaders hoped that by heating up the conflict on the Golan Heights (the war of attrition included artillery, tank and air battles) they would be able to prevent the oil-rich states from lifting the oil embargo against the United States. While Syria stepped up its level of fighting, the Soviet Union urged the Arab states in very strong terms to maintain their oil embargo. Thus, on 12 March, Radio Moscow broadcast:

> If today some Arab leaders are ready to surrender in the face of American pressure and lift the ban on oil before the demands [for a total Israeli withdrawal] are fulfilled, they are challenging the whole Arab world and the progressive forces of the entire world which insist on the continued use of the oil weapon.[8]

While urging the continuation of the oil weapon, the Soviet media also belittled Kissinger's mediation efforts, with *Pravda* on 17 March calling them 'a mountain that gave birth to a mouse'. Nonetheless, Kissinger's diplomatic efforts were successful, and on 19 March the oil embargo against the United States was lifted by the major oil-producing Arab states, although as a sop to the Syrians Algeria stated that it would re-examine its embargo policy on 1 June. In any case, Arab unity on the oil embargo was clearly broken as Libya and Syria refused to go along with the majority decision to lift the embargo.

The termination of the oil embargo can be considered a significant defeat for Soviet diplomacy in the Middle East. The Soviet leadership had come out strongly for the maintenance of the oil embargo as a means of keeping the Arab world unified against the United States, and the USSR had greatly profited from the disarray in both NATO and the EEC caused by the embargo. Egypt's decision to support an end to the embargo – despite all the aid the USSR had given Egypt before and during the October War – was yet another indication of the sharp diminution of Soviet influence in Egypt and the corresponding rise in American influence.

Following the end of the oil embargo, the USSR sought to improve its ties with Iraq, Libya and the Palestine Liberation Organisation to balance its losses in Egypt. Nonetheless, the central Soviet concern during the post-embargo period was its relations with Syria. The Soviet leaders were clearly concerned that Syria might follow Egypt's example and move towards the West in return for economic and technical aid. The Syrian government's decision on 13 March to lift restrictions on the movement of private capital in and out of Syria and to permit the Syrian private sector to sign loan agreements with foreign investors must have added to the Soviet concern.[9] By supporting Syria in its war of attrition on the Golan Heights against Israel, the Soviet leaders hoped to avert a Syrian turn to the West while at the same time isolating Sadat as the only Arab leader to have reached an agreement with Israel. Yet in pursuing their policy of encouraging Syrian belligerence, the Soviet leaders had to toe a very narrow diplomatic line. A new summit meeting with the United States was on the horizon, and important strategic arms limitation issues between the two superpowers were under active consideration. Consequently, the Soviet leaders adopted a policy of support for Syrian belligerency while at the same time maintaining close contact with Kissinger's mediation efforts. This dual policy would underscore Soviet support for the Arab cause while the series of meetings between Kissinger and top Soviet leaders would help to create a positive atmosphere for the convening of a summit conference between Nixon and Brezhnev.

The first high-level Soviet–American meeting after the lifting of the

oil embargo came on 29 March when Kissinger journeyed to Moscow
for talks with the Soviet leadership. While strategic arms issues were the
main topic of consideration, the two superpowers also discussed the
Middle East situation. The final communiqué, however, stated only that
the 'two sides would make efforts to promote the solution of the key
questions of a Near East settlement'.[10] At the same time the Soviet leaders
went out of their way to emphasise their support for President Asad
during his visit to Moscow in mid-April. Asad was met at the Moscow
airport by all three of the primary Soviet leaders (Brezhnev, Kosygin
and Podgornyi), and the Syrian president's visit received major
front-page coverage in both *Pravda* and *Izvestiia*. The Syrian side, for its
part, as the joint communiqué on the conclusion of Asad's visit states
're-emphasised the importance of the Soviet Union's participation in all
stages and in all areas of a settlement aimed at establishing a just and
lasting peace in the Near East".[11] When Gromyko met Kissinger at the
end of April in Geneva as the American Secretary of State was en route
to the Middle East for further negotiations with Syria and Israel, they
were said to have

> exchanged opinions concerning the current situation in the talks on
> the Near East settlement and concerning the next stage of these
> talks. The two sides agreed to exert their influence in favour of a
> positive outcome of the talks and to maintain close contact with each
> other while striving to co-ordinate their actions in the interests of a
> peaceful settlement in the region.[12]

The Syrian–Israeli disengagement agreement, finally concluded at
the end of May, set up a UN force on the Golan Heights (renewable
semi-annually) between the armies of Israel and Syria and returned to
Syria all the land it had lost in the 1973 war as well as the city of
Quneytra lost in 1967. Soviet comment on the agreement, however,
stressed two main points rather than relating to its details: that the
USSR had played a major role in bringing about the agreement, and
that it was only the first step towards a more comprehensive
settlement. *New Times* associate editor Dmitrii Vol'skii, in an article
reviewing the agreement, took the opportunity to warn the Arabs that
it was not in their interest to have the USSR 'squeezed out' of the
peacemaking process.[13]

In the atmosphere of the Syrian–Israeli disengagement agreement,
the United States set the date of Nixon's visit to the USSR and the
Soviet leadership could perhaps hope that the momentum towards

'irreversible détente', interrupted by the October war, had now been restored. At the same time, as a result of the disengagement agreement, American prestige rose sharply in the Arab world, and it appeared to many observers that the United States was in the process of replacing the Soviet Union as the dominant foreign influence among the Arabs, a view that was to be reinforced by Nixon's triumphant tour of the Middle East in mid-June.

As might be expected, Soviet reporting of the Nixon visit to the Middle East played down its significance. This was in clear contrast to the Soviet media's treatment of Nixon's visit to the USSR later in the month which was hailed as proof that détente was working. While the primary Soviet interest in the summit was to achieve progress in the areas of strategic arms limitation and Soviet–American trade, the Middle East also received its share of attention at the summit. Interestingly enough, in the section of their final communiqué dealing with the Middle East, Brezhnev and Nixon devoted considerable attention to the Palestinian problem — something the Soviet leadership was to capitalise on after the summit.

> Both sides believe that the removal of the danger of war and tension in the Middle East is a task of paramount importance and urgency, and therefore, the only alternative is the achievement on the basis of Security Council Resolution 338 of a just and lasting peace settlement, in which should be taken into account the legitimate interests of all peoples in the Middle East, including the Palestinian people, and the right to existence of all states in the area.
> As co-chairmen of the Geneva Peace Conference on the Middle East, the USSR and the USA consider it important that the conference resume its work as soon as possible with the question of other participants from the Middle East to be discussed at the conference. Both sides see the main purpose of the Geneva Peace Conference, the achievement of which they will promote in every way, as the establishment of a just and stable peace in the Middle East.
> They agreed that the USSR and USA will continue to remain in close touch with a view to co-ordinating the efforts of both countries towards a peaceful settlement in the Middle East.[14]

While the Soviet leadership may have welcomed the summit as an indication that Soviet–American relations had returned to their prewar level of friendship, it was still faced with the problem of reversing the pro-American trend in the Middle East. It was to set about solving this problem as soon as the summit had been concluded.

3. From Moscow to Vladivostok: Soviet Policy towards the Middle East between the Summit Conferences

Following the summit, Soviet propaganda gave great attention to the final communiqué's emphasis on the role of the Palestinians in a peace settlement. This was part of the Soviet drive to reinforce the USSR's relations with the PLO as a counter to Sadat's westward move and the unwelcome possibility of a similar move by Syria. With the reconvening of the Geneva Peace Conference under active discussion, the Soviet leaders increased their efforts to persuade the PLO to participate in the Geneva Conference with the ultimate goal of creating a Palestinian Arab state on the West Bank and in Gaza. *Izvestiia*, in a key article on the Middle East, stated:

> Back in November 1947, the 1947 UN General Assembly adopted a resolution on the division of Palestine into two independent states — Jewish and Arab. Israel was created in 1948. The Arab Palestinian state never became a reality . . . The Palestinian Arabs must now have the opportunity to decide their own fate. The Geneva Peace Conference on the Near East can and must be the most suitable place for a discussion of their legitimate rights.[15]

The Soviet embrace of the Palestinian cause reached a new high at the end of July with Arafat's visit and the unprecedented coverage the Palestinian question received in he Soviet central press.[16] Soon after Arafat's departure, however, the Soviet Union was confronted with a problem of far greater significance than the role of the PLO in the Geneva talks — the resignation of US President Richard Nixon who had been the architect of the US détente policy with the USSR. While Gerald Ford, his successor, pledged continuity in America's relations with the Soviet Union (the pledge was given wide play by the Soviet press), nonetheless the accession to power of a man neither burdened by Watergate nor wedded to détente must have been of great concern to the Soviet leaders.

Gerald Ford came to power in the United States at a time when politics in the Middle East were in a state of flux. The Arab—Israeli conflict, in particular, which had been temporarily defused by the Syrian—Israeli disengagement agreement, looked as though it might be headed once again for war.

The Soviet leadership had contributed to the new round of Middle East war talk by a sharp increase in shipments of sophisticated arms to Syria in July and August, which raised the fear in Israel that Syria was acquiring the capacity to wage war against Israel all by itself. The Israelis were concerned that Syria might launch a pre-emptive attack with its newly obtained SCUD surface-to-surface missiles, possibly after the termination of the mandate of the UN force on the Golan Heights on 30 November. This fear led to renewed Israeli arms requests to Washington and a one-day practice call-up of Israeli reserves which, in turn, alarmed the Arabs. As talk of war returned to the Middle East, the Soviet position improved, since in case of any resumption in major fighting the Arabs would be in need of large amounts of Soviet weaponry, although the Arab states had taken steps to limit this dependency on Moscow by moving to establish their own arms industry and searching for weapons in Western Europe and the United States.[17]

In an attempt to keep the momentum for peace created by American diplomacy from breaking down, Kissinger and Ford entertained a parade of Middle East leaders in August and September as the United States sought to work out the optimum approach for the next stage of the peace talks. Visiting Washington during this period were Egyptian Foreign Minister Ismail Fahmi, Syrian Foreign Minister Abd al-Halim Khaddam, Jordan's King Husayn, Saudi Arabian Foreign Minister Umar Saqqaf, and finally, in mid-September, Israel's new Premier, Yitzhak Rabin. Following meetings with Ford and Kissinger, Rabin presented a formula for Arab 'non-belligerency' which he said would be an acceptable price for another Israeli withdrawal. In return for a further withdrawal in Sinai, he stated, Egypt could demonstrate its good intentions by ending its economic boycott against Israel or taking a similar action.[18] While one of the goals of Rabin's trip to Washington was to co-ordinate strategy in the peace negotiations, a second goal was to acquire sufficient weaponry should the peace negotiations fail. Rabin seemed to have been successful in his arms quest, because in a news conference on 13 September the Israeli Premier stated: 'We reached an understanding on our on-going military relationship in a concrete way with concrete results'.[19]

As might be expected, the Soviet leadership, unhappy that Washington continued to be the centre of Middle East diplomacy, seized upon Rabin's visit to Washington along with Ford's and Kissinger's warnings at the United Nations in mid-September about the high price of oil[20] to undermine the United States' position in the Arab world. The Soviet media also carried numerous reports about massive US arms shipments to Israel and about US military and economic threats against the Middle East oil producers.[21]

In any case, it was with this background of Arab irritation over the

United States' policies that Kissinger embarked on yet another trip to the Middle East in early October. The main target of the US Secretary of State's diplomacy was Egypt, as both the United States and Israel felt that another Israeli—Egyptian agreement would be the logical next step in the process of securing a final Arab—Israeli peace settlement. Unfortunately for Kissinger, however, Sadat was not to prove as accommodating to the United States as on previous occasions. The Egyptian leader, who desired to maintain his position as leader of the Arab world, was unwilling to agree to the cessation of the Arab economic boycott against Israel desired by Rabin or make any other political concessions to Israel in return for another Israeli withdrawal. He was, moreover, anticipating a Brezhnev visit with the concomitant political, military and economic expectations which he could not afford to jeopardise. In these circumstances, Kissinger's diplomatic efforts made little progress during his October visit to Cairo, although Sadat did agree to accept a six-month extension of the United Nations force in the Sinai Desert — possibly because, without a resumption of Soviet arms deliveries, he was unable to demonstrate that he could exercise the option of returning to war. Indeed, it was in a quest for arms that Fahmi now prepared for a further visit to the Soviet capital. His talks there resulted in promises of renewed arms supplies, as well as agreement that 'complete and final settlement of the Middle East crisis can be achieved only within the framework of the Geneva conference'.[22]

The Rabat conference in October seemed to improve the Soviet position. It not only declared that the PLO was the 'sole and legitimate representative of the Palestinian people and had the right to establish the independent Palestinian authority on any liberated Palestinian territory',[23] a position the USA would find difficult to endorse if it was also hailed by the Soviet media as proof of the Arab states' growing unity 'on an anti-imperialist basis',[24] although in fact Arab unity at Rabat was not as strong as the Soviet press made it appear. Libyan leader Muammar Qadhdhafi boycotted the conference, and Iraqi leader Saddam Husayn stated at the end of the meetings at Rabat that 'should the PLO go to Geneva or become a party to the contacts being held with the United States, Iraq's commitment to this draft resolution was to be null and void'.[25]

Moreover, the Middle East appeared even closer to war, particularly after Arafat's speech at the UN on 13 November in which he repeated his call for the dismantling of Israel and threatened that if his demands were not met the PLO would continue its terrorist attacks.[26] The

Syrian government, moreover, refused to state whether it would permit a six-month extension for the mandate of the UN force on the Golan Heights, which was due to expire at the end of the month, a ploy it was to use again. The Israelis, not wishing to be caught by surprise as they were in October 1973, began to prepare for war. Following a report that twenty Soviet ships were unloading arms at Syrian ports, the Israelis began to mobilise reservists and move them to the Golan Heights. True, with a summit conference between Ford and Brezhnev scheduled for 23 November, the Soviet leadership clearly had no desire to alienate important segments of American public opinion by supporting the PLO's demands to liquidate Israel — particularly with new agreements on strategic arms limitation to be discussed at the summit and the USSR's need for American technological assistance and long-term credits for its new five-year plan which was then under preparation. Yet such a situation clearly provided opportunities for use of Soviet leverage. Although it was the personal intervention of Kissinger that succeeded in calming the situation,[27] it is quite possible that Ford told Brezhnev at Vladivostok to make clear to the Syrians the need to accept an extension of the UN force. Given Syria's need for a continued supply of Soviet weaponry to fight a new war, the USSR was not without leverage in this situation. In any case, at the end of November Syria did agree to extend the UN force, although to what degree the Syrian decision was due to Soviet pressure, American inducement,[28] internal politics or Egypt's unwillingness to support Syria in a new war at that time, is not yet known.

The Middle East occupied a relatively small section of the communiqué issued by the two leaders at the conclusion of their summit at Vladivostok. Brezhnev and Ford were said to have

> reaffirmed their intention to make every effort to promote a solution of the key issues of a just and lasting peace in accordance with United Nations Resolution 338, with due account taken of the legitimate interest of all peoples of the area, including the Palestinian people and respect for the right of all states in the area to independent existence. The sides believe that the Geneva Conference should play an important role in the establishment of a just and lasting peace in the Middle East and should resume its work as soon as possible.[29]

While rather vague as to details, the communiqué appears to have been a compromise between the two sides. On the one hand, the statement supporting the right of all Middle Eastern states to 'independent existence' explicitly repudiated the PLO plan to dismantle Israel. Indeed, the Soviet Union's support of the Palestinian Arabs, at least as reflected in the joint communiqué, was weaker than in the Nixon–Brezhnev communiqué issued five months earlier. On the other hand, however, by agreeing to a speedy resumption of the Geneva Conference the United States appeared to be acceding to the Soviet desire to play a more active role in the peace negotiations. Nonetheless, since no date was set for the resumption of the conference, and since similar language had been used in the July communiqué, the United States kept alive the possibility of more activity by the peripatetic Kissinger.

Thus ended both the summit conference and the immediate threat of war in the Middle East. It was not to be long before Kissinger was again on his way to the Middle East in another attempt to work out an Egyptian–Israeli disengagement agreement.

4. *From Vladivostok to the Collapse of the Kissinger Mission*

The central Soviet concern during the November 1974–March 1975 period was that another American-orchestrated disengagement accord would be realised. To thwart such an eventuality, the Soviet leadership sought to capitalise on its relations with the PLO in an atmosphere of enhanced PLO prestige following the Rabat conference and Arafat's appearance at the UN. When Arafat visited Moscow in late November 1974, the Soviet media gave a great deal of emphasis to his statement hailing the USSR as 'a true and sincere friend of the Arab peoples'.[30]

Nonetheless, despite the Arafat visit to Moscow, and Arab unhappiness about rumoured American plans to seize Arab oilfields,[31] by February 1975 conditions appeared ripe for another Kissinger shuttle in the Middle East. As a result, the USSR stepped up its efforts to prevent a partial settlement as Soviet Foreign Minister Andrei Gromyko visited Syria and Egypt in early February, prior to Kissinger's trip to the two Arab states. In Damascus, Gromyko received Syrian agreement for the immediate resumption of the Geneva Conference and even got Syrian consent to have the date of the meeting set for 'no later than February or early March 1975' – an action aimed at enabling Moscow to prevent any major accomplishments by Kissinger before the conference resumed its work. Syria also again agreed to Soviet participation 'in all areas and at all stages' of Middle East peace efforts, thereby ensuring, at least on paper, that the USSR would not again be isolated from any peace settlement that Kissinger might be able to work out. In return, the Soviet Foreign Minister emphasised the USSR's willingness to continue 'to strengthen the defence capability of Syria' and even went so far as to indicate the USSR's preference for Syria as the leader of the Arab anti-imperialist coalition:

> The Soviet Union gave a high approval of the efforts made by the Syrian Arab Republic to strengthen inter-Arab solidarity and to consolidate the Arab states' unity of action to counteract the plans of imperialism and international Zionism.[32]

Thus the USSR began to openly back Syria as the centre of an Arab grouping of states that would, the Soviet leaders hoped, support Soviet policy irrespective of any action taken by Egypt, with which their relations were again deteriorating. For his part, Asad was in need of Soviet aid, given the unlikelihood of another Israeli withdrawal on the Golan Heights prior to a final peace settlement, and Israel's stated unwillingness to attend any peace conference to work out a final settlement so long as the PLO was allowed to attend. Indeed, the impasse between Israel and Syria became very severe at this point because Syria refused to attend any peace conference unless the PLO attended as an equal partner.

Gromyko's reception in Cairo was considerably cooler than the one he received in Damascus. The joint communiqué issued at the conclusion of his talks with Sadat stated that they had taken place in a 'friendly and businesslike atmosphere' – a clear indication of very low-level co-operation. Nonetheless, Egypt was to agree to an 'immediate resumption of the Geneva talks' – although, unlike in Syria, no fixed date was set – and the Egyptians also agreed that the USSR should participate in 'all areas and all stages' of a Middle East peace settlement.[33] Evidently the Soviet leadership hoped that Gromyko's mission had succeeded in averting any new 'separate deal' inimical to Soviet interests, and a *New Times* article describing Gromyko's trip to the two Arab capitals stated:

> What is especially important is that these visits have demonstrated anew that the Soviet Union and the Arab countries agree in principle on the approach to a Middle Eastern settlement. For it is no secret that there has been considerable speculation on this score in the Western (and not only the Western) press. . .[34]

In addition to Gromyko's visit to the region and the somewhat enhanced Soviet position there, a number of obstacles seemed to be interfering with the continued upsurge of US successes in the region as Kissinger set out in early March on what was earmarked as the decisive shuttle to bring about a second-stage disengagement between Egypt and Israel.[35] US brandishing of the threat to seize Arab oilfields, the Cyprus conflict and the resultant deterioration in the relations of both Greece and Turkey with NATO and the United States, and South-east Asian developments where the Cambodian government of Lon Nol was on the verge of being toppled, were all having this effect. In particular, it may well have been the feeling in both Cairo and Damascus that just as the US Congress had tired of pouring aid into Cambodia and South Vietnam, so too would it eventually tire of aiding Israel.

Moreover, despite Egypt's continued professions about Arab unity during the shuttle, and despite the strong bargaining position the resumption of Soviet arms supplies gave Sadat, it is clear that Syria, as well as the Soviet Union, was very concerned about the possibility that Sadat might agree to a second-stage disengagement agreement with Israel. To combat the possibility of being isolated against Israel should this occur, the Syrian government, in early March, offered to join the PLO in a joint command[36] and also signed a far-reaching economic and political agreement with its erstwhile enemy, the regime of King Husayn of Jordan.[37] At the same time, by taking the first steps towards a PLO–Syrian–Jordanian alignment, Asad was also moving towards a position of leadership in the Arab world. The USSR strongly endorsed the effort by Asad to establish the PLO–Syrian–Jordanian alignment, *inter alia* because it had the potential of leading pro-Western Jordan into the Soviet camp, thereby helping to establish the 'anti-imperialist' Arab unity the USSR desired.[38]

The Israelis, meanwhile, cognisant of the fact that they were almost totally dependent on Iranian oil should they give back the Abu Rodeis oilfields which Sadat demanded, also took a hard bargaining stance with Kissinger. Indeed, for the first time since the October war, Israel seemed to unite, with public opinion backing Premier Rabin's opposition to Kissinger's terms, as such hardliners of the right as General Arik Sharon joined such 'doves' of the left as Aryeh Eliav and Abba Eban to demand meaningful concessions from Egypt before any settlement could be agreed upon. The result was the failure of Kissinger's mission, the temporary end of the US diplomatic initiative in the Middle East and an opportunity for the Soviet Union to move to the centre of Middle East diplomatic manoeuvring.

5. *From Disengagement Failure to Disengagement Success: Middle East policy April–September 1975*

The failure of Kissinger's Middle East disengagement efforts led President Ford to call for a total reassessment of US policy towards the Middle East, and the US temporarily stepped back from its central position in Middle East diplomacy. With the USA abandoning centre stage, the Soviet Union took the initiative in trying to secure a Middle East settlement through its own diplomatic efforts. A parade of visitors from Arab countries arrived in Moscow in April, Kosygin visited Libya and Tunisia in May, and the Soviet leadership made a number of gestures towards improving relations with Israel. Nonetheless, the USSR proved no more successful in promoting a Middle East peace settlement than the USA had been.

Taking advantage of the pause in the US momentum, the Soviet Union took the initiative for the first time since the 1973 war. It called once again for a resumption of the Geneva Peace Conference to work out a settlement that would secure a total withdrawal of Israeli forces from all Arab territory occupied in the 1967 Six Day War, establish a Palestinian state, and guarantee the right to existence of all states in the Middle East — including Israel.

It was to forge a united Arab stand on a peace settlement of this nature that representatives of Egypt, Iraq, Syria and the PLO were invited to Moscow in April. The Soviet leadership's self-imposed task was not facilitated by growing dissensions in the Arab camp on other issues: Syria and Iraq were heavily at odds over the amount of water Syria was willing to allow to flow into Iraq from the Euphrates Dam; Egypt and Libya were at loggerheads; and fighting was going on in Lebanon. Only between Syria and Egypt had the situation improved due in part to the failure of Kissinger's mission. The first to arrive in Moscow was the Iraqi regime's 'strongman', Saddam Husayn. Soviet Premier Aleksei Kosygin, in his welcoming speech, urged the Arabs to take a more unified stand lest they be at a disadvantage in dealing with the USA and Israel at the Geneva Conference.[39] The joint communiqué issued at the end of Husayn's visit showed that the measure of agreement was limited to an affirmation of the need for the 'cohesion of the Arab states on an anti-imperialist basis', and the need to strengthen Arab co-operation with the socialist countries, along with the 'legitimate right of the Arab people of Palestine to self-determination'.[40]

Following Husayn to Moscow was Egyptian Foreign Minister Ismail

Fahmi. Once again, disagreements were evident in the discussions between the two sides, although *Pravda* stated that Egypt did agree that 'any partial measures and decisions on them must be a component, inalienable part of a general settlement, and must be adopted in the framework of the [Geneva] conference on the Near East'[41] – a stipulation that Egypt was to show no hesitation in disregarding several months later.

The third in the parade of Middle East visitors coming to Moscow in April was Syrian Foreign Minister Khaddam. The joint communiqué issued at the conclusion of Khaddam's visit denounced 'separate agreements'. Yet here too there was clear evidence of disagreement. Although the USSR hailed Syria for its 'efforts to consolidate Arab solidarity and strengthen the Arab countries' unity of action', the Syrians would not endorse Gromyko's statement to his Syrian colleague that no peace was possible without the guarantee of Israel's right to exist, and that the USSR was prepared to guarantee Israel's existence.[42] Damascus was not yet ready to embrace this Soviet position on the prerequisites for a Middle East peace settlement.

The next Arab visitor to the Soviet capital, Yasir Arafat, was even less tractable. The most both sides were able to agree on was the need for the PLO and the Arab states to co-ordinate their efforts 'against any bilateral separate deals outside the context of a comprehensive settlement of the Arab–Israeli conflict',[43] with Arafat supporting the Soviet position that the policy of partial settlement was 'aimed at dividing the Arab countries' and 'isolating them from their valuable allies, the Socialist countries, and drawing them into the sphere of imperialist domination'.[44]

One week after Arafat's departure from Moscow, Kosygin himself left the Soviet capital for a journey to Libya which, over the last year, had become one of the Soviet Union's primary allies in the Middle East despite their disagreement over an Arab–Israeli peace settlement. Despite the Libyan government's stated opposition to the existence of the state of Israel, Kosygin publicly reiterated the three-pronged Soviet solution for the Middle East conflict – including the passage which called for the guaranteeing of the 'independent existence and development of all states in the region'. In addition, Kosygin, mindful of the strained relations between Libya and Egypt, sought to play down the seriousness of the differences dividing the Arab world, urging the Arab states to greater unity to solve their problems.[45]

In summing up Kosygin's visits to the two countries, *Izvestiia* stated that they had demonstrated the importance of Soviet–Arab co-operation and had shown that despite 'differences among the Arab countries in their approaches to the settlement of the Near East conflict', the Arab countries would 'be able to overcome these disagreements, put the fundamental interests of the Arab world first and foremost, and subordinate their actions to the strengthening of unity in the anti-imperialist struggle'.[46]

While the Soviet leadership was seeking to produce a co-ordinated and unified Arab approach to the peace talks, it did not overlook the necessity of gaining Israeli agreement for the Soviet peace plan. Moscow sent two reportedly high-ranking diplomats to sound out the Israelis on possible terms for reconvening the Geneva Conference.[47]

Despite all these diplomatic efforts, however, the Soviet leaders proved no more successful than the United States had been in working out the mechanics of a peace settlement. By the end of May, Washington had resumed the initiative. On the eve of the Sadat—Ford meeting in Salzburg, the Soviet media attacked both the USA and Egypt, comparing the latter's stand with the 'principled position' of Syria:

> People in some Arab capitals continue to maintain that the "key to peace" in the Near East is in the hands of the USA which supposedly is able to exert some kind of decisive pressure on Israel . . . Experience has shown that certain circles in the USA have no intention of exerting pressure on Israel, and particularly not in the Arabs' favour. For these circles, especially after the loss of South Vietnam, the Arab—Israeli conflict is only a means of consolidating their positions in the Near East, which have been seriously undermined as a result of the social and national liberation revolutions in the Arab countries . . . What was Egypt's attitude to the Kissinger plan? The very fact that talks were held with the American Secretary of State was evidence that Cairo is not rejecting the search for an accord on the question of a partial withdrawal.
>
> Syria's position is very clear. It would regard an Egyptian—Israeli agreement as a separate agreement, one at variance with the spirit of Arab unity . . . [This is] in keeping with Syria's principled position which organically links a Near East settlement with the creation of an independent Palestinian Arab State.[48]

Syria was indeed building up its position as a potential alternative to Egypt. Syrian—Jordanian relations reached a high point when Asad visited Amman in mid-June and the Syrian and Jordanian governments announced the formation of a permanent joint High Commission to co-ordinate military, political, economic and cultural policies.[49] This may well have appeared to Moscow as yet another step towards the creation of a Syrian–Jordanian–PLO entente which would isolate Egypt and become a centre of 'anti-imperialist Arab unity' in the Arab world.[50] Yet even Syria was developing economic relations with the West, and with the United States in particular,[51] while Sadat journeyed to Salzburg via Damascus, which at least implicitly indicated Syria's support for the trip. Moreover, Khaddam visited Washington in July, showing that the Syrian government continued to keep its diplomatic options open. As the United States leadership stepped up its efforts to achieve the disengagement agreement, the Soviet leadership increased its public attacks on Egyptian policy. Yet these did not deter Sadat from working out a three-year disengagement agreement with Israel, under Kissinger's mediation, in the latter part of August. Throughout these negotiations, *Pravda* kept up its efforts to isolate Sadat. It stressed that Israel was making concessions that were 'militarily meaningless',[52] and that the negotiations ignored such important questions as a withdrawal from the Golan Heights and from the banks of the Jordan as well as a recognition of the legitimate rights of the Palestinian Arabs.[53] The Soviet press denounced the agreement as a threat to Arab unity[54] and quoted Khaddam's denunciation of the agreement as 'not a step towards peace, but a step towards war'.[55]

The USSR proved unable to prevent the second Israeli–Egyptian disengagement agreement. Given these Soviet efforts, however, one must question Kissinger's and Ford's evaluations that the USSR deliberately kept quiet during the Middle East negotiations lest it upset détente and prevent Ford's journey to Helsinki for the European Security Conference.[56] It would appear, rather, that despite the Soviet leadership's strong opposition to the second Egyptian–Israeli disengagement agreement, it proved powerless to prevent it.

6. From the Second Egyptian–Israeli Disengagement Agreement to the Riyadh Conference

The Soviet leadership was clearly discouraged by the second Egyptian–Israeli disengagement agreement which heralded both an increase in American influence in the peace-settlement process and a further erosion of the Soviet position. Following the agreement, the USSR redoubled its efforts to isolate Sadat and denigrate his domestic and foreign policies. At the same time, the USSR drew closer to Syria which considered itself abandoned by Egypt in the Arab confrontation with Israel, found itself confronted by a civil war in Lebanon, and seemed to be playing the role of leader of the anti-imperialist bloc of Arab states ascribed to it by the Soviet Union.

To show its displeasure over the interim agreement, the USSR boycotted the signing ceremony in Geneva. Interestingly enough, the United States also did not attend the session, despite all the hard work Kissinger had put in to secure the agreement — reportedly to avoid embarrassing the USSR.[57] (Whether the USSR would have stayed away from such a ceremony in deference to the USA if Soviet representatives had worked out an agreement in the face of US opposition, is a very open question.) Indeed, the Soviet leadership probably interpreted the American action as just an indication of weakness.

In the wake of the new agreement Soviet media attacks on the Sadat regime's foreign policy increased in intensity, reaching a new crescendo on the eve of the Sadat trip to the United States at the end of October.[58]

Meanwhile, just as in the period following the failure of Kissinger's mission in March, a parade of high-ranking Arab visitors came to Moscow. This time, however, the visitors not only came from the 'progressive' Arab states and organisations (Iraq, Syria, Libya and the PLO), but also from such conservative states as Jordan and Kuwait. The key to Soviet policy in the Arab world *vis-à-vis* the conflict and its settlement, however, remained Syria. Asad came to Moscow on 9 October and the joint communiqué issued after the meeting stated that 'no one would be allowed to disrupt or damage' the friendship between the two states.[59] The trip was a profitable one for the Syrians: Asad was promised new shipments of Soviet weapons, including MiG-23s, which more than made up for Egypt's pulling out its warplanes from Syria as relations between the two Arab nations sharply deteriorated. One week later, Asad announced his refusal to enter into negotiations with the USA on a disengagement agreement similar to that worked out by Egypt and Israel.[60] The Syrian stand scuttled American moves to keep the shuttle momentum alive.

The MiG-23s arrived in Syria in the middle of November, thereby strengthening Syria's position as yet another deadline for the extension of the mandate for the UN force on the Golan Heights approached.[61] Syria used the approaching deadline to strengthen its demand for changes in the UN Security Council Resolutions 242 and 338 favourable to the Palestinians, as its price for renewing the mandate. When the USA opposed the Syrian position, Asad reduced his requirements to a demand that the PLO be permitted to participate in the Security Council debate on the Middle East in January 1976. The

USA did not oppose this Syrian ploy, probably in order to keep the momentum towards a peace settlement (or at least the appearance of such a momentum) alive. This Syrian manoeuvre, backed by the USSR won the PLO increased diplomatic stature by enabling its representatives to address the Security Council for the first time, and won Syria new prestige in the Arab world as well, confirming its position as champion of the Palestinians.

The Soviet Union meanwhile was continuing to demand the reconvening of the Geneva Peace Conference, with the full participation of the PLO. On 9 November, just a few days after Sadat's visit to the USA (26 October to 5 November), the Soviet government transmitted to Washington an official Note suggesting a joint initiative to reconvene the Geneva Conference with the full participation of all concerned, including the PLO 'from the very beginning' and 'on an equal footing'. This was clearly intended to undermine a continued US–Egyptian dialogue on a peace-making process alternative to and outside Geneva. On 18 December it rejected the American counter-proposal to hold a preparatory conference without the PLO as 'an intention to avoid convening the Geneva Conference',[62] Now the Soviet leaders sought to use the January 1976 Security Council debate on the Middle East, at which the PLO would be represented, as a vehicle for speedily reconvening the Geneva Conference. A Soviet government peace proposal put out on the eve of the meeting was explicit on this point:

> The main result of the discussion of the Middle East situation in the Security Council should be the creation of the necessary conditions for the resumption and effective work of the Geneva Conference.[63]

The substance of the peace plan was not new, as once again the threefold Soviet plan was unfurled. The only difference was an even stronger emphasis than before on the rights of the Palestinians, as the statement called for ensuring the legitimate rights of the Palestinians 'including their inalienable right to the creation of their own state', and emphasised the opinion of the 'overwhelming majority' of states that all the directly interested parties, including the Palestine Liberation Organisation, should take part in the Geneva Conference's work from the very beginning with equal rights.

The Security Council debate, however, proved ineffectual as the United States vetoed an anti-Israeli resolution. Moreover, while the prestige of the PLO and the Palestinian Arabs may have been increasing on the world scene, their position in Lebanon was becoming ever more

precarious as they had to contend not only with the Christian
Maronites, but also with an increasing Syrian intervention in the civil
war.[64]

The Soviet Union continued, however, to underline its close
relations with Syria. In Brezhnev's address to the 25th Party Congress,
Syria headed the list of the USSR's Arab friends. In the same speech
the secretary-general reiterated the three points of the Soviet peace
plan: Israeli withdrawal from all territory captured in the 1967 war; the
recognition of the 'legitimate rights' of the Palestinians, including their
right to a national state; and the guarantee of the security of all states
in the region and their right to independent existence and development.
In addition, Brezhnev once again stated the USSR's willingness to
participate in international guarantees for the security and borders of
all the states in the Middle East. Brezhnev added that he was prepared
to work to end the arms race in the Middle East (long an American
goal), but only after an overall settlement had been reached.[65]

The relatively optimistic presentation by Brezhnev of the USSR's
position in the Arab world at the 25th Party Congress, however, was
soon overtaken by events, while his peace plan was to fail to receive
support from either the Arabs (except for some Arab Communist
leaders attending the Congress in Moscow) or the Israelis. The first blow
to Brezhnev's analysis of Soviet–Arab relations came less than three
weeks after the Party Congress when Egyptian President Anwar Sadat
abrogated the fifteen-year Treaty of Friendship and Co-operation
signed with the USSR in 1971.[66] Secondly, the situation in Lebanon
had also deteriorated. What made matters worse for the Soviet leaders
at this point was that the United States, which had long been inactive in
the Lebanese crisis, suddenly dispatched a special envoy, L. Dean
Brown, to Lebanon to try to mediate the conflict; while the US Sixth
Fleet was moved to a position near Lebanon as a precautionary measure
in case an evacuation of US citizens was ordered. Brown's mission,
moreover, was dispatched after talks in Washington between King
Husayn, now one of Asad's closest Arab allies, and the Ford
administration, and the Soviet leaders must have clearly feared that
since both the United States and Syria had the common goal of
restricting the leftist Muslims and Palestinians in Lebanon, the two
nations might well co-ordinate their actions. It was against this
confused background of communal conflict, widespread fighting,
growing hostility among key members of their 'anti-imperialist' Arab
coalition, and the possibility of increased Syrian–American
co-operation, that the Soviet leadership suddenly unveiled yet another

Middle East peace plan on 29 April.[67]

Using the civil war in Lebanon as the reason for its call for a 'radical' solution of the Middle East conflict, the Soviet statement once again stressed the three central components the Soviet leaders saw necessary for a peace settlement. The USSR, in a change from earlier peace statements, also acknowledged the possibility of a two-stage Geneva Conference — something advocated previously by the United States (as we have seen) — wherein the initial stage would 'solve all the organisational questions that might arise'. Nonetheless, by stipulating that the Palestine Liberation Organisation had to take part in *both* stages of the conference (which it wanted resumed, 'without delay'), the Soviet leaders seem to have negated the possibility of its taking place since the USA, to say nothing of Israel, refused to deal with the PLO until it recognised Israel.[68]

The Soviet peace proposal led neither to a general peace in the Middle East nor to peace in Lebanon. Instead, fighting again increased, with ever-growing evidence of a rupture between Damascus and the PLO. Moreover, a successful mediation effort by Saudi Arabia, which was a significant contributor of assistance to the Syrian economy, seemed likely to pull Syria into the American-supported Egyptian– Saudi axis with all the implications this had for an Arab–Israeli settlement as well.

This then was the context of a Soviet decision to send Premier Aleksei Kosygin to visit Iraq and Syria.[69] Despite the difficult circumstances of the visit, in view especially of Syria's major offensive in Lebanon on the eve of Kosygin's arrival, the Soviet Premier praised the Syrians for resisting private deals like the Sinai II agreement.[70] The joint communiqué that summed up the talks in the Syrian capital again endorsed the Geneva Conference with the participation of the PLO 'from the very start and on an equal footing'.[71]

Throughout the summer the Lebanese situation worsened from the Soviet point of view, the considerable Syrian force fighting that of Junblat and the Palestinians and finally inflicting heavy defeats on them.[72]

The deteriorating situation was to cause the USSR to launch yet another Arab–Israeli peace initiative at the beginning of October. Unlike the April initiative, however, this was given to the states concerned (the USA, Egypt, Syria, Jordan and Israel), as well as to the PLO, before it was made public by *Pravda* on 2 October. Moscow once again cited events in Lebanon as the reason for the need for an overall peace settlement, and called for the resumption of the Geneva

Conference in the October–November 1976 period – that is, almost immediately. In addition to the three by now traditional points in the Soviet peace plan (the need to ensure Israel's independent existence and security was specifically spelled out this time), the new Soviet proposal also called for the cessation of the state of war between the Arab states and Israel.[73] While this was clearly a gesture towards Israeli demands, the Soviet Union's adherence to the principle of PLO participation in both stages of the Geneva Conference as well as on an equal footing continued to eliminate the chances of a quick resumption of the Geneva Conference.

The Soviet peace plan did not bring peace to Lebanon, although there was a temporary lull in the fighting as Syria, having once again proved its military superiority over the Palestinians, halted before its forces would have crushed them. A lasting ceasefire was finally achieved in Lebanon in October 1976, though not under Soviet mediation but that of Saudi Arabia, the USSR's *bête noire* in the Middle East, at a major Arab conference in Riyadh.

7. From the Riyadh Conference to Asad's Visit to Moscow

In addition to the Lebanese peace agreement, another major diplomatic development to come from the Riyadh conference – one that was hardly more pleasing to Moscow – was the reconciliation between Syria and Egypt. With the American elections due in the very near future and a general expectation that the USA would move for a Middle East peace agreement soon afterwards, it seemed certain that both Syria and Egypt realised that their bargaining position *vis-à-vis* Israel would be much stronger once their quarrel was patched up. In addition, their main financial supporter, Saudi Arabia, had a significant amount of economic leverage to indicate to both states that it was in their interest to cease their conflict. As a result, Syria ended its propaganda attacks on Egypt over the Sinai II agreement, while Egypt ended its attacks on Syria for its intervention in Lebanon. The fact that Saudi Arabia had successfully mediated the end not only to the Lebanese war but also to the Syrian–Egyptian rift, served to underline its growing importance in Arab affairs.

By early November, in addition to their concern about developments in Lebanon and the increasingly important role of Saudi Arabia in Arab politics, the Soviet leaders now faced a change of leadership in the United States with which relations had cooled considerably over the past twelve months.[74] Once the election campaign was over (the USSR attributed a large part of the cooling off of Soviet–American relations to campaign pressures) the Soviet leadership set about sending signals to the incoming Carter administration that it was interested in improved relations and would look forward to Soviet—American co-operation in reaching a new strategic arms agreement and a Middle East settlement.

A major signal to the Carter administration came during the meeting of the American—Soviet Trade and Economic Council at the end of November 1976 when Brezhnev appealed for an end to the 'freeze' on the strategic arms discussions and for a new agreement based on the Vladivostok accord. He also used the opportunity to call for an end to the US trade discrimination against the USSR, stating that US firms lost between \$1·5 and \$2 billion because of it.[75] Two weeks later *Pravda* published a major article by Georgii Arbatov, director of the Soviet Institute for the Study of the United States (SShA), evaluating the state of US—Soviet relations. After criticising the 'enemies of détente', Arbatov praised President-elect Carter's 'positive' statements about improving Soviet—American relations and seeking ways to limit arms. Arbatov then went on to call for the resumption of the Geneva Middle East Peace Conference as quickly as possible.[76] The most important Soviet signal, however, came the day before Carter's inauguration when, in a speech in Tula, Brezhnev, noting that the SALT I agreement expired in October, appealed for the 'consolidation' of the Vladivostok accord and for a resumption of the Geneva Middle East Peace Conference.[77]

While looking towards improved relations with the United States, Moscow also sought to rebuild its position in the Middle East. Soviet relations gradually improved with Syria following the end of the fighting in Lebanon — the USSR agreed tacitly to Syrian domination there.[78] It also sought to bring Libya and Iraq to the Soviet view of a Middle East settlement. In early December Libyan leader Muammar Qadhdhafi visited the USSR. In his dinner speech welcoming Qadhdhafi, Soviet President Podgornyi reiterated the Soviet position that 'a settlement in the region was dependent on Israeli troop withdrawals from land occupied in 1967', thus, tacitly at least, indicating that Israel was justified in holding all the land it had up to 4 June 1967. Podgornyi also called for ensuring the right of the Palestinians to have their own state, and for the resumption of the Geneva Conference where a full settlement of the Arab—Israeli conflict could be worked out.[79]

As had been the pattern in previous Soviet—Libyan meetings, the Libyans were very frank in stating their opposing positions. Qadhdhafi presented Libya's solution to the Arab—Israeli conflict — 'the expulsion of the racists [Israelis] from Palestine'. Realising that his views differed very sharply from those of his Soviet hosts, the Libyan President then made a gesture towards their position by stating 'of course we respect the viewpoint of others'. He went on, however, to deprecate the importance of convening the Geneva Conference.[80]

As might be expected, the communiqué issued at the end of the four days of meetings between Qadhdhafi and the Soviet leaders omitted any reference to the Geneva Conference or Israel's right to exist.[81]

The next rejectionist front leader to visit Moscow was Saddam Husayn of Iraq. Unfortunately for the Soviet leaders, however, they met with little more success with Husayn than they had with Qadhdhafi. In his welcoming speech, Kosygin put forth the position that a settlement required the withdrawal by Israel from all territories occupied in 1967 and he openly stated that peace and security could not be established in the Middle East without guaranteeing the right of independent existence to all the states involved in the conflict, and unless the state of war among them was ended. Kosygin also emphasised the necessity of ensuring the right of the Palestinians to set up their own state, and he advocated the resumption of the Geneva Conference — even if it should experience 'difficulties'.[82] Saddam Husayn, for his part, took a hard line on a peace settlement although he was not quite so explicit as Qadhdhafi, stating that while Iraq favoured peace and stability, it rejected those plans which impose 'capitulationist decisions on our people to rob them of their historic rights'. However, he made no mention of the lack of desirability of a peace conference.[83] In the final communiqué the two sides agreed that a Middle East settlement could come about only if 'all occupied Arab territory' was liberated and the 'legitimate and unalienable national rights of Palestine's Arab people be completely satisfied' — terminology open to varied interpretations.[84]

Just prior to his visit at the end of January, *Pravda* printed an extensive article by Pavel Demchenko citing the general readiness in the Middle East for an overall settlement of the Arab—Israeli conflict and for the resumption of the Geneva Conference, indicating that the PLO was ready to settle for a West Bank—Gaza state and would even go to a peace conference — if invited under the proper circumstances.

Lately, statements have been appearing more and more frequently in the Arab and Western Press saying that attempts to solve the Middle East problem in parts or by stages have failed ... Even the creator of 'diplomacy by small steps', Henry Kissinger, was forced to state

recently that 'the moment has come when the all encompassing
approach logically became the next step'.

There is also much talk in foreign newspapers that 1977 is the time
for resuming the Geneva peace conference on the Middle East . . .
Egypt and Syria recently published a communiqué proclaiming full
support for the Geneva Conference . . . Jordan is also prepared to
participate in the conference. As for the Palestine Liberation
Organisation, its position was set down in the 13th session of the
National Council of Palestine in 1974 and calls for 'the
establishment of independent national power of the people in any
part of the Palestinian land that is liberated'. It appears from a
number of statements by PLO leaders that such power can be
established on the West Bank of the Jordan and in the Gaza Strip.
The National Council favours PLO participation in the search for a
Middle East settlement, provided the Palestinian question is treated
as a political question, i.e. that the aim is to satisfy the people's
national rights and is not limited solely to the refugee problems.[85]

While Demchenko emphasised the willingness of the Arab states to
go to Geneva, he neglected to mention that by the end of January both
Syria and Egypt had spoken of a link between a Palestinian entity and
Jordan in a possible gesture to Israel to expedite the beginning of peace
negotiations. Such a development could hamper the independence of
action of the PLO, something neither its leaders nor the USSR wanted.
In addition, the PLO did not appear to be as forthcoming as
Demchenko indicated. Indeed, the Palestine National Council meeting,
initially scheduled for December 1976, was postponed until March
1977 while its Central Committee, meeting in Damascus on 12
December, made no decision about a willingness to set up a West
Bank–Gaza state or even form a government-in-exile to attend a
Geneva-type peace conference.

While the Soviet leaders had at least made an effort to win the Arab
rejectionists over to their point of view on Israel's right to exist, they
did not prove successful and there is, of course, a real question as to
how hard they tried. Following the events in Lebanon, Iraq and Libya
were the two strongest allies the USSR had left in the Arab world and
the Soviet leadership may not have wished to alienate them by pressing
too hard on this point – particularly since if the main confrontation
states (Israel, Egypt, Syria and Jordan) agreed on a peace settlement,
there was little either Iraq or Libya could do to prevent one.

As the USSR was endeavouring to secure a resumption of the

Geneva Conference in order to bring about its conception of an
Arab–Israeli peace settlement, the newly inaugurated American
President, Jimmy Carter, was trying to promote a settlement as well.
After dispatching his Secretary of State, Cyrus Vance, to the Middle
East in February, Carter invited to Washington a series of Middle
Eastern leaders, beginning with Prime Minister Yitzhak Rabin of Israel.
Carter sought to set his Israeli visitor at ease at the beginning of their
talks by publicly coming out for 'defensible borders' for Israel and
indicating that these borders might extend beyond the 'permanent and
recognised borders' reached in a peace settlement.[86] As might be
expected, such a pronouncement was strongly opposed by Arab leaders
and exploited by the Soviet press.[87] One week later, however, in
response to a question in his Town Meeting visit to Clinton,
Massachusetts, Carter stunned the Israelis by publicly coming out for a
'homeland' for the Palestinians. Although his speech emphasised a
Model II plan for peace, where Israel would be a fully accepted member
of the Middle East community with ties of trade, tourism and cultural
exchange with its Arab neighbours, Jordan, Lebanon, Egypt and Syria,
and that the Palestinians had to give up their 'publicly professed
commitment to destroy Israel',[88] nonetheless this was the first time an
American President had ever publicly mentioned a Palestinian
homeland. It would appear that Carter was deliberately signalling the
Palestinians, since the Palestine National Council was meeting in Cairo
at that time amid a great deal of speculation that it would moderate its
position towards Israel. Carter apparently hoped that by enunciating
the term 'Palestinian homeland', he might reinforce trends for
moderation among the Palestinians by indicating that the USA was
willing to come out in support of a Palestinian entity of some type.
Given the fact that Syria and Egypt had earlier spoken of such an entity
linked to Jordan, Carter's comment that 'the exact way to solve the
Palestine problem is one that first of all addresses itself right now to the
Arab countries'[89] may have been seen as support for such a position.
Indeed, the Soviet leadership may well have been concerned that were a
Palestinian state to be linked to Jordan, which had established close ties
to Syria, then yet another instrument which it hoped to use to oppose
US policy in the Arab world might be lost.[90]

Carter's hopes for moderation at the Palestine National Council
session, however, were not realised. Militancy won out and there was no
change in the Council attitude towards Israel, with Article No. 9 of the
fifteen-point programme specifically calling for the 'liberation of all the
occupied Arab lands' and for the 'return of the national established

rights of the Palestinians without peace, reconciliation, or
recognition'.[91] While neither the USSR nor the USA could have been
pleased at the militancy against Israel evidenced by the Palestine
National Council meeting, the former may have at least drawn comfort
from Article No. 4 of the programme which rejected 'all kinds of
American capitulationist settlements and all liquidationist projects'.[92]
In addition, Article No. 8, which called for 'strengthening the Arab
front . . . in order to cope with the imperialist and Zionist designs', was
similar to the Soviet goal of establishing an anti-imperialist Arab unity,
albeit for a different ultimate purpose.[93] In commenting on the
Council session one week later, *Pravda* columnist Iurii Glukhov hailed
the Palestinian readiness to deal with progressive, democratic forces in
Israel (Article No. 14 of the programme), although he conspicuously
failed to mention the council's statement that these forces had to be
anti-Zionist — thus eliminating a number of Zionist Jews who advocated
the establishment of a Palestinian state alongside Israel.[94] Finally,
Glukhov endorsed as a 'just demand' the council demand (Article No.
15) that the PLO be represented as an 'independent member in all
conferences and meetings bearing on the Palestine problem', a position
effectively negating a number of proposals for a joint Palestinian—
Jordanian entity at the Geneva talks.

   While President Carter was apparently trying to signal the Palestinian
Arabs at their council meeting with his statement about a Palestinian
homeland, Soviet Party leader Brezhnev was also sending out signals.
Relations with the United States, which looked promising at the start
of the Carter administration, had deteriorated sharply because of US
advocacy of the Human Rights issue. With Secretary of State Cyrus
Vance on his way to Moscow to begin the negotiations on a new
strategic arms agreement, Brezhnev used the opportunity of a speech to
the Soviet Trade Unions Congress (much as he had done with his earlier
speech at Tula), to urge an improvement in Soviet—American relations,
and he offered another Soviet Middle East peace plan as part of his
signal.[95] He talked of the need for 'concerted action' by both the USA
and the USSR 'to achieve a just and lasting peace in the Middle East',
and went on to speak in detail about a Middle East peace settlement.
Interestingly enough he began his discussion by stating that while it
looked as if the Geneva Conference is 'gradually becoming more of a
reality', he went on to say that the Conference was 'not an end in itself'
and that 'the main thing is that its work should yield fruitful and just
results'. Perhaps indirectly indicating to the Palestinians and other
Arabs that they would have to deal directly with Israel, Brezhnev then

stated 'it goes without saying that the drawing up of peace terms in all details is primarily a matter for the conflicting sides'. Following this caveat, he then discussed the four-point peace plan first mentioned in October 1976 which stipulated (1) the total withdrawal of Israeli troops from lands occupied in 1967; (2) the securing of the inalienable rights of the Arab people of Palestine, including their right to self-determination and statehood; (3) the right of all states in the Middle East to 'independent existence and security'; and (4) the termination of the state of war between Israel and its Arab neighbours. Brezhnev then went on, however, to make a number of additional points which seemed directed at gaining Israeli and US approval. In the first place he spoke of a stage-by-stage Israeli withdrawal, perhaps to give Israel a greater sense of security about withdrawing, although his timetable of 'several months' indicates that this was more of a gesture than a genuine attempt to allay Israel's security concerns. Secondly, Brezhnev spoke of clearly defined border lines between Israel and its Arab neighbours after an Israeli withdrawal, borders that would be 'final and inviolable'. In another apparent attempt to make Israel feel more secure, Brezhnev also spoke of the establishment of demilitarised zones on both sides of the respective borders (but only if the respective states agreed) and the stationing of a UN emergency force or UN observers in these zones for 'some clearly stipulated period of time'. Such a situation would prevent the unilateral expulsion of the UN troops which was one of the causes of the 1967 war. Brezhnev also spoke of guarantees for any peace settlement, indicated as the USSR had done in the past that the Soviet Union was prepared to be a guarantor; and he suggested that the guarantor states could have observers in UN contingents 'in the respective [demilitarised] zones'. Finally, after stating that these were the USSR's 'preliminary ideas' about a peace settlement which it was 'not imposing on anyone', Brezhnev stated the Soviet Union's receptivity to other peace plans and once again offered to reach an agreement to help end the arms race in the Middle East once a Middle East peace settlement was reached.

The latest detailed Middle East peace plan, which went further to meet Israeli demands than any other Soviet offer since the 1973 war, remained an essentially Model I plan, which Israel rejected. Despite the plan, the Soviet leadership's talks with Vance did not go well, although the disagreements were not so much on the Middle East as on strategic arms. *Pravda*'s description of the talks cited the two nations' agreement that co-ordinated actions by the US and USSR 'are essential for the achievement of a just and durable peace in the Middle East' and noted that an agreement had been reached to hold a Vance–Gromyko meeting in Geneva in May to 'broaden the exchange of opinions on the Middle East, including the question of the resumption of the Geneva Conference'.[96]

The interim period between the proposed Soviet–American discussions on the Middle East was to prove an active one indeed in Middle East diplomacy. President Carter continued his round of talks with Arab leaders, seeing Anwar Sadat and King Husayn in Washington and arranging to meet Hafiz Asad in Europe. The Soviets themselves were not idle, as first Tunisian Foreign Minister Hedi Nouria, then Arafat and later Asad journeyed to Moscow.

When Arafat arrived in the USSR he met first Andrei Gromyko and then Brezhnev. Radio Moscow reported 'a thorough exchange of views' on the Middle East situation between Gromyko and Arafat, and noted the 'urgent need to resume as soon as possible the work of the Geneva Conference' – a major change from the degree of necessity noted by Brezhnev in his Trade Union speech discussion of Geneva only two weeks before.[97]

Brezhnev himself met Arafat the same day and *Pravda* printed a report of the meeting, together with a picture on its front page.[98] Brezhnev hailed the Palestinian resistance movement and once again stated that the USSR considered the creation of an independent Palestinian state 'an inseparable part of an all-encompassing Middle East settlement'. For his part, Arafat thanked the USSR for its support of the Palestinian Arabs' struggle for 'their legitimate national rights' and reaffirmed that the Palestinians would continue to fight against the 'intrigues of imperialism and reaction'. Given the obvious disagreements between the two sides, no joint communiqué was issued, although, for the Soviet leadership, the visit had the positive effect of reaffirming Soviet–Palestinian relations and their joint opposition to US peace initiatives, after a number of Palestinians had criticised the Soviet Union for a lack of support in their battles against Syria during the Lebanese civil war.

One week later Hafiz Asad journeyed to Moscow. He was welcomed at the airport by Leonid Brezhnev, a clear signal from the Soviet leadership of its desire to improve relations with Syria. At a dinner honouring Asad, Brezhnev urged co-ordination of action on the Middle East.[99] In addition, however, Brezhnev reiterated to Asad the Soviet position that Israel had the right to 'state independence and a secure existence'. Interestingly enough, while also coming out for a Palestinian state he stressed the point that 'not a single decision affecting the Arab people of Palestine should be taken without the Palestinians or against their will'. While Brezhnev made this assertion in the context of a statement advocating the convocation of the Geneva Conference 'without delay' (thus apparently backtracking from the position he took on the urgency of reconvening Geneva in his Trade Union speech one month before) the implications of his comments appeared contradictory. Indeed, it seemed to indicate that if the Palestinians refused to recognise, or live in peace with Israel, even under the Soviet peace formula, the USSR would necessarily have to acquiesce in their decision. While the Soviet leaders may have intended this statement to oppose 'reactionary' Arab attempts to impose a peace settlement on the Palestinians 'against their will', such phraseology is open to different interpretations and the PLO leadership may yet invoke it to oppose the Soviet peace plan.

Asad in his reply did not address himself directly to a settlement, although he called for a complete Israeli withdrawal from lands occupied in 1967 and recognition of the Palestinian Arabs' right to self-determination. He also supported the Soviet Union's call for the rapid reconvening of the Geneva Conference.[100]

The communiqué issued at the conclusion of Asad's visit referred to 'a constructive exchange of opinions on a number of issues, including the ways of achieving a just and lasting peace in the Middle East'. It included only those two aspects of a settlement that Syria advocated: the total withdrawal of Israeli troops from all Arab territory occupied in 1967, and the satisfaction of the national rights of the Arab people of Palestine, including their right to creation of their own independent state. The other Soviet principle, stating the right of existence of all states in the Middle East, was conspicuous by its absence from the communiqué and there was also no mention of the termination of the state of war between the Arabs and Israel. It also called for the 'earliest possible convocation of the Geneva Conference', emphasising the 'importance of the role of the USSR as co-chairman'.[101]

The very limited measure of agreement achieved between the USSR and Syria during Asad's visit, and the strong disagreement between Moscow and the PLO evidenced during Arafat's visit, indicated the limited degree of influence the USSR enjoyed *vis-à-vis* its two closest partners among the parties directly concerned in the Arab—Israeli conflict.

Conclusions

This study has examined Soviet policy towards the Arab—Israeli conflict in the larger context of Middle Eastern politics since the

Arab—Israeli war of 1973. On the basis of the evidence available, it would appear as if the USSR is indeed interested in an Arab—Israeli settlement, if one can be reached on Soviet terms. The Soviet plan for a settlement is essentially a Model I peace plan where Israel would withdraw from all the territory it captured in 1967, but have its sovereignty over its 4 June 1967 borders acknowledged by the Arabs and possibly guaranteed by the USSR and the United States. In addition, a Palestinian state would be created on territory to be evacuated by Israel on the West Bank and Gaza Strip areas. To make such a plan more agreeable to Israel, the USSR has also suggested a staged withdrawal — albeit over a short period of time — and the establishment of demilitarised zones on both sides of the border with the stationing of UN forces in these zones for a specified period of time, as well as a 'normalisation' of Soviet—Israeli relations.

Such a plan would be very much in the Soviet Union's interest for a number of reasons. In the first place it would preserve the state of Israel whose existence has become an important part of Soviet strategy in the Middle East. For a number of years the USSR has sought to consolidate what it has termed 'anti-imperialist Arab unity' around Arab enmity towards Israel which the USSR portrays as the linchpin of Western imperialism in the Middle East. The mere fact of an Israeli withdrawal to the prewar 1967 lines would not remove the potential threat of a future Israeli attack on the Arabs, nor the memories of Israeli occupation of Arab lands in the post-1967 period. Indeed, by supporting a Model I peace plan (and opposing the concept of a Model II peace where Israel would have trade, cultural and diplomatic relations with its neighbours) the USSR would apparently hope to keep at least a certain amount of latent hostility alive in the Arab—Israeli relationship, thereby forcing the Arabs to keep at least a modicum of unity to confront the putative Israeli threat. The Soviet leaders evidently hope they could then exploit that unity to enhance their own position in the Middle East and weaken the position of the United States.

A second benefit for the USSR of such a plan would be the termination of the American role as mediator in limited Arab—Israeli disengagement agreements. This role has brought the USA a great deal of prestige in the Arab world since the 1973 war as Kissinger was able to demonstrate to the Arabs that it was the United States, and not the Soviet Union, which was able to secure Israeli territorial withdrawals. Once a final, as opposed to another partial, agreement was reached, the necessity for American mediation would be ended, and the Soviet leaders may reason that this would lead to a drop in US prestige and influence in the Arab world, as well as an end to the quarrels between the Arab states over the disengagement agreements which have impeded the Soviet Union's drive to help create the 'anti-imperialist' Arab unity it has sought.

Yet another benefit of such a plan would be that, by preserving Israel, the United States would not be alienated. Given the strong emotional and political ties between Israel and the United States, which have been reiterated by the new US President, Jimmy Carter, on a number of occasions, the USSR would clearly jeopardise even the remnants of détente that still exist, and the chances for a Senate ratification of another SALT agreement, by working for Israel's destruction. It is for this reason, if no other, that the Soviet leadership, in speeches to Arab leaders as well as in its peace plans, has endorsed Israel's right to exist as an independent state. Indeed, the Soviet leaders may well recall the sharp deterioration in Soviet–American relations following Soviet aid to the Arabs during the 1973 war; and, particularly at a time when both Soviet–American and Sino–Soviet relations are strained, the Soviet leadership would obviously not like to witness the further deterioration of Soviet–American relations that would be caused by any Soviet support of a plan to destroy Israel. Concomitantly, the establishment of a Model I Arab–Israeli peace would also lessen the possibility of a superpower conflict over an Arab–Israeli war which could lead to a nuclear confrontation, yet another consequence of a peace agreement most welcome to the Soviet leadership.

A fourth benefit for the Soviet Union from its peace plan, if it were accepted, would be the establishment of a Palestinian state. Given current trends in Arab politics, the Soviet leadership obviously hopes that such a state would be an ally of Soviet policy in the Arab world and would help combat American influence in the region. Given the fact that Libya and Iraq, the Soviet Union's most important Arab allies after the Lebanese civil war, are on the periphery of the Arab world as well as being mistrusted by their fellow Arabs, the USSR would clearly benefit from having a close ally in the very centre of the Middle East. In addition, the Kremlin obviously believes that such a state, sandwiched between a hostile Israel and an equally hostile Husayn regime which has not forgotten PLO attempts to overthrow it, and under probable pressure from Syria as well, would be dependent on Soviet support and hence would have an interest in maintaining close relations with the USSR.

How would the USSR like to achieve such a settlement? Soviet leaders have most often pointed to the Geneva Conference as a vehicle for reaching a settlement, although they have differed among themselves somewhat over the urgency of convening the conference. An examination of the course of Soviet policy since the 1973 war indicates that Soviet calls for the resumption of the Geneva Conference were usually at their strongest when it appeared that the United States was going to secure a diplomatic success in its mediation efforts and the USSR faced the possibility of being frozen out. This was particularly evident in the period from February 1974 to March 1975 when Kissinger's first attempt to negotiate a second Israeli–Egyptian agreement failed, and in the period from April to October 1976 during the escalating civil war in Lebanon when the USSR saw developments there moving in a direction inimical to its interests. In such a situation, the call for the reconvening of the Geneva Conference was a Soviet effort to regain some diplomatic momentum by participating as a co-equal with the United States in a major meeting dealing with the Middle East.

It should also be noted that the dynamics of a reconvened Geneva Conference could be hoped to give the USSR the opportunity to champion the Arab cause, while isolating the United States as the supporter of Israel, thus enabling the USSR to regain some of the influence it lost to the United States in the Arab world since 1973. While the USSR has also, on occasion (such as in Brezhnev's Trade Union speech in March 1977), played down the urgency of reconvening Geneva, this would appear a tactical rather than a strategic policy, and the very reversal of Brezhnev's statement on the urgency of Geneva first by Radio Moscow and then by Brezhnev himself (all within the space of one month) indicates that the USSR would much prefer to reconvene a Geneva Conference, even if the Arab states were not united in their policies, and even if the conference were to encounter 'difficulties' (to use Kosygin's term), rather than wait for the United States to work out yet another settlement — and obtain Arab appreciation for its efforts.

One of the obstacles facing the reconvening of the Geneva Conference, however, has been the refusal of the PLO to agree to live in peace with Israel and the refusal of both Israel and the United States to meet it until it takes such a position. It was for this reason, perhaps, that the USSR sought to use the Security Council debate on the Middle East of January 1976, in which the PLO was invited to participate, as a device to facilitate the reconvening of Geneva and possibly even to serve as a partial substitute for it. This ploy proved unsuccessful, however, as Israel boycotted the session because of the PLO presence, and the United States maintained its support of Israel to the point of

vetoing an anti-Israeli resolution. It would appear that unless the USSR
or the Arabs can persuade the United States to allow the PLO to
participate in Geneva without a change in its position towards Israel, or
the Palestine National Council reverses its March 1977 decision and
agrees to live in peace with Israel, it is unlikely that Geneva will be
reconvened. Indeed, Brezhnev's hesitancy about the urgency of
reconvening Geneva in his March 1977 Trade Union speech may have
been directly related to the uncompromising position on Israel adopted
by the Palestinians at the Palestine National Council meeting. All in all,
since the Soviet Union is now on record as demanding the participation
of the PLO from the beginning and on an equal basis in any Geneva
discussions, the prospect of an early convening of a Geneva Peace
Conference is not bright, unless some sort of diplomatic device for the
mutual recognition of Israel and a Palestine government-in-exile can be
arranged just prior to the opening of the Conference – a rather
doubtful prospect given the stated position of the PLO.

Given this situation, what are the Soviet leaders likely to do in the
future? In the absence of any forward movement in Geneva, due to
PLO opposition to Israel's existence, there exists the possibility that the
United States, with an activist President, will again seize the initiative.
Indeed, with Carter clearly sketching out the basic elements of what he
feels to be a fair and equitable settlement of the Arab–Israeli conflict,
using such terms as 'defensible borders' for Israel (albeit with only
minor modifications from the 1967 prewar lines), and a 'Palestinian
Homeland', the Soviet leaders face the prospect that additional interim
agreements leading, ultimately, to a final settlement may be worked out
under American auspices – a situation they clearly do not want. In
addition, as a number of Arab countries, particularly the confrontation
states surrounding Israel (Syria, Jordan and Egypt), concentrate their
energies on economic development, they may be far less willing to go to
war against Israel once again – particularly an Israel assumed by the
Arabs to be armed with nuclear weapons[102]– and they may well be amenable to a peace accord reached under American auspices if it can enable
them to regain the lands lost in 1967. Assuming the United States main-
tains its close ties with Saudi Arabia, whose influence in Arab politics has
been steadily increasing since 1973, then the main Arab confrontation
states, Egypt and Syria, backed by Saudi Arabia, may well pressure the
PLO leadership to accept a tie with Jordan and thereby work out an
arrangement with Israel even, if necessary, by forcing changes in that
leadership. There would be little the USSR could do to avert such a
development, which holds the possibility of greatly curbing, if not
eliminating, the PLO's freedom of manoeuvre, since Soviet influence

over the Arab states is very limited indeed. If one measure of a state's influence over another is its ability to force the elite of the influenced state to take actions which it would otherwise oppose, the USSR has proved singularly ineffective in influencing even its primary arms clients in the region. In the case of Egypt, which in recent years has broken away from its once very close relationship to the USSR, one can point to many occasions on which the Sadat regime has opposed Soviet pressure. The Syrian ruling elite, under the leadership of Hafiz Asad, has similarly opposed Soviet pressures on a number of occasions.

These examples, together with a number of others that could be examined, clearly indicate the inability of the Soviet Union to influence Arab elites to take actions against their will in matters of importance to them. Consequently, should the elites of the Arab confrontation states ever decide to enter into a peace agreement with Israel, it is unlikely that the USSR could exercise influence over any one of them to prevent a peace agreement from being signed. In such a situation, the USSR might, of course, seek to try to effect an elite change in these states to bring to power other elites who would be more favourably inclined to Soviet policy. Nonetheless, when one examines the elite changes that have occurred in Syria and Egypt over the last seven years, it becomes clear that Soviet ability to effect elite change is also very limited. Indeed, Asad overthrew the more pro-Soviet Salah Jadid in November 1970 and Sadat, in 1971, successfully withstood a coup attempt by Ali Sabri and others, who had close ties with the USSR.

The USSR can be expected to utilise its extensive propaganda apparatus, as well as the Arab communist parties which it controls, to denounce a US-mediated peace agreement – much as it did when the Sinai II agreement was concluded. It is doubtful, however, whether such propaganda attacks would have any major effect if the majority of the Arab world (Egypt, Syria, Jordan, Saudi Arabia and Kuwait) were to endorse the agreement. Indeed, even when Egypt was isolated in its decision to accept the Sinai II agreement, the Soviet propaganda campaign proved unable either to prevent the agreement or to overturn it (or Sadat) once it had been signed.

The USSR may also threaten to withhold, or actually withhold, arms from Syria and Egypt while simultaneously increasing arms shipments to these two states' main adversaries, Iraq and Libya, which would support the USSR in opposing a US-arranged peace agreement. Yet this would be done for their own reasons, such as Libya's quarrel with Egypt and Iraq's confrontation with Syria. In any case, Libya and Iraq are currently the 'odd men out' of the Arab world, greatly mistrusted by their Arab neighbours, and their opposition to any peace agreement could not be expected to prevent the primary Arab confrontation states or their supporters, Saudi Arabia and Kuwait (which also mistrust Libya and Iraq), from coming to an agreement with Israel. At most, a loose, not very effective coalition of anti-agreement forces might form composed of Libya, Iraq, whatever Palestinian elements are not included in, or do not agree to, a peace agreement, Algeria, South Yemen and potential opposition groups in Egypt, Syria and Jordan. Here again, however, the effect of such a Soviet action does not appear to be too great and will certainly not upset the balance of power in the region. Sadat has already begun looking around in the West for weapons and to other Soviet arms clients and to China for spare parts. Since, after a settlement with Israel, Egypt's need for a large standing army would diminish (as would Israel's) a cut-off of Soviet arms could be expected to be absorbed while the Egyptian army switched over to a Western armament system. Even such a reduced Egyptian army would be more than a match for Soviet-armed Libya which would not be so foolhardy as to attack Egypt lest Sadat be provoked into annexing the oil-rich country. In the case of Syria, the situation is somewhat more complex, but essentially similar. A cut-off of Soviet arms would clearly weaken the Syrians in the confrontation with Iraq, which, however, would be unlikely to go to war for a number of reasons. In the first place, it would be faced not only with a Syrian army which could expect at least political support from the USA (and which, after a peace settlement with Israel, could move at least some of its troops to the Iraqi border — much as it did at the height of the Lebanese civil war), but also a hostile Saudi Arabia to the south, an Iran with which relations are, at best, lukewarm to the east, and with a restive Kurdish population in its northern mountains. Syria, of course, could also be expected to seek military assistance in the West where it has already begun to seek trade and economic assistance. One should add at this point that it is not at all certain that the USSR would totally eliminate its arms aid to Syria and Egypt if an American-sponsored peace agreement is signed. Perhaps mindful of the damage caused to its relations with Yugoslavia and Albania when it totally severed military aid, the Soviet Union may well decide to continue military aid to both Arab countries, albeit probably at reduced rates, to preserve a modicum of influence within the officer corps of each country and to prevent the two Arab states from becoming totally dependent on Western military assistance.

It may well be that active Soviet opposition to any American-arranged peace agreement could also provide a rallying point for counter-elites in each of the Arab confrontation states which, in the long run, might have the ability to seize power and then turn to the USSR for arms aid and diplomatic support. Yet, given the relative stability of the Husayn, Sadat and Asad regimes, this does not appear to be an immediate concern let alone a development Moscow could rely upon to bring about any long-run change in the attitude to it of successor leaderships.

Thus, faced by the unwelcome possibility of an American-orchestrated peace agreement which it is unlikely to be able to prevent, the USSR may try to pressure the leaders of the PLO to change their position *vis-à-vis* Israel in order to go to Geneva where, the Soviet leaders could argue, the PLO, backed by the USSR, would get a better deal than it would get from a peace settlement worked out under American auspices. Unfortunately for Moscow, it has very limited leverage on the constituent elements of the PLO, and such pressure might well be ineffective, unless the Palestinians see it in their own interest to change their programme.

One should also consider the possibility that the USSR might choose to acquiesce in US peacemaking efforts for a limited period of time, hoping that they might fail either in crystallising or in being implemented. Moscow may assume that given its ties with the PLO in the past, it may be able to have influence in any Palestinian or Palestinian—Jordanian entity which is created by the peace settlement. Similarly, since the Soviet leadership takes, to use its terminology, a 'strategic' (long-term) view of Middle East developments, it may reason that the conservative monarchies of Saudi Arabia, Kuwait and the United Arab Emirates may soon be replaced by radical regimes of the Iraqi type which would appeal to the USSR for support, and that the Sadat regime, beset by economic problems, may yet fall, to be replaced by a more radical regime. The Soviet leadership may also reason that conflict over the high price or availability of oil may split the conservative oil-producing states from their current alignment with the United States — a development that could spur them to turn to the USSR for support and protection. Such a policy of 'watchful waiting' and exploiting regional developments rather than opposing a US-mediated peace settlement would also be less damaging to Soviet—American relations, particularly in the 1978—9 period when the USSR will be intent on securing a strategic arms agreement and possibly economic agreements as well.

In sum, therefore, the Soviet plan for a Middle East peace settlement would be a Model I arrangement which would achieve an Israeli withdrawal from its 1967 conquests while leaving sufficient tension in the Arab–Israeli relationship for the USSR to exploit in order to further its goals in the region, primarily the weakening and ultimate elimination of Western influence from the oil-rich and strategically-located Arab world. The main vehicle the Soviet leaders see to achieve such a settlement is the Geneva Conference, but a combination of increasing Soviet support for the PLO and Palestinian Arab obduracy on the issue of living in peace with Israel makes the convening of such a conference in the near future unlikely. Given this situation, the USSR may be faced by yet another American effort to achieve an Arab–Israeli settlement, and there would appear to be little the USSR could do to prevent such a settlement from taking place if the Arab states involved were committed to it. Nonetheless, since the Soviet leadership takes a long-term view of Middle Eastern events, it may choose to acquiesce in an American-arranged peace plan – should it prove successful – in the hopes of improving Soviet–American relations in the short run while exploiting Middle Eastern developments to undermine US influence in the Middle East in the medium and long run.

Notes

1. The text of Security Council Resolution 338 is in Walter Laqueur (ed.), *The Israeli–Arab Reader* (New York: Bantam Books, 1976), p.481.

2. For a discussion of the differing American peace conceptions, see Steven L. Spiegel, 'The United States and the Middle East Crisis', *Middle East Review*, IX, 13 (Spring 1977), pp.25–33.

3. See *Pravda*, 10 and 16 November 1973, for implicit criticism of Sadat for accepting the prisoner exchange agreement without demanding Israeli withdrawal to ceasefire lines of 22 October, urged by the Soviet Union. Cf. Andrei Kirilenko's speech at the 56th CPSU Anniversary, *Pravda*, 7 November 1973.

4. See Baruch Gurevitz, 'The Soviet Union and the Palestinian Organisations', in this volume.

5. For Gromyko's remarks on Israel and its borders, see Yaacov Ro'i, 'The Soviet Attitude to the Existence of Israel', in this volume, pp.232–3. Excerpts quoted here are taken from *Current Digest of the Soviet Press* (henceforth *CDSP*), XXV, 51, pp.1–4.

6. *Pravda*, 25 January 1974 (translated in *CDSP*, XXVI, 4, p.25). For further details of Fahmi's visit to Moscow, see Ro'i, 'The Soviet Union and Egypt: the Constraints of a Power-Client Relationship', in this volume.

7. *Pravda*, 8 March 1974. For the Soviet role in the achievement of the Syrian–Israeli disengagement agreement, see also Galia Golan and Itamar Rabinovich, 'The Soviet Union and Syria: the Limits of Co-operation', in this volume.

8. *R. Moscow*, 12 March 1974, cited in UPI report from London in *New York Times*, 13 March 1974.

9. See the report in *Middle East Monitor* (henceforth *MEM*), IV, 7 (April 1974), p.1.

10. *Pravda*, 29 March 1974. For further discussion of Soviet–US relations in this period, see Galia Golan, 'The Arab–Israeli Conflict in Soviet–US Relations',

in this volume.

11. *Pravda*, 17 April 1974 (translated in *CDSP*, XXVI, 16, p.6). For Asad's visit, see also Golan and Rabinovich, 'The Soviet Union and Syria', in this volume, p.219. |

12. *Pravda*, 30 April 1974 (translated in *CDSP*, XXVI, 17, p.14).

13. 'Step Towards Settlement', *New Times*, 23 (1974), p.9.

14. The text of the communiqué is found in *New Times*, 28 (1974).

15. *Izvestiia*, 9 July 1974 (translated in *CDSP*, XXVI, 27, p.21).

16. See lengthy articles in *New Times*, 32 (1974), pp.26–31; *Izvestiia*, 30 July 1974. The same issue of *New Times* carried a front-page editorial supporting the PLO and a two-page interview with Yasir Arafat. For Arafat's visit to Moscow, see Gurevitz, 'The Soviet Union and the Palestinian Organisations', in this volume, p.261.

17. *MEM*, IV, 11 (1 June 1974) p.1. According to a report by Joseph Fitchett in the *Christian Science Monitor*, 23 December 1974, Egypt had also contacted Iran in an effort to gain access to sophisticated military weaponry. Egypt had already approached Western markets (cf. Ro'i, 'The Soviet Union and Egypt', in this volume, p.187) and was later to make extensive military purchases in France, Britain and the United States.

18. Cited in report by Bernard Gwertzman in *New York Times*, 16 September 1974.

19. Cited in a report by Bernard Gwertzman in ibid., 14 September 1974.

20. For the texts of Ford's and Kissinger's UN speeches, see the news releases of the Bureau of Public Affairs of the US Department of State for 18 and 23 September 1974.

21. Cf. editorial in *New Times*, 38 (1974), p.17; *Pravda*, 29 September 1974.

22. 'Fruitful Talks', *New Times*, 43 (1974), p.17. For Fahmi's October 1974 visit to Moscow, see Ro'i, 'The Soviet Union and Egypt', in this volume, p.189.

23. *MEM*, IV, 21 (15 November 1974), pp.2–3.

24. Dmitry Volsky, 'After the Rabat Meeting', *New Times*, 45 (1974), p.11.

25. Cited in *MEM*, IV, 21 (15 November 1974), p.4. The Iraqi leader's statement also clearly demonstrated that despite extensive Soviet military aid, and assistance in the war against the Kurds, on this important issue the two states were diametrically opposed, because the USSR had strongly advocated a PLO role at Geneva.

26. The text of Arafat's speech was printed in *New York Times*, 16 November 1974.

27. For a good analysis of the 'war scare' see the report by John Cooley in *Christian Science Monitor*, 18 November 1974.

28. In mid-November the United States promised to sell a large quantity of grain to Syria. The deal, like that with Egypt to which the United States also promised a large quantity of grain in the early part of the month, was long-term, low-interest and low-price and, in the grain-short world of 1974, held political significance.

29. The text of the communiqué is in *New York Times*, 25 November 1974.

30. *Pravda*, 28 November 1974.

31. The March 1975 issue of *Harpers* detailed the hypothetical American seizure of the Saudi Arabian oilfields for which some voices in the USA were calling.

32. *Pravda*, 4 February 1975 (translated in *CDSP*, XXVII, 5, p.15).

33. Ibid., 6 February 1975 (translated in *CDSP*, XXVII, 5, p.16). For Gromyko's Cairo visit, see Ro'i, 'The Soviet Union and Egypt', in this volume, p.191.

34. D. Antonov, 'Urgent Tasks', *New Times*, 7 (1975), p.6.

35. Cf. report by Joseph Harsch in *Christian Science Monitor*, 7 March 1975.

36. Cited in Associated Press Report from Damascus, *New York Times*, 9 March 1975.

37. See *MEM*, V, 5 (15 March 1975), p.2 for a description of the agreement.

38. *Izvestiia*, 15 April 1975.

39. *Pravda*, 15 April 1975.

40. Ibid., 17 April 1975.

41. Ibid., 23 April 1975.

42. Ibid., 24 and 27 April 1975. See Golan and Rabinovich, 'The Soviet Union and Syria', in this volume, p.222.

43. *Pravda*, 5 May 1975.

44. A. Usvatov, 'Palestinian Delegation in Moscow', *New Times*, 19 (1975), p.24.

45. *Pravda*, 14 May 1975 (translated in *CDSP*, XXVII, 20, p.10).

46. *Izvestiia*, 21 May 1975 (translated in *CDSP*, XXVII, 20, p.14).

47. Cf. reports by Dev Muraka in *Christian Science Monitor*, 25 April 1975, and Wolf Blitzer in the *Jerusalem Post* of the same date. See also Ro'i, 'The Soviet Attitude to the Existence of Israel', in this volume, p.241.

48. *Izvestiia*, 29 May 1975 (translated in *CDSP*, XXVII, 22, p.10).

49. *Al-Hawadith* (Beirut) cited in Associated Press report in the *Jerusalem Post*, 29 August 1975.

50. For a more detailed treatment of the Syrian–Jordanian rapprochement, see Robert O. Freedman, 'Lebanon, The Soviet Union and the Syrian–PLO–Jordanian Entente' in Anne Sinai and Allen Pollack (eds.), *The Syrian Arab Republic* (New York: American Academic Association for Peace in the Middle East, 1975), pp.86–9.

51. See the reports by John Cooley in *Christian Science Monitor*, 26 June and 23 July 1975.

52. *Pravda*, 12 August 1975.

53. Ibid., 18 August 1975.

54. Ibid., 26 August 1975.

55. Ibid., 29 August 1975.

56. Cf. report by Godfrey Sperling in *Christian Science Monitor*, 21 August 1975.

57. Reuters report from Geneva in *New York Times*, 5 September 1975.

58. The Soviet attacks also concentrated on Sadat's opening of the Egyptian economy to foreign capital, with *Pravda* on 23 November 1975 going so far as to infer that Egypt was losing its 'economic independence'. See Ro'i, 'The Soviet Union and Egypt', in this volume, pp.182–3 and 189.

59. *Pravda*, 11 October 1975.

60. *Ar-Ray al-Amm* cited in Associated Press report from Kuwait in *New York Times*, 19 October 1975.

61. Cf. report by Bernard Gwertzman in ibid., 18 November 1975.

62. *Pravda*, 20 December 1975. For the Soviet proposal, see TASS in Russian for abroad and in English, 10 November 1975/*SWB I*, 12 November 1975. The US suggestion was presented to the Soviet embassy in Washington on 1 December, see *Department of State Bulletin*, LXXIV, 1906 (5 January 1976), pp.12–13.

63. *Pravda*, 10 January 1976. The statement is translated in *CDSP*, XXVIII, 2, p.6.

64. See Golan and Rabinovich, 'The Soviet Union and Syria', in this volume, pp. 224–6.

65. *Pravda*, 25 February 1976 (translated in *CDSP*, XXVIII, 8, p.7).

66. See Ro'i, 'The Soviet Union and Egypt', in this volume, pp.201–211.

67. *Pravda*, 29 April 1976. Translation issued by *Moscow News*, 19 (15–22

May 1976).

68. On 29 April 1976, the author happened to be conducting interviews at the United States State Department when the Soviet Peace Plan was received via teletypewriter. He was informed that the USSR had not given the document to the United States before making it public.

69. For details of Kosygin's visit, see Golan and Rabinovich, 'The Soviet Union and Syria', in this volume, p.226.

70. *Pravda*, 3 June 1976.

71. Ibid., 4 June 1976.

72. See Golan and Rabinovich, 'The Soviet Union and Syria', in this volume, p.226.

73. *Pravda*, 2 October 1976.

74. Soviet activity in Angola, together with a primary campaign against the conservative Republican Ronald Reagan, had put President Ford on the defensive about Soviet–American relations and he had announced in a 1 March TV interview that the word 'détente' was no longer a proper one to describe these relations (see *Washington Post*, 3 March 1976). In addition, following an unsuccessful visit to Moscow in January 1976 Kissinger had announced to the Senate Finance Committee that because of Angola the Ford administration no longer planned to ask Congress to lift the trade restrictions it had voted against the USSR and stated that he now opposed the multi-billion dollar US investments in the USSR to develop Soviet oil and natural gas that he had previously advocated (see *New York Times*, 31 January 1976). In mid-March three Soviet–American cabinet-level meetings were cancelled by the USA (*Washington Post*, 16 March 1976) and, perhaps most serious of all to the Soviet leaders, progress in SALT was virtually halted – a delay Brezhnev publicly decried in a speech to the Conference of European Communist Parties at the end of June – *Pravda*, 30 June 1976.

75. *Pravda*, 1 December 1976.

76. Ibid., 11 December 1976.

77. Ibid., 19 January 1977.

78. See, 22 December 1976, and Golan and Rabinovich, 'The Soviet Union and Syria', in this volume, p.227.

79. *Pravda*, 7 December 1976.

80. Ibid.

81. Ibid., 10 December 1976.

82. Ibid., 2 February 1977.

83. Ibid.

84. Ibid., 4 February 1977.

85. Ibid., 27 January 1977 (translated in *CDSP*, XXIX, 4, p.26).

86. Cited in *Near East Report*, XXI, 11 (16 March 1977), p.42. Subsequent US statements, however, referred only to 'minor modifications' of the 1967 borders.

87. *Pravda*, 12 March 1977.

88. Cited in *Near East Report*, XXI, 12 (23 March 1977), p.47.

89. Ibid.

90. Soviet concern was expressed by *R. Peace and Progress*, 22 March 1977/*FBIS III*, 23 March 1977. See also *Izvestiia*, 5 April 1977. Oleg Alov, writing in early March in *New Times*, 12 (1977), pp.4–5, criticised both Sadat's plan for a confederation between Jordan and a Palestinian entity and Israel's demands for a Model II peace settlement, enunciated in a speech by Rabin.

91. The fifteen-point Palestine National Council Programme was translated in *FBIS, Daily Report*, 21 March 1977.

92. Cf. Victor Bukharov, 'The Palestinians' Stand', *New Times*, 15 (1977),

p.10.

93. *R. Moscow* in Arabic, 23 March 1977/*FBIS III*, 24 March 1977, emphasised this point.

94. *Pravda*, 27 March 1977. Cf. Gurevitz, 'The Soviet Union and the Palestinian Organisations', in this volume, p.275.

95. The text of the foreign policy section of Brezhnev's speech was translated in *New Times*, 13 (1977), pp.4—7.

96. *Pravda*, 1 April 1977.

97. *R. Moscow*, 6 April 1977/*FBIS III*, 6 April 1977.

98. *Pravda*, 8 April 1977.

99. Ibid., 19 April 1977. The speech received first-page coverage.

100. Ibid.

101. Ibid., 23 April 1977.

102. For an Arab view expressing the certainty that Israel has nuclear weapons, see 'Israel's Nuclear Weapons — Are They in Safe Hands?' in *The Middle East*, 20 (June 1976), pp.25—8.

PART 5 CONCLUSIONS

12 THE SOVIET UNION IN THE MIDDLE EAST: PROBLEMS, POLICIES AND PROSPECTIVE TRENDS

Dina Spechler

The Soviet Union has been actively involved in the Middle East for over two decades. Throughout that period Soviet interests in the area have never been purely regional. Soviet behaviour has always been shaped and constrained by the USSR's chief global interests and aims. These have been to counter the strategic threat posed by the Western alliance and to undermine or reduce the relative political, economic and military strength of the West while avoiding a direct confrontation with it.

Insofar as a presence in the Third World, including the Middle East, has bolstered the strength and enhanced the strategic capability of the Western alliance, the USSR has attempted to eliminate or curtail that presence and substitute its own. It has sought political influence with local regimes and political groups so that they would reject ties with the West and co-operate with the USSR. As an area directly adjacent to it, the Middle East has played a particularly important role in the USSR's global strategy. The Soviets have tried to establish a military presence there which would enable them to counter or deter the military threat posed by Western forces positioned on their southern and south-western borders. Since the 1960s, with the forward deployment of the Soviet navy, the USSR's key interest in the Middle East has been to secure naval and air bases to provide support facilities and air cover for its Mediterranean fleet. A secondary objective has been to establish a presence in the Persian Gulf which would enable it, should the need arise, to secure or interdict Middle Eastern oil supplies.

To achieve these objectives Soviet policy has been to seek allies among regimes which show signs of radicalism, i.e. discontent with Western influence and with political and economic arrangements inspired or imposed by Western powers. The USSR has tried to encourage the anti-Western inclinations of these regimes, offering economic and military aid to induce and enable them to cut their ties with the West. It has used this aid to promote social and economic change in accord with the Soviet model, on the theory that the more nearly these regimes adopt that model, the more likely they will be to co-operate with the USSR.[1]

In the decade preceding the October War, Soviet attention and aid were directed to the FLN in Algeria, the Baʻthist regimes in Syria and Iraq and the nationalist government in South Yemen. But the cornerstone of Soviet strategy in the Middle East was Egypt. Egypt under Nasir was militantly anti-Western. Nasir introduced far-reaching socialist reforms, including extensive nationalisation of private property. In exchange for substantial Soviet aid, he gave the USSR a decisive say in the character of the Egyptian economy and economic development. Few realms of Egyptian life remained free of Soviet influence: the USSR became deeply involved in the operations of the one political party, the Arab Socialist Union, as well as in local government, the secret police, the army, the educational system and the governmental propaganda organs.[2]

The basis of the close Soviet–Egyptian relationship was strong mutual need. Nasir needed the USSR as a supplier of arms. Given his ambition to lead not merely Egypt but the Arab world, he had to be prepared to avenge Arab and Palestinian rights in armed conflict with Israel. The USSR needed Egypt because it was uniquely positioned and equipped not merely to supply it with the air and naval facilities it required, but to give it entrée into the Arab world as a whole, and Africa.

The relationships between the USSR and its Arab allies were not without strains and tensions. One source of conflict was the role of the Communist Party, which Egypt and Algeria were bent on suppressing, and in whose demise in those countries the Soviets ultimately acquiesced. Far more problematic for the USSR was the question of Egyptian and Syrian initiation of a war against Israel. Although the Soviets encouraged Egyptian and Syrian militancy in the weeks preceding the June 1967 war, they did not desire an outbreak of fighting and were surprised when it occurred. The course of the war both embarrassed and alarmed the Soviets. Although a hasty resort to the hotline and spectacular Israeli successes on the battlefield prevented an American intervention in this instance, the Soviets could not be sure what the United States might do in a new round of hostilities. And although the USSR had been unable and unwilling to intervene, it paid a considerable political price for not doing so, as it displayed weakness to the West and to its Communist allies and less than complete loyalty to its Arab friends. The Soviets saw that it would be harmful, perhaps fatal, to their position in the Middle East to fail again to support their allies in time of war. Yet intervention carried with it the terrible risk of a superpower confrontation.

In the light of these concerns, the Soviets concluded after the Six Day War that they had more to lose than to gain from another full-scale war in the Middle East. Hence while they rearmed Egypt and Syria, they also unilaterally imposed certain restraints on their resupply programme. They avoided providing any Arab country with a quantity and assortment of weapons which would tempt it to challenge Israel singlehandedly. This meant that no Arab country would be likely on its own to start a war it could not win, a war which the Soviets would surely be called on to win for it. Moreover, despite the political costs involved, they allowed Israel to retain ultimate military superiority over all the Arab states together. They refused to grant any combination of Arab countries the arms they would have needed to wage an all-out war against Israel.[3] As neither superpower could afford to let its friends lose in an all-out war, a US—Soviet confrontation would be very likely if one were to break out. Thus such a war had to be prevented at all costs.

But the costs were high. When Nasir died in 1970, a new leadership came to power in Egypt which was far less enamoured of its Soviet connection. More a pragmatist and technocrat than ideologue, Sadat was less sympathetic than his predecessor to anti-imperialist rhetoric and socialist solutions. He believed that Egypt had stagnated under Soviet tutelage and that Soviet intervention in his country's affairs was as humiliating and oppressive as colonial rule and its neo-colonial aftermath had been. And perhaps most critical for the Soviet position in Egypt, he chafed under the restraints the Soviets had imposed on his weapons acquisition programme. His decision to expel the twenty thousand Soviet advisers and technicians present in Egypt in July 1972 was a product of all these grievances, combined with the belief that if the Russians stayed, they would succeed in overthrowing him.[4]

In the fifteen months between their expulsion and the October War, the Soviets attempted both to restore their influence in Egypt and cultivate alternative allies in the Arab world. Yet they still maintained the self-imposed restraints on weapons deliveries which had done so much to undermine their position in the country most valuable to them. That Egypt continued to be of vital importance to Soviet Middle Eastern and global strategy was indicated by Soviet behaviour during the war. The thrust and timing of Soviet diplomacy — the USSR's efforts to arrange a ceasefire — were based on the military situation on the Egyptian front and were co-ordinated with the Egyptians alone (not the Syrians, Iraqis or Palestinians). In apparently supplying Egypt with surface-to-surface missiles capable of carrying nuclear warheads, then threatening to intervene on Egypt's behalf, the USSR took major risks on behalf of its ally. Either act could have triggered American entry into the war and the confrontation the Soviets so wished to avoid.[5]

The October War and its Aftermath

The October War exerted a profound impact on the politics of the Middle East. In the course of the war and its aftermath the stakes of the political game there changed dramatically, as did the relative positions of the players. The most important new phenomenon in the postwar situation was the determination of the Arab oil exporters, first manifested during the war, to unite in wielding the oil weapon for their joint political and economic ends. Of crucial importance, too, was the willingness of the major non-Arab exporters to give the Arabs at least partial support, in the realm of price policy. At first this new situation seemed clearly to work to the advantage of the USSR and the detriment of the West. As the Soviets were themselves net oil exporters to the West, higher oil prices would substantially improve their terms of trade and increase their hard currency earnings. Western interest in investing in Soviet oil resources would surely rise, as a result of fear of a prolonged or renewed Arab oil embargo. At the same time, difficulties in procuring oil would place the Western economic system under great strain, and this would generate sharp conflicts within the Western alliance and social unrest in each of the member countries. The Soviets expected nothing less than a complete 'change in the correlation of forces between the Third World and the West'. This, they assumed, could only benefit the USSR for it would make the Third World, especially the Middle East, more independent of the West and free to develop links with the USSR.[6]

However, it soon became apparent that the situation was far more complicated and ambiguous than it had seemed at first. It was far from clear who would benefit and who would lose. Much would depend on the initiatives the major players might take and their ability to turn to their advantage the new situation in which they found themselves.[7]

The spectre of an embargo enormously enhanced the urgency and importance to the West of ensuring the supply of Middle Eastern oil. It suddenly became a major concern of the entire Western world to mollify the Arabs and to settle the conflict between them and Israel so as to reduce the likelihood that the embargo might be reimposed. At the same time, the unprecedented increase in the price of oil enacted during the war and the subsequent increases triggered by that step created vast new wealth in the Middle East. This meant that there were major new opportunities for all extra-regional powers, both West and East, to do profitable business. The oil producers were suddenly prepared to pay hard currency for enormous quantities of industrial and military technology, not merely for themselves but for the less well-endowed confrontation states. The question was, whose arms and whose equipment would be purchased with the new wealth?

With the newly apparent importance of controlling the flow of oil and the new opportunities to be exploited in cornering Middle Eastern markets, both the United States and the Soviet Union had stronger reasons to want to play a role in the region and to reduce the influence the other superpower exerted there. For its part, the United States was prepared to undertake a major diplomatic and economic offensive to achieve this end. Much more than at any previous time in the history of the Arab—Israeli conflict, America was ready to offer political support and economic aid to Israel's enemies. And just when its role as supplier of arms to the Arabs was becoming economically attractive to the Soviet Union, the United States and Western Europe indicated that they, too, needed hard currency and were willing to break with past policy and do business.

If the stakes of the Middle Eastern game had increased, so had the costs and difficulties of playing. There was a time when the USSR could simply have underbid any Western competitors which might have emerged, offering prices so low and terms so favourable as to be irresistible. But now the Arabs were demanding (and were prepared to pay for) the most advanced and expensive technology available or on the drawing boards. These were not items which the Soviets could virtually give away, as they had done some of their World War Two vintage equipment.[8]

With alternative sources of arms potentially available to them, the USSR's traditional friends, Egypt, Syria and Iraq, would now be far less dependent on it, as would be any new allies which it might wish to acquire. In each of the confrontation states, although most noticeably in Egypt, there was greater willingness to co-operate with the United States, even to change internal economic arrangements and policies to accommodate American lenders and investors. At the same time, the influence of the USSR's chief opponents in the Arab world, the oil-rich, conservative Persian Gulf states, increased. When Saudi Arabia began to use its new wealth to play an active role in Middle Eastern politics, the Soviets had to contend with a very serious and intensely hostile antagonist.

Partly as a result of pressure from the Saudis, who did not want to be called on to impose another unprofitable embargo, partly under the pressure and inducements of the Americans, who did not want to endure one, and partly for reasons of their own, the confrontation states began to evince somewhat more interest in a political solution to the Arab—Israeli conflict than they had in the period preceding the war. At the same time, bolstered by the belief in their recent victory, they stiffened their terms. Not merely Israeli withdrawal 'from occupied territories' but the creation of a Palestinian homeland now became the demand of even the least radical Arab states. As for the more radical states, those least amenable to Saudi or American influence and least damaged by recurrent war with Israel (Iraq, Libya, South Yemen and Algeria), they continued to reject the notion of peace on any terms.

In this new postwar situation the position of the USSR would prove to be far weaker than it had been before the war. Contrary to Soviet expectations, the changes in the regional and international distribution of wealth and influence which were generated by the employment of the oil weapon were in many ways harmful to Soviet interests. However, the full impact of the changes wrought by the war did not reveal itself immediately. It took at least a year for each of the major actors to define and embark on his postwar course. For the USSR the first year after the war was a time of stocktaking, of repeated reassessments, reviews of options and shifts in the emphasis, even direction, of policy to adjust to the new and changing reality. Only by the end of that year did the full outline of Soviet postwar policy emerge.

The USSR in the Postwar Period: Resolving the Conflict

For all the ambiguity of the postwar situation, the war itself had taught the Soviets one clear lesson. However useful the Arab—Israeli conflict may have been in giving the Soviets an entrée into the Middle East, the USSR could not control this conflict and risked a great deal by its perpetuation. The USSR had preferred that the Arabs use political, rather than military, means to recapture the territories they lost in 1967. But so long as it felt compelled to arm the Arabs as a means of ensuring their friendship, it had little leverage over them. It had not been able to keep them from going to war. Moreover, self-restraint in the supply of arms was not enough to enable the USSR to avoid being drawn into their war. Even carefully trained and equipped Arab troops, constrained to waging a limited war for limited objectives, had found and could again find themselves in danger of annihilation, desperately in need of direct Soviet assistance. And this was assistance which no superpower could easily refuse its client. It was imperative that the USSR find a way to maintain its position in the Middle East which would eliminate the need for such assistance, and with it, the risk of confrontation with the United States.

There was clearly only one way to reach this objective. One had to arrive at a 'reliable' and 'stable' settlement of the Arab—Israeli conflict.[9] If it were to serve Soviet interests, however, such a settlement would have to do more than simply reduce the likelihood of a new outbreak of fighting. It would have to formalise and legitimise the USSR's presence in the Middle East and bolster its status as a superpower. This it could do by providing for a long-term Soviet role as a co-guarantor or enforcer of the peace, which would permit the USSR to place troops, technicians and inspectors in the area as part of a peacekeeping force.[10] The settlement had to be one for which the USSR could claim credit, hence one which it played a major part in achieving. At the same time, it would have to be a settlement for which the Soviets would want to claim credit, thus one which went a considerable distance towards meeting Arab demands. The USSR had little direct interest in the territorial arrangements which would be made in a settlement. The important thing was to arrive at a formula which all sides could accept. It would clearly have to entail substantial Israeli withdrawals, but just how substantial was a subject on which the Soviets could take a variety of positions, depending on which seemed tactically optimal at a given moment.[11]

The primary objective of Soviet policy in the immediate postwar period was to arrive at a settlement of this kind — one tailored to Soviet interests, beneficial to the Arabs and achieved (or seemingly achieved) through Soviet efforts on their behalf. It was with this goal in mind that the Soviet Union co-operated with the United States in setting up the Geneva Peace Conference. Since this was a forum in which the Soviets could play an equal and leading role in the proceedings along with the United States, they were particularly eager to convene it and tried hard to persuade all the parties concerned to conduct negotiations there.[12]

If a settlement were to be arrived at, one had, as Soviet Foreign Minister Gromyko declared when the Conference opened, to be realistic, to take into account the most fundamental interests of the parties concerned. With the matter of a settlement at last 'moved off dead centre' as a result of the war, the Soviets attempted to go to some lengths to assure both sides that their basic concerns would be respected and at the same time to refrain from supporting extreme positions that would only bar an agreement. To satisfy the Arab confrontation states they insisted on Israel's withdrawal from all the territories it had occupied in the 1967 war — but not from any other territory the Arabs might claim. For the Palestinians this meant participation in the peace negotiations and some form of national entity to be arranged in those negotiations[13] — but not the destruction of Israel or its incorporation into a secular democratic state in all of Palestine, or even necessarily the right to return and live within the territory of the Israeli state. For Israel this meant Arab recognition of its right to exist, its territorial integrity, and the inviolability and legitimacy of its 4 June 1967 borders. It meant demilitarised zones, manned by international personnel, if Israel wanted them. And it meant that the provisions of the peace settlement would be incorporated in public documents that would have the force of law, not merely in secret understandings or private assurances which Israel's foes or friends could more easily repudiate. This was the essence of what the Soviets dearly sought for themselves and their allies in Eastern Europe: formal, legally binding international affirmation of territorial acquisitions obtained in the course of a defensive war, but hitherto not granted formal acceptance by the entire international community.[14] In their eyes this package represented no small gain for Israel. The one thing the Israelis would have to forfeit was a claim to territory beyond their 1967 borders. Their occupation of this territory was the 'root cause' of the conflict. Once they demonstrated some willingness to relinquish it, the Soviets hinted, the Israelis would clear away the chief obstacle to good relations with the USSR as well as to peace in the Middle East. Such was the position the Soviets took in the first months after the war, in an intensive effort to forge a settlement and lessen the risks of their involvement in the Arab–Israeli dispute.[15]

Would appeals to reason on both sides and offers of Soviet patronage or friendship be enough to induce the parties to the dispute to reconcile their differences along the lines the Soviets proposed? No, the Soviets quickly concluded, they would not. One had to apply pressure. But what kinds of pressure could the USSR apply? There were few effective instruments at the Soviets' disposal. From the Palestinians one could withhold full diplomatic support or recognition, and for the time being, the Soviets did this. From a recalcitrant confrontation state one could withhold weapons — but only at the risk of undermining completely one's position in the area.

Reportedly, the Soviets threatened to cut off arms supplies to Syria unless it agreed to participate in the Geneva Conference.[16] Where the United States and Israel were concerned, there was nothing the USSR

could, or was prepared to do directly. (It was not, for example, ready
to make its agreement to nuclear arms limitation contingent on
American exertion of pressure on Israel.[17]) But if the Soviets
themselves lacked leverage over the Americans and the Israelis, the war
had shown that the Arabs had at their disposal an extremely powerful
weapon — even more powerful than the threat of war. This was the oil
weapon, particularly the oil embargo. The potency of this weapon had
been vividly demonstrated during the war. Without it the United States
might ultimately have withheld or delayed its support for a ceasefire,
thereby placing the Egyptians in great danger and the USSR in an
acutely difficult position. As the Soviets saw it, the chances of reaching
a settlement were vastly improved by and indeed might hinge on the
continuation of the embargo. Hence they undertook a major campaign
to persuade the Arab oil exporters to maintain it until Israel showed
some sign that it was ready to make the concessions the Soviets deemed
essential to a settlement.[18]

Adjusting to New Realities

The Soviet Union's support for the use of the oil embargo may have
been tactically necessary to the achievement of one of its key regional
goals — settling the Arab–Israeli conflict. It may have seemed at first
that it would also serve the USSR's larger global interests. But it soon
became apparent that this policy was at odds with the Soviets' chief global
aim in the immediate postwar period: development of détente. From the
Soviets' point of view, their conduct during and after the war was very
much in keeping with the spirit of détente. They had helped to arrange a
ceasefire, although it was politically damaging to themselves to do so,
and had offered the United States an opportunity to work jointly with
the USSR in enforcing it. But the view from America was quite
different. The massive Soviet air and sealift to Egypt and Syria and the
Soviet threat to intervene unilaterally to rescue Egypt's Third Army
had convinced many Americans that the USSR had decided to abandon
détente in an effort to bolster its position in the Middle East. Soviet
exhortations to the Arabs to impose and maintain the embargo were, in
effect, a last straw. At the beginning of November 1973, President
Nixon asked Congressional leaders to postpone action on what was one
of the Soviet Union's chief objectives in seeking détente, a bill granting
it most-favoured nation status in trade with the United States. The
Administration put the Soviets on notice: we won't help your economy
while you're trying to strangle ours.[19] At the same time, Secretary of
State Kissinger, angered by what seemed to him to be a breach of trust

and personal affront on the part of the Soviet leaders, resolved that it was no longer in America's interest to co-operate with the Soviet Union in the Middle East. The USSR, he concluded, had done much more to aggravate than to prevent or control the crisis in the region. The cause of peace would best be served by reducing as far as possible Soviet influence there. If such a policy were a violation of détente, it would only be a response to an evident Soviet decision not to apply détente to the Middle East.

Kissinger apparently resolved that the time was right to capitalise on Sadat's irritation with the Soviets and Saudi Arabia's traditional hostility to them in order to promote the emergence of an American–Saudi–Egyptian alliance. This alliance would be united both by a strong economic stake in peace and by opposition to the USSR.

It would serve the triple purpose of ensuring to the United States the goodwill of the world's largest oil exporter, undermining the Soviet position in the Middle East and defusing, if not resolving, the Arab–Israeli conflict. It would be open-ended: other Middle Eastern powers would be welcome to join. Contacts with the Saudis and the Egyptians were followed by a Kissinger trip to Damascus, where it was agreed that the USA and Syria would open interest sections in one another's capitals. Resumption of diplomatic relations, broken off by Syria in June 1967, was clearly on the agenda.

What the Arab members of this prospective alliance desired most urgently was a de-escalation of tensions in the area and some tangible evidence of Arab gains from the war. The United States, having won credibility in Egyptian eyes by imposing a ceasefire on the advancing Israelis, was in an ideal position to mediate between the two sides. Kissinger proceeded forthwith to arrange an exchange of prisoners between Israel and Egypt (7 November 1973) and an Israeli–Egyptian disengagement agreement which restored to Egypt the east bank of the Suez Canal (18 January 1974). He then turned to Syria with an offer to negotiate similar agreements between it and Israel. The United States made no effort to co-ordinate these activities with the Russians, in effect freezing them out of the diplomatic process in the Middle East.

Kissinger's moves put the Soviets in a difficult dilemma. They were greatly disturbed by the new direction of American policy and dismayed by the success it was having. But at the same time they recognised the necessity of the steps Kissinger was taking. At present, the 'urgent, top priority task', Gromyko had told the Geneva Conference, is to obtain an effective disengagement of troops.[20] The Soviets also realised that American mediation was essential to accomplish this task. Only the United States enjoyed the confidence of both sides. But the Soviets could not allow the Americans to go on monopolising the peacemaking process and cultivating US—Arab ties at the expense of the USSR. In the wake of the Egyptian—Israeli disengagement agreement, Soviet policy had, therefore, two objectives: to convince all the parties concerned that the USSR must be included in all future disengagement and peace negotiations and to dissuade the Soviets' erstwhile allies from developing any closer relations with the United States.

In accord with the first objective, the Soviets' public and private reaction to Kissinger's activities in Egypt was mild: critical (on the grounds that Kissinger had not obtained enough for the Egyptians) and yet supportive.[21] They hurriedly invited the Egyptian foreign minister, Fahmi, to Moscow (21—24 January 1974). There they assured him of their interest in developing and strengthening Soviet—Egyptian relations, chided him for not including the USSR in the Egyptian—American discussions and pressed him to agree to closer co-ordination of policy with the Soviets in the future. The USSR, they urged, should participate in all stages of any negotiations relating to a peace settlement.[22] In Syria the Soviets disparaged Kissinger's mediation. Gromyko travelled to Damascus (7 March 1974) to encourage the Syrians to hold out for better terms, thus injecting the USSR into the Syrian—American discussions and intimating to the Syrians that they would be better off if they involved the Soviets in their subsequent dealings with the United States. The USSR also supported Syria's decision to conduct a war of attrition against Israel on the Golan Heights. The chances that this might erupt into full-scale war were slim, but it might annoy the Americans enough to dampen the emerging Syrian—American friendship, while convincing them to apply more pressure on Israel. It might in addition persuade the Arab oil exporters that this was no time to lift the embargo, an essential bargaining card even in this preliminary part of the peace negotiations.[23]

It soon became apparent that these Soviet efforts to counteract the new line in American policy were of little avail. On 13 March 1974, probably under American and Saudi urging, Syria took a major step towards fostering closer relations with the United States. Reversing a decade of movement towards socialism, the government removed restrictions on the flow of private capital into and out of the country and announced that the private sector could sign loan agreements with foreign investors. To the Soviets, who believed that a country's economic policies were the best indicator of its commitment to friendship with the USSR and the best predictor of its foreign policy, this was a very bad omen indeed. But a graver blow was yet to come. Egyptian President Sadat turned a deaf ear to the USSR's overtures. Not only did he decline to co-ordinate his policies more closely with the Soviets. He had become convinced that his American connection was his best hope for obtaining what he most needed, the return of the Sinai Peninsula to Egypt. Thus he agreed to use his influence with the Arab oil producers on behalf of the United States to persuade them to end their embargo. His efforts were successful, and on 19 March 1974 it was announced that the embargo was being lifted. The key lever the Soviets had hoped to use to forge the settlement they wanted was thus lost to them, thanks in part to the intercession of their own ally.

Reassessment and Policy Change

These events were enough to convince the Soviets that a reassessment of their Middle Eastern strategy was in order. It was time to re-examine the question, what were the Soviets' interests in the area and how might they best promote them. In particular, the Soviet Union had to decide who would in the future be its most likely and valuable allies in the region, what it would need to do to ensure their loyalty, and what price it would be worth paying to secure it. These were not questions to be resolved quickly or easily. This reassessment proved to be a major undertaking, to which diplomats in the field, foreign ministry personnel in Moscow and experts in each of the academic institutes dealing with the Third World were asked to contribute.[24] Initiated in the spring of 1974, it found its first expression in policy in the late spring and early summer, but was not completed until the end of that year.

The Soviets had no immediate explanation for Egyptian and Syrian behaviour. But the question of immediate relevance for policy was what, if anything, to do about it. How could the USSR convince its long-time friends to maintain their 'special relationship' with the USSR, rather than to allow themselves to be drawn into the American orbit? And if it failed to convince them, what could it do to maintain its position in the Middle East? In the case of Egypt, the decision was, as it had been after the July 1972 expulsion, to apply pressure. Hoping to discredit Sadat in the eyes of the Egyptian public and the Arab world as a whole, the Soviets printed Arab press criticism of Sadat as a traitor to Nasir's heritage.[25] They reportedly suspended all weapon deliveries to Egypt at this time[26] and turned down Egypt's urgent request for deferment of its huge debt to the USSR.[27] Towards Syria the Soviets adopted a different approach. Syria had been a good deal more reticent in accommodating the United States and more willing to co-operate with the Soviet Union.[28] Hence the Soviets had reason to believe that in its case positive inducements would be more effective. Moreover, these could be used to signal Sadat as to the rewards he could expect if he changed course. At the beginning of April the USSR delivered to Syria a large quantity of weapons, including for the first time the highly advanced MiG-23s, much coveted by both Syria and Egypt. Syrian President Asad was then given a lavish welcome in Moscow, promises of still more military aid and reportedly a twelve-year deferment of Syria's debt.[29] He, in turn, provided his hosts with the quid pro quo they desired, confirmation of the importance of Soviet participation 'in all stages and in all areas' of a peace settlement.[30]

Pressure on Egypt and inducements to Syria were not enough in view of the possibility, real, if small, that both tactics might fail and the USSR would lose its two chief allies in the Arab world. The Soviets now resolved to strengthen their relations with other old friends and seek out new ones in an effort to hedge their bets. The two countries to which they turned after the lifting of the embargo were Iraq, with which the Soviets had intermittently enjoyed good relations for more than a decade, and Libya, hitherto bitterly hostile to the USSR. The choice was dictated first by the interest evinced by these two states in ties with the USSR. Both were on poor terms with most of their neighbours and without friends in the Arab world. Soviet friendship was a way for both governments to break out of isolation and gain diplomatic and material support.[31] Both had in effect drawn closer to the USSR as a result of their opposition to the removal of the oil embargo. Both were notably anti-American. They provided the Soviets with an opportunity to form tactical alliances based on mutual opposition to the growth of American influence in the Middle East. Moreover, Iraq had steadily worsening relations with Syria, as had Libya with Egypt. Soviet moves to cultivate these two countries could serve as an implicit threat to Syria and Egypt that if they continued to respond to American blandishments, the USSR might turn elsewhere. In the event of a conflict it might actually back their opponents.

Iraq and Libya were also of significant strategic value to the Soviets. Iraq, located on the Persian Gulf, was able to supply them with naval facilities and airfields. These would be useful in the event of the USSR wishing to interdict or credibly threaten to interdict Western oil supplies. Libya's airfields and naval bases were close to NATO facilities. In addition, both countries were of interest to the USSR in their capacity as oil exporters. Both were able to guarantee the USSR a substantial supply of oil, to be used by its East European allies or resold for hard currency in Western Europe. And in the wake of the October War, both were accumulating large reserves of hard currency which they were prepared to spend on Soviet arms. Thus within days of the lifting of the embargo, Soviet Defence Minister Grechko made a visit to Baghdad to discuss Soviet–Iraqi military co-operation, and Soviet President Podgornyi met Libyan Premier Jallud in Paris. A month later Jallud went to Moscow, where he, too, met Grechko. While there, he arranged to purchase Soviet arms and reportedly agreed to Soviet use of Libyan airfields.[32]

These Soviet–Iraqi and Soviet–Libyan ties were an indication that the Soviets were groping for a new strategy in the Middle East. One apparent objective of the new strategy was to make the USSR's position in the region less dependent on the course of the Arab–Israeli conflict and the Soviet role in that conflict. The Soviets, so it seemed, were seeking to transfer their competition with the United States to new grounds, outside the centre and towards the periphery of the Middle East. There they could capitalise on the radicalism or anti-Americanism of local regimes or their desire to forge a connection with the USSR in order to exert pressure on the United States. The new policy reflected changes in Soviet strategic interests. These were partly the result of the enhanced importance of obtaining access to Middle Eastern oil and gas in the wake of the October War, and partly of new developments in American strategic weapons deployment. These developments were making bases en route to the Indian Ocean as important as facilities in the eastern Mediterranean.[33] The new policy also reflected an awareness of new profits to be made in the Middle East and a determination to share in them. By the end of 1975 it had become clear that there had been a marked increase in Soviet interest in relations with countries possessing exportable quantities of oil and natural gas. Not merely Iraq and Libya, but also South Yemen, Somalia, Iran, Algeria and Afghanistan (a natural gas producer) notably increased their share of Soviet economic or military aid in 1974–5.[34]

Setbacks and Responses

The new developments in Soviet Middle Eastern policy did not mean that the USSR was no longer interested in the Arab–Israeli conflict. It was still of great importance to the Soviets to achieve a settlement of that conflict and to do so on their own terms. For this purpose, allies on the periphery of the Middle East were of little value. It was still vitally important to the USSR to exert a predominant, if not exclusive influence on the politics and policies of Egypt and Syria and prevent further American inroads there.

From this point of view, the measures taken after the lifting of the oil embargo had little success. Between April and July 1974, the Soviets suffered a series of severe setbacks. Sadat did not succumb to Soviet pressure. Rather, he turned his country decisively away from the Soviet Union, both in its foreign and its domestic policies.

In April the Egyptian President announced that he was ready to purchase weapons in the West. In the same month he steered through parliament a number of laws designed to change the basic orientation of the Egyptian economy, directing it away from socialism and reliance on the USSR and towards expansion of the private sector and intercourse with the West. The United States quickly reciprocated. President Nixon asked Congress for $250 million in aid to Egypt, thereby reversing almost two decades of American policy. The American position, not merely in Egypt, but in Syria as well, was given a major boost by the conclusion of the Syrian–Israeli disengagement agreement in May, and a much-publicised Nixon tour of the area in June. Immediately after the Nixon trip US–Syrian diplomatic relations were renewed and Syria announced it was ready for 'dialogue' with any foreign capital which wanted to participate in Syrian development. A month later, in July, the National Congress of the Ba'th Party called for the continued Syrian support for step-by-step diplomacy. A *pax Americana* seemed clearly in the making.

The policy review and reappraisal initiated by the USSR in the early spring were resumed with new intensity. Step-by-step diplomacy initially had been useful to the Soviets to ensure that they would not again be called on to rescue their clients through direct intervention. But now, once the Syrian–Israeli disengagement had been arranged, it was essential to prevent any more American-engineered agreements. They only reduced the chances of a settlement of the kind the Soviets sought, while bolstering the position of the United States in the area. And it was clear that something had to be done to reverse or at least hold back the surging tide of American influence. But what else could the Soviets do, beyond holding out a carrot to Syria and a stick to Egypt, while making approaches to other Middle Eastern states more peripheral to the conflict?

Pressure on Syria was at this juncture too risky. President Nixon's aid request to Congress in April had included $100 million for a special fund, generally assumed to be intended for Syria. Should the USSR now threaten to withhold aid, the Americans would surely step in to fill the breach. In the light of Egypt's imminent 'defection', the

USSR could be left without airfields or ports essential for the operation of its Mediterranean fleet. But maintenance of current aid levels was also clearly not sufficient to counter American competition. The Soviets decided on a major increase in the quantity and quality of aid. The Syrian share in new Soviet offers of economic aid to Third World countries increased by nearly 50 per cent in 1974–5.[35] And in July–August 1974 the USSR sharply increased its shipments to Syria of advanced weapons, including offensive, ground-to-ground missiles. So anxious were the Soviets to satisfy their now-crucial ally that, for the first time in the history of their involvement in the Middle East, they appeared to be violating one of their own cardinal rules with regard to weapon supplies. Syria, it seemed, was beginning to acquire the capacity to wage war on Israel by itself, by means of a pre-emptive attack.[36] You need not rely on the Americans, the Soviets were in effect telling the Syrians. You will be able to regain your territory by war or threat of war – and you can do so even without Egyptian co-operation.

It was not enough, however, to lure the Syrians. One had, too, to deter the United States from expanding its involvement with them. There was little the USSR could do to accomplish this, other than what it had tried before. Earlier in the year it had backed Syria's war of attrition in part to dampen a US–Syrian rapprochement. Now it resorted to similar tactics. In the autumn of 1974, as the date of expiration of the mandate of the United Nations observer force on the Golan Heights approached, it encouraged the Syrians to remain ambiguous as to their intentions. Tension would mount, the Soviets probably calculated, the United States would be alarmed, and the American image of Asad as a man of peace, worthy of US support, would be shattered. At the same time, Sadat would find it difficult to co-operate with American efforts, already initiated, to negotiate a second set of disengagement agreements. Support for Syrian militancy was becoming a regular feature of Soviet Middle Eastern diplomacy, now increasingly aimed at preventing the growth of American influence in the region at the expense of the USSR.

Another option open to the Soviets was to try to convince the United States of the futility of its attempt to exclude the USSR from peace negotiations. It was very likely in pursuit of this option that the Soviets resolved in the summer of 1974 that the time was ripe for a major display of friendship for the Palestine Liberation Organisation. The USSR had hitherto held back from making such a display. It was not sure that a terrorist organisation, lacking international legitimacy, possessing uncertain backing among the population it claimed to represent, and committed to the destruction of Israel (hence opposed to a peaceful settlement of the conflict), was indeed a desirable ally. But, just as the Soviets had decided that it was necessary to maintain tactical alliances with two states whose views on the resolution of the Arab—Israeli conflict were equally far from their own, so they apparently concluded that a link with the PLO was unavoidable. On 30 July 1974, soon after the Syrian Ba'th Congress disappointed the Soviets with its decision to co-operate with further American initiatives, a PLO delegation was invited to Moscow. There the Soviets told the Palestinians they would support the creation of an independent Palestinian state — not in place of, but alongside Israel. To compensate for their insistence on a 'mini-state', the Soviet leaders agreed to the opening of a PLO office in Moscow (a form of recognition virtually equivalent to that accorded to foreign governments). Moreover, the communiqué at the end of the visit 'noted with satisfaction' the Arab states' recognition of the PLO as the 'sole legitimate representative' of the Palestinian people. Indirect as it was, this was the first time the Soviets had officially accorded the PLO such recognition.[37]

This gesture, followed in the autumn by an enthusiastic demonstration of support for the Palestinians and the PLO at the United Nations and a Brezhnev speech affirming the right of the Palestinians to a state of their own, probably had a number of motives. With the Soviet position apparently deteriorating in Egypt and Syria, this was a way to assure the USSR the friendship of a group which enjoyed great popularity in the Arab world and pre-empt an American bid for its friendship. It was also a good way to embarrass the unfaithful Egyptians.[38] But the most important reason for the visit and subsequent displays of recognition and support was to communicate with the United States. The Americans had always followed the Israeli lead in ignoring the Palestinians or treating them simply as refugees, whose status would have to be provided for in the context of a settlement between Israel and its neighbouring states. It was now in the interest of the USSR to convince American policy makers that internationally recognised Palestinian rights extended beyond compensation and/or return; that these rights could not be implemented in piecemeal agreements between Israel and the confrontation states, but only in a comprehensive settlement to which the Palestinians were themselves a party; that the PLO alone had the stature to represent the Palestinians in negotiating such a settlement; and (most important) that the USSR, too, must be included in such negotiations, for only it had sufficient influence with the PLO to induce it to make peace with Israel. Soviet gestures towards the PLO in the summer and autumn of 1974 were undoubtedly intended to make this case.

The most difficult problem for the Soviets in the wake of their summer setbacks was to decide what to do about Egypt. The Soviets had a great deal invested in Egypt. For nearly two decades their closest friend in the Middle East, indeed in the Third World as a whole, Egypt was a kind of showcase to all developing nations, a demonstration of the generosity with which the USSR rewarded those who co-operated with it.[39] To be repudiated by it now was acutely embarrassing. It was also a blow to Soviet strategic policy. If Soviet strategic interests were shifting southwards, this was a gradual process, not yet complete. For the present, the American Sixth Fleet in the eastern Mediterranean was still a very tangible threat which had to be neutralised, and Egyptian naval facilities were vital for this purpose. Syrian harbours were too small and Libyan bases too far away to be good substitutes. Yet it was far from clear what the USSR could do to dissuade Egypt from turning to the West. The American option – the promise of peaceful recovery of Egyptian territory through US mediation – was too attractive to be forgone, and the Soviets could offer no equivalent. To a war-weary Egypt, pushed in the direction of the United States by its Saudi benefactors, even the promise of Soviet arms was not so appealing.

The Soviets tried, nonetheless. As pressure did not seem to be working, they attempted conciliation. When Sadat made his April 1974 announcement that he was prepared to purchase Western arms, Brezhnev responded with two friendly notes, and arms shipments were reportedly resumed.[40] In October, Egyptian Foreign Minister Fahmi was invited to Moscow, where he was promised the MiG-23s his country had been requesting for over two years. A date was set for a Brezhnev visit to Cairo.

There could not have been complete and firm agreement within the Soviet leadership on this course, however, for apparently without any further 'provocation' on Egypt's part, Brezhnev's visit was suddenly cancelled at the end of December 1974. As Egyptian–American talks on a second disengagement got underway early in the new year, the Soviets appear to have decided that the time had come to give up on Sadat and cut their losses in Egypt. The weapons the Egyptians received in January and/or February 1975 seem to have been the last they obtained from the USSR. On a visit to the Middle East in early February Soviet Foreign Minister Gromyko hailed Syria, not Egypt, as

the leader of the Arab states opposed to Zionism and imperialism.[41]
What Gromyko had in mind became clear early in March, when Syria
offered to unite with the PLO in a 'joint command' and signed a broad
agreement on economic and political co-operation with Jordan.[42]

Until the summer of 1974 the USSR had hoped and tried to unify
the Arab world. Believing that only with a united front could the
necessary conditions be won from Israel, they had tried to resolve or
diminish inter-Arab conflicts, especially those between Egypt and the
other key actors in the Arab—Israeli conflict. The lifting of the oil
embargo all but shattered whatever unity had persisted after the war.
The communiqué following the mid-summer PLO visit indicated that
the Soviets were reconsidering their approach. By the winter of
1974—5, they were prepared to try a different strategy. They began to
encourage the emergence of a broad new coalition under Syrian
leadership. The new grouping, the Soviets hoped, would be friendly to
the USSR and support its inclusion in the peace negotiations. It would
exclude and isolate Egypt until such time as Cairo realised the error of
its ways and abandoned the American option. And it would
demonstrate to the United States that it could not reach its goals in the
Middle East by excluding the Soviet Union. The Soviets would have to
be brought in so as to secure the co-operation of all key Middle Eastern
parties.

With regard to Egypt itself, the Soviets now (in the winter of
1974—5) concluded that it must be taught a lesson. Sadat had hoped to
have the best of both worlds — the friendship of both superpowers. If
the Soviets themselves were enjoying a détente with the United States,
why could their allies not do the same? But the Soviet Union was not
willing to tolerate such an interpretation of détente. Sadat would have
to accept friendship on Soviet terms or not at all. Beginning in the
spring of 1975 the Soviets refused Egypt any new military aid, withheld
spare parts for weapons already supplied, and even intervened to
prevent it from acquiring those parts elsewhere. They applied economic
pressure. Vital industrial spare parts were likewise held back, economic
and technical aid was delayed, and repeated requests for a debt
moratorium were denied. The Soviets refused to sign new trade
agreements unless Egypt agreed to make large debt repayments. So
extreme was the pressure that by the end of 1975, Egypt had become a
net exporter to the Soviet Union. Ultimately, the Soviets hoped, this
pressure would lead to the overthrow of Sadat. They encouraged his
domestic opponents and revived the Egyptian Communist Party,
reportedly instructing it to work for a change of regime in Egypt.[43]

The New Policy: a Trial Period

By early 1975 the main outlines of Soviet Middle Eastern policy in the postwar period had become clear. The principal objectives of the USSR were twofold: first to strengthen its now shaky position and weaken that of the United States in the area, and second to move the peace negotiations from an American-dominated forum to one in which the USSR played an important role and could obtain the kind of settlement it wanted. It was attempting to achieve these goals in two ways: by cultivating allies who were hostile to American diplomatic efforts and unlikely to respond to American blandishments (as well as unlikely to receive them); and by punishing Sadat, while offering military, economic and political co-operation to an alliance of forces which (hopefully) would both isolate Egypt and support the Soviet approach to a Middle East settlement.

This was not a strategy destined for short-term success. It was thwarted from its inception by the appeal of the American option for Egypt and other Arab states and by the disparity in goals, priorities and outlook both between the Soviet Union and its allies and among those allies themselves.

The first test of this strategy came in February–March 1975, when Kissinger resumed his shuttle diplomacy in an effort to secure a second Egyptian–Israeli disengagement agreement. The Soviets were adamantly opposed to Kissinger's mission and greatly encouraged when it failed in late March 1975, although they themselves could claim little credit for the failure. The collapse of the Kissinger shuttle provided them with an excellent opportunity to promote their own approach to a Middle East settlement, a renewal of the Geneva Peace Conference.

Moving quickly to exploit this opportunity, the Soviets invited each of their key allies and even their erstwhile ally Egypt to Moscow in April 1975, to discuss a reconvening of the Conference. They presented their own plan for peace, involving Israel's withdrawal to its 1967 borders; implementation of Palestinian rights, including the right to an independent state; and guarantees of security to all states in the area, including Israel. Libya, not invited to these discussions, was accorded a visit by Kosygin the following month.

The Soviets were dismayed to find that only Egypt was prepared to support their plan! The Libyans and the Iraqis were still opposed to all negotiations with Israel, regardless of the forum. The PLO would not agree to go to Geneva without an amendment of United Nations Security Council Resolutions 242 and 338 on which the conference was based. Nor would it agree to recognise Israel's existence. Syria, while prepared to support the resumption of the Geneva talks with PLO participation, was unwilling to give explicit recognition to the existence of Israel, much less its 1967 borders.[44] Even if convened, the Soviets realised, the Conference could only fail.

There was very little the Soviets could do at this point. They qualified their insistence on Geneva in their public statements with the proviso that it needed 'thorough preparation', and when Kissinger again resumed his shuttle in late July 1975, they encouraged Arab criticism of his efforts. This was of no avail. The real opportunity to prevent another disengagement agreement had been lost in the spring, when disagreements with their allies prevented the Soviets from offering any alternative. From Sadat's point of view, the gains to be made from a major Israeli withdrawal and return of Egyptian oil fields, likely to be accompanied by more Saudi financing and American military aid, outweighed the prospective losses from withheld Soviet aid and denunciations by the Soviets' Arab allies. The second Egyptian–Israeli disengagement agreement was signed on 1 September 1975. The Soviets were angered, especially by its provisions for stationing American personnel in the Sinai, but a special strategy session of the USSR's Middle Eastern ambassadors hurriedly convened in Moscow could think of no more creative response than vehement criticism. The situation was not improved in subsequent months. Stepped-up Soviet military aid to Syria and direct official recognition of the PLO as the sole legitimate representative of the Palestinian people[45] did not produce any major change in the positions of these two parties.

In the course of the next year (autumn 1975–autumn 1976) it became increasingly clear that the Soviets' strategy was bearing no fruit. Their alliance with radical forces in the Arab world, while financially lucrative,[46] was producing no benefits in the arena of the Arab–Israeli conflict. Pressure on Egypt was not having the desired effect. Buttressed by American support, Sadat had begun retaliating against the USSR by restricting its access to vital naval facilities. As the months went by, Egypt's relations with the United States grew warmer, while the Soviet position in Egypt deteriorated steadily. Finally, in March 1976, the Egyptians abrogated their fifteen-year Treaty of Friendship and Co-operation with the USSR. A tremendous blow to Soviet Third World diplomacy, this step left the Soviet Union with almost no political links with Egypt and no military facilities there.[47] Reconvening of the Geneva Conference was becoming less and less probable. The American administration, involved in an election campaign and hesitant to make major foreign commitments or appear excessively co-operative towards the USSR, was uninterested. The PLO, with little prospect of receiving Israeli recognition, saw no reason to agree to a peace proposal involving co-existence with Israel. And Syria, amply supplied with Soviet weapons, had no incentive to relinquish its claim to what it considered its southern province, the territory on which the Israeli state had been established.

From the Soviet point of view, even worse than the intransigence of what were now its two chief allies was the increasingly acrimonious conflict between them in Lebanon, where the civil war had erupted in April 1975. The PLO, hoping to exploit the Lebanese war to strengthen its position in the country, found itself thwarted by Syria, which had similar ambitions. By the spring of 1976, Egypt, Libya and Iraq, all opposed to Syrian aggrandisement, were aiding the PLO and Lebanese Leftist Muslims against Syrian-commanded Palestinian forces co-operating with Lebanese Christians. Embarrassed and dismayed by this situation, the Soviets tried to mediate the conflict, inviting a PLO delegation to Moscow at the beginning of April 1976 for this purpose. The failure of their mediation effort was critical, for the Americans and the Saudis quickly stepped in to fill the breach. A United States emissary was dispatched to Lebanon in the same month, and the prospect of a *Pax Americana* in still another Middle Eastern arena began to loom on the horizon. When even the threat of withholding arms did not seem to affect the Syrians, the Soviets sent their own intermediary, Premier Kosygin, to the area. The very night he arrived (31 May 1976), the Syrians sent a fully-fledged army of regular Syrian troops into Lebanon, clearly in defiance of their Soviet patrons. In the end it was the Saudis, ready and able to commit their oil wealth to the endeavour, who were successful not only in achieving a durable ceasefire in October 1976, but in reconciling Egypt and Syria.

The Soviets were now (in October 1976), faced with the near-collapse of their Middle Eastern strategy. The alliance they were attempting to build had apparently dissolved. For the foreseeable future, there could be no hope of a Syrian–PLO 'Joint Command'. Jordan was still friendly towards Syria and the USSR. But despite a visit by King Husayn to Moscow in June 1976, it had rejected Soviet offers of an anti-aircraft missile system accompanied by Soviet technicians. Supplied with Saudi dollars, it had chosen a more expensive American system instead, thereby dashing Soviet hopes of developing Jordanian–Soviet ties. Egypt, far from isolated, was on good terms with both Syria and the PLO. Worst of all, both the American and the Saudi positions had been strengthened by the crisis.

The United States had increased its contacts with Syria and the PLO. Saudi Arabia had emerged as the most influential power in the Arab world, perhaps the only force capable of unifying it. It was clear that it now could and would play a crucial role in any negotiations aimed at resolving the Arab—Israeli conflict. And it was most unlikely to support a role for the USSR, either in achieving or in implementing a settlement.

A Last Effort

Was there anything the Soviets could do to salvage their badly damaged position? The one possibility they had never fully explored in formulating their postwar Middle East policy was an approach to the Israelis.[48] Foreign Minister Gromyko had attempted to be generous towards Israel in his speech to the Geneva Conference following the war. But the deterioration of Soviet—Egyptian relations soon afterwards had forced the Soviets to move in the direction of the more radical Arab states and leaders. This had militated against the adoption of a softer stance towards Israel. Now (in the autumn of 1976), for lack of any better option, anxious to get a process of negotiation going, the Soviets resolved to try conciliating Israel. If Israel's most pressing concerns could be attended to and its worst fears allayed, perhaps it would then be more forthcoming. Perhaps it would make the kind of gesture to the Arabs necessary to produce concessions from them.

What made this strategy particularly promising at this time was the prospect that the forthcoming American elections might bring to office a new president and with him a new secretary of state less committed to shuttle diplomacy and more amenable to Soviet—American co-operation in the Middle East. A new man in the White House, with four years to go before another election, might be more willing than President Ford had been to bring the kind of pressure to bear on Israel which would be necessary for any settlement to be reached. He would be more likely to do so if he believed the Soviets were also pressing their allies for important concessions.

It was probably with calculations of this sort in mind that at the beginning of October 1976, when a Saudi-engineered ceasefire in Lebanon seemed imminent, the Soviets issued a new peace plan. They knew that one of the things the Israelis desired most keenly was a public affirmation by their Arab neighbours that they were no longer at war with Israel. This was in Israeli eyes a *sine qua non* of any settlement: without it one could not begin to trust Arab intentions towards Israel. Israeli Prime Minister Rabin had proposed that if a treaty of peace were too difficult for them to sign, the Arabs might agree instead simply to end the state of war with Israel. The Soviets now seized on this suggestion. Their October peace plan incorporated not only the three elements they had previously proposed (Israeli withdrawal from the territory it had occupied in 1967, guarantees of the security of all states in the area, and implementation of Palestinian rights, including that of statehood), but also the provision that there should be a termination of the state of war between Israel and its neighbours.[49] A major Brezhnev speech in March 1977 went even further to accommodate Israel. It revived for the first time the plan Gromyko had presented to the Geneva Conference in December 1973: 'final and inviolable' borders, internationally guaranteed, accompanied by demilitarised zones and a United Nations observer force. More than that, Brezhnev took into account Israel's reluctance to complete a troop withdrawal in a single stroke, before it was sure of Arab intentions to live in peace with it. He proposed a step-by-step withdrawal which could take place over a period of time. And holding out the prospect of ending the terrible strain on the Israeli economy resulting from arms expenditures, he suggested that with a settlement, the arms race in the Middle East might be ended.[50]

For this strategy to work the Soviets had to persuade the Americans not merely to go to Geneva, but also to exert the necessary pressure on Israel. Fortunately for the USSR this was not difficult to do. The new American President came to office convinced by his advisers that step-by-step diplomacy had exhausted itself and that the next objective of American policy in the Middle East had to be a comprehensive settlement. Moreover, meetings with each of the major Middle Eastern leaders soon persuaded him that American pressure on Israel was necessary for the sake of a secure energy supply to the United States as well as for peace in the Middle East. In March 1977 Carter became the first American President to voice support for a 'Palestinian homeland'. This move, raising the possibility of US–PLO co-operation, was not entirely pleasing to the USSR. More to Soviet liking was the conclusion reached by Carter in the autumn of 1977 that American efforts to bring Arabs and Israelis together would fail unless they received Soviet backing. A joint Soviet–American communiqué on 1 October 1977 affirmed the belief of both parties that 'the only right and effective way' to resolve the Middle East conflict was 'negotiations within the framework of the Geneva Peace Conference'. The two sides also announced their joint intention 'to facilitate in every way' the resumption of the Conference within three months. The Soviets at last had been thrust squarely into the midst of Middle East peace negotiations. One of their most important objectives in the postwar period seemed to have been accomplished.

Persistent Problems and Dilemmas

The change in American Middle East policy in the first year of the Carter administration constituted a major victory for Soviet diplomacy – the most important success for the USSR in four years of almost unmitigated frustrations and setbacks. But the American decisions to follow the USSR in recognising Palestinian national rights and to bring the USSR itself back into the peace negotiations by no means solved all the problems confronting the Soviets in their dual quest for a settlement and a stronger position in the Middle East.

If the United States has been more willing to co-operate with the USSR, the Saudis have remained as determined as ever to undermine the Soviet position in the Middle East and are increasingly prepared to use their resources and influence to accomplish this. Saudi Arabia took the initiative in drawing up a plan and providing the money to induce Somalia to end its military co-operation with the USSR and buy Western arms. It has been aiding moderate forces in South Yemen and helping to repress Communists in the Sudan. It has been underwriting Jordanian arms acquisitions from Western sources. And it has been providing several billion dollars yearly to subsidise both Egypt's arms purchases in the West and its economic development along non-socialist lines.[51]

The appeal of the Saudi-backed 'American option' to Egyptian President Sadat has been the principal problem for the USSR in the Middle East in the postwar period. For nearly two decades Soviet policy in the area had centred on Egypt. It was based on the assumption that a deep and abiding interest in preventing Western domination of the Middle East united the two countries. The Soviets were, therefore, astonished by Sadat's decision to turn to the West and to Arab friends of the West for political, economic and even military support. The USSR has found itself virtually impotent in the face of this decision: the new oil wealth has made it impossible for it to compete.[52] Moreover, the Soviets are not really prepared to enter into a competition. They might have entertained the idea at an earlier stage of Soviet–Egyptian relations, when Egypt had received less Soviet aid and was viewed as something less than a fully-fledged ally. But by the time of the October War, Egypt was indeed an ally, an important part of the Soviets' strategic defence system, for whose sake the Soviets had

risked a superpower confrontation.[53] And détente or no détente, no
superpower could tolerate close political, economic and military
co-operation by one of its allies with members of a rival alliance system.
But if there was nothing the USSR could or would offer to deter such a
development, there has been no pressure it could safely exert to halt it.
The Soviets have been unable to reform or overthrow Sadat; they have
only succeeded in antagonising him.

The American decision to involve the Soviet Union in the Middle
East peace process has in no way solved this problem. The American
move did not reflect a diminished interest in Egypt. Sadat, thoroughly
embittered by Soviet moves against him, cannot be expected to 'recant'
so long as Western and conservative Arab support for him is
forthcoming. On the contrary, he is becoming one of the USSR's chief
opponents in the Middle East. The timing of his decision to go to
Jerusalem in November 1977 was almost certainly linked to the
issuance of the US–Soviet communiqué the previous month. Sadat has
no interest in bolstering and legitimising the Soviet role in the Middle
East. His direct approach to the Israelis was probably designed in part
to circumvent the USSR. Thus, as a result of his hostility to the Soviet
Union, largely provoked by the Soviets' own actions, the USSR has
already found its one important success in the postwar period slipping
away from it. Future peace negotiations may very well proceed without
it, and any settlement which might be reached may well exclude it.
Neither the increasingly influential Saudis, nor Israel, hardly moved by
or even cognisant of the USSR's gestures towards it, is likely to oppose
such a development.

Egypt's 'defection' is also an ongoing problem because the USSR has
failed to find an adequate substitute for it in the Arab world. The allies
the Soviets have tried to cultivate as alternatives to Egypt have many
shortcomings. The PLO, as an organisation committed to no distinct
social programme, and Libya, a reactionary Muslim state, are
ideological embarrassments to the USSR. None of the Soviets' present
friends has the influence or authority Egypt has enjoyed in the Arab
world; none is potentially a major force for spreading Soviet influence
in the Middle East. None can compensate in a strategic sense for the
loss of Egypt.

What makes the USSR's present allies most problematic is the gap
between their own needs and priorities and those of the Soviets
themselves. Ironically, among the Middle Eastern leaders the USSR has
sought to cultivate, only President Sadat has actively desired a
settlement. Unlike Egypt, Libya and Iraq have suffered little from the
conflict with Israel. Hence a militant, uncompromising stance, including

refusal even to negotiate with the Zionist state, yields considerable political mileage for their leaders. With a political base among homeless, radicalised refugees who likewise have not lost family and friends in fighting Israel, the severely divided leadership of the PLO has been able to agree on little more than non-recognition of Israel.[54] And Syrian President Asad, member of a minority group, in need of a popular cause to retain the loyalty of an ethnically diverse population, has found it politically expedient to stand behind the PLO on this issue.

The Soviets, while having no direct stake in the existence of Israel, are aware that Arab recognition of it is indispensable for a settlement. Throughout the postwar period they thus have tried assiduously to persuade their allies to take this step. However, they have lacked the leverage necessary to accomplish this. They have had only one means of pressure at their disposal, the supply of arms, and this they could not use. They have feared that by suspending arms deliveries they would not only lose valuable hard currency, but drive their only remaining allies into the arms of Western suppliers. Because of Egypt's 'defection', the Soviets have thus been forced into an alliance with parties over whom they have had little influence and with whom they have had severe disagreements, yet whose co-operation they are compelled to seek. As a result, they have found their two chief goals in the region incompatible: they have been unable to build their position in the Middle East while at the same time making any meaningful contribution towards achieving a settlement of the key conflict there.

This dilemma is unlikely to be resolved in the near future. Even if the United States again comes to the Soviets' aid and persuades its friends to assign a role to the USSR in the negotiating process, the Soviets are likely to find themselves faced with the choice of either ignoring and abandoning their own allies or boycotting the negotiations and any settlement they might produce. Their alliance with radical elements in the Arab—Israeli conflict, adopted in part so as to make themselves indispensable to a settlement, may ultimately prevent them from becoming a party to one. Whether, in such a situation, the Soviets would be prepared to use their arms supplies as a form of pressure and to break with their allies if it fails, would depend on just how attractive the settlement is to them. Egypt, Israel and Saudi Arabia can probably be relied on to ensure that it would have very little to offer the USSR.

Prospective Trends

Given the frustrations its involvement in the Arab—Israeli conflict has brought the USSR, one can well imagine that within its foreign policy establishment there have been those who have questioned the wisdom of prolonging that involvement. Indeed, there is reason to think that after both the 1967 and 1973 wars, voices in the Party and military maintained that continued political, economic and military support for the Arab participants in the dispute was not in the Soviets' interests.[55] The case against involvement has, if anything, become stronger in the period since the October War. The danger of a superpower confrontation in the event of a new outbreak of fighting has in some respects increased. This is because the destructive power available to both sides is now far greater than it was before the war. With the delivery of SCUD ground-to-ground missiles to Syria, the possibility of nuclearisation of the conflict is greater. Hence the likelihood that one or both sides would need superpower intervention to save it from a catastrophic defeat has also increased. Even if a confrontation could be avoided in the event of a new war, détente would be very severely set back. Moreover, with the increasing sophistication of the weapons demanded and deployed by both sides, the cost of providing arms is now much higher.[56] Domestic resentment of Soviet aid to the Arab combatants has not diminished as a result of the October War; it is sufficiently intense for the Soviets to avoid giving their own people any indication of the scale of their contributions.[57] At the same time, the gains to the USSR from involvement in the conflict have been diminishing and will probably continue to do so. As it has been pointed out, the Soviets' current allies among the parties to the dispute are of less strategic value and are in some respects a political burden. In the future, as the USSR's aircraft carriers become operational and as the United States deploys submarines equipped with longer-range missiles in the Indian Ocean instead of the Mediterranean, the potential strategic gains from links with the confrontation states will decline even further.

Despite these considerations, however, it is likely that the Soviet Union will opt to stay involved in the conflict. If a settlement is arranged, it will not eliminate all tensions between Israel and its neighbours. But it will reduce the chances of a major war erupting and hence the likelihood of a superpower confrontation. If no settlement is arrived at, or if one which is arranged does not provide a role for the USSR, the Soviets would find it very difficult simply to withdraw from the conflict. Such a step would be too great a blow to Soviet prestige, too clear a sign of Soviet weakness *vis-à-vis* the United States. Moreover, with the Arab combatants now able to draw on the enlarged revenues accruing to the oil producers in the region, the Soviets may find the burden of aid declining and the possibility of recouping past investments increasing. Also, whatever its strategic requirements may be in the long run, in the near future the Soviet Union will still need air and naval bases in the eastern Mediterranean. It must still counter the American Sixth Fleet, and its sole completed aircraft carrier has been in port for repairs almost from the time it was launched. In the long run, bases relatively close to the Soviet Union will be useful links between it and sea and air forces deployed at greater distances.[58] It would take a bold leader indeed, with unchallengeable authority in foreign affairs, to reverse two decades of policy while arguments such as these could be adduced against him. Such a leader is not likely to emerge in the USSR for the foreseeable future.[59]

Thus whether or not a settlement is reached, and if it is, whether or not it provides the USSR with a role as guarantor of the peace, the Soviet Union is likely to continue offering arms to Israel's opponents. (They, in turn, suspicious of Israel's intentions and probably not reconciled to its permanent existence, are likely to want them.) But one can expect the Soviets to make a concerted effort both to reduce the costs of involvement and to ensure significant gains from it in the form of political or economic compensation. The Soviets have already shown a marked preference for trade, rather than aid, in their dealings with the Middle East. Already we have evidence of pressure, not merely on Egypt, but on Syria too, to pay back at least some of its debts to the USSR. Egypt and Jordan, and on some occasions Syria, have been told they must pay for new arms in hard currency. And the USSR has already begun to demand political concessions from all three of these countries in return for its arms.[60]

While the USSR stays involved in the Arab–Israeli dispute, it is also likely to seek other ways of maintaining a position in the Middle East which entail fewer risks. Military aid as a percentage of total Soviet aid to the region declined in 1974–5, perhaps indicating a future preference for a type of assistance less fraught with danger for the USSR.[61] Brezhnev has more than once expressed interest in limiting the arms race in the Middle East.[62] Soviet arms deliveries might go on, but in the context of an agreement prohibiting the supply of nuclear and perhaps certain other offensive weapons to the area. The Soviets may seek to become involved in areas where the United States does not have as long-standing and clearly articulated a commitment or where it is more likely to view Soviet advances as reasonable and thus tolerable. Recent increases in Soviet interest in the Red Sea area meet the first criterion, and new efforts to cultivate Turkey and Afghanistan the second. Moreover, the USSR may try to reduce the political and

economic risks of involvement. It has begun to spread its aid
commitments more evenly among a larger number of regimes. It has
also begun to make more extensive use of the Communist parties of the
Middle East, reviving the Egyptian party, encouraging the Jordanian
and Israeli parties to form national fronts, and co-ordinating its
criticism of President Asad's moves in Lebanon with the Syrian
party.[63] This may presage a future tendency to depend more on local
Communists in policy formulation and implementation, as the USSR
can be more assured of their loyalty than that of non-Marxist,
nationalist regimes and movements.

At the same time, we may begin to see the Soviets modify somewhat
the criteria they employ when they select their allies. It has been
pointed out that in the past they were eager to cultivate regimes which
showed interest in socialist reforms. They assumed that progress
towards socialism was an irreversible process, particularly if supported
by Soviet aid and guidance, and that a socialist orientation implied
friendship and co-operation with the USSR. In the course of the
reassessment sparked by Egypt's 'defection', these assumptions were
sharply challenged. Soviet sources now explicitly recognise that until
the process of building socialism is complete, regressions are always
possible, and that even a country well on its way to socialism can be
induced to turn away from the USSR.[64] In the future this may mean
that the USSR will be more cautious, that it will insist on more
thoroughgoing reform before extending a large amount of aid to a
regime which appears or claims to be socialist. What is even more likely
is that the Soviet Union will attempt to reduce its vulnerability to the
surprises and contradictions of Middle Eastern politics. It will try to
formulate a policy whose success or failure will not depend so heavily
on the political orientation of Arab regimes. It may display less concern
for effecting socialist transformations and less readiness to make large
economic commitments in order to achieve them. It probably will be
more willing to ignore the political complexion and socio-economic
character of its potential friends, while selecting its allies simply on the
basis of their political, economic or strategic significance for the USSR
and their willingness to co-operate with it. Backing for the PLO,
expanding ties with Libya, and overtures to Jordan already indicate a
growing disregard for ideological niceties. Significant postwar increases
in aid to Iran, Turkey and Afghanistan, approaches to Kuwait, and
feelers extended even to Saudi Arabia, likewise point in this
direction.[65]

It would appear, in sum, that as a result of the new situation confronting the USSR in the postwar period, a situation drastically altered by the use of the oil weapon, the USSR has begun to modify its Middle Eastern policy in a number of important ways. The changes in the global and regional distribution of wealth and influence brought on by the employment of the oil weapon created a series of acute problems for the USSR. Serious US competition for the favour of its long-term chief ally led to the formation of a burdensome alliance, which in turn prevented the USSR from taking any meaningful steps to achieve the peace it sought. Four years of diplomatic effort thus did not bring the USSR the settlement it wanted or substantially increase the likelihood that it would obtain it.

But if the use of the oil weapon created severe problems for the USSR in the Middle East, it has also given rise to new interests and opportunities for it. The Soviet stake in gaining access to and controlling the supply of Middle Eastern oil and gas increased substantially, as did the USSR's opportunity to gain from the export of arms, equipment and expertise to the area and the export and re-export of oil to the West. The new wealth in the Middle East opened up to the USSR prospects of reducing the economic burden of its involvement in the Arab—Israeli conflict. The increased value of Middle East oil and gas gave the USSR an incentive to shift its effort and attention in new directions, possibly entailing for it less political, economic and military risk. The new trends in Soviet Middle Eastern policy towards economisation, risk limitation, and the pursuit of economic and strategic advantage without regard for ideological considerations, reflect the Soviets' effort to exploit these opportunities and respond to these incentives. How successful they will be in the pursuit of their new interests and objectives remains to be seen. How their policies in the region will affect their global interests is likewise an open question. Will an energetic drive to gain access to Middle Eastern oil, accompanied by a stepped-up effort to penetrate Western oil markets, promote détente or engender new tensions in the Soviet relationship with the West? Will the risks of a US—Soviet confrontation diminish as the USSR redirects its energies in the Middle East, or will there be an even more intense and dangerous superpower competition to sell arms and gain influence in the resource-rich states of the region? Only when the answers to these questions become clear will we know whether the USSR's altered Middle Eastern policy is truly serving its interests and whether the USSR is better off in a regional and international order vastly changed by the use of the oil weapon.

Notes

1. See Oded Eran, 'The Soviet Perception of Influence: the Case of the Middle East', in this volume.

2. See Yaacov Ro'i, 'The Soviet Union and Egypt: the Constraints of a Power-Client Relationship', in this volume. For the amount of Soviet aid to Egypt under Nasir see Gur Ofer, 'The Economic Aspects of Soviet Middle Eastern Policy', Tables 3.1 and 3.2, in this volume.

3. See Amnon Sella, 'Changes in Soviet Political-Military Policy in the Middle East after 1973', in this volume.

4. See Sella, 'Changes in Soviet Political-Military Policy', and Ro'i, 'The Soviet Union and Egypt', both in this volume.

5. Both steps threatened to alter the balance of power in the Middle East in a major way, hence the possibility of a strong American reaction had to be contemplated. On the question of the delivery of SCUDs to Egypt see Sella, 'Soviet Political-Military Policy', in this volume. On the threat to intervene see Galia Golan, *Yom Kippur and After: The Soviet Union and the Middle East Crisis* (Cambridge: Cambridge University Press, 1977), pp.120–5.

6. See Dina Spechler and Martin Spechler, 'The Soviet Union and the Oil Weapon: Benefits and Dilemmas', and Eran, 'The Soviet Perception of Influence', both in this volume.

7. See Spechler, 'The Soviet Union and the Oil Weapon', in this volume. this volume.

8. Sella, 'Soviet Political-Military Policy', in this volume.

9. The quoted words are those of Soviet Foreign Minister Andrei Gromyko in his speech to the Geneva Peace Conference. (TASS in English, 21 December 1973/*FBIS III*, 26 December 1973.)

10. The USSR has often expressed its readiness to guarantee a settlement and its desire to participate in a peacekeeping force. See Gromyko's speech to the Geneva Peace Conference, TASS in English, 21 December 1973/*FBIS III*, 26 December 1973; Ro'i, 'The Soviet Attitude to the Existence of Israel', in this volume.

11. See Ro'i, 'The Soviet Attitude to the Existence of Israel', in this volume.

12. This was apparently one of the main reasons why the Soviets invited a delegation of Palestinian leaders to Moscow to meet Politburo members at the end of November 1973. See Baruch Gurevitz, 'The Soviet Union and the Palestinian Organisations', in this volume. For Soviet efforts to persuade the Syrians to go to Geneva, see Galia Golan and Itamar Rabinovich, 'The Soviet Union and Syria: the Limits of Co-operation', in this volume.

13. In one of its first postwar statements on the Middle East, the USSR came out officially for the first time in favour of implementing Palestinian 'national' (as opposed to simply 'legitimate') rights. It did so in a joint Soviet–Yugoslav communiqué issued at the close of a visit by Tito to Moscow (TASS, 15 November 1975). See Gurevitz, 'The Soviet Union and the Palestinian Organisations', in this volume, p.3. While not yet an unambiguous declaration in favour of Palestinian statehood (that would come later when tactically needed), this move was intended to assure sceptical Arab observers that in seeking a settlement, the Soviets would continue to champion their cause and would not sell them out in the name of risk-avoidance or superpower harmony. Moreover, it appeared desirable from the Soviet point of view that a settlement establish a state friendly to itself in the heart of the Middle East. A Palestinian state, indebted to the USSR for its very existence, might be a useful and reliable ally.

14. The Israeli borders which the USA was prepared to support were those gained in the defensive war of 1948–9. Acceptance of the Soviet Union's

post-World War Two borders was finally granted at the European Security Conference which met in Helsinki in July 1975. Mr Philip Windsor of the London School of Economics has pointed out that the Soviets were successful only in obtaining recognition of the inviolability of the borders created after World War Two, not their finality. Thus when they subsequently renewed their support for final borders for Israel (in March 1977), they were offering Israel more than they themselves had received. (Discussion at the *New Outlook* Conference, Tel Aviv, 18 November 1977.)

15. Gromyko, Speech to Geneva Peace Conference: Soviet–Yugoslav Communiqué, 15 November 1973.

16. See Sella, 'Soviet Political-Military Policy', in this volume.

17. US–Soviet relations were the USSR's top priority. Attainment of Soviet goals in this arena could not be made to depend on the achievement of the USSR's objectives in the Middle East. See Galia Golan, 'The Arab–Israeli Conflict in Soviet–US Relations', in this volume.

18. The USSR had previously urged the use of the oil weapon and applauded the wartime decision to deploy it. For the postwar campaign, see *Izvestiia*, 30 December 1973, 6 January 1974; *New Times*, 8 (1974), p.16. The campaign was intensified in March 1974, when OAPEC and OPEC met to consider lifting the embargo (*R. Peace and Progress* in Arabic, 11, 12, 14, 15, 17 March 1974; *R. Moscow*, 12, 13, 17 March 1974; *Pravda*, 16, 17 March 1974). See Robert O. Freedman, *Soviet Policy Toward the Middle East Since 1970* (New York: Praeger Publishers, 1975), pp.137–40, and Golan, *Yom Kippur and After*, pp.198–9.

19. The *New York Times*, 5 November 1973, cited in Freedman, *Soviet Policy Toward the Middle East*, p.133.

20. Gromyko, Speech to the Geneva Peace Conference.

21. For Soviet criticism of the prisoner exchange, see *Pravda*, 7, 10, 16 November 1973, cited in Freedman, *Soviet Policy Toward the Middle East*, p.135. For the Soviet response to the Egyptian–Israeli disengagement agreement, see Ro'i, 'The Soviet Union and Egypt', pp.184–5 and n.13.

22. *Pravda*, 25 January 1974.

23. See *Pravda*, 8, 17 March 1974, for disparaging remarks regarding Kissinger's efforts and Soviet insistence that Syria procure from him a timetable for Israel's withdrawal. For interpretation of Soviet conduct in Syria at this time, see Golan and Rabinovich, 'The Soviet Union and Syria', in this volume.

24. See Eran, 'The Soviet Perception of Influence', and Sella, 'Soviet Political-Military Policy', both in this volume.

25. *Pravda*, 25 March 1974.

26. *Le Monde*, 18 April 1974, cited in Golan, *Yom Kippur and After*, p.211.

27. *Al-Ahram*, 14 April 1974, cited in Golan, *Yom Kippur and After*, p.212.

28. Syria had not followed Egypt in expelling Soviet personnel and had continued to tolerate Soviet combat personnel on its soil and a major Soviet presence in its ports and airfields. (See Sella, 'Soviet Political-Military Policy', in this volume. Syria kept the Soviets informed on the progress of its disengagement talks, while it is generally believed that Egypt did not (see Freedman, *Soviet Policy Toward the Middle East*, p.137), or did so partially and sporadically (see Ro'i, 'The Soviet Union and Egypt', in this volume, n.11). Syria also cooperated with the USSR in opposing the lifting of the oil embargo.

29. Golan and Rabinovich, 'The Soviet Union and Syria', in this volume, p.219.

30. *Pravda*, 17 April 1974.

31. Freedman, *Soviet Policy Toward the Middle East*, pp.68–9, 142.

32. On the content of Grechko's Baghdad visit, see *Pravda*, 27 March 1974.

The Jallud-Podgornyi meeting took place on 7 April 1974 and Jallud's Moscow visit on 14–20 May 1974. Information on Jallud's visit comes from *R. Tripoli*, 29 May 1974, and *Air International*, III, 3 (1974), p.107, both cited in Golan, *Yom Kippur and After*, pp.200, 241.

33. See Sella, 'Soviet Political-Military Policy', in this volume.

34. Ofer, 'Economic Aspects', in this volume.

35. Ofer, 'Economic Aspects', in this volume, Table 3.4.

36. Sella, 'Soviet Political-Military Policy', in this volume.

37. See Gurevitz, 'The Soviet Union and the Palestinian Organisations', in this volume, and Galia Golan, 'The Soviet Union and the PLO', *Adelphi Papers*, 131 (1977).

38. See Ro'i, 'The Soviet Union and Egypt', in this volume, and Freedman, *Soviet Policy Toward the Middle East*, pp.154–5.

39. See Ro'i, 'The Soviet Union and Egypt', in this volume.

40. There is much disagreement about when the shipments were resumed. Freedman in *Soviet Policy Toward the Middle East*, p.141, and Sella in 'Soviet Political-Military Policy', in this volume, imply this happened soon after Sadat's announcement. But Golan, in *Yom Kippur and After* asserts that arms shipments were halted at this time and not resumed until the autumn of 1974 (pp.211, 311n.).

41. *Pravda*, 4 February 1975. The Syrians reciprocated by agreeing that the Geneva Conference should resume within a month – before any new disengagement agreement was likely to be completed.

42. For Soviet enthusiasm for this alignment, see *Izvestiia*, 15 April 1975.

43. See Ro'i, 'The Soviet Union and Egypt', and Ofer, 'Economic Aspects', both in this volume.

44. For the Soviet position at this time, see Gromyko's speech in the presence of Syrian Foreign Minister Khaddam, *Pravda*, 24 April 1975. On the positions of the Arabs see Gurevitz, 'The Soviet Union and the Palestinian Organisations', in this volume; Golan, 'The Soviet Union and the P.L.O' (*Adelphi Papers*); and Golan and Rabinovich, 'The Soviet Union and Syria', in this volume.

45. This occurred in a Soviet–Kuwaiti communiqué on 5 December 1975.

46. See Ofer, 'Economic Aspects', in this volume, on Soviet gains from arms sales.

47. See Ro'i, 'The Soviet Union and Egypt' and Sella, 'Soviet Political-Military Policy', both in this volume, for the implications of this step for the USSR.

48. For some tentative efforts in this direction, see Ro'i, 'The Soviet Attitude to the Existence of Israel', in this volume.

49. *Pravda*, 2 October 1976. See Robert Freedman, 'The Soviet Conception of a Middle East Peace Settlement', in this volume.

50. See Freedman, 'Soviet Conception', in this volume.

51. *International Herald Tribune*, 23 December 1977.

52. Since the October 1973 war, the wealthy Arab oil states and Western countries combined gave Egypt more economic aid than the USSR did in two decades (Ofer, 'Economic Aspects', in this volume).

53. See note 5.

54. See Gurevitz, 'The Soviet Union and the Palestinian Organisations', in this volume, and Golan, 'The Soviet Union and the PLO' (*Adelphi Papers*). PLO head Yasir Arafat has himself wavered on the issue of recognition of Israel. In September 1977 he told American television interviewer Barbara Walters that he would grant it if Israel would recognise the PLO. No other PLO spokesman has taken this position, nor has the organisation as a whole endorsed it. Arafat himself

has since assumed a much more negative posture towards Israel.

55. For reference to the 1967 debate on Soviet Middle Eastern policy, see Ro'i, *From Encroachment to Involvement* (New York: Wiley, 1974), p.459. Apparently all Soviet involvement in the Third World has been questioned since 1973. See Eran, 'The Soviet Perception of Influence', in this volume.

56. See Ofer, 'Economic Aspects', and Sella, 'Soviet Political-Military Policy', in this volume.

57. Theodore Friedgut, 'The Domestic Image of the Arab–Israeli Conflict in the Soviet Media', in this volume.

58. See Sella, 'Soviet Political-Military Policy', in this volume.

59. All members of the Soviet leadership group have a strong stake in preventing the emergence of any one figure with unchallenged authority in any sphere. They are very likely to unite against any one of their members who seems to be acquiring it.

60. On trade versus aid, see Ofer, 'Economic Aspects', in this volume. Compare the rates of growth of the averages given for 1971–3 and 1974–5 in Tables 3.3, 3.4 and 3.5. Also compare the amounts involved. On debt repayments, see Ofer, 'Economic Aspects', in this volume. On payment for new arms, see Ofer, 'Economic Aspects', in this volume, and Golan, *Yom Kippur and After*, p.169. On the demand for political concessions, see Sella, 'Soviet Political-Military Policy', in this volume, and Golan, 'The Arab–Israeli Conflict in US–Soviet Relations', in this volume, n.3.

61. See Ofer, 'Economic Aspects', in this volume, Table 3.1.

62. In his speech to the Twenty-fifth Party Congress in February 1976, as well as in his above-mentioned March 1977 speech, delivered to the Soviet Trade Unions Congress.

63. See Gurevitz, 'The Soviet Union and the Palestinian Organisations' and Eran, 'The Soviet Perception of Influence', both in this volume.

64. Eran, 'The Soviet Perception of Influence', in this volume.

65. A parliamentary delegation from the USSR visited Kuwait at the end of February 1974; a Kuwaiti delegation went to Moscow in December 1975, and an arms deal was concluded in November 1976. For favourable Soviet comments on and rumours of contacts with Saudi Arabia, see Golan, *Yom Kippur and After*.

AUTHORS

Oded Eran is Senior Research Fellow of the Russian and East European Research Center and the Center for Strategic Studies of Tel Aviv University. He is preparing a book on the foreign policy-oriented research institutes of the USSR Academy of Sciences.

Robert Owen Freedman is Dean of the Graduate School and Professor of Political Science at Baltimore, Hebrew College. His books include *Economic Warfare in the Soviet Bloc: A Study of Soviet Economic Pressure Against Yugoslavia, Albania, and Communist China* (New York: Praeger, 1970) and *Soviet Policy Toward the Middle East Since 1970* (New York: Praeger, 1975).

Theodore Herzl Friedgut is Lecturer in Russian Studies at the Hebrew University of Jerusalem and the author of *Political Participation in the USSR* (Princeton University Press, forthcoming) and articles on Soviet internal politics.

Galia Golan is Senior Lecturer in Political Science and Russian Studies at the Hebrew University of Jerusalem and Director of its Soviet and East European Research Center. Her books include *The Czechoslovak Reform Movement: Communism in Crisis 1962–1968* (Cambridge University Press, 1971), *Reform Rule in Czechoslovakia: The Dubcek Era 1968–1969* (Cambridge University Press, 1973) and *Yom Kippur and After: The Soviet Union and the Middle East Crisis* (Cambridge University Press, 1977).

Baruch Gurevitz is Lecturer in Russian History at Tel Aviv University and Senior Research Fellow of its Russian and East European Research Center. He is the author of articles on Soviet nationality problems and a book on National Communism in the Soviet Union, to be published by the University of Pittsburgh.

Gur Ofer is Associate Professor of Economics and Russian Studies at the Hebrew University of Jerusalem. He is the author of *The Service Industries in a Developed Economy: Israel as a Case Study* (New York: Praeger, 1967) and *The Service Sector in Soviet Economic Growth: A*

366

Comparative Study (Harvard University Press, 1973) and numerous articles on Soviet and East European economics.

Itamar Rabinovich is Associate Professor of Modern Middle Eastern History at Tel Aviv University. His books include *Syria Under the Ba'th 1963–66* (Jerusalem and New York, 1973) and *From June to October: The Middle East Between 1967–1973* (Co-editor with Haim Shaked) (New Brunswick, New York, 1977).

Yaacov Ro'i is Senior Lecturer in Russian History at Tel Aviv University and Director of its Russian and East European Research Center. He is the author of *From Encroachment to Involvement: A Documentary Study of Soviet Policy in the Middle East, 1945–1973* (Jerusalem: Israel Universities Press, 1974) and *The Soviet Union and Israel, 1947–54: Soviet Decision Making in Practice* (New Brunswick, New Jersey: Transaction, forthcoming).

Amnon Sella is Lecturer in Russian Studies and International Relations at the Hebrew University of Jerusalem and the author of articles on Soviet military policy. He is preparing a book on Soviet military and political conduct in the Middle East from 1970 to 1977.

Dina R. Spechler is Lecturer in Political Science at Tel Aviv University and the author of *Domestic Influences on Soviet Foreign Policy* (University Press of America, forthcoming).

Martin C. Spechler is Lecturer in Economics at the Hebrew University of Jerusalem and author of articles on Soviet economics.

POSTSCRIPT TO CHAPTER 3

This paper was completed in March 1977 and was based on information available at that time, which included figures on Soviet aid and trade through 1975. Since then more information has become available and new developments have taken place in the Middle East. The most important of their new developments, related to our subject matter is the expulsion of the Soviet Union from Somalia and its stepped-up involvement in Ethiopia. Most of the new figures, for 1976, and the recent events support the main line of argument and conclusions of this paper. It so happened, however, that one major source of information, the CIA report on 'Communist Aid and Trade to the Less Developed Countries of the Free World, 1976', presented data on a non-comparable basis with those of previous years, which makes it very complicated to incorporate into our previous data. For this reason and because of time pressure, I left the paper in its March 1977 version. A number of specific updating points may however be warranted.

(1) The new data on military aid provided by the CIA incorporate now the new higher *dollar* prices for Soviet military equipment incorporated in the revision of the CIA estimates of the Soviet military budget. Total military aid is now estimated at 17.2 billion rubles through 1976, 15 through 1975, as compared with 9.5 billion rubles on the basis of previous estimates. 1.2 billion rubles of the difference represent an increase in the estimate of military deliveries during 1975, very likely revealing the true extent of the Libyan arms deal. However, the geographical distribution of Soviet MA remain basically as concluded in the paper with continuation of the same trends observed there.

(2) Specifically, even more MA and economic aid are now reported to be directed towards the oil countries — Libya, Iraq, Algeria, Iran and Afghanistan. The largest arms deal in 1976 was a 1 billion ruble agreement with Iraq, but supplies continued to flow to Libya and Algeria. Increased economic relations are reported with Iran, Afghanistan and the above-mentioned countries. The above-mentioned source is now talking much more openly on the hard-currency aspects of arms deals with oil countries. At present hard-currency incomes from arms sales are estimated to earn about 1.5 billion dollars a year.

(3) The new Ethiopian adventure of the Soviet Union is certainly a deviation from the general trends described in the paper. It proves that

Soviet interests in the region, especially in the direction of the Horn of Africa, the Indian Ocean and Africa in general is still intensive and go beyond the economic interests emphasised in the paper.

(4) Finally the accumulating evidence up till now seems to support the view that the Soviet Union is faced with a serious shortfall of oil from its own sources as compared with both its plans and needs. The accepted view is that during the early and mid-80's not only will it not be able to spare oil for hard currency exports, but that it may have to import oil in order to satisfy its minimum requirements as well as those of Eastern Europe. Since the Soviet Union will not be able to pay for such imports in hard currency, it should certainly be even more interested in exchanging soft goods for oil and hard currency with the oil countries of the Middle East. However, under a highly adverse local energy crisis, the Soviet Union may be 'forced' to encourage an internal coup d'etat in one of the rich oil countries of the region by which it may hope to acquire oil at less than the commercial prices. Since everybody seems to agree that the Soviet energy problem is a temporary one, such exploitation should likewise not last too long. It is still my conviction that the Soviet Union will do the utmost to avoid such a development and to stay self-sufficient in energy even in the short run. Only a major emergency will 'force' it to engage in an adventure of the kind described here — an adventure with very high risks and a steep political price.

INDEX OF PERSONS

INDEX OF SUBJECTS